Roberta V. Hughes Wright, a lifelong resident of the Detroit area, maintains a legal practice in Michigan. She is also a member of the Bar of the District of Columbia and has been admitted to practice before the U.S. Supreme Court. Wright holds a J.D. from Wayne State University and a Ph.D. in education from Wayne State University. She is presently married to Dr. Charles H. Wright, a retired physician who is founder of Detroit's Museum of African American History and president of the Michigan Support Group for Penn Center on South Carolina's St. Helena Island, and she has a daughter and son.

Wilbur B. Hughes III is a native Detroiter who currently lives in Farmington Hills, Michigan. A graduate of Howard University School of Law, Hughes serves as general manager and a member of the board of directors of Detroit Memorial Park Association. As an active member of the American Cemetery Association, he has visited many of the nation's burial grounds. He previously served as staff assistant to the House Committee on the District of Columbia and was staff writer and historian for the District of Columbia *Southwestern* newspaper. Hughes is married to the former Adawork Tsadik.

Dr. Michael L. Blakey, author of the Foreword, is Director of the New York African Burial Ground Project at Howard University, where he is also associate professor of anthropology and curator of the university's W. Montague Cobb Human Skeletal Collection, the third largest collection in the nation.

Westley W. Law, author of the Preface, is a revered griot in Savannah, Georgia, who has devoted his life to civil rights and historic preservation. He helped transform the historic King-Tisdell Cottage into a museum of African American history.

D1091350

Historic Black Landmarks: A Traveler's Guide

"An important contribution to American society."
Washington Post

Foreword by Robert L. Harris Jr., Africana Studies and Research Center, Cornell University. By George Cantor, 6" x 9" paperback, 372 pages, photos and maps, ISBN 0-8103-9408-1.

African America: Portrait of a People

"Thoughtfully addresses the challenges and triumphs of Black Americans during the last 400 years."
Christian Science Monitor

By Kenneth Estell, 7.25" x 9.25" paperback, 791 pages, 200 photos, ISBN 0-8103-9453-7.

Black Firsts

"A superb historical study of black achievement."
Houston Chronicles

By Jessie Carney Smith, 7.25" x 9.25" paperback, 530 pages, 200 photos, ISBN 0-8103-9490-1.

The Essential Black Literature Guide

Published in association with the Schomburg Center for Research in Black Culture, one of the world's foremost facilities dedicated to the preservation and interpretation of black cultural artifacts.

By Roger M. Valade III, 6" x 9" paperback, 446 pages, 150 photos, ISBN 0-7876-0734-7.

Epic Lives

"Reading it was like having a steaming cup of tea with some of the most ... creative and bold women in our nation."
Detroit Free Press

Foreword by Stephanie Stokes Oliver, editor, *Essence* magazine. By Jessie Carney Smith, 7.25" x 9.25" paperback, 100 photos, ISBN 0-8103-9426-X.

Milestones in 20th-Century African American History

A day-to-day, year-by-year account of Black America's political and cultural development.

By Alton Hornsby Jr., 7.25" x 9.25" paperback, 530 pages, 100 photos, ISBN 0-8103-9180-5.

LAY DOWN BODY

LIVING HISTORY IN AFRICAN AMERICAN CEMETERIES

With love and appreciation to our family
for their timeless and unfaltering support,
and to those in repose,
whose memories surfaced so realistically during our research

LAY DOWN BODY

Roberta Hughes Wright
and
Wilbur B. Hughes III

Gina Renée Misiroglu,
Managing Editor

LIVING HISTORY IN AFRICAN AMERICAN CEMETERIES

Detroit • New York • Washington, D.C. • Toronto

LAY DOWN BODY

LIVING HISTORY IN AFRICAN AMERICAN CEMETERIES

Published by Visible Ink Press™
a division of Gale Research Inc.
835 Penobscot Building
Detroit, MI 48226-4094

Visible Ink Press is a trademark of Gale Research Inc.

Cover photograph of "Farewell to Eugene" by Romare Bearden courtesy Estate of Romare Bearden.

Most Visible Ink Press™ books are available at special quantity discounts when purchased in bulk by corporations, organizations, or groups. Customized printings, special imprints, messages, and excerpts can be produced to meet your needs. For more information, contact Special Markets Manager, Visible Ink Press, 835 Penobscot Bldg., Detroit, MI 48226. Or call 1-800-776-6265.

Art Director: Tracey Rowens

Library of Congress Cataloging-in-Publication Data

Hughes Wright, Roberta

Lay down body: living history in African American cemeteries/ Roberta Hughes Wright and Wilbur B. Hughes III; Gina Misiroglu, managing editor; foreword by Michael L. Blakey; preface by W. W. Law.

p.   cm.

Includes bibliographical references (p. 313) and index.

ISBN 0-7876-0651-0

1. African Americans—Funeral customs and rites—History. 2. Cemeteries—United States—History. I. Hughes, Wilbur B. III. II. Misiroglu, Gina Renée. III. Title.

E185.86.H84 1995

393′.08996073—dc2095-22925

CIP

Printed in the United States of America
All rights reserved
10 9 8 7 6 5 4 3 2 1

CONTENTS

FOREWORD

*L**ay Down Body: Living History in African American Cemeteries* is a timely, thoughtful, and broad-ranging discussion of the African American cemetery. Without proclamation, but simply by virtue of the connections these authors choose to make, cemeteries are shown to resonate with a people's sense of self. African American identities are entombed, marked, fought for, preserved, celebrated, symbolized, mourned, and incorporated in the cemeteries they describe. These memorialized identities are sometimes neglected, lost, or later restored to memory. Once the corporal remains of a human life have been planted under earth, chances are good that they will be encountered again.

Of course many of the world's greatest monuments represent elaborate burials, such as the great pyramids of the Nile Valley or the mausoleums of the Ashanti nobility. Yet the simplest of societies have also engaged that fundamental act of humanity that cemeteries represent. Indeed, like the making of stone tools and fire, the uniquely human practice of burying the dead sets people apart from the rest of the natural universe. Our species has carefully buried the dead—has made family cemeteries—since paleolithic times. Each time that anthropologists rediscover these ancestors of deep time, our knowledge of who we were and how we have come to be is enriched. Neanderthals having the most rudimentary culture have left these simple monuments to themselves. Enslaved Africans in the Americas had even less control over the course of their lives than those most ancient people. Their very membership in the human family was denied, and even today that humanity is questioned in the societies that slavery built. Yet even those who owned plantations succumbed to a certain level of negotiation with those who were enslaved. Basics of food, shelter, social, and cultural life would be required if this unalterably human labor were to be made useful to Europeans. The cemetery was one such necessary concession. Here in the solemn dignity of funerary ritual, the community would come together to remember, pay respect, and hope for another life.

Lay Down Body tells of the great variety of African American cemeteries in all parts of the continent. The descriptive documentation of the whereabouts of African American cemeteries is important enough, and that is only the framework of this compelling book. We learn, furthermore, about the landscape and modest monumental structures that are apparent in a rich accompaniment of beautiful photographs. The authors explain how these cemeteries were founded, along with the symbolism entailed in burial practices and monuments. Yet these historic properties are no more nor less than the centerpiece of the story told.

This is a book about the living. Through the use of diverse sources, including oral history, historical text, news articles, and archaeological insights, the authors weave together the lives of communities of ancestors and communities of living descendants—lives of hardship, despair, courage, triumph, discrimination, disregard, respect, reverence, neglect, revitalization, war, love, tranquility, and political struggle. The story of cemeteries is not unlike that of the people who create them, indeed the authors tell us that "struggle and conflict" often surround African American efforts to preserve their cemeteries at the end of the twentieth century.

The themes of this book resonate deeply with my own personal, professional, and cultural experiences. I have directed the New York African Burial Ground Project, which this book describes, for three years. As the earliest large African cemetery yet uncovered in North America, the African Burial Ground and the study of its ancestral remains is special for many people throughout the African Diaspora. The work in which my staff and I are involved concerning the African Burial Ground is principally that of biological anthropologists who seek to learn about ancestral lives. Using scientific methods, we reconstruct the health, population structure, traumas, and cultures of the people by examining their skeletons and burial artifacts.

Yet the personal and cultural experiences I share with the rest of the African American community have always been important to my appreciation of what we are doing here. The pitched struggle waged by the descendant African American community to preserve the African Burial Ground was phenomenal. As an insensitive Federal Government agency and their anthropologist contractors persisted in disrespecting the living and the dead, we saw the ire of our community come to bear with extraordinary unity and commitment. The African Burial Ground was saved, though only in part, by dedicated community activism. These events showed clearly that respect (and disrespect) for the dead could not be readily distinguished from respect (and disrespect) for the living. *Lay Down Body* tells of the pervasive and ongoing struggles of African Americans to define themselves as who they know themselves to be, despite the challenging conditions all along the road home. To the extent that we lose our cemeteries, we lose recognition of much of who we are in the larger sense of the family, community, and nation. And oh, how the authors convey who and what we are!

Finally, I am impressed by how practical the information of this book is. Anyone wanting to preserve a threatened cemetery will obtain a wealth of practical knowledge about how to lay out a preservation plan, utilizing the successful experiences of others who have met that challenge. Cemeteries are as important to the binding together of a people as any of the other cultural values with which they are associated. How we take care of our ancestral monuments reflects how we care for and think of ourselves. The admonition of *Lay Down Body* is clear. If we do not protect our cemeteries, no one else will.

MICHAEL L. BLAKEY

Project Director, New York African Burial Ground Project,
Howard University
April 16, 1995

Dr. Roberta Hughes Wright and Wilbur B. Hughes should and do have a longterm interest in African American cemeteries. Dr. Wright's father (and Hughes's grandfather), Robert I. Greenidge, a physician educated at Wayne State University's Medical School, was one of the original investors, in 1926— and subsequently a board member—of Detroit Memorial Park Association. Hughes has carried on the tradition in his position as general manager and board member of the cemetery, which is one of the oldest and most profitable African American enterprises in Michigan. Not only has it been a growth business for nearly seventy years, but it has provided lowcost loans to eligible borrowers, expanded its operations to a second site, and commissioned Dr. Wright to write the history of the cemetery, *Detroit Memorial Park Cemetery: The Evolution of an African American Corporation,* published in 1993. Since that time, Dr. Wright's interest in cemeteries has increased, and she and her son have visited and recorded the history of many African American burial grounds nationwide.

It appears to me that even as we examine houses and other structures in the study of our community and our history, we must also go back and look at burial grounds. That examination is basic and germane to the development of any future records, collections, or museums. In many cases, the physical structures that were associated with people of the past no longer exist and are not being preserved. Even many families who own their ancestors' home eventually move away and allow the houses to fall. Consequently, the only tangible evidence left to reflect what our beings were are those tombstones and mausoleums. We are able to recall the presence of families, sometimes, but often with intermarriage and the disappearance of descendants, families are completely demolished.

To a certain extent, in my estimation, the preservation effort is basic. It appears to me that the slave graves, with a few exceptions, constitute only a spot, leaving no other evidence of those burials. The first perpetuation of graves appears to have sprung either from the free Blacks who had the means for a proper burial and a tombstone, or from enslaved Blacks who were highly esteemed in the domestic service. Sometimes the families they served buried them in their white family plots, as a member of the family. Others provided a Black cemetery plot, sometimes with appropriate markers.

That marked the beginning of tangible burials. Yet while numerous well-preserved burial sites still function today, many cemeteries lie in neglect. We know that many are nearly inaccessible, hidden among bushes, trees, and other growth. I hope that once this book is in the hands of caring readers, our community will again turn its attention to these neglected old burial sites. We should not allow the sites to fall into greater disuse and disrepair.

Studying cemeteries can be very rewarding on a more personal level as well. Searching burial grounds and reading stones can be of great help to the family genealogist, and researching the records found in tombstone archives may turn up a sought-after relative.

Lay Down Body: Living History in African American Cemeteries, both a record of African American people and a call to action, whets the appetite of the curious and the caring.

W. W. LAW
Savannah, Georgia

ACKNOWLEDGMENTS

We are profoundly indebted to the many people who have assisted us with this book. Thanks go to each and every one of them. Unfortunately, we may have inadvertently missed listing a few persons; they are also thanked.

Gratitude of the highest order goes to those who provided special assistance by contributing to the text. Their contributions made a big difference in the scope and quality of the book. Appreciation goes to:

American Cemetery magazine, for use of excerpts from Melissa Johnson Williams and John L. Konefes's article about the environmental aspects of embalming, and from John E. Sterling's June 1995 article about headstone databases.

The American Genealogical Research Institute staff for information reprinted from their publication *How to Trace Your Family Tree.*

Bantam, for use of Maya Angelou's poem "Elegy: For Harriet Tubman and Frederick Douglass," reprinted by permission from *Maya Angelou Poems,* Bantam, 1981, 1986.

Michael L. Blakey, project director of the New York African Burial Ground Project at Howard University, for contributing the foreword for this book.

The Boston Parks & Recreation Department for *The Boston Experience: A Manual for Historic Burying Grounds Preservation,* second edition, 1989, which comprised much of our chapter on burial ground preservation.

Billie Burn, for the use of information from her comprehensive study *An Island Named Daufuskie,* and for our interview at the Daufuskie Island dock.

Citadel Press, for the use of excerpts from William Wells Brown's *The Negro in the American Rebellion: His Heroism and His Fidelity,* Citadel Press, 1971.

Hennig Cohen for use of his "Burial of the Drowned among the Gullah Negroes," reprinted by permission from *Southern Folklore Quarterly,* Vol. XXII (1958), pages 93, 95-96.)

Vennie Deas-Moore for "Treading on Sacred Grounds," reprinted with the permission of the National Trust for Historic Preservation, copyright 1993 by Lynette Strangstad. Deas-Moore has served as assistant folklorist for the Smithsonian Institute's office of Folklore Program and Howard University's Institute for Urban Affairs and Research. She is consultant for both the South Carolina ETV Network and the McKissick Museum at the University of South Carolina.

Dodd, Mead & Co., for use of "Big Sixteen," "The Bury League," "Concerning the Dead," "Go Down Death," and "Voices in the Graveyard," from *The Book of Negro Folklore,* copyright 1958 by Langston Hughes and Arna Bontemps.

Durham Service Corps, for use of Lacretia Wilkerson and Isaac Johnson's interview with Mr. Willis G. Carpenter, first published in the Corps' pamphlet, *Reclaiming Yesterday—The Geer Cemetery Project.*

Harold Ober Associates, Inc., for use of "The Negro Mother," by Langston Hughes, reprinted from *Selected Poems of Langston Hughes,* published by Alfred A. Knopf, copyright 1959 by Langston Hughes.

"If Winter Comes," by Edna Gullins, reprinted by permission from *Negro Voices,* edited by Beatrice M. Murphy, 1938.

Wesley W. Law, Savannah, Georgia's famed griot, for his assistance with the Savannah story and for this book's Preface.

"My Epitaph," by Lewis Grandison Alexander, reprinted by permission from *Negro Voices,* edited by Beatrice M. Murphy, 1938.

The National Trust for Historic Preservation, for use of "Cleaning Burial Markers" and "Maintaining and Preserving Burial Sites," reprinted by permission from *Information* (newsletter), information series No. 76, 1993.

Elaine Nichols for "Rediscovering Our Roots Through Jumping the Broom," from *The Last Miles of the Way: African-American Homegoing Traditions, 1890—Present,* copyright 1989 by Commissioners of the South Carolina State Museum. This directory features a wealth of data about the cultural heritage of African Americans in South Carolina and accompanied an exhibition on display at the South Carolina State Museum from June 4, 1989, to December 1, 1989.

Chris Nordmann for the chapter "Genealogy for the Beginner," adapted from "Basic Genealogical Research Methods and Their Application to African Americans," *African American Genealogical Sourcebook,* edited by Paula K. Byers, copyright 1995 by Gale Research.

Sandlapper Publishing, Inc. for use of "Early One Morning" from *Reminiscenses of Sea Island Heritage,* by Ronald Daise, copyright 1986 by Sandlapper Publishing, Inc.

Harriet Jackson Scarupa for information from the excellent article in *American Visions,* June 1994, "Learning from Ancestral Bones: New York's Exhumed African Past."

The *Tennessee Tribune,* for use of its "Tribute to Tennessee's Black Civil War Soldiers," first published in vol. 2, no. 2, February 1993.

Sharyn Thompson, for use of "Tallahassee's Old City Cemetery," reprinted by permission from her pamphlet "Florida's Historic Cemeteries: A Preservation Handbook," published by the Historic Tallahassee Preservation Board of the Florida Department of State.

Mrs. Bertha Smith and the Moving Star Hall congregation for their arrangement of the song "Lay Down Body," Ethel Raim for her lovely transcription, and Guy and Candie Carawan for bringing the song to our attention through their book *Ain't You Got a Right to the Tree of Life? The People of Johns Island, South Carolina—Their Faces, Their Words, and Their Songs,* University of Georgia Press, copyright 1989 by Guy and Candie Carawan.

Dr. John A. Wright for information from *St. Louis Black Heritage Trail,* edited by Diane Scollay, Shirley Wittner, and Carol Shoults.

We are so very grateful for assistance from Charles Alexander of Detroit, Michigan, for initial keying of the manuscript; Edward J. Allen of Beaufort, South Carolina; Link Fannie Allen of Boston, Massachusetts; George Alston of St. Helena, South Carolina; the American Cemetery Association; Link Cheryl Anderson of Denver, Colorado; Link Lucille Barbour of Atlantic City, New Jersey; Richard Barnett of Hattiesburg, Mississippi; Harriet Barnwell of Beaufort; Angela Bates of Nicodemus, Kansas; Robin Benedict of Fort Lauderdale, Florida; Evelyn and John Bingham of Detroit; Charles Blockson of Temple University, Philadelphia, Pennsylvania; Charles Boland of Lexington, Kentucky; Letitia and Carl Bolden of Detroit; Catherine Bowser of Truxtun (Portsmouth), Virginia; Alphonso Brown of Charleston, South Carolina; Dr. Margaret Burroughs of Chicago, Illinois; Juan Byars of Hilton Head Island, South Carolina; and Frank Bynes, historian and funeral director in Savannah, Georgia.

We also have abiding gratitude to Charletta J. Campbell of Henning, Tennessee; Emma Campbell and Emory Campbell of Hilton Head Island, South Carolina; James Cato of Beaufort; Michael Cohen of Hilton Head Island; Montrose Cunningham of Dallas, Texas; Century Funeral Home of Hattiesburg; Link Mary Chapman of Des Moines, Iowa; Richard F. Dabbs of Mayesville, South Carolina; Natalie and Ron Daise of Beaufort; Alvin Dahmer and Ellie Dahmer of Hattiesburg; Deborah Dandridge of Chicago; Link Helen Davis of Boston; Emily and Herbert DeCosta of Charleston; the Reverend Kenneth Doe of St. Helena Island, South Carolina; Kathryn Rainbow-Earhart, M.D., of Topeka, Kansas; John M. Estes Jr., Connecting Link of Des Moines; the Fairfield County Museum of Winnsboro, South Carolina; and Carolyn Fisher of Hilton Head (formerly of Dayton, Ohio).

We also owe thanks to Marie Gadson of Coffin Point, St. Helena Island; Helen Galloway of St. Helena; Doris Grant of Hilton Head Island; attorney Fred Gray of Montgomery and Tuskegee, Alabama; Sharony Andrews Green of

Detroit; Dr. Patricia Guthrie of San Leandro, California; Juanita Halfacre of Canfield, Tennessee; Axel Hansen, M.D., of Nashville, Tennessee; Laura Hansen of New York City; Dr. Necia Harkless of Lexington; Jerry Henderson of Austin, Texas; Valentine Hill of Bloomfield Hills, Michigan; Mrs. Lula Holmes of St. Helena Island; Dorothy Houston of Memphis, Tennessee; and Venida Smith Hudley of Coppell, Texas; and Dr. Harris Huntley of Birmingham, Alabama.

We also appreciate the assistance of Mildred Jefferson of Charleston; Lois Jenkins of Beaufort; Angelyne Johnson of Savannah; Audrey Johnson of St. Helena Island; Delores Johnson of Chicago; Matthew Jones of Savannah; Hazel Lee of Detroit; Bertram Lippincott III of Newport, Rhode Island; John Luke of Detroit; Edna K. Luten of Savannah; Malcolm Macdonald of Tuscaloosa, Alabama; Marshel's Wright-Donaldson Funeral Home; Gwen and Robert Mason of Washington, D.C.; Joan Maynard of Brooklyn; Mae Mendoza of Beaufort; Robert L. Moseley Jr. of Nashville; Dr. Henry Moses of Nashville; and the North American Black historical Museum and Cultural Center of Canada.

We are indebted, also, to Penn Center, St. Helena Island; John L. Poston Jr. of Memphis; Kathy Ramsey of Detroit; Winona Rawls of Detroit; Ed Robinson of Birmingham; Link Dr. Nellie Roulhac of Philadelphia; Dr. Lawrence Rowland of Beaufort; Denise Rowson of Durham, North Carolina; Jean Sanders of Compton, California; Beth Shepard of Boston; Mrs. Agnes Sherman of St. Helena Island; Helen Sheumaker of Lawrence, Kansas; Rosa and Charles Simmons of Hilton Head Island; Brenda Simon of Burton, South Carolina; Josie Skanes of Birmingham, Alabama; Gerhard Spieler, county historian of Beaufort; Dr. Rowens Stewart of Detroit; Denise Stinson of Detroit; Lynette Strangstad of Charleston; and Julia Thompson of Hattiesburg.

Many thanks, also, to John E. Walker of Phoenixville, Pennsylvania; David Wallace, M.D., of Cleveland Heights, Ohio; I. E. Washington of Augusta, Georgia; Dennis Watson of Dallas; Roy O. West of Richmond, Virginia; Barbara and Perry White of Hilton Head Island; Charles White of New Jersey and Hilton Head Island, South Carolina; Frances White of Detroit; Nathaniel White of Hilton Head; Rita White of Bala Cynwood, Pennsylvania; the Reverend Horace Williams of St. Helena Island and Beaufort; Cynthia Wilson of Tuskegee; Vernon Wimbrough of Portsmouth, Virginia; Byrd E. Wood of Washington, D.C.; Jack Wood of Jackson, Tennessee; Yvonne at Wright-Donaldson Funeral Home in Beaufort; Myrtle Yancey-Mitchell of Lexington; and Elizabeth Yates of Indianapolis, Indiana.

This book could not have been completed without the guidance of managing editor Gina Renée Misiroglu—ever creative, professional, and thorough. Amy Inouye and Charles Mitchell lent invaluable researching skills. Many thanks to the Visible Ink Press team, including developmental editor Christa Brelin, publishers Martin Connors and Diane Dupuis, and editors Dean Dauphinais and Leslie Norback. For permissions research, thank you Margaret Chamberlain and Maria Franklin. Art director Tracey Rowens created a beautifully designed book.

Author Wright's daughter and author Hughes's sister, Dr. Barbara Hughes, deserves a big thanks for her constant assistance and especially for monitoring the chapter on genealogy. Other family members who were always there to help and give suggestions were Blythe Lelia Allen; Brett William Allen; and Christina Barbara Hughes.

Photographs appearing in *Lay Down Body* were received from the following sources:

Augusta, Georgia cemetery photos, from the Reverend A. C. Redd.

Beaufort National Cemetery plaque from Joseph W. Smith.

Charleston, South Carolina photos, from Julius Watson.

Cover photograph of "Farewell to Eugene" by Romare Bearden courtesy Estate of Romare Bearden.

Daufuskie Island Center, from Joseph W. Smith.

Map of African Burial Ground (New York City) location, copyright 1994 by Steve Harper, Office of Public Education and Interpretation of the African Burial Ground.

Pedigree chart and family tree, copyright 1982 by Rosemary A. Chorzempa, *The Family Tree Workbook: Genealogy for Beginners,* Dover Publications.

Portrait of George Washington Carver, from AP/Wide World Photos.

Portrait of Alex Haley, from AP/Wide World Photos.

Portrait of Benjamin E. Mays, from AP/Wide World Photos.

Portrait of Elijah McCoy, from The Granger Collection, New York.

Portrait of Gen. Robert Smalls, from The Granger Collection, New York.

Portrait of Emmett Till, from AP/Wide World Photos.

Portrait of Maggie L. Walker, from The Granger Collection, New York.

Portrait of Dinah Washington, from AP/Wide World Photos.

Portrait of Whitney Young Jr., from Gerald Davis/Archive Photos.

All other photographs were taken by the authors on their various trips—author Hughes with his lovely, supportive, and helpful wife, Adawork Tsadik Hughes, and author Wright with her husband, Charles H. Wright, M.D., who was most helpful in spite of the fact that he was simultaneously writing his own book, *The National Medical Association Demands Equal Time: Nothing More, Nothing Less.*

The trouble with us," lamented Booker T. Washington, "is that we are always preparing to die. You meet a white man early in the morning and ask him what he is preparing to do . . . he is going to start a business. You ask a colored man . . . he is preparing to die."

Whether you agree with this or not, and we see it as a gross overstatement, there is no doubt that, "when de Lord calls us home to walk de golden streets," it's important to go in style. But going "in style" isn't always easy.

As this book's first chapter shows, on the slave ships Africans frequently turned to death, either by forced starvation, by starving themselves, or by leaping into the ocean. Some believed that if they were killed they would return again to their own country. In other words, many of the slaves may have taken solace in the thought that after death, they would return to Africa.

So mixed is the record of funeral procedures during slavery, it is impossible to extract the truth. It is known that some "masters" permitted funeral rites while others objected strongly. Some objected to the use of African drums to announce funerals, some banned singing at slave wakes, and others outlawed Black preachers at slave funerals. Often funerals were only allowed at night.

At the cemetery, the open grave waited, frequently dug along an east-west axis by slaves who knew not to violate the West African strictures against burying a person "crossing in the world." As a rule, each plantation had its own burial ground, but sometimes towns or churches provided a small cemetery in which the slaves of various owners were laid to rest.

Natural weathering, vandalism, neglect, abandonment, agricultural practices, encroachment by development, and industrial pollution all pose threats to these and other African American cemeteries. Why is this important? Because many cemeteries represent the culture of Black America. The sites are significant because burial practices tend to be among the most conservative, or least changed, factors of a group's material culture. The oldest and most persistent values are sometimes preserved only in cemeteries.

Lay Down Body: Living History in African American Cemeteries is the story of struggle. It tells of the struggles of Black people to maintain a vestige of our African American heritage, including efforts to maintain ownership of our burial grounds. In showing how even the most modern of the twentieth-century Black cemeteries reflect traditions of Africa, we glimpse the similarity in the rites, including the ceremony, the music, the mourning habits, and the family outings at the cemetery. The effort to maintain pride and tradition has been affected also, in some areas, by the intrusion of developers usurping the hallowed grounds for new construction.

This book is not an attempt to list or categorize all the African American cemeteries in the United States, nor is it a book about African American cemetery decorations or grave artistry. Other books have beautifully illustrated many of the unique and elaborate decorative settings found in cemeteries, particularly throughout the South.

Instead, *Lay Down Body* concentrates on the struggle and the conflict. We have selected representative cemeteries throughout the United States and Canada and recounted recent stories about the "digging up" of cemeteries where slaves were buried. In the chapter called "The Cradle," we focus on the first, often trouble-plagued cemeteries of the southeastern Sea Islands and nearby areas. Cemeteries both large and small in other parts of the United States and Canada relate to the conflict as well. In "Cemeteries Coast to Coast," we begin with the earliest cemeteries, located in the Southeast, and continue northward and westward to examine burial grounds throughout the continent. In "Genealogy for the Beginner," we provide examples of family trees and discuss how cemeteries themselves, along with cemetery, church, and other records, can help the family historian track down "lost" ancestors. Burial societies and lodges, stories and tales, preservation of historical burial grounds, environmental and business concerns, and an overview of funeral customs and trends complete the story.

Readers will notice that we have varied our use of such terms as African, Negro, Colored, Black, and African American. Our intent has been to use the terms as they were accepted during various periods in our history; that is, using *African* to describe those born in Africa, then *Negro* and *Colored* when describing African Americans during the period up through the 1960s, when *Black* became popular and, indeed, powerful. We employ the term *African American* throughout the book, believing that it best describes our past heritage and our present legacy.

Another concern of ours was the use of the word *slave*. Because the word is used so much throughout history, we have repeated it many times. We strongly believe, however, that people are not born slaves; rather, they are *enslaved*, and we prefer to use the latter term whenever possible.

Our hope is that, in reading this book, you will find enjoyment in the stories of preceding as well as prevailing burial customs and traditions. This, then, might spark your interest for exploring deeper into how our cultural and artistic expressions survived, arising often from unbelievably difficult obstacles and barriers. What thoughts do you envision when looking at a solitary, weather-worn stone marker standing deep amidst nature's foliated debris? Let your imagination soar.

LAY DOWN BODY

LEADER: *Lay down body,*
GROUP: *Lay down a little while.*
LEADER: *Lay down body,*
GROUP: *Lay down a little while.*

LEADER: *Oh, my body now,*
GROUP: *Lay down a little while.*
LEADER: *Oh, my body now,*
GROUP: *Lay down a little while.*

LEADER: *Down in the graveyard,*
GROUP: *Lay down a little while.*
LEADER: *Down in the graveyard,*
GROUP: *Lay down a little while.*

LEADER: *I know you tired,*
GROUP: *Lay down a little while.*
LEADER: *I know you tired,*
GROUP: *Lay down a little while.*

LEADER: *Come from a distance,*
GROUP: *Lay down a little while.*
LEADER: *Come from a distance,*
GROUP: *Lay down a little while.*

LEADER: *Ain't you had a hard time?*
GROUP: *Lay down a little while.*
LEADER: *Ain't you had a hard time?*
GROUP: *Lay down a little while.*

LEADER: *Last December,*
GROUP: *Lay down a little while.*
LEADER: *Last December,*
GROUP: *Lay down a little while.*

LEADER: *Tedious was my journey,*
GROUP: *Lay down a little while.*
LEADER: *Tedious was my journey,*
GROUP: *Lay down a little while.*

LEADER: *Rocky was my road, Lord,*
GROUP: *Lay down a little while.*
LEADER: *Rocky was my road, Lord,*
GROUP: *Lay down a little while.*

LEADER: *Ain't you got somebody gone?*
GROUP: *Lay down a little while.*
LEADER: *Ain't you got somebody gone?*
GROUP: *Lay down a little while.*

LEADER: *I got somebody gone,*
GROUP: *Lay down a little while.*
LEADER: *I got somebody gone,*
GROUP: *Lay down a little while.*

LEADER: *Just keep a-rollin',*
GROUP: *Lay down a little while.*
LEADER: *Just keep a-rollin',*
GROUP: *Lay down a little while.*

LEADER: *Body, ain't you tired?*
GROUP: *Lay down a little while.*
LEADER: *Body, ain't you tired?*
GROUP: *Lay down a little while.*

LEADER: *Body, ain't you lonesome?*
GROUP: *Lay down a little while.*
LEADER: *Body, ain't you lonesome?*
GROUP: *Lay down a little while.*

LEADER: *Body, ain't you weary?*
GROUP: *Lay down a little while.*
LEADER: *Body, ain't you weary?*
GROUP: *Lay down a little while.*

LEADER: *Lay down body,*
GROUP: *Lay down a little while.*
LEADER: *Lay down body,*
GROUP: *Lay down a little while.*

ARRANGEMENT BY
MRS. BERTHA SMITH
AND THE
MOVING STAR HALL
CONGREGATION

SITES, SUPERSTITION, AND STORIES

NOW IN THE QUIETNESS OF THE GRAVE
I BEGAN TO UNDERSTAND WHAT HAPPENED.
IT ALL OCCURRED BECAUSE I DID NOT KNOW
THE MEANING OF A WORD.
WHEN I WENT TO WORK ON JUDGE SNYDER'S PLANTATION,
HE CLASPED HIS HANDS OVER HIS FAT BELLY AND SAID,
"I ALWAYS BELIEVE IN GIVING A NIGGER A **SQUARE** DEAL"
WHEN SETTLING TIME CAME THAT FALL
AND I DISCOVERED THAT I OWED THE JUDGE A HUNDRED
DOLLARS MORE
THAN THE PROCEEDS FROM MY TWENTY BALES OF COTTON,
I ACCUSED HIM OF CHEATING ME.
HE STRUCK ME AND I SLEW HIM.
I WAS LYNCHED.
NOW I REALIZE THIS OCCURRED BECAUSE I DID NOT KNOW
THE MEANING OF THE WORD **SQUARE**.

—HARVEY M. WILLIAMSON

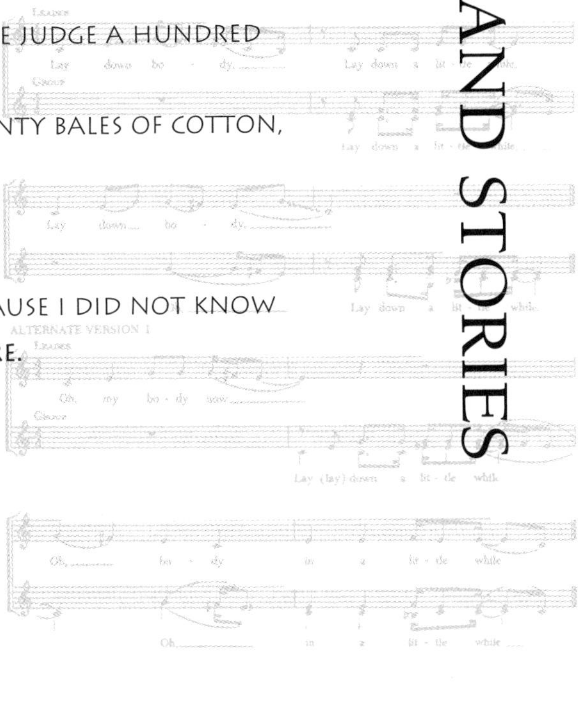

On the numerous plantations dotting the fertile land of the Old South, there was one thing that even the most hard-hearted master was never quite willing to deny his slaves. Contemporary accounts dating from the 1700s reflect the Negroes' insistence that proper

1

attention be paid to their dead. They could not bear that their loved ones be interred without ceremony. A funeral was, to these early generations of African Americans, a pageant, marked by the gathering of kindred and friends from far and near. A funeral usually became an all-day meeting—often in a grove—and it drew white and black alike. A related demand—for the slaves knew how to make their demands—was that the Negro preacher "should preach the funeral." In matters of death, at least, the wishes of the slaves usually prevailed.

Along with their burial customs, those enslaved and transported from Africa brought with them to the Americas their ancient storytelling traditions. While slaveholders went to some length to eradicate tribal languages and customs, present-day literature abounds with a wealth of songs and stories that have survived in a continuation of the strong African oral tradition. Such folktales—usually animal stories involving the spider, the jackal, the hare, the fox, or the tortoise—reflect the tribal roots of these African people.

Among the many traditional stories and tales carried over from the homeland are "preacher tales." Such Negro religious tales were primarily told to entertain the listeners. These included both stories told by the preacher from his place in the pulpit and the stories told about the preacher when he had stepped down among his congregation. In addition, the singing of Negro spirituals added to the spirit of the occasion—be it a funeral, a wedding, or a Sunday service.

James Weldon Johnson, a prominent writer of prose and poetry, recognized in the sermons of the old-time Negro preacher an important form of folk expression. He reproduced a number of these in verse, including "Go Down Death," a poem taken from a funeral sermon. The old-time Negro preacher who created such sermons belonged to a unique breed. Inspiring, entertaining, comic—when comedy was needed—he was in every sense the shepherd of his flock. It was he who eased the hard journey of the congregation with the comforting sentiment, "You may have all dis world, but give me Jesus."

When reading these stories and poems, or listening to renditions of the old songs, in addition to being entertained one can hear the messages that once spoke to the very hearts and souls of both the enslaved and the newly freed. Later generations of blacks, although not enslaved themselves, still have a deep and abiding sense of the hurt and humility endured by their brothers and sisters. Little has changed . . . yet much has changed. There is no way to measure the *progress* of the African American. Some believe that the oppression and degradation experienced by so many under the yoke of slavery was so effective that their effects will echo for generations to come. Others feel that their nation's chronicle of slavery can be revisited and embraced as just that—a history from which to learn and grow and change.

LAY DOWN BODY

First Burials

The horror stories describing enslavement, death, and "first burials" are beyond interpretation or present-day understanding. It seems appropriate to begin our story with the early burials of native Africans who were captured and removed from their homeland. The history of the slave ship *Henrietta Marie*—brought to light through the underwater exploration of members of the National Association of Black Scuba Divers—provides an illustration of this early era. The *Henrietta Marie* was a 120-ton merchant vessel of seventy feet or so that set sail for the United States in September 1699. Her story is typical of the horribly devastating plight endured by enslaved Africans during what was termed "the middle passage."

The *Henrietta Marie* participated in the seventeenth- and eighteenth-century "triangular slave trade," in which merchants navigated the lucrative loop from West Africa through the Caribbean to New England and back. Ships sailed this infamous slave-trading triangle for more than three hundred years, with their cargo of tens of millions of abducted Africans.

On average, the sea voyage ended in death for one out of every eight black passengers; the mortality rate for the transatlantic voyage sometimes climbed as high as 50 to 60 percent. Not surprisingly, a "slave ship" was invariably trailed by a school of sharks. A few captains operated as so-called "loose packers," but the majority were "tight packers," believing that an excessive loss of life would be more than offset by a larger cargo. Disease took its toll, especially when the ship was struck with an epidemic of scurvy or the flux. Suicides, loss of the will to live, and slave mutinies provided greater risks and additional increases in the number of lives lost. But in spite of it all, the slave trade flourished.

The remains of the *Henrietta Marie,* which sank in the early 1700s, were discovered in 1972, about thirty-five miles west of Key West, Florida, across the open waters where the Atlantic Ocean and the Gulf of Mexico merge. Artifacts recovered from the ship—now on display at Key West's Mel Fisher Maritime Heritage Society—reflect her grisly purpose. Shackles of all sizes, glass beads, decayed elephant tusks, and other such items were found. Exploration of the wreck determined that the ship's human cargo was wedged beneath the deck and manacled firmly in place for the grueling three-and-a-half-month voyage across the Atlantic to the Americas. Each person was restricted to a space of only about five-and-a-half feet by eighteen inches. The hold—about ten feet deep and twenty feet wide—was "home" to 250 or more Africans who, along with hungry rodents, were forced to remain there, sweating, relieving themselves, and getting sick, for the duration of the voyage. Death and disease were rampant; the callous, imperious enslavers simply tossed the bodies of those who perished into a "watery grave."

The watery grave of the "middle passage" would give way to land-bound slave cemeteries, many of which have been dismantled or destroyed over the intervening years. As is shown in the following narratives that focus on areas such as New York City and Dallas, shovels and bulldozers preparing land for new construction have come to a halt after the discovery of old slave cemeteries full of skeletal remains. These cities have worked around these "forbidden" areas and have many times provided plaques, parks, and tourist walks for spectators to read about and view the sites.

In 1992, the National Association of Black Scuba Divers sank a one-ton concrete and bronze monument at the site of the wreckage of the *Henrietta Marie*. It read:

Henrietta Marie
In memory and recognition of the courage,
pain and suffering of enslaved African people.
Speak her name and gently touch
the souls of our ancestors.

Slave Cemeteries in the Americas

Slave cemeteries are not confined to any one section of the country. In most areas where bodies have been found, the discoverers are initially amused and surprised to uncover clumps of bones and artifacts. In some instances, these unknowing amateur archaeologists have not been particularly concerned about the significance of their findings. However, public reaction upon learning what has been unearthed—particularly by the African American and Native American communities—has been intense. The excavators have been forced to stop, assess, and redirect their efforts before proceeding. In most cases, as with the Old Quarters Cemetery in Virginia, homage has been paid in some manner to the dead.

TRIBUTE PAID AT THE
OLD QUARTERS CEMETERY

In a pasture next to an old slaves' cemetery in Montross, Virginia, about five hundred people gathered one hot July day in 1991 to pay homage to a forgotten Virginia aristocrat and an enduring ideal—freedom. According to a story in the *New York Times*, the setting was apt. The northern neck of Virginia, wedged between the Potomac and Pappahannock Rivers, was the birthplace of a number of Americans inextricably linked with the concept of Liberty. George Washington was born a few miles from here, as were James Madison and James Monroe. But unlike Robert Carter III, the wealthy planter who was honored that day, none of those familiar figures felt compelled to extend freedom to the dark-skinned people who served as their slaves.

"He was a man ahead of his time," said Nancy Carter Crump, a distant relative of Carter. Two hundred years before, Carter, who owned sixty thousand acres across eighteen plantations and was considered one of the wealthiest men in Virginia, stunned his family, friends, and neighbors by filing a

deed of emancipation, or manumission, thereby setting free more than five hundred "Negroes and mulatto slaves" who were his "absolute property."

"I have, for some time past, been convinced that to retain them in slavery is contrary to the true principles of Religion and Justice and, therefore, it is my duty to manumit them," Carter wrote in the document filed on August 1, 1791—more than seventy years before Abraham Lincoln issued the Emancipation Proclamation. Historians believe Carter's action to have been perhaps the largest individual act of emancipation to occur in American history.

Knowledge of Carter and his deed has been lost to all but a few historians and local admirers. He lies buried in an unmarked grave near the side of his mansion, Nomini Hall, which burned in 1850. In 1988, parishioners of the New Jerusalem Baptist Church erected a small monument on the site of the Old Quarters Cemetery, a burial ground for slaves from surrounding plantations that lies on a now-wooded hillside that tumbles down to a rushing creek.

THE AFRICAN BURIAL GROUND UNEARTHED

In 1741, what would become known as the "Great Negro Plot" took place in New York City. Meeting in upper Broadway's Hughson's Tavern, a slave cabal planned to burn down the entire city. A mysterious series of fires followed, prompting a citywide investigation and the roundup of scores of black slave suspects. During the trial that followed, the prosecutor accused the tavern owner, a white man named John Hughson, of allowing the defendants to use his tavern as a meeting place, arguing that plans to take over the city were initiated with Hughson's knowledge.

A sixteen-year-old barmaid and indentured servant named Mary Burton sealed the fate of many of the suspects by giving incriminating testimony. Of the thirty-five people eventually convicted in the plot, thirteen black men were burned at the stake; the rest were hanged, along with Hughson, two white women, and another white man. It is believed that all those executed may have been buried in the Negroes Burying Ground.

The Negroes Burying Ground was a cemetery used by the African population of New York during the British colonial era. Among those interred there were both free and enslaved peoples, most of whom had been uprooted from their homelands and forcibly transported to North America. Until recently, the existence of the burial ground was known to only a few scholars immersed in the fields of colonial New York history and African American studies.

It is still unknown exactly when the burial ground was first used. The earliest historical reference found to date is a letter written by chaplain John

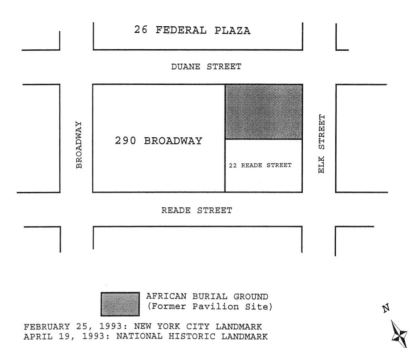

26 FEDERAL PLAZA

DUANE STREET

BROADWAY

290 BROADWAY

22 READE STREET

ELK STREET

READE STREET

AFRICAN BURIAL GROUND
(Former Pavilion Site)

FEBRUARY 25, 1993: NEW YORK CITY LANDMARK
APRIL 19, 1993: NATIONAL HISTORIC LANDMARK

N

A tribute to the African Burial Ground, located on the corners of Elk and Duane Streets, "is dedicated to the people who are buried here and to all who were enslaved in the city's early history from 1626 until July 4, 1827, Emancipation Day in New York."

Sharpe in 1712, wherein he made note of Africans burying their countrymen in the "town common," a block of land that today encompasses City Hall Park and an area several blocks north. For the remainder of the eighteenth century, the Negroes Burying Ground was pictured on maps and referred to in land surveys. While the beginning date remains uncertain, more than two hundred years have passed since the closure of the cemetery in 1794.

The Negroes Burying Ground was rediscovered in 1991, when construction began on a new, $276-million office tower. The graveyard had been the site of one of New York City's earliest landfill projects, and workmen and experts alike were surprised to discover graves anywhere from sixteen to twenty-eight feet below street level. After the first examples of colonial cultural materials—objects made, used, or modified by people—were discovered, archaeologists were called in and began unearthing skeletal remains from what they believed at the time to be an eighteenth-century cemetery.

Further investigation determined that the area was one of the oldest vestiges of the black community in New York City. After considerable fanfare, federal officials decided that archaeology would take precedence over construction. The site was described by the government as "the only colonial-period African American cemetery to be excavated in the United States." Unfortunately, this decision spawned considerable political bickering when it was determined that excavation would result in a four-month, $6-million delay in construction.

The government wanted to end the painstaking excavation by dental pick and spoon in favor of a faster approach employing wide shovels. Using what he called the "coroner's method," John Rossi, project manager for the pending thirty-four-story federal office tower, argued that only one day would be needed to clean a skeleton, remove it, and place it in a box still surrounded by soil, rather than the three to five days predicted by archaeologists. Several prominent black New Yorkers petitioned the government to allow the excavation to continue at a more deliberate pace, citing the site's historical importance and cultural significance.

"It's bad enough that some of the bodies that may be in those tombs were discriminated against in life," commented New York State Senator David A. Patterson. "But now, they're being discriminated against in death." Rossi's method was put on hold pending a ruling from Washington, D.C., and the archaeological method of excavation continued. During the early days of the excavation, ninety-three skeletons were unearthed in the city block bounded by Broadway, Duane, Reade, and Elk Streets. Historians and archaeologists now believe that the locale once served as a cemetery for black New Yorkers, as well as a potter's field and a Revolutionary War burial ground, before it was closed in 1794. Experts associated with the project believe that as many as twenty thousand African men, women, and children were buried in the original cemetery, which once covered more than five acres, or about five city blocks.

About 40 percent of the remains discovered at this Manhattan site were those of children below the age of twelve. This suggests that the death rate for African American children in colonial New York City was relatively high, especially when compared with the estimated rate of death for similar children in other northern port towns during the same period. Small pox, measles, diphtheria, whooping cough, chicken pox, and scarlet fever were often fatal to children during the colonial era—a time when there were no known cures for such illnesses.

Records show the frequency of death among young, enslaved Africans in the eighteenth century to be more than twice that of their free, European-born counterparts. Often black children—particularly infants—were not wanted by New York slave owners because they required care, food, and living space, and distracted their parents from their other duties.

All of the bodies found that dated from that period were buried in coffins, heads pointing west. Most were clad in shrouds that had long since disintegrated. Experts puzzled over one mystery: the skeleton of a black man whose grave contained four buttons of a type found on a British marine officer's coat of the late 1700s. Who was he? And why would he have a garment of that kind? Such questions have yet to be answered.

In the early part of 1992, New York City archaeologist Daniel N. Pagano stated that on February 14, during the process of pouring a concrete footing on the east side of the site—where it had already been determined that graves were most probably located—jawbones, leg bones, and arms bones were scooped up by the backhoe.

Upon discovering that they were bringing up bones, all work in the area stopped. Plans were made to test the entire area under an archaeologist's supervision. Alan Greenberg, project executive for the General Services Administration (GSA), said that construction crews had relied on an out-of-date drawing to gauge which part of the site was deemed "culturally sterile"— that is, unlikely to yield remains or artifacts to archaeologists working on the excavation. An amended drawing, made after a more recent investigation, had shown the limits of the "sterile" area more precisely, but it never arrived at the field office. Mr. Greenberg attributed this to a "simple human error or miscommunication." Then-Mayor David N. Dinkins was described as "exceedingly distressed that, despite a memorandum of agreement that protected the area, twenty burials were destroyed."

The existence of the African Burial Ground (as the site was renamed after its rediscovery) is strong evidence that enslaved Africans in colonial New York City built a lively communal and spiritual life despite their legal and social disenfranchisement. It would appear that, contrary to the assumptions of many historians, slavery in northern cities did not isolate enslaved Africans from one another, but instead provided the impetus for the growth of a uniquely African American society and culture.

In addition, the rediscovery of the African Burial Ground has changed the way future urban archaeology will be conducted. Standard archaeological testing procedures, particularly in this area of Manhattan, will now need to consider the possibility of deeper deposits due to the shifting land gradations caused by continued urban development.

In November 1993, after the site at Elk and Duane Streets had been declared a National Historic Landmark, local African Americans paid tribute to the African Burial Grounds during a candlelight ceremony in lower Manhattan. Howard Dodson, director of the Schomburg Center for Research in Black Culture, observed: "The African Burial Ground offers proof of what has indeed been our role in New York and America. Our role and social influence was a well-kept secret. Now we have the kind of evidence that establishes Africans as having a private claim—a real investment in America."

A number of West African chiefs and delegates paid a visit to Howard University on August 2, 1995, where anthropologists are studying the bones found in the African Burial Ground project. According to Patrice Gaines of the *Washington Post,* Nana Oduro Numapau II, president of the Ghana National House of Chiefs, reflected, "This is clear evidence, indeed, [that] these are our brothers and sisters who were enslaved. Normally when we go to a cemetery, we go home to have a day of mourning. I want to declare this a day of mourning for African people."

In a September 1992 article in the *Detroit News,* reporter Bruce Frankel recorded anthropologist Sherrill Wilson's thoughts on the burial ground,

LAY DOWN BODY

thoughts that mirror the sentiments of historians and citizens familiar with this special site: "It's a rare window into the past, where we can learn from those people what they can never tell us."

ANCIENT GROUNDS BENEATH THE NEW YORK METROPOLIS

In a 1993 article for the *New York Times,* Steven Lee Myers addressed the political issues surrounding the unearthing of citywide cemeteries. Equating such activities to opening a Pandora's box, Myers wrote that efforts to study the remains of Manhattan's Negroes Burying Ground helped focus attention on the scores of other cemeteries throughout New York City, including those beneath such established sites as Washington Square, the Waldorf-Astoria Hotel, and LaGuardia Airport. Attempts to save other cemeteries have had mixed results and have incited considerable controversy.

"In Queens," reported Myers, "Mandingo Osceola Tshaka, the retired [Broadway] singer, has succeeded in forcing the Department of Parks to delay a $1.2 million renovation of a playground, Everett P. Martins Field in Flushing, after he came forward with evidence that the tiny park served as the Colored Cemetery of Flushing for much of the 1800s. Mr. Tshaka began his campaign [in the summer of 1992] after he found a 1919 survey showing four marble tombstones and newspaper clippings suggesting that hundreds of people may have been buried there until after the Civil War.

"The cemetery, on 46th Avenue at 165th Street, had gradually deteriorated into a weedy lot until the city acquired it in 1913 and later turned it into a park. [A newspaper article] in 1936 told of how workers digging the park's wading pool unearthed 'bones galore and rare pennies . . . that had covered the eyes of the dead.'" The article noted that there was no way to identify the graves, Myers explained, "so the digging was continued. . . . [In 1993] the Department of Parks . . . agreed to delay the renovation until archaeologists could study the graves." Plans to renovate the park have been canceled; the site is presently maintained by the Queens Department of Parks and Recreation.

Other slave cemeteries dot the countryside stretching to the north of New York City, including one on the south side of Phillips Road, just west of Fishkill Creek, in Hopewell Junction, Dutchess County. The site was once the property of the Storms, a family of Dutch descent. The slaves buried in the cemetery were the property of different branches of the Storm family, who shared this common burial ground for their human chattel during the eighteenth and nineteenth centuries. Restoration of the site has been undertaken by the black community of nearby Poughkeepsie.

Another cemetery for "colored inhabitants" of the nineteenth century is located in Westchester County, adjacent to Rye's Greenwood Union

Cemetery. The land for the cemetery was donated by Elizabeth and Underhill Halstead in 1860 for use as a cemetery for black residents of "Rye Town" and for black Civil War veterans. It was donated to the Rye trustees "and their successors in office forever" for use as a "cemetery or burial ground for the colored inhabitants." The Town of Rye and the City of Rye began a dispute over the cemetery and its maintenance; eventually the cemetery was forgotten. In 1981 the local newspaper took up its cause once again and the neglected cemetery was cleaned up to some degree by volunteers. But the dispute rekindled as to which government was responsible for its maintenance. In 1986, the burial site received a historic marker from the Westchester Tricentennial Commission.

Mount Moor Cemetery, considered to be the oldest African American cemetery in Rockland County, is located in the town of Clarkston, West Nyack. It contains grave sites dating back to the pre–Civil War period. The original burial grounds were purchased by a small group of black residents in 1849; the cemetery was expanded by an additional land purchase in 1855. Many black veterans of the Civil War, Spanish-American War, and other wars are buried here.

Weeksville, a nineteenth-century African American community located in the ninth ward of Brooklyn, was named for James Weeks, a black man who purchased land from the Lefferts family estate in 1838. A civic organization, the Society for the Preservation of Weeksville and Bedford-Stuyvesant History, has been established to restore the site's historic structures. Joan Maynard, in her 1983 booklet "Weeksville: Then and Now," traces the area's history from its inception as the Dutch colony of New Amsterdam in 1638. In 1646, she notes, eleven Africans were captured at sea and brought to port by the Dutch West India Company, a gigantic slave-trading operation. Some of the men remained under slavery, while others—as free blacks—purchased land that was eventually confiscated. By 1790, one-third of the county's population were slaves, making Kings County the largest slave-owning region in New York State. Maynard writes of New York's free black population:

> In the late 1700s and the early 1800s, most free blacks lived in Manhattan. They had formed many religious, social, educational, and economic organizations before the abolition of slavery in New York State in 1827. The influence of free blacks in Manhattan was enormous on their brothers and sisters in Brooklyn. The role of the black church was especially important in the lives of the people.

> In Brooklyn, churches like the Bridge Street Church, incorporated in 1818, became a station or terminal on the Underground Railroad. Siloam Presbyterian, 1847; Concord Baptist, 1848; and others formed the core of the earliest black settlement in Brooklyn. They were located near the present day downtown area of the Borough. The opening of the Brooklyn Bridge in 1883 brought new waves of settlers to Kings County and changed much of the character and identity of the early black enclaves.

L A Y   D O W N   B O D Y

The village of Brooklyn received a charter as a city in 1834; by 1896 it had greatly increased in size. The city of Brooklyn, Kings County, was incorporated as a borough of the city of New York in 1898. Under the ward system of government, the hamlet of Bedford was a part of the original town of Brooklyn. Weeksville, a part of the ninth ward, became a Bedford neighborhood.

Near this small African American community, also within the ninth ward of Brooklyn, once stood the Citizens Union–Mount Pleasant Cemetery. Its history illustrates an all too familiar struggle. On September 1, 1851, Alexander Duncan, Robert Williams, and Charles Lewis purchased twenty-nine and a half acres of land from white landowner Johnson Leake for use as the Citizens Union Cemetery. Two months later, they formed the Citizens Union Cemetery Corporation, sold the land to the corporation, and invited others to purchase stock.

Duncan, Williams, and Lewis represented families who had been banned from burial privileges in the area's "white" cemeteries. Theirs would be a burial ground open to the colored members of the community: Fees charged for opening and closing graves were low, and other minor fees and charges were sometimes waived altogether in cases of extreme poverty.

When the corporation began to suffer losses in May 1853, the three founders and other stockholders reorganized, changed the name to Mount Pleasant Cemetery Association, and began operating as Mount Pleasant Cemetery in June of the following year. This did not solve their growing problems—financial and otherwise—which included an award by the court in favor of original landowner Leake, who regained title to the property. Leake had no use for the cemetery, so he sold it back to Duncan, then acting as association agent.

In 1869 an event occurred that at the time appeared to be a problem, but may actually have been a blessing. The city purchased a section of the land, prompting the Mount Pleasant Cemetery Association to request to sell the rest of the land for noncemetery purposes (the Eastern Parkway now covers the location). The cemetery organization was, behind the scenes, thick with conflict, misrepresentation, and personal squabbling. And the surrounding neighborhood considered the cemetery a "nuisance." In order to sell the land, according to Maynard, the cemetery had to "remove from said burial grounds, the remains of all bodies buried and now remaining therein and all monuments and headstones and reinter them to some suitable burial ground, purchased by the association for that purpose."

The cemetery association purchased a one-acre plot at neighboring Cypress Hills Cemetery and hired two men to move all of the bodies. During the process, the association discovered, to its dismay, several bodies that had been interred surreptitiously in unmarked graves, apparently by Duncan. These were removed by steam shovel and dumped along the roadside; in 1872 the board of trustees sold the Citizens Union–Mount Pleasant Cemetery land.

EXCAVATING THE FREEDMAN'S CEMETERY

In July 1990 Rod Richardson of the *Detroit News* reported on a Dallas, Texas, freeway-widening project that had been placed on hold after initial excavation had uncovered a layer of Dallas history; namely, the bodies of hundreds of former slaves and black settlers who lay buried in forgotten graves just north of the downtown area. Richardson reported that archaeologists had been called in to relocate some of the remains before work could resume on the expressway expansion through the city's center.

Road work on Dallas's North Central Expressway came to a halt after a backhoe scraped across what turned out to be portions of caskets, wooden markers, and gravestones. As more and more graves were uncovered in the path of the freeway—some containing historic relics—the official calculation for the length of time needed to complete the archaeological dig was revised from a few weeks to two years.

"It is an emotional, archeological, and historical issue," commented archaeologist (Ms.) Jerry Henderson, who oversaw the job for the State Highway and Transportation Department. "Let's face it: The people who were buried here were wronged. And it's up to us to see that their final resting place is restored and their memories preserved." More than one thousand graves were eventually identified; of those, about five hundred were moved to accommodate the freeway expansion project.

In August 1990, Lisa Belkin reported in the *New York Times* that the aptly named Freedman's Cemetery had been the burial site of as many as two thousand freed slaves and their descendants. Although few written records remain, Henderson speculated that most of the black Dallas residents buried there were interred between 1861 and 1925. More than a century ago, the area was dubbed North Dallas Freedmen Town, after the emancipated slaves who lived there. It was virtually wiped out in the 1940s, its cemetery partially desecrated, when construction began on the North Central Expressway.

A point of pride among local black residents between the Civil War and the Depression, the cemetery is not much to look at today. Over the years, its few stones have been flattened by vandals and its grounds either littered with decades of accumulated trash, partially capped by concrete, or transformed into a rarely used children's park.

The plot, which once extended over two acres, would still be a park today had it not gotten in the way of the state's plans to widen the expressway. Beginning in early 1991, residents and officials began paying attention to the cemetery. The widening was delayed for several years while workers restored parts of the original grounds and sorted through neglected decades of black history in Dallas.

Residents of Dallas who had relatives buried in the cemetery were overwhelmed by the restoration effort after years of neglect. "In my lifetime, it's

a wonderful thing to see," said Dr. Robert Prince, a local physician whose family Bible documents at least four great-aunts and great-uncles at rest somewhere amid the jumble of graves.

Shortly after the plans to widen the highway were announced, Henderson took a walk around the area to study the possible effects of the proposed construction on both the environment and the historical integrity of the area. She found a sign for "Freedman's Memorial Park" that claimed the park as the site of a former cemetery. It is illegal in Texas to cover a burial plot without moving the bodies.

Henderson began to research the size of the original grounds and her best sources turned out to be the memories of Dallas citizens, particularly Prince, who had written records dating from the 1860s and a colorful oral history from earlier still. Prince, who was born in 1930, believes that the land was originally a slave cemetery; the reason that no one has discovered written records dating prior to the Civil War is because slaves were not allowed to read or write.

After the war ended, he speculated, many of the two hundred thousand newly freed slaves in Texas headed toward the cities to be closer to the Freedmen's Bureaus that were established during Reconstruction. They settled in places that were familiar; in Dallas it was the area around the slave cemetery where they pitched tents and eventually built a community.

The land that would one day house part of the cemetery was owned by William and Elizabeth Boales, former slaveholders who agreed to sell the one-acre parcel to a group of freedmen in 1869 for $25, a substantial price for the time. A decade later, an adjacent acre was bought by a larger group of freedmen for $425, payable over two years. Prince's great-grandfather, Dock Rownen, was the last surviving member of that group.

Prince recalls walking through the grounds with his great-uncles, who would point to plots marked only with wooden crosses and tell him which relative was buried in each. He remembers them telling of the 1870s, when a railroad was built through the two acres, covering many of the graves.

And he himself recalls when the original North Central Expressway was dug along the path hewn by that railroad—and still more graves were lost. Prince claims that his family was offered $10 by the state for each relative whose grave could be proved to have been moved or destroyed during the construction.

Prince watched for nearly fifty years, as the few remaining granite headstones were vandalized and the abandoned land became the property of the city. He was saddened when the land was made into a playground in 1965. As recently as five years ago, Prince asked the Parks Department to turn the park into a memorial containing a plaque or monument commemorating the site. His suggestion was not approved.

Soon after Henderson learned of the cemetery, she contacted Prince. She explained that Texas law simply required that the graves be moved. But before that was done, she wanted to excavate the entire area. "We need to know how it was laid out originally, so we can maintain its integrity," she told him. "Families were buried together. We need to keep them together."

The excavation proceeded slowly. The gray clay at the site, which stuck to the tops of the coffins when wet, cracked along the edges of the lids when it dried in the sun. During such dry periods, each of these revealed coffin outlines was traced with a piece of string and nailed to the ground for future reference. Hundreds of string outlines eventually filled the lot.

Along the way, Henderson and a half-dozen assistants discovered trinkets that had been left in the graves as gifts: a casing that once held a pocket watch, a palm-size doll carved in stone, a tiny glass vase. Only two headstones were found. One, marked only with the initials *A. T.*, was planted firmly at the foot of a grave. The other belongs to Emma, daughter of one Mary McCune, born June 29, 1855, who died May 5, 1903. Her stone was discovered lying on its side, away from any grave site. Descendants of Emma McCune contacted the highway department after reading about the stone's discovery. Archaeologists will use what they learned about McCune's life and death, along with other such information, to help piece together the Freedman's Cemetery's past.

The reinterment of the bodies posed several problems. With insufficient space to allow for reinterment in the portion of the original cemetery remaining, the archaeology crew searched for space within the limits of Calvary Street. Once called Lemmin Avenue, Calvary Street had been thought to serve as the southern boundary for Freedman's Cemetery. Once the street was donated by the city of Dallas and the pavement removed, however, 133 more burials were identified. Another option, involving acreage to the south of Freedman's Cemetery, proved more fruitful. The property had been foreclosed on and was owned by the Federal Deposit Insurance Corporation (FDIC), who cooperated with the city of Dallas to provide the land needed to relocate all the graves. A December 2, 1994, ceremony marked the closing of the eight-year project, as the last of the remains were buried in the reconfigured Freedman's Cemetery. According to Montrose Cunningham of the Texas Department of Transportation's Public Information Office, the city of Dallas plans to erect a $2 million memorial over the site.

EXCAVATING THE NEW GUINEA CEMETERY

Edna K. Luten is secretary and one of several hard-working members of Savannah, Georgia's Eugenia Cemetery Historical Society, which has undertaken the task of rejuvenating the New Guinea Cemetery. Luten reports that during the period when Negroes were held in bondage, an area located on Savannah's Old Montgomery Cross Road was set aside for slave burials. A for-

mer plantation, the property was sold to the Chatham County Commissioners for use as a prison where inmates would live self-sufficiently, raising all that they ate. The deed stipulated that the Negro cemetery must remain as a burial ground.

Down through the years, the fact that the county owned the New Guinea Cemetery was forgotten, although area residents continued to bury ex-slaves and descendants there. In 1953, realizing the importance of keeping the graveyard clean, a group of people from community churches began to hold monthly meetings on cemetery grounds. They established a five-dollar cleaning fee per burial and ten cent contributions per member per meeting. They also sold fish and chicken dinners in order to pay attorney Harry Ginsburg to do research on the cemetery land.

Ginsburg's research revealed that the property was indeed owned by the county; the deed was recorded in the Chatham County Courthouse. In 1980 the Department of Transportation decide to widen Old Montgomery Cross Road, planning to move the dead and relocate them elsewhere. After months of meeting, wrangling, and arguing with county commissioners, the Eugenia Cemetery Historical Society was offered the deed to a portion of the cemetery, set off by a brick fence. The county's roadwork ended up encroaching only fifteen feet into the north side and fifteen feet onto the south side.

The society was asked to provide a list of officers, trustees, and meeting dates for county review. On May 6, 1992, after four weeks of legal advertisement, the society was notified of the date for the planned sale. Their president, trustees, and members met with county officials on June 1, 1992, and bid one dollar for the land. The deed to the cemetery property was presented and accepted, officially giving members of the Eugenia Cemetery Historical Society title to the land where their descendants lie buried and which they continue to maintain today. For more information about the purchase of Eugenia Cemetery, please turn to pages 115–117 in the next chapter.

WESTWOOD CEMETERY

Wellington-Oberlin, in Lorain County, Ohio, became the site of a slave rescue that was said to have raised nationwide consciousness of the antislavery movement. In 1858, John Price, a fugitive slave living in Oberlin, fell into the hands of four slave catchers using the ruse of offering him a job picking tomatoes at a local farm. However, halfway to Wellington, a small town south of Oberlin where the slave catchers intended to put Price on a train bound for Kentucky, they were spotted. A crowd gathered and freed Price.

Up to the Civil War Lorain County served as a passage for many fugitive slaves heeding the instructions of abolitionist Frederick Douglass, who counselled following the North Star to freedom in Canada. Oberlin's Westwood Cemetery is now the final resting place for many of these fugitive slaves, as well as area activists. In fact, Westwood lays claim to being one of the first cemeteries in the United States to bury all races together, with no distinction made between blacks and whites. The cemetery now provides many visitors with a reflective, meditative setting in which to explore the histories of those who effected vital changes in U.S. civil rights.

Many famous African Americans have called Lorain County home for varying amounts of time. **John Mercer Langston** was perhaps Oberlin's most famous African American. The son of an enslaved mother and white father, he was born into slavery on a Virginia plantation. Langston moved to Oberlin for an education and became the first black attorney in Ohio, the first black to practice law before the U.S. Supreme Court, and the first black to be elected to any office in the nation. He was also the first black homeowner on Oberlin's East College Street, a prestigious address then shared by only the city's most prominent and wealthy citizens. Langston served on the board of education in Oberlin for eleven years and was responsible for the formation of the 127th Colored Ohio Volunteer Infantry. He was a president of the Equal Rights League—the forerunner of the National Association for the Advancement of Colored People (NAACP)—and fought hard against slavery and for the enfranchisement of blacks; became inspector general of the postwar Freedmen's Bureau; established the law department; and eventually became president of Howard University. Langston served as minister to Haiti in 1877 and later became the first and, as yet, only black congressman from Virginia.

Other activists from Oberlin, Ohio who are buried at Westwood Cemetery include:

> **Lewis Clarke**—Known for being the "real George Harris," Clarke's life formed the basis for that character in Harriet Beecher Stowe's *Uncle Tom's Cabin*. He made a daring escape from slavery and risked recapture by appearing as a speaker at abolitionist meetings in the free states. When Clarke died, the governor of Kentucky ordered that his body lie in state so that people could pay homage to the ex-slave who made an impact on pre–Civil War history.

> **John Copeland**—Copeland was an Oberlin carpenter and freeborn black who was the son of a slave. He was very active in the Oberlin Anti-Slavery Society and was well known for his fiery activism. Copeland played a role in the Wellington-Oberlin slave rescue, and it was rumored that he escorted fugitive slave John Price to freedom in Canada. Copeland was in the rifle works at Harpers Ferry when it was assaulted by Lee's troops. As a result, he was wounded, captured, and almost lynched on the spot. After a local minister saved him, he was charged with treason, convicted, and sentenced to be hanged. He said before his execution, "If I am dying for freedom, I could not die for a better cause—I'd rather die than be a slave!" He was hanged, after John Brown, on December 16, 1859. Like others, his body was stolen by medical students from Winchester Medical College. At the request of

the deceased's family, James Monroe traveled to Virginia to retrieve Copeland's body but was unable to do so. A memorial service was held for Copeland and fellow-activist Shields Green on Christmas Day, 1859, at the First Church in Oberlin.

Marie DeFrance—DeFrance was the only single black woman who owned her own business in Oberlin during the period. Called Millinery M. DeFrance, her shop was located at 24 South Main Street. She operated it for thirty-five years while living with her mother at 103 East College Street.

Lee Howard Dobbins—Dobbins was a four-year-old slave child who, in 1853, died in Oberlin on his way to freedom in Canada. His mother had died in slavery; his adoptive mother was forced to leave the boy behind in Oberlin because he was too ill with consumption to travel. Dobbins died several days later in the care of an Oberlin family. A funeral was held in Oberlin's First Church, where over one thousand attended.

Shields Green—Green was a runaway slave from South Carolina and a newcomer to Oberlin when he left to help John Brown. His real name was Esau Brown; he used Shields Green for the sake of anonymity. He escaped to Canada but later moved to Rochester, New York, and became a servant to Frederick Douglass. Green decided to join John Brown's army against the wishes of Douglass, who knew the raid meant certain death. Green was hanged for his participation on December 16, 1859, alongside John Copeland.

Mary Kellogg—A Louisiana slave who was willed by her father to the wife of Oberlin College president James Fairchild, Kellogg was the mulatto daughter of a wealthy plantation owner. Arriving at Fairchild's home at the age of forty-three, Kellogg was immediately emancipated but remained with Fairchild and his family as their servant.

Sarah "Margu" Kinson (Green)—Green was the youngest passenger on the slave ship *Amistad* when the slaves aboard successfully mutinied. The ship floated into Long Island Sound in 1839, where, fortunately for those on board, the slave trade was illegal. After a long court battle, the slaves were freed by the Supreme Court in 1841. "Margu," as she was called, was from Kaw Mendi, West Africa. She was the first female foreign student and first African to study at an American college—Oberlin College. After spending time at Oberlin, Margu returned to Africa as a missionary.

Lewis Sheridan Leary—Leary, along with fellow-Oberlinite John Copeland, was in the rifle works at Harpers Ferry when it was assaulted. He died the next day after being shot and wounded. Leary was twenty-four years old at the time of his death. His body, along with two others, was stolen by local medical students; he was eventually buried at John Brown's farm in North Elba, New York, along with others killed during the raid. Previous to the raid, Leary played a role in the Wellington-Oberlin slave rescue but was not indicted. He is also known for his address to a meeting of the anti-slavery society, where he said, "Man must suffer for a good cause."

John H. Scott—Scott was a freed slave who became a harness and trunkmaker in Oberlin. He joined the Fifth Ohio Cavalry in 1865. Scott also gained a reputation as a fervent temperance man. In one instance, he became incensed when an Elyria beer company sent a wagon to Oberlin to sell its product, believing that black residents were being targeted as the wagon's best patrons.

Orindatus S. B. Wall—This emancipated slave was the son of a slave woman and a wealthy planter. Active with John Mercer Langston (his brother-in-law) in recruiting black troops to serve in the U.S. Army, Wall became the first regularly commissioned black captain in the army early in 1865. He was a member of the first graduating class of Howard University and went on to become a lawyer in Washington, D.C.

Africanisms and Burial Customs

Africanisms involve a body of knowledge that is often passed down from the oldest living members of the community. The encompassing expressions, sayings, and superstitions relate to music, dance, religious beliefs and practices, and the arts. Many of the stories and superstitions relating to death and burials are still told and believed today, especially in the Southern United States. Since the Sea Islands, particularly, have strongly rooted Africanisms, their culture is assured of a continued relationship with the African homeland. The countries of Angola and Sierra Leone are most commonly thought of as having the closest identification to their African heritage.

The psychic atmosphere that encompassed African village life was—and in some instances, still is—rooted in a belief in mystic powers. Many manifestations of this belief remain with us today. There exists, however, a distinction between those that have become integrated into the African American belief system and those that are "lighthearted" mental challenges. The dividing line is hazy; each must make the determination for himself:

- Every effort must be made to carry out the wishes of the dead, carefully. For if this is not done, the dead person will haunt the family or the individual responsible for going against his wishes.

- The dead look out for their loved ones.

- If a dog howls or a rooster crows in the doorway, it is a sign that someone will die.

- When an individual is asleep, his spirit leaves his body. Therefore, if you harass him and he wakes up before his spirit has returned, he will die.

- Don't kill a bluebird—this means bad luck—and if a spider descends on a string of his web, don't let him rise again. This means death.

- If anyone is lying down, don't step over him or you'll catch all of his sickness and possibly die.

Reverend A. C. Redd of Augusta, Georgia, a trustee of Penn Center in St. Helena, South Carolina, provides a list of Africanisms in *African American Funerary Practices* that helps illustrate some of the superstitions and words of advice that prevailed in times past. Others are definitions of much-used terms:

- Animism: The belief that natural phenomena and animate and inanimate things have an innate soul or spirit.

- Breaking dishes: This act releases the spirit.

- Secondary burials/presermons: Final ceremonies that also mark the end of mourning.

- Decoration of graves with household items or personal possessions: This reflects the belief that items are there for the spirit.

- The soul leaves the body via the mouth.

- Importance of being buried feet facing east: To allow rising at Judgment Day; otherwise the person is in the crossways of the world.

- Singing style: Rhythm is emphasized more than melody or harmony during grave-side hymns.

GO DOWN DEATH

DAY BEFORE YESTERDAY MORNING
GOD WAS LOOKING DOWN FROM HIS GREAT,
    HIGH HEAVEN
LOOKING DOWN ON ALL HIS CHILDREN
AND HIS EYE FELL ON MY SISTER CAROLINE
TOSSING ON HER BED OF PAIN
AND DEATH HEARD THE SUMMONS,
AND HE LEAPED ON HIS FASTEST HORSE,
PALE AS A SHEET IN THE MOONLIGHT.
UP THE GOLDEN STREET DEATH GALLOPED,
AND THE HOOF OF HIS HORSE STRUCK FIRE FROM
    THE GOLD,
BUT THEY DIDN'T MAKE NO SOUND.
UP DEATH RODE TO THE GREAT WHITE THRONE,
AND WAITED FOR GOD'S COMMAND.
AND GOD SAID: GO DOWN DEATH, GO DOWN,
GO DOWN TO SAVANNAH, GEORGIA,
DOWN IN THE YAMACRAW,
AND FIND SISTER CAROLINE.
SHE'S BORNE THE BURDEN AND HEAT OF THE DAY,
SHE LABORED LONG IN MY VINEYARD,
AND SHE'S TIRED—
SHE'S WEARY—
GO DOWN, DEATH, AND BRING HER TO ME.

—JAMES WELDON JOHNSON

- If it rains while a man is dying, or if the lightning strikes near his house, the devil has come for his soul.

- It is thought to be bad for anyone to work around a dead person when he is tired, that is, in a weakened condition where spiritual harm might result.

- Among the West Africans, an old saying existed about the need to dig a grave over several days, because of the danger that a fatigued worker might perspire and allow a drop of sweat to fall in the excavation. The ghost could then utilize this to take with him the soul of the one who had labored too hard.

- Always cover the body; never place it directly on the ground.

- A dead person's spirit remains on earth and can do good or evil.

- Coins were placed on the eyes of the dead to keep them closed. However, coins were also sometimes placed in the hands as the deceased person's contribution to the community of the ancestors—or perhaps, as a token for admittance to the spirit world.

- Ceremoniously broken possessions of the deceased should be placed on top of the grave to prevent the spirit from returning to this world in search of them. Breaking objects also breaks the chain of death, or saves other family members from immediately following the deceased in death. Lamps found on the graves symbolically provided light for the spirit searching for home. Bed frames were also placed on graves so that the spirits could rest while journeying home.

The Book of Negro Folklore provides a startling and exciting look at the many superstitions concerning the dead. According to this source, all over the South—as well as in the Bahamas—the spirits of the dead have great power, which they use chiefly to harm.

- Frequently, graveyard dust—often called "goofer dust"—is required in the practice of hoodoo (a black version of the familiar word "voodoo").

- The Ewe-speaking peoples of the west coast of Africa all make offerings of food and drink—particularly libations of palm wine and banana beer—upon the graves of the ancestor. In America the spirit is always given a pint of good whisky.

- It is well known that church members are buried with their feet to the east so that they will arise on that last day facing the rising sun. Sinners are buried facing the opposite direction. The theory is that sunlight will do them harm rather than good, as they will no doubt wish to hide their faces from an angry God.

L A Y   D O W N   B O D Y

- Ghosts cannot cross water—so if a hoodoo doctor wishes to sic a dead spirit upon a man who lives across water, he must first hold the mirror ceremony to fetch his victim from across the water.

- People who die from the sick bed may walk any night, but Friday night is the night of the people who died in the dark—those who were executed. These people have never been in the light. They died with a black cap over the face. Thus, they are blind. On Friday nights they visit the folks who died from sick beds and they lead the blind ones wherever they wish to visit.

- Ghosts feel hot and smell faintish. According to testimony, all except those who died in the dark may visit their former homes every night at twelve o'clock. But they must be back in the cemetery at two o'clock sharp or they will be shut out by the watchman and must wander about for the rest of the night. That is why the living are frightened by seeing ghosts at times. Some spirit has lingered too long with the living person it still loves and has been shut out of its resting place.

Calling Upon the Spirits

Perhaps the simplest way for an ordinary person to see ghosts is to look back over his or her own left shoulder, though the same result may be accomplished by looking through a mule's ear; by punching a small hole in your ear; by looking into a mirror with another person; by breaking a raincrow's egg into some water and washing your face in it; or by breaking a stick in two.

Some say that if you go to the graveyard at twelve o'clock noon and call the name of anyone you know who has died, his or her spirit will answer you, though generally the procedure is more complicated. Some suggest that you go to a graveyard at twelve o'clock noon or midnight and take with you a piece of mirror and a pair of new steel scissors. At exactly twelve o'clock, hold up the mirror before your eyes and drop the scissors on the ground. Call upon that person with whom you desire to talk. You'll see his or her reflection in the mirror and can ask of that person what you please. The blades of the scissors will begin to work of their own accord, metaphorically cutting away any doubt or fear that might arise in your mind.

Another method involves putting half a dozen pure white dinner plates around the table at home, and then proceeding into the graveyard at twelve noon. Call the name of a dead acquaintance. His or her spirit will answer you at once.

- Dirt from sinners' graves is supposed to be very powerful, but some hoodoo doctors will use only dirt from the graves of infants. They say that dirt from a sinner's grave is powerful enough to kill, but the spirit is likely to get unruly and kill others for the pleasure of killing. It becomes too dangerous to commission.

- The spirit newly released from the body is likely to be destructive. This is why a cloth is thrown over the face of a clock in the death chamber and the looking glass is covered over. The clock will never run again, nor will the mirror ever cast any more reflections, if they are not covered so that the spirit cannot see them.

- When it rains at a funeral it is said that God wishes to wash the tracks of the deceased off the face of the earth, they were so displeasing to him.

- If a murder victim is buried in a sitting position, the murderer will be speedily brought to justice. The victim sitting before the throne is able to demand that justice be done. If he is lying prone he cannot do this.

- A fresh egg in the hand of a murder victim will prevent the murderer from going far from the scene. The egg represents life; the dead victim is holding the life of the murderer in his hand.

- Sometimes the dead are offended by acts of the living and slap the faces of the living. When this happens, the head is slapped one-sided and the victim can never straighten his neck. Speak gently to ghosts, and do not abuse the children of the dead.

- At any time, anywhere, it is not good to answer the first time your name is called. It may be a spirit and if you answer it, you will die shortly. They never call more than once at a time, so by waiting you will miss probable death.

This list by no means exhausts the monumental collection of sayings, beliefs, and superstitions that exist around burial traditions, but these are among the most lively and thought-provoking.

Stories and Folktales Through the Years

There are many stories and folktales that have been carried down through the years. During the days of enslavement, the historical presence of Africa helped to insure the survival of families in the culture. Language usage, folktales, and religious practices from the homeland were the source of an almost limitless number of songs, spirituals, and stories passed on from generation to generation. With their imagination and ingenuity, the enslaved would, untiringly, try to amuse themselves. Sometimes, sitting in the sultry summertime with its accompanying humiliations—mosquitoes, sand flies, and plagues of smallpox—the repetition of stories was inevitable. The beauty of the spoken word shone brightly, lending meaning to the past and nurturing the strength and hope needed for times to come. A few of the favorite stories are included here.

"VOICES IN THE GRAVEYARD"

As with many of the stories and folktales included in this section, little is known about the origin of "Voices in the Graveyard." However, the story,

beloved by most who hear it, maintains a cadence and flow that reflect both the fun and sense of mischief of the narrative.

One night two slaves on the Byars plantation entered the potato house of the master and stole a sack of sweet potatoes. They decided that the best place to divide them would be down in the graveyard, where they would not be disturbed. So they went down there and started dividing the potatoes.

Another slave, Isom, who had been visiting a neighboring plantation, happened to be passing that way on the road home, and, hearing voices in the graveyard, he decided to stop and overhear what was being said. It was too dark for him to see, but when he stopped he heard one of the thieves saying, in a singsong voice, "Ah'll take dis un, an' yuh take dat un. Ah'll take dis un, an' yuh take dat un."

"Lawd, ha' mercy," said Isom to himself, "Ah b'lieve dat Gawd an' de debbil am down hyeah dividin' up souls. Ah's gwine an' tell ol' Massa."

Isom ran as fast as he could up to the master's house and said, "Massa, Ah's passin' th'oo de graveya'd jes' now, an' what yuh reckon Ah heerd? Gawd an' de debbil's down dar dividin' up souls. Ah sho' b'lieves de Day ob Jedgment am come."

"You don't know what you are talking about," said the master. "That's foolish talk. You know you are not telling the truth."

"Yas, sah, Massa, Yas, sah, Ah is. Ef yuh don' b'lieve hit, cum go down dar yo'se'f."

"All right," said the master, "and if you are lying to me I am going to whip you good tomorrow."

"Aw right, Massa," said Isom, "case Gawd an' de debbil sho' am down dere."

Sure enough when Isom and the master got near the graveyard they heard the singsong voice saying, "Yuh take dis un, an' Ah'll take dat un."

"See dar, didn' Ah tell yuh, Massa?" said Isom.

In the meantime the two slaves had almost finished the division of the potatoes, but remembered they had dropped two over by the fence, where Isom and the master were standing out of sight. Finally when they had only two potatoes left, the one who was counting said, "Ah take dese two an' yuh take dem two over dere by de fence."

Upon hearing this, Isom and the master ran home as fast as they could go. After this the master never doubted Isom's word about what he saw or heard.

"EARLY ONE MORNING" AND OTHER SEA ISLAND TALES

"Early one mornin', Death come creepin' in m'room!"

Martha Jenkins of Coffin's Point Plantation in St. Helena Island, South Carolina, tells an eerie tale set forth in *Reminiscences of Sea Island Heritage:*

> My cousin an' some other boys went huntin' one day, an' they hunt all through the graveyard. An' while they was in there, he pick up this clock off of one of the graves an' brought it home an' clean it up. After cleanin' it, it start to run. So he put it on his dresser in his room.
>
> That night after he went to bed, ev'rytime he doze off, that thing tell him: "Bring my clock back!"
>
> That went on all night. An' early the nex' mornin,' he got his brother with him, an' he took that clock back! An' that person did not bother him anymore!

The Sea Islands are noted as a haven of lingering spirits. Tales of haints and hags abound, as well as belief in root doctors, hoodoo, or black magic. A dying custom, most probably of African origin, called for placing a dead person's personal effects—pipes, pots, pans, jewelry, and clocks—upon his or her grave. Accordingly, a person's "spirit," when freed from the grave, would "go after" whoever disturbed its grave site. Jenkins continues:

> My grandaunt died an' they give us [Jenkins, her sisters, and brother] all her things: broom, bucket, dipper an' a rockin' chair. So that night [after the burial], she came in the house an' she played with everything that they give us. An' she did that all night! The rocking chair creaked, the water dipper clanged against the metal bucket, and the broom's sweeping sounds spooked the listeners' ears until morning.

Another custom witnessed on St. Helena Island was the placing of a dollar bill in the first grave of a cemetery before the casket was lowered. The action was to "pay the ground" for receiving the dead. And a deceased person's family members younger than age six were passed once back and forth over the opened casket to keep the dead person's spirit from bothering them.

Because it was believed that the spirits of the dead roamed about, particularly in graveyards, cemeteries were shunned as much as possible. Jenkins begins another tale:

> One day we went in the graveyard to get some hick'ry nuts. An' while we was there getting those nuts, we heard these footsteps! We listen for awhile . . . but after we didn't hear them again, we didn't think anything about it.

When we hear it again, it was right up on us! We then turn and run, but we remember what our dad use to say: "If anything scare you an' you run, make sure you don't fall. Because if you do an' that thing stop over you, you will die!" So I don't think any one of us fall—because every one of us is still here today!

Another traditional bogey, the hag, still haunts the minds of those who believe in it. Whenever a person is unable to sleep soundly or awaken completely, and has a frightening feeling of being smothered and weighted on their face and chest, and "hearing" screams that are inaudible—it is said that they are being "ridden" by a hag.

A hag, supposedly, straddles an individual's face and "rides" them, causing disorientation and panic. Unbelievers say that the state of being hag-ridden arises from poor blood circulation, nervousness, or excessive worrying.

Tale bearers, though, declare that hags are ordinary community members who are empowered to shed their human skins, change their forms to become invisible, and torment others by "riding" them. One could rid himself of a hag by throwing salt at it (in which case it could not return to its human skin and, consequently, would die) or by cursing at it vehemently. Others would pray. Babies were protected by placing matchsticks in their hair. Embellishments of the belief include:

- A hag sucked the blood out of an individual and sold it for profit; hence, if a supposedly poor neighbor spoke frequently about visits to distant places, he or she was labeled a "hag."

- A hag was any elderly family member who wanted to get back at someone who had wronged or annoyed him or her.

- If a broom was placed near the doorway, a hag, even in its human form, would not enter someone's house.

TALES OF BROTHER RABBIT

Storytelling was one of the slaves' most successful methods of maintaining their native language and remembering their customs. In order to placate eavesdropping slaveholders, the slaves used Brother Rabbit—sometimes "Bra Rabbit" or "Brer Rabbit"—as their hero, often representing him as a helpless creature. They wittingly, however, gave their hero characteristics that allowed him to "outdo" bigger and stronger animals. Brother Rabbit was cunning, amusing, and even sometimes naive.

A group of St. Helena Island residents and students under the direction of Penn Center's executive director, Emory Campbell, and project director, Walter R. Mack, compiled a compelling booklet called *Five Gullah Folktales*.

These tales exemplify those that were derived from African folklore and have existed in the Sea Island culture (South Carolina, Georgia, and Florida) for more than two hundred years. What follow are the Gullah versions—a language that combines West African dialects with English—and the English version of a story recorded by Matthew Polite.

Bra Rabbit an Bra Shaak: Gullah Version

Dere was a island, an Bra Rabbit he had ta go oba dere ta marry dis couple. So, wen he got down dere, ebrybody don leabe Bra Rabbit.

So, Rabbit play a trick. Call Bra Shaak ta take him oba on dis islant. So, Bra Shaak come, you kno, an Rabbit got on de shaak back an went on cross, come ta de islant. Come back down again. De people done leabe him again. He hadn't pay Bra Shaak nottin, now.

So, he call Bra Shaak again. Bra Shaak come back. Come sho, an Rabbit got on Shaak back an e take him back oba.

So, Bra Rabbit ta keep from pain Bra Shaak, he said, "Hmmm, Bra Shaak, A smell you back fin stink."

Bra Shaak say, "Wa you say Bra Rabbit?"

"Man, we mos git ta sho!"

Wen dey git ta sho dat he could jomp off, he say de same ting again. An Bra Shaak look aroun. Bra Rabbit jomp op an gone.

Now Bra Shaak he gone study way how ta ketch Bra Rabbit. He went on de sho an play ded. De people come by an carry de nyews ta Bra Rabbit. Bra Rabbit comin back now ta preach his funeral. An Bra Shaak gon habe de chance ta ketch Bra Rabbit.

So, Bra Rabbit said, "Why, Shaak can't be ded! Man, bot Shaak can't be ded! Him just bring me oba yestaday."

Day tell um, "Well, bot Shaak's ded now."

So, Rabbit went down dere wid his Bible, you kno. He didn't get close ta de shaak. Bra Rabbit suppose be smaat. He wouldn't git close ta de shaak.

So, Rabbit went aroun an say, "You kno, wen somebody ded, dey habe a different scent."

He git op close nough ta smell de scent. "Oh no, Bra Shaak ent ded!"

An you kno one ting, dey could neba git Bra Rabbit ta go close ta de shaak. Cause ef anybody ded, dey gone smell. Bot dey ent neba git Bra Rabbit. Bra Rabbit stay faa nough dat dey couldn't ketch um.

LAY DOWN BODY

Brother Rabbit and Brother Shark: English Version

There was an island, and Brother Rabbit had to go over there to marry a couple. So, when he got down there everybody had left Brother Rabbit.

So, Brother Rabbit played a trick. He called Brother Shark to take him over to the island. So, Brother Shark came, you know, and Brother Rabbit got on the Shark's back and went on across to the island. He came back down again. The people had left him again. Now, he hadn't paid Brother Shark anything.

So, he called Brother Shark again. Brother Shark came back. He came ashore, and Brother Rabbit got on the Brother Shark's back and Brother Shark took him back over.

So, Brother Rabbit, to keep from paying the Shark, said, "Hmmm, Brother Shark, I smell your stinking back fin."

Brother Shark said, "What did you say, Brother Rabbit?"

"Man, we almost have gotten to shore!"

When they got to shore so he could jump off, he said the same thing again. And Brother Shark looked around. Brother Rabbit jumped up and left.

Now Brother Shark thought of a way to catch Brother Rabbit. He went on the shore and played dead. The people came by and carried the news to Brother Rabbit. Brother Rabbit was coming back now to preach Brother Shark's funeral. Now Brother Shark's going to have a chance to catch Brother Rabbit.

So, Brother Rabbit said, "Why, Brother Shark can't be dead! Man, but Brother Shark can't be dead! He just brought me over yesterday."

They told him, "Well, Brother Shark is dead now."

So, Brother Rabbit went down there with his Bible, you know. He didn't get close to the shark. Brother Rabbit is supposed to be smart. He wouldn't get close to the shark.

So, Brother Rabbit went around and said, "You know, when somebody's dead, they have a different scent."

He got up close enough to smell the scent. "Oh no, Brother Shark isn't dead!"

And you know one thing, they could never get Brother Rabbit to go close to the shark. Because if anybody's dead, they're going to smell, But they never got Brother Rabbit. Brother Rabbit stayed far enough away so they couldn't catch him.

THE WRONG MAN IN THE COFFIN

This is another delightful story that is amusing and fun. One wonders, here, if maybe this story doesn't hit a little too close to home. Perhaps the character Sadie was as serious as she was witty.

You know de chu'ch folks in de Bottoms hab a love for big funerals. 'Reckly attuh freedom, dey hab de funerals on Sunday, 'caze de boss-mens don' 'low' no funerals in de week-a-days. Nowadays, dey hab al funerals on a Sunday jes' for de sake of de love of big funerals.

In dem days comin' up, womens ain't gonna talk 'bout dey men folks while dey's livin'. Dey wanna keep folks thinkin' dey hab a good man for a husband, but dese days an' times hit's a lot diffunt. De gals what ma'ied nowadays talk 'bout dey husbands to any an' evuhbody. You can heah 'em all de time talkin' 'bout "dat ole scoun'al ain't no 'count." Dey say, "If'n you been ma'ied a yeah an' yo' husband ain't nevuh paid a light bill, ain't never paid on de insu'ances, what you think 'bout a scou'al lack dat?"

One time dere was a han' what died on de old McPherson fawm by de name of Ken Parker. De membuhship of de Salem Baptis' Chu'ch think Ken's a good man, 'caze he hab a fine big family an' he 'ten' chu'ch regluh as de Sundays come. De pastuh think he a Good Christun, too. So when he git up to preach Ken's funeral, he tell 'bout what a good man Brothuh Ken was, 'bout how true he was to his wife, an' what a good providuh he done been for his family an' all lack dat. He keep on an' keep on in dis wise, but Ken's wife Sadie know de pastuh done errored; son she turn to de ol'es' boy, Jim, an' say, "Jim, go up dere an' look in dat coffin an' see if'n dat's yo' pappy in dere."

BIG SIXTEEN

A complex story, "Big Sixteen" carries a message of strength. Langston Hughes and Arna Bontemps immortalized it in their 1958 collection, The Book of Negro Folklore.

It was back in slavery time when Big Sixteen was a man and they called 'im Sixteen 'cause dat was de number of de show he wore. He was big and strong and Ole Massa looked to him to do everything.

One day Ole Massa said, "Big Sixteen, Ah b'lieve Ah want you to move dem sills Ah had hewed out down in de swamp."

"I yassuh, Massa."

Big Sixteen went down in de swamp and picked up dem 12 x 12's and brought 'em on up to de house and stack 'em. No one man ain't never toted a 12 x 12 befo' nor since.

So Ole Massa said one day, "Go fetch in de mules. Ah want to look 'em over."

Big Sixteen went on down to de pasture and caught dem mules by de bridle but they was contrary and balky and he tore de bridles to pieces pullin' on 'em, so he picked one of 'em up under each arm and brought 'em up to Ole Massa.

He says, "Big Sixteen, if you kin, ketch de Devil."

"Yassuh, Ah kin, if you git me a nine pound hammer and a pick and shovel!"

Ole Massa got Sixteen de things he ast for and tole 'im to go ahead and bring him de Devil.

Big Sixteen went out in front of de house and went to diggin'. He was diggin' nearly a month befo' he got where he wanted. Then he took his hammer and went and knocked on de Devil's door. Devil answered de door hisself.

"Who dat out dere?"

"It's Big Sixteen."

"What you want?"

"Wanta have a word wid you for a minute."

Soon as de Devil poked his head out de door, Sixteen lammed 'im over de head wid dat hammer and picked 'im up and carried 'im back to Ole Massa.

Ole Massa looked at de dead Devil and hollered, "Take dat ugly thing 'way from here, quick! Ah didn't think you'd ketch de Devil sho 'nuff."

So Sixteen picked up de Devil and throwed 'im back down de hole.

Way after while, Big Sixteen died and went up to Heben. But Peter looked at him and tole 'im to g'wan 'way from dere. He was too powerful. He might git outa order and there wouldn't be nobody to handle 'im. But he had to go somewhere so he went on to hell.

Soon as he got to de gate de Devil's children was playin' in de yard and they seen 'im and run to de house, says "Mama, Mama! Dat man's out dere dat kilt papa!"

So she called 'im in de house and shet de door. When Sixteen got dere she handed 'im a li'l piece of fire and said, "You ain't comin' in here. Here, take dis hot coal and g'wan off and start you a hell uh yo'own."

So when you see a Jack O'Lantern in de woods at night you know it's Big Sixteen wid his piece of fire lookin' for a place to go.

"DIXIE"

Oh, I wish I was in the land of cotton,

Old times there are not forgotten,

Look away,

Look away,

Look away, Dixie land.

In Dixie land where I was born

Early on a frosty mornin'

Look away,

Look away,

Look away, Dixie land.

Hurray, Hurray,

In Dixie land, I'll take my stand

To live and die in Dixie.

Away, away, away down South in Dixie.

Away, away, away down South in Dixie.

Ben and **Lee Snowden's** gravestone in a small cemetery north of Mt. Vernon, Ohio, reads: "They taught 'Dixie' to Dan Emmett."

"'Dixie,' the anthem that has been a fixture at rallies 'away down South' for more than one hundred years, may have been written by this black family—and Yankees, no less," asserts *Detroit Free Press* reporter Phillip Rawls.

The popular notion was that white minstrel performer Daniel Decatur Emmett wrote the song; his performance of it on Broadway in 1859 is the earliest on record. Now, authors Howard L. and Judith R. Sacks speculate that Emmett learned the song from the Snowdens, a family of black musicians who also lived in Emmett's hometown of Mt. Vernon, Ohio. Apparently, the Snowdens lived across the street from a tavern and stagecoach stop. They started entertaining travelers in 1850 with a style that later became parodied in minstrel shows.

"They were performers primarily for white audiences," Sacks says of the Snowdens. "White folks wrote to them constantly asking for songs they had heard them perform." The matriarch of the Snowden family, Ellen Cooper Snowden, was born a slave in Maryland in 1817. When she was ten, her owner freed her and sent her to Mount Vernon, on the Ohio frontier, to work for his cousins. So why would the descendants of a freed slave "wish I was in the land of cotton"?

Speculation is that there were no other blacks in Mt. Vernon. They were not lamenting slavery, but there was a strong sense of loss of family, tradition, and culture. To be in the North and be free was not always an entirely positive experience for an African American, especially one without family.

Over the years, the words to "Dixie" have changed many times. Some versions have up to ten stanzas, but the two stanzas printed here are generally in use today.

Stories of Today

The narratives related to burial customs and cemeteries most pointedly pay tribute to African American heritage. From stories of death are reflected stories of life. African Americans recall how they shed their identity during slavery; even in the postbellum years there remained an uneasiness about oneself. The telling of tales, the belief in voodoo or hoodoo, the singing of spirituals: all were important ways of finding a comfort spot and assessing one's self-worth.

In time, as blacks became increasingly educated and socialized within their new homeland, there still remained a common bond and a common experience in being black and encumbered by continued social and political indignities.

As one reads of the black cemeteries and black towns that arose between the 1800s and the early 1900s, one can't help but sense an attempt to deal with an increasing frustration over adverse conditions. The separation of black towns from the established "white" communities developed from a social and political environment that excluded blacks from the "larger world." This, too, caused the proliferation of black cemeteries, the chance to create havens of peace and freedom through the legal means of possession and ownership.

ONE SMALL TOWN IN MISSISSIPPI

Many people are familiar with Fannie Lou Hamer, the legendary civil rights leader who began picking cotton and ended up exciting an entire nation with her impassioned plea for racial justice at the 1964 Democratic National Convention. A close friend of hers relates the following story, which took her by surprise as the phone rang one day in 1972:

> Mrs. Hamer described how, on the previous night, a carload of white boys in a small town in Mississippi had shot and killed a black girl who had just graduated from the formerly all-white high school. As Mrs. Hamer shouted her anger over the phone, I could hear the dead girl's mother wailing in the background.
>
> The senseless slaying set off days of protest marches and drew reporters from around the world. After the funeral, I rushed along back streets to get a good place at the town cemetery. But when I got there, there were no gravediggers. And no grave site. Then it hit me. They were burying the slain girl in "the colored cemetery."

Rediscovering Our Roots Through Jumping the Broom

During the antebellum period, black Americans customarily gathered for burial ceremonies to perform a traditional dance which had great religious and cultural significance. Known as the Circle Dance in West and Central Africa, it was and is called "ring shouts" or "plantation walk-around" in black American culture. Although styles of shouts vary greatly from community to community, they share basic similarities. All ring shouts combine music and dancing in a counterclockwise circle. In some cases, the feet are never lifted from the floor, but are shuffled one in front of the other.

These words are spoken with complete wonder and respect by Elaine Nichols, curator of the South Carolina State Museum in Columbia, who recorded her knowledge of early African customs in her pamphlet "The Last Miles of the Way."

A growing number of African Americans have begun to reexamine slavery, remembering it through ritual and ceremony, in an attempt to celebrate the spirit of ingenuity and survival that existed in the face of suffering. It is not unusual to find African Americans celebrating history by incorporating the customs of their forefathers, especially burial customs, such as the ring shouts.

continued on next page

I found the funeral—at a poorer, leaner, almost grassless version of the first cemetery. Later, when I told Mrs. Hamer, she shook with bitter laughter. "You," she said, "should know better."

Mrs. Hamer went on to explain that while segregation was officially dead, blacks seldom asked to be buried in the white cemeteries. They wanted to be buried with their friends and relatives in the "colored cemeteries." But in the rare cases when a black person did want to be buried in the "white cemetery," something—money, lack of space, lack of "reservations"—almost always seemed to deter them.

There was something particularly painful about the thought that—even in death—blacks were segregated.

STORIES FROM FLORIDA

In 1970, a cemetery in Fort Pierce, Florida, refused to bury a twenty-year-old black man slain in the Vietnam War because of a "Caucasian only" deed restriction. The burial proceeded only after a federal judge ruled that such clauses were unconstitutional. His mother apologized for all the trouble. "I just wanted him there because it was better kept than the other cemetery," she says.

In 1986, as fifty people watched, Dania, Florida, officials unveiled a granite monument designed to lay to rest a sign from the town's past. The monument publicly recognized a sad event from 1940, when the remains of blacks were dug up from the city's cemetery to make room for more white graves. The black remains were then reburied in a new "colored cemetery"—literally on the other side of the railroad tracks. Thereafter, many black families were never able to locate the graves of their loved ones.

But on that day the city commission discarded the unofficial names Westside Cemetery and Dania Colored Cemetery and officially combined the two under the name Westlawn Memorial Cemetery.

LAY DOWN BODY

At the dedication, a black man, Marvin Merritt, put aside his past bitterness and reminded those assembled of the common resting place that awaits the faithful of all races. "When the trumpets of the Lord shall sound and all these days are past, all these bones are going to rise up and God is going to take them all in His hand," Merritt said.

And all the people said, "Amen."

In 1988, as part of an out-of-court settlement, Deerfield Beach, Florida, dug up the body of **Mayo Howard,** a twenty-eight-year police veteran, from a public cemetery historically used for blacks and buried him in another public cemetery historically used for whites. Howard's wife Evelyn claimed that the city had refused her original request to bury her husband, an African American, in the historically white cemetery. Mrs. Howard's lawyers called segregated cemeteries one of the last entrenched vestiges of American segregation, and alleged that across the South, there were still countless cemeteries with old "Caucasian only" restrictions.

In July 1991, the *Washington Post* printed the story of a 104-year-old black Florida woman, Ada Dupree, who was denied her wish to be buried in the all-white cemetery in Esto, the town she helped settle. She was interred in an all-black burial ground seven miles away.

Dupree's family took her silver coffin across Florida's panhandle, from Esto to Graceville, and buried her as some Esto residents made public apologies for anonymous racist threats directed at the Dupree family.

Several dozen relatives were joined by a dozen white friends as they prayed, sang and paid respects to the oldest citizen of Esto, a town of 250 near the Alabama border.

Dupree wanted to be buried in Esto, where she moved in 1902 and cared for many white families who settled there. "If anybody deserved to be

continued from previous page

Although such introspection is not new, some recent scholars say that this celebration, recently inspired by the Afrocentric movement, represents a transition from shame and denial about slavery to an embrace of that painful past. The unsealing of memory has taken place in many ways. Across America, black couples jump over a broom to seal the bond of matrimony, a ritual created by slaves, who were often forbidden to marry.

Harriette Cole, an editor at *Essence* magazine and the author of *Jumping the Broom*, says that the flourishing of such rituals shows that many blacks are beginning to understand that they do not have to reach back to Africa for tradition. "We can go to our grandparents, our great-grandparents. We have family we can trace back to slavery," Cole says.

And the customs continue. According to Nichols, many years ago—to protect children from spirits and to alleviate any fears of the dead—children were sometimes passed over a deceased person's coffin. Babies and young children were passed over the coffin of their relatives, especially deceased parents and grandparents. The preservation of this custom, occasionally still practiced in the Carolina low country, is one example of cultural continuity in both form and function. It keeps the child from fretting or being afraid of the dead, and it keeps the spirit from claiming the life of the child. Any attempts by the spirit to haunt or harm the child are thwarted.

continued on next page

continued from previous page

Although some might perceive the adherence to such a custom as strange, others see within the act a respectful observance of tradition. Ms. Thomas, manager of the Shrine of the Black Madonna bookstore in Atlanta and creator of its exhibit, "The Black Holocaust," which has drawn more than fifty thousand visitors, explains the resurgence of interest in the slave trade and black rituals quite succinctly: "Every group of people is allowed to remember the past and pay homage to those who have come before them. Why shouldn't we? It's that whole ritual of memory and honor. That's part of being human."

buried there, it was she. She was there before any white person was," said a white mourner. Relatives had changed their plans to bury Dupree at the Esto Farm Cemetery after callers threatened to "shoot up the hearse and any black mourners."

The Duprees were the only black people in Esto for many years. Ada's husband, Gilbert, died in the 1940s.

FREEDMAN'S VILLAGE

The January 1985 issue of *Crisis* magazine includes an interesting story written by Major General Jerry R. Curry, Deputy Commanding General of the U.S. Army. He writes:

One summer day last year, I was riding one of my favorite mounts along the north wall of Arlington National Cemetery. Just inside the wall was a marker stone with the chiseled words, "Jubal Diggs, A citizen," . . . I wondered why the phrase, "A citizen?" Most of those resting beneath the greening sod of Arlington National Cemetery were citizens, but "citizen" wasn't written on their marker stones.

A few weeks and much research later, an intriguing bit of history yielded its secrets. Between 1864 and 1866, approximately 3,800 Civil War "Contrabands," which was the name at that time for Negro refugees or escaped slaves, were buried in Section 27.

Section 27, just inside the north wall of the cemetery, is near the Netherlands Carillon, where three or four times a day its chimes melodiously drench the air with sweet sound.

In 1863, a Contraband Camp was established at the Arlington Estate of Robert E. Lee. It sprawled north from what are now the Amphitheater and Tomb of the Unknown Soldier to Section 27. Diseases, such as smallpox and typhoid fever, remained rampant in the camp, and many now buried in Section 27 died of these and other diseases.

In 1865, the camp was renamed "Freedman's Village." Over 1,000 people lived there in approximately 100 one-and-a-half story frame houses. Each family was given a plot of land to farm and was paid $10 a month by the federal government, which charged $3 a month to rent. Families worked in various trades and skills. . . .

About 1890, the Government bought the land back from them and helped them relocate to other areas, so the area of the now active cemetery could be expanded. This was accomplished with a minimum of discomfiture to the families scattered throughout the area and neighboring states. One of those who relocated was Mr. James Parks. He was "born a slave" in 1845 and was owned by the Curtis-Lee Estate.

Even though Mr. James Parks was a free man, he decided to stay on at the Arlington Estate and work for wages. He continued to work there for many years. . . . When the Curtis-Lee Estate became Arlington Cemetery, Mr. Parks again elected to stay on to work as an employee of the cemetery . . . . Mr. Parks was so well respected and loved that, upon his death in 1929, the Secretary of the Army made an exception to policy and directed that he be buried in Arlington National Cemetery.

Back along the north wall, also buried in Section 27, are Union soldiers with the notation on their marker stones of "USCT," which stands for United States Colored Troops. The casualties of the Freeman's Camp combine with the USCT war casualties and all are interred in a beautiful and peaceful location in Arlington National Cemetery. Together they total more than 5,000.

Most of the slaves buried at the Slave Burial Grounds at Mount Vernon did not know freedom in their lifetimes. Yet, they rest in peace and honor no less than their American citizen brothers and sisters of Freedman's Village who lie buried in Section 27 of Arlington National Cemetery.

In October 1992, a *Cleveland Plain Dealer* article highlighted the 130th anniversary memorial service held in the Freedman's Village section of Arlington National Cemetery in Arlington, Virginia; the address was by Ohio representative Louis Stokes. The site has gained increasing notice recently among the four million tourists who visit the cemetery each year. On this October day, veterans, historians, and government officials gathered to honor forgotten heroes whose graves are marked simply, "civilian" or "citizen."

Efforts by the Committee to Memorialize African Americans of the Civil War, as well as by Representative Stokes, recently led to the graves being refurbished and information about the site being added to tourist brochures. Dismayed by the lack of maintenance and recognition of the site, Stokes, in 1992, won approval for spending $250,000 in federal funds to upgrade and designate the area.

Cemetery administrators unveiled a handwritten burial registry restored by staff at the Library of Congress that will enable visitors to locate ancestors'

THE NEGRO MOTHER

CHILDREN, I COME BACK TODAY

TO TELL YOU A STORY OF THE LONG DARK WAY

THAT I HAD TO CLIMB THAT I HAD TO KNOW

IN ORDER THAT THE RACE MIGHT LIVE AND GROW,

LOOK AT MY FACE—DARK AS THE NIGHT—

YET SHINING LIKE THE SUN WITH LOVE'S TRUE LIGHT.

I AM THE CHILD THEY STOLE FROM THE SAND

THREE HUNDRED YEARS AGO IN AFRICA'S LAND.

I AM THE DARK GIRL WHO CROSSED THE WIDE SEA

CARRYING IN MY BODY THE SEED OF THE FREE

I AM THE WOMAN WHO WORKED IN THE FIELD

BRINGING THE COTTON AND THE CORN TO YIELD.

I AM THE ONE WHO LABORED AS A SLAVE

BEATEN AND MISTREATED FOR THE WORK THAT I

     GAVE—

CHILDREN SOLD AWAY FROM ME, HUSBAND SOLD, TOO.

NO SAFETY, NO LOVE, NO RESPECT WAS I DUE.

THREE HUNDRED YEARS IN THE DEEPEST SOUTH

BUT GOD PUT A SONG AND A PRAYER IN MY MOUTH

GOD PUT A DREAM LIKE STEEL IN MY SOUL.

continued on next page

graves or research village history. Mobile tours of the cemetery now note Freedman's Village and Section 27. There are approximately ten thousand burials in Section 27. Burials are mixed, but include nearly four thousand former residents of Freedman's Village and thousands of combat troops.

SERGEANT BRENT WOODS RECEIVES HIS RITES WITH HONOR

Sergeant Brent Woods, a former slave who was buried in obscurity in 1906, was finally awarded the Congressional Medal of Honor—the nation's highest decoration—for bravery during the Indian Wars. In 1984 he was honored with full military rites at Mill Spring National Cemetery near Somerset, Kentucky.

Lorraine Smith of Somerset learned of Woods's heroism through records in the National Archives in Washington, D.C. Woods joined the army in 1873 at the age of eighteen and became a sergeant, but was demoted to private five times. Smith believes that the demotions came because of his race, "but each time," she said, "he did something outstanding, so they'd raise him back to sergeant."

In an 1881 incident, Sergeant Woods's cavalry company was trapped by a group of Apaches in a New Mexico canyon. After the commanding officer was killed and the second in command deserted the company, Woods took charge, helped a group of civilians to safety, and led his company in a successful attack.

Woods retired from the army in 1902 and returned to Pulaski County, his birthplace in south central Kentucky, where he spent the last four years of his life in relative obscurity. He was buried beneath an unmarked headstone in a cemetery in downtown Somerset, Kentucky, that has since been abandoned. Lorraine Smith's research efforts into Woods's heroism eventually led to the 1984 ceremony at the Mill Spring National Cemetery, where Woods's remains were moved.

COFFINS WASHED AWAY

The tiny farm town of Hardin, Missouri, was turned topsy-turvy during the summer of 1993 when the Missouri River barreled through its streets like white water rapids. The flood destroyed the Assembly of God Church, the city hall, grain bins, houses, and barns, and cut off electricity, running water, and phone service. Residents were already devastated by the catastrophe when the unthinkable happened: The river washed away the town cemetery where most of the area's deceased were interred. Close to nine hundred coffins and burial vaults floated downstream toward St. Louis, Missouri, and the Mississippi River. At one point, the nine-acre cemetery was under about thirty feet of water.

The river carved out the cemetery's oldest section, where inadequate records and memories have yielded few clues as to who occupied the graves. The section, for example, included a segregated acre where blacks were buried decades ago, many in unmarked graves. After the flood, the county coroner and others marked newly dug graves for identified bodies, but placed others in huge mass graves.

The American Cemetery Association (ACA), which was founded in 1887 and comprises cemeteries and funeral homes in more than twenty countries, contributed more than $20,000 to the Missouri Funeral Directors Association. The ACA thus demonstrated a spirit of helping one's neighbors in a time of distress and bereavement and brought different segments of the funeral and remembrance industry together to accomplish a common goal. The organization later contributed additional money directly to the fund for the Hardin town cemetery.

continued from previous page

NOW, THROUGH MY CHILDREN, I'M REACHING THE
   GOAL
NOW, THROUGH MY CHILDREN, YOUNG AND FREE,
I REALIZE THE BLESSINGS DENIED TO ME.
I COULDN'T READ THEN. I COULDN'T WRITE.
I HAD NOTHING, BACK THERE IN THE NIGHT.
SOMETIMES, THE VALLEY WAS FILLED WITH TEARS.
BUT I KEPT TRUDGING ON THROUGH THE LONELY
   YEARS.
SOMETIMES, THE ROAD WAS HOT WITH SUN,
BUT I HAD TO KEEP ON TILL MY WORK WAS DONE.
I HAD TO KEEP ON! NO STOPPING FOR ME—
I WAS THE SEED OF THE COMING FREE.
I NOURISHED THE DREAM THAT NOTHING COULD
   SMOTHER
DEEP IN MY BREAST—THE NEGRO MOTHER.
I HAD ONLY HOPE THEN, BUT NOW THROUGH YOU,
DARK ONES OF TODAY, MY DREAMS MUST COME TRUE.
ALL YOU DARK CHILDREN IN THE WORLD OUT THERE,
REMEMBER MY SWEAT, MY PAIN, MY DESPAIR,
REMEMBER MY YEARS, HEAVY WITH SORROW—
AND MAKE OF THOSE YEARS A TORCH FOR TOMORROW.

continued on next page

continued from previous page

MAKE OF MY PAST A ROAD TO THE LIGHT

OUT OF THE DARKNESS, THE IGNORANCE, THE NIGHT.

LIFT HIGH MY BANNER OUT OF THE DUST,

STAND LIKE FREE MEN SUPPORTING MY TRUST.

BELIEVE IN THE RIGHT, LET NONE PUSH YOU BACK,

REMEMBER THE WHIP AND THE SLAVE'S TRACK.

REMEMBER HOW THE STRONG IN STRUGGLE AND
STRIFE

STILL BAR YOU THE WAY, AND DENY YOU LIFE—

BUT MARCH EVER FORWARD, BREAKING DOWN BARS.

LOOK EVER UPWARD AT THE SUN AND THE STARS—

OH, MY DARK CHILDREN, MAY MY DREAMS AND MY
PRAYERS

IMPEL YOU FOREVER UP THE GREAT STAIRS—

FOR I WILL BE WITH YOU TILL NO WHITE BROTHER

DARES KEEP DOWN THE CHILDREN OF THE NEGRO
MOTHER.

—LANGSTON HUGHES

THE BLACK MINERS CEMETERY

Some of the most frequently visited cemetery grounds on the West Coast lie quietly nestled in a valley just outside the small city of Roslyn, Washington. Surrounded by the thick pines of the Cascade Range, this quaint setting has, surprisingly, become a bustling, but still folksy, town. Made popular as the filming location for the recent television series *Northern Exposure,* the town attracts as many as twenty-four thousand tourists a year, most of whom are surprised when they are encouraged to visit one of Roslyn's twenty-five cemeteries.

Roslyn prides itself on its cemeteries, most which are adjacent to one another. Some have the original moving turnstiles, and fences are maintained to provide an orderly procession of visitors and to keep away herding animals and foraging wildlife. Each cemetery has its own character.

Roslyn was founded in 1886, when the Northwestern Mining Company discovered millions of tons of coal waiting to be tapped in huge veins under the town, which in its heyday had a population of six thousand. A small city bustling with a melting pot from all different racial and ethnic backgrounds, the miners were quick to organize and establish fraternal lodges of social orders and ethnicities.

Some miners and their families belonged to more than one lodge at a time, and could choose between a variety of cemeteries that offered some form of perpetual care, but not all those in the community could afford such a fitting tribute. Many burials remain unmarked, while some graves are outlined by rocks, large and small, as well as markers without names.

The lack of marked graves is most apparent at Mount Olivet, the black miners cemetery established in 1888. The miners and their families buried in these grounds were among the first blacks to settle in Washington and buy cemetery property in the valley. Mount Olivet is now a barren hill said to be filled to capacity with more than two hundred burials, although at first glance it is hard to believe judging by the dozen or so remaining markers.

LAY DOWN BODY

Many of the unmarked graves are those of Roslyn's young children and victims of infant mortality. Sickness, epidemics, plagues, and outbreaks of fatal diseases took their toll in the city around the turn of the century, often taking the lives of the young and the weak.

Often parents were not able to afford a fitting burial or monument. Instead they would get boxes from local grocers—designed to hold long, oversized macaroni—to serve as makeshift coffins. These macaroni box burials were common throughout several of the city's cemeteries.

Roslyn's coal mining days came to an end in 1964, when Northwest Mining pulled out of town. Over the years since then, the cemeteries fell into disrepair from lack of maintenance, but a sense of camaraderie and pride eventually filled the local community and prompted its residents to ensure that the town's cemeteries be well maintained. A common sight in recent years—whenever the weather allows—are groups of townspeople working in the town's cemeteries, cleaning them up and working together to revitalize a piece of their town's heritage.

THE CRADLE: THE SEA ISLANDS AND SOUTHEAST

I KNOW MOON-RISE, I KNOW STAR-RISE,

LAY DIS BODY DOWN.

I WALK IN DE MOONLIGHT, I WALK IN DE STARLIGHT,

TO LAY DIS BODY DOWN.

I'LL WALK IN DE GRAVEYARD, I'LL WALK THROUGH

DE GRAVEYARD,

TO LAY DIS BODY DOWN.

I'LL LIE IN DE GRAVE AND STRETCH OUT MY ARMS,

LAY DIS BODY DOWN.

I GO TO DE JUDGEMENT IN DE EVENIN' OF DE DAY

WHEN I LAY DIS BODY DOWN,

AND MY SOUL AND YOUR SOUL WILL MEET IN DE DAY,

WHEN I LAY DIS BODY DOWN.

—AUTHOR UNKNOWN

There are hundreds, if not thousands, of sea islands along the Georgia, South Carolina, and Florida coasts—settings for some of the most unique burial sites imaginable. Much of the area, particularly in South Carolina, is also known as the Low Country. Burial grounds of the Sea Islands and the Low Country are predominantly family- or church-related. Most exist without a state mandate for perpetual care.

The lush magnificence surrounding many of these cemeteries is unexcelled. Tropic-like landscapes reveal nature at its finest. Live oak trees laden with Spanish moss and green- to brown-leafed palmetto trees tower over scrub bushes and wildflowers that display their blooms amid clumps of fallen leaves, some so old they appear petrified.

Set within this scene are granite memorials to forgotten loved ones: upright, tilted, or ground level, some with legible inscriptions and others on which the message has faded with time. Often the markers have been home-made, constructed of material of traditional significance.

Most of the cemeteries in this region are located beside a river or marsh and are less than ten acres in size. Walking through the grounds requires stepping high to avoid stumbling over tree roots and scattered, matted brush. There is no symmetry, no order or plan, to the location of the markers. A family member visits the burial ground prior to the funeral, selects a spot for the grave, and informs the funeral home so that digging can commence. Care is taken to try to avoid disturbing areas where there are burials without markers.

Because these cemeteries are often "just across the way" or "down by the church," they are as familiar as the local school, the church, or the general store. Children here do not view the cemeteries as scary or haunted as they do in other areas of the country. And for both residents and visitors of these special areas the fascination and quest for knowledge about death and burial rituals remains fervent and real.

Daufuskie Island, Hilton Head Island, Beaufort, St. Helena Island, Low Bottom, Charleston, Columbia, and Winnsboro, South Carolina; and Savannah, Georgia, introduce the Sea Islands and the Low Country cemeteries. The mossy fringe of the Sea Islands edges a 250-mile stretch of southern coastline reaching from northern Florida up to Charleston. The islands—marshy, low land veined by numerous tidal streams—appear everywhere.

Because the deep waterways offer good harbors, captive Africans were put ashore here off ships hailing from West Africa or the Caribbean. The slave population—by 1860 more than four hundred thousand in South Carolina alone—provided the muscle for plantations of rice, indigo, and cotton. During the Civil War, General Sherman issued Special Field Order Fifteen, reserving land for former slaves. Unfortunately, the order was widely ignored within a year, and many whites held onto their land and bequeathed it to their heirs.

Several fairly large parcels of land, however, were purchased and kept by the freedmen—those blacks emancipated at the end of the war—who now began to receive wages for their labor. They planted crops and built houses, churches, and, of course, cemeteries. On St. Helena Island, in particular, much of the area is divided into communities that maintain the same names as the plantations before the war. In fact, it is still common for residents to ask each other, "What community do you live in?" rather than, "What street do you live on?"

Further north, in South Carolina, are Columbia's Randolph Cemetery and, a little farther north, Winnsboro's Camp Welfare Cemetery. The quaint town of McClellanville lies further east, in a wildlife and National Forest area just a sandspit from the Atlantic Ocean. McClellanville is the hometown of Vennie Deas-Moore, previously assistant folklorist at the Smithsonian Institute's Office of Folklore Program and Howard University's Institute of Urban Affairs and Research. Woven within her sensitive recollections are the traditions that still remain and shadows of the history lost in many similar coastal towns.

> Over a small graveyard alongside my family's church, Old Bethel A.M.E., hover the spirits of my ancestors. African American burial traditions in McClellanville . . . still reflect the belief that at death, the physical body is lowered into the soil, but the soul/spirit remains among the living. This spirit must be satisfied and not disturbed. The belief [holds] that these spirits have an invisible circle of spiritual bonding with their family and loved ones. My mother often talks about how I was passed across the coffin of my grandfather. The belief was that since I was still a tiny, weak soul—only a baby and the youngest of my family—my grandfather could come back and take me with him, causing my death at this young age. Passing me across broke that spiritual bond.

> In earlier times a broken wooden wagon wheel was placed on the grave, breaking the spiritual links, so that the spirit would not tantalize the living. Today floral designs are arranged in the shape of a broken wheel. The yucca plant is frequently planted among the graves. This thorny bush makes it difficult for the spirit to roam about the graveyard. Sweet-smelling plants are also found among the foliage. The dead are attracted to the sweet smell of the gardenia bush. One lady chuckles as she tells me, "I not too long ago dug up a large gardenia bush out of my yard because it was drawing too many spirits to my house."

> Immediately after death, open vessels of water are emptied, so the roving spirit will not remain in the home. Broken plates, drinking containers, and utensils, items last used by the deceased, are placed on the grave site. One may also find medicine bottles, furniture, cigar boxes, doll heads, and other personal items.

Deas-Moore also offers these words of advice to those who visit a cemetery: "Do not cross over the grave, walk around. . . . Do not stand on top of the grave. . . . Do not point at the grave or your finger may drop off. . . . Do not remove grave goods or you will carry the discontented spirit with you." She further explains the importance of family traditions within burial services and cemetery maintenance:

The family plot is an important part of African American family structure. As death comes, each member must be placed within the family plot, so that the family will remain together. This may mean bringing the body from miles away. Some family plots are likened to gardens. The care of these plots is restricted to the family. It is the responsibility of the family to maintain the spiritual, as well as physical, continuity of the grave site. There is usually a grave keeper, but his responsibility is to maintain the overgrowth of the cemetery, taking care not to disturb the grave sites. Another important role of the grave keeper is to watch the cemetery against intruders.

Conservation of African American cemeteries means "let it be." It is not unusual to find an African American grave completely overgrown, especially when burials are no longer taking place. This does not necessarily signify neglect, but is done so that the dead will not be disturbed.

Whether intentional or not, the coming of resort developers to the South Carolina coastline has erased many remote African American burial grounds. The grave sites of slaves, remnants of the southern plantations, have vanished forever without any records of their existence. Someone once told me that what was once her family's burial site is now a golf course. The opportunity for preservation is past, except for a few elders with memories of where their ancestors' physical bodies were once buried. As for the souls or spirits, who knows?

Deas-Moore's story reflects the kind of generational, hand-me-down history that exists among many African Americans. The history of Deas-Moore's parents and her parents' parents is preserved through word-of-mouth, a tradition that is commonplace throughout the South and other regions. When researching the various cemeteries, it was found that often very sketchy information exists, precisely because word-of-mouth acts in place of conventional recordkeeping in many small towns. For this reason, interviews with local residents must supplement death certificates and other facts found in city and county records offices, if any documents of this type existed. In the descriptions that follow, information is sometimes missing, but even what is missing speaks to the flavor of the particular burial site.

Daufuskie Island, South Carolina

Daufuskie Island lies between Hilton Head and the Tybee Islands along the Atlantic Coast. It was the first inhabited Carolina sea island and is part of the southernmost tip of South Carolina territory. Without a bridge, the island—two-and-one-half miles wide by five miles long—is bordered on the north by the Cooper River, on the east by Calibogue Sound and the Atlantic Ocean, on the south by Mongin Creek, and on the west by New River.

In recent years, when property, especially beach property, had been nearly depleted on other islands in Beaufort County, all eyes focused on Daufuskie. By 1990 developers were on the scene with bulldozers and earthmovers. Trees were cut and burned and roads changed drastically. Residents, who once walked the seven-mile stretch of beach to gather clams, oysters, conch, arrowheads, and shells, found they could no longer do so.

Much of the island, however, has remained undeveloped, and visitors arrive daily to take in its natural splendor. It takes twenty to thirty minutes by ferry to reach the island; ferries make the run several times each day from docks in neighboring Hilton Head Island and Savannah, Georgia, both less than twenty miles away. In addition, private boats frequent the waterways with country club members and golfers headed for the island's new and expensive "play areas." Buses wait at Daufuskie's dock for tourists; their guide-bus drivers constantly circle the island, providing visitors with a running narrative of what is and what was.

For some who knew the island in years past, there is sadness. Some of the blacks who remain have fought the system, winning in a losing kind of way. Native islanders who had to sell their land because of high taxes and those who now look out their windows and see guard towers and gates have a feeling of hopelessness. The gates barricade the entrances to the costly private clubs built on the land that they and their neighbors once owned. However, some of the native islanders are not as concerned about the changes. Jobs are guaranteed to all residents who apply, and this has been particularly helpful to the young islanders who rely on after-school jobs.

An interesting account of traditional rites of burial on the island is included in the book *An Island Named Daufuskie,* by Billie Burn. The story of the struggle as it relates to the island's cemeteries touches one's heart; it prompted a special trip to Daufuskie to meet Ms. Burn, who has been a resident of the island since 1935. Serving both as island postmaster and school bus driver from 1963 until the early 1980s, Burn has accumulated a limitless cache of wonderful stories.

A trip to Daufuskie in the 1990s is a far cry from the homey aura of the "tugboat" trip that was taken in the 1960s, although regular tourists can still travel by slow boat from Hilton Head and Savannah. In the 1960s, Daufuskie was called a black island. Although large portions of land remained in the hands of whites, blacks were visually and importantly dominant. Tourists visited the island regularly, some expressly to sample the delicious seafood and mouth-watering crab cakes sold at the dock by the native islanders. But now only a handful of African Americans remain on the island, left behind by those who left by choice and those who sold their property because of the inability to pay the increasingly high property taxes.

But even in this smaller black community, some oral traditions still remain. Here is what Burn relates about burial practices on the island:

Seeing that the dead have a decent burial is a very important segment of Daufuskie life. Black undertakers, in years past, were Joseph Haynes, Mose Ficklin, Joseph Grant, and Sarah Grant. Each of them kept a supply of $100 caskets on hand at all times.

Joe Grant was Sarah's husband; and when he passed away in 1962, Sarah took his place and was the last undertaker on the island. She was already the midwife, which caused a person on the island to remark, "Granny bring 'em 'n she take 'em away." When Sarah ceased from her work, an undertaker had to be summoned from the mainland.

He would come over and prepare the body right in the home. Sometimes a family could not afford to buy a casket. In this case, a local carpenter was called upon to make a pine box coffin, which cost, if anything, very little.

At a person's death, the one officiating laid the body out in the home on a "cooling board" which was usually an ironing board. The body was bathed (the men shaved) and then dressed in the Sunday-best clothes. Coffee grounds and turpentine were placed in the body cavities to prevent seepage and odors. If it was in the summer, the burial was usually the same day. But if the body was held over and the weather warm, the casket was placed on the front porch, where there was plenty of air and a person stood guard all night. Or, if the body stayed inside, fans kept the body cool. "Wakes" were held each night prior to the burial. Relatives and friends would be present to mourn the passing of a loved one. Food and drinks would be available to sustain them.

Persons digging the grave were usually friends of the family or in later years the county road workers, among whom were Joseph Bryan, Daniel (Fastman) Mitchell, Clarence and Willis Simmons, Frankie Smith, and Thomas Stafford.

Customarily, the preacher conducted the funeral at the home, but if the body came from Savannah, it was sometimes moved from the boat to the church, or in most cases, from the dock to the cemetery with a grave-side service.

Following the service, in the early years, the casket was then placed in a wagon pulled by oxen or a horse. A procession of mourners walked behind the wagon and sang all the way to the cemetery. The casket was opened so that everyone could file past and see the loved one for the last time. Black and white people attended all funerals.

According to the black tradition, before the body was placed in the ground, if there was a surviving child or grandchild, this child would be lifted over the casket so that the child would not fret for his parent or grandparent, and so that the spirit of the dead person wouldn't take the child to the grave with him or her. Facing the east, the casket was lowered into the ground and the dirt was rounded over the grave. A piece of oak limb was shoved into the ground as a head marker. All of the things that the person used during his/her illness were placed on the grave. Everything the dead needed would be right there, and they would have no reason to return for anything.

Contents of the bottles of medicine were spilled and the bottles inverted; cups, saucers, toothbrushes, drinking or reading glasses, spoons, knives, forks, clocks, razors, false teeth, combs—all were sticking out and highly visible in this mound of dirt. Unless the funeral came from Savannah, floral arrangements were few.

Established during the plantation days, there were actually eight cemeteries on the island. However, the pyramid-type vault for [the white] Mongin family at Haig's Point, by the eastern gate, was moved circa 1880 to Bonaventure Cemetery in Savannah, Georgia. Now, there are seven cemeteries, one for white people, known as the Mary Dunn Cemetery, and six for the blacks. These six are: Bloody Point, Cooper River, Fripp, Haig's Point, Maryfield, and Webb. The two largest and most active have been the Cooper River and Maryfield cemeteries.

Land for the cemeteries was acquired in various ways. There were eleven plantations on the eve of the Civil War: Benjie's Point, Bloody Point, Cooper River, Eigleberger, Haig's Point, Mary Dunn, Maryfield, Melrose, Oak Ridge, Piney Islands, and Webb Tract. Titles to Daufuskie land changed hands often and most of it was under absentee ownership for sometime. When Union warships headed for South Carolina waters, planters left Daufuskie before the invasion. They forsook everything they possessed, including fields white with cotton, waiting to be picked. The land went into Union hands as abandoned land or for nonpayment of taxes.

Some of the land was returned to the planters after the War but often with the provision that the ex-slaves be allowed to remain on the land and to retain crops of the season, harvested or unharvested. On 28 December 1865 an agreement gave land to twenty-two former slave families for one year. Two-and-one-half acres in the corn field and two-and-one-half acres in the cotton field were allotted to each family. The War had changed things. Those whites that regained control of their plantations now had to pay wages to former slaves for their labor. Land was most often set aside by the planters for burial grounds, previously for the enslaved and, later, for the ex-slaves.

An Island Named Daufuskie further reports that several of the native islanders were consulted as to who was buried in which cemetery. Burn herself acknowledges the sketchiness of island history: "It is very difficult to try to remember the names of those who have been dead for so many years. . . .

L A Y   D O W N   B O D Y

If anyone is omitted, it is only because that person's name could not be recalled. Some of the cemeteries have very few headstones."

But the lack of history exists only insofar as the recording of actual names. One step onto any of the Daufuskie Island cemeteries and one can't help but notice how each exudes its own special history. Each cemetery is its own treasure, its own private historical landmark. It's the sheer "charm," if that word is appropriate to describe a cemetery, of these tucked-away burial sites that captures the imagination. And they are certainly a contrast to some of the bigger, better known, and more immaculately kept cemeteries of the Southeast.

BLOODY POINT CEMETERY

When the first white men set foot on Carolina soil, they displayed their guns, hoes, axes, knives, and other farm tools. Native Americans, whose ancestors had been on the island for thousands of years, watched patiently as the white settlers shot deer, planted seeds, and cut down trees. After some years of life together, during which the Indians traded corn, beans, squash, furs, and finally acres of land for cheap trinkets from the white men, the first skirmish began. This greed and abuse led to the Indian Uprising of 1715. The beach sand on the "point" was left red with the blood of those slain.

A second skirmish occurred a few years later when the settlers fought Native Americans they had accused of looting. They killed twenty-eight Indians, and for the second time the beach was crimson with blood. The third skirmish took place in 1728. This time a Yamassee war party surprised the settlers, and white men's blood was spilled on the beach. After 1715 the area had become known as Bloody Point, and the later battles helped cement the name forever.

Burials in Bloody Point Cemetery, a black cemetery situated on the west side of Bloody Point by the waters on Mongin Creek, began in the 1800s. As noted in *An Island Named Daufuskie,* many of the markers at this cemetery have been vandalized, and only four remain:

James Jones Jr.
Born April, 6, 1886
Died October 16, 1909
Sweet Be Thy Sleep

William (Dollar Bill) Bryant
Husband of Alice Bryant
Died October 21, 1930
Age 52 years

Grace Ficklin
Was born on Daufuskie
May 15, 1874

Died February 5, 1939
In Her Own Home Age 65
At Rest

In Memory of Silas Bryan
Born January 10, 1884
Died January 24, 1945

Joseph Michael does not have a headstone, but his granddaughter, Frances E. Jones, states that he was born in 1865 and died November 7, 1933. Cleveland Bryan has a record of his little brother being buried at Bloody Point: **Thomas Bryan Jr.**, born Friday, May 12, 1916; died Thursday, November 3, 1916.

Also buried here is **Pender Hamilton**, the cook for Michael Doyle, who was responsible for erecting the Bloody Point light tower; and **Jimmy Lee**, a basket maker on the island.

The names of the following black people could be remembered, but their birth or death dates have passed from knowledge: **Best:** Florence; **Brown:** Isaac (Son); **Bryan:** Martha, Nathanal, Robert Jr., Silas; **Sylvia:** William; **Hamilton:** Morris, Pender; **Heyward:** Flora, Leotha; **Jackson:** George, London, Mary; **Lee:** Henrietta, Jimmy; **Mongin:** "Crab," Hezekiah (Kyah), Lemon (Robinson); **Robinson:** Charles, Edward, Ollie; **Walker:** Hester, Simon.

COOPER RIVER CEMETERY

Cooper River Plantation consists of about seven hundred acres. Its land was confiscated by Union troops during the Civil War, but in 1867 the former owner redeemed the property and divided it into small tracts, which he sold to former slaves. One of them, Cato McIntire, bought a choice piece of land containing the two-story mansion house, which stood until fire destroyed it in 1940.

The cemetery is situated on the west side of the plantation, on the bank of the Cooper River. It was here that the African American communities in Daufuskie, Hilton Head Island, and elsewhere mobilized when construction began on a house and pathway to be built on a portion of cemetery land.

In the fall of 1990, residents of Daufuskie Island filed a suit in county court, charging the Melrose Company and Cooper River Landing Company, Inc., with trespassing and desecrating the graveyard. The two had joined together to lease the home and pathway illegally constructed on cemetery land. The Melrose Group Limited Partnership used the new house as a reception center and transportation office.

The lawsuit sought an end to the "trespass" of cemetery boundaries—first plotted in 1884—unspecified compensatory and punitive damages, and

restitution. Specifically, the lawsuit charged a Daufuskie Island businessman with building a house atop a black cemetery, and held that a dock leading to the property from the Cooper River cut off access to the cemetery from the water. The plaintiffs argued that the dock interfered with a burial tradition of native Sea Islanders, who believe that water is the gate to their spiritual world and that the water serves as a channel for the spirits of the dead to return to their native Africa. The Beaufort County master in equity (a circuit court judge in civil cases) remarked during the hearing, "Now, all that's a bunch of junk insofar as I'm concerned. If the spirit can go to Africa by the water, this 'bridge' ain't going to stop it."

Cooper River Cemetery lies on the west side of the plantation, on the bank of the Cooper River.

The 1884 Daufuskie plot-map indicates that the cemetery, used primarily by black native islanders, was originally intended to cover one acre. A half-acre portion with headstones was fenced off when the house was built; the remaining half-acre became part of the property leased by the Melrose Company.

On January 25, 1991, islanders scored a victory when Judge Thomas Kemmerlin of Beaufort's Court of Common Pleas ruled that the lawsuit against the developers for desecration of the African American graveyard on Daufuskie Island, South Carolina, could proceed. He rejected the developers' request to have the suit dismissed with a simple statement: "All right-thinking people would sympathize with ones whose loved ones' graves have been disturbed, as perhaps they were here."

The Melrose Company agreed to move its Reception Center, built on top of burials at the Cooper River Cemetery, as part of an out-of-court settlement in 1993.

At the hearing on January 15, 1991, the judge's small courtroom was packed to overflowing with plaintiffs and their supporters. The case also attracted a lot of media attention, including NBC-TV and several magazines and newspapers. Lawyers for Melrose Company argued that the developers had clear title to the cemetery land because of a "quiet title" action. "Quiet title" is a legal action that enables a prospective land buyer or owner to insure their ownership of the land by notifying anyone with possible claims to the land and then cutting off their rights to it.

The developers tried to have the case dismissed at the hearing, and attorney Lewis Pitts of the Christic Institute (now the Southern Justice Institute)—a nonprofit group that helps needy people with problems like land questions, property taxes, and questionable losses of land and cemeteries—argued that denying the plaintiffs the right to bring their suit to court would deny them their right to due process under the U.S. Constitution.

The judge's ruling meant that the case could go to the next step of discovery. "We will be taking depositions from the defendants in the case, to show that they knew what they were doing all along," said Pitts. "They saw the cemetery as valuable waterfront and they were determined to make money off it."

Plaintiff Lillian Spencer, a retired mathematics teacher whose grandmother is buried in Cooper River Cemetery, cited a similar case, where devel-

LAY DOWN BODY

opers in Georgia also built on top of a graveyard called Richmond Hill. Her father's relatives are buried there, and the owners went so far as to name their new development after the graveyard.

"Destruction of graveyards is part of the genocidal effect of the so-called 'New Plantations' being developed in the low country area of South Carolina," Pitts continued. "These areas depend on cheap black labor, theft of black land, and destruction of black communities and culture. It used to be indigo, rice, or cotton plantations; now it's golf, tennis, and equestrian plantations. It's all based on economics and racism."

The June 25, 1993, edition of the *Savannah Morning News* reported good news about the outcome of the lawsuit and plans to continue the fight for justice:

> The Melrose Co. Reception Center will be relocated away from its current waterfront site by the end of 1993, according to the terms of the out-of-court settlement reached in June of 1993. [Mr. Pitts stated] "[T]his is a good first step to reclaim African American heritage and culture on Daufuskie. We consider the agreement an important victory, an important first step toward achieving reparations for the people of Daufuskie who've had so much taken from them for so many years."

As part of the cemetery settlement, a nonprofit Cooper River Cemetery Preservation Society was formed, with the six plaintiffs as officers, to preserve and restore the cemetery. Following are the headstones that have been found at Cooper River:

James Givens
Born February 13, 1906
Died November 30, 1943
Age 37

Lizzie McIntire
Born 1865
Died February 27, 1921
Age 56

In Memory of N. Simmons
Born January 31, 1933
Died July 24, 1945

Willie Hudson
Born June 6, 1870
Died October 28, 1942

In Memory of Cato McIntire (II)
Born April 20, 1908
Died May 27, 1936
Age 28

Cato McIntire once owned the mansion house in the Cooper River region, where he is now buried.

"My Beloved Husband"
Cato McIntire
Born April 27, 1847
Died October 27, 1919
"Resting with Jesus"

Lottie Carter
Born September 6, 1906
Died March 3, 1937
Age 31

In Memory of Rebecca Chisolm
Born July 4, 1872
Died March 1, 1960
"At Rest"

L A Y   D O W N   B O D Y

Tina Jenkins
Born June 2, 1883
Died January 1, 1941

In Memory of Elizabeth Riley
Born October 27, 1882
Died August 13, 1948

Robert Hamilton
Age 66 (Born 1851)
Died March 31, 1917

Gabrial Washington
South Carolina
Pvt. 1cl

321 Serv. Bn
Died June 11, 1943

Prophet Jenkins
Georgia
803 Co Trans. Corp.
Died August 28, 1957

In Memory of
Benjamin Riley
Born May 26, 1916
Died July 2, 1939

There are also headstones with the inscriptions:

Brown, Derald
July 24, 1964–July 26, 1964

Hamilton, Jane
died 1962
(Hamilton donated land for the school that bore her name.
After the school was abandoned she lived in the school
building until her death.)

The following are among those with names and dates, but no stone
markers:

Michael, Margaret (Peggy)
May 30, 1865–April 17, 1963

Stafford, Charlease Marie (stillborn)
December 31, 1966

Washington, Agnes
February 28, 1894–August 22, 1971
(Agnes Washington was one of the cooks at Melrose
Plantation.)

Washington, Lillie Mae
1954–1963

Wilson, Paul
March 27, 1927–September 6, 1968
(Paul Wilson was a relative of Jane Hamilton. He lost sight in
one of his eyes and one day he slipped and fell into New
River at the public landing. His body was found two weeks
later.)

The following have no dates on markers: **Brisbane:** Charlotte;
Brown: Jackson; **Chisolm:** Reverend; **Grant:** Priscilla; **Hamilton:** Bunkum,
Lexi, Robert Jr.; **Houston:** Jeremiah; **Manuel:** Amelia; **Mitchell:** Victoria;
Riley: Joe, Julia.

FRIPP CEMETERY

This black cemetery on Mary Dunn Plantation is located by the bank of the New River on property that now belongs to a member of the Ward family. The plantation is named after Mary Martinangele Dunn, who had owned the last of her family's slaves.

Two of the cemeteries are on land that belonged to the Martinangele family: Mary Dunn Cemetery for the white population, and Fripp Cemetery for the black population. Fripp Cemetery was probably started by Mary Foster Martinangele to bury slaves after she purchased the property in 1762. Mary's daughter, Mary Martinangele Dunn, owned the three hundred acres of the family land that would become known as Mary Dunn Plantation.

In 1874 Dunn sold all her property, with the exception of the four acres she stated as being a burial ground. She sold this property to her brother-in-law, William Fripp Chaplin Sr., who had it surveyed in lots and sold, mostly to blacks, many of whom were Mary Dunn's former slaves.

Richard Fuller Fripp Sr. was left in possession of the land that held the cemetery. He continued to allow blacks to bury their dead there; hence the name Fripp Cemetery. It is unknown whether any tombstones remain, but the following list of some of those buried at Fripp Cemetery were either some of Mary's slaves or descendants of her former slaves: **Bryan:** Abraham, Aleck, Baccus Sr., Baccus Jr., Ben, Biggam Sr., Biggam Jr., Clara, Cynthia, Ella, Ellen, Ernestine, Essie, Flora, Janie, Molly I, Molly II, Patsy, Paul, Richard; **Holmes:** Tom (Rose Brisbane's first husband); **Mack:** Miriah Bryan (cook for Fuller Fripp).

HAIG'S POINT CEMETERY

Haig's Point Plantation, consisting of approximately 358 acres, was sold in 1850 to Squire Pope Jr. It was later combined with the adjacent Freeport Plantation and grew to 958 acres. When northern troops invaded Daufuskie Island in 1861, they took possession of the entire plantation. The mansion was torn down, and the heavy timbers and even the nails were salvaged to use for building roads to more easily move troops during the Civil War. The Haig's Point Cemetery is unique among Sea Island burial grounds as one of only two sites located away from either water or marshlands—the other is the cemetery at Webb Tract. Haig's Point Cemetery is located just east of the Savannah Walk, off Haig's Point Road, and contains graves bearing the following markers:

> **John Stafford**
> 1888–1944
> He Kept the Faith

Kate Holmes
Born Barnwell, S.C.
July 4, 1868
December 19, 1945

Doctor Mills
Born April 18, 1866
Died August 17, 1917

In Memory of
Kattie Byers
1889–1950

May Hamilton
Co. B.
21 U.S.C.I.

In Memory
Elizabeth F. Holmes
Born August 3, 1903
Died 1959

Mrs. Adres
Born 1834 (85 years old)
Died June 25, 1919

In Memory
Samuel Holmes
Died June 8, 1969
(Samuel Holmes was a carpenter who built several houses on Daufuskie. He had a horse named Friendship that carried Samuel and his box of tools to every job.)

The following have small foot-markers provided by the funeral home:

Ida Holmes
Infant
Died, 1921

Ida Holmes
Teenager

Nora Lawrence
Died 1956
(Mother of Johnny Hamilton)

These are the names of people buried with no markers but some dates remembered: **Stafford:** Herbert, 1918–June 26, 1968; **Stafford:** Lula, 1882–July 27, 1964; **Young:** Tara "Missy," August 17, 1893–February 23, 1965; **Frazier:** Fred; **Holmes:** Theresa J., Rubin; **Lawrence:** Frank; **Mills:** Jim, Susie; **Rivers:** Dan, Prince; **Simmons:** Milton, Pink, Rufus; **Smalls:** Ben, Lucie, Maggie; **Wiley:** Jane; **Williams:** Margaret; **Young:** Leroy.

MARYFIELD CEMETERY

This black cemetery borders a marsh on the west side of Maryfield Plantation, located near what is now known as Governor's Point. Haig's Point, the area's main road, leads down to Governor's Point Road. In its heyday, Maryfield Plantation consisted of 530 acres. Confiscated during the Civil War, the land was later redeemed by its former owners, then surveyed and laid off in forty-two lots that were sold to former slaves and their families. A group of spiritual black men got together and, on January 29, 1881, purchased twelve acres for $82. The First Union African Baptist Church was built on this land, but burned in 1884; pleas for funds to help the rebuilding effort appeared in the Savannah newspaper. A new church was constructed just south of where the original church had stood; both it and a black school still remain on the plantation. Maryfield Cemetery is thought to be the most popular and probably, at over ten acres in size, the largest black cemetery in the area. A great number of markers still stand at the site. Following is a list of those with dates:

THE BENTLEY FAMILY:
Charley, December 31, 1875–March 24, 1944
Eddie, February 28, 1909–June 15, 1954
Janie, April 8, 1908–August 8, 1979
Mingo, May 26, 1906–September 26, 1936
Robert, April 10, 1902–February 5, 1953

THE BRYAN FAMILY:
Alfred (Plue) August 1, 1899–December 11, 1941
Anthony William, January 26, 1953–March 7, 1956
Arthur, Died January 6, 1938
Elizabeth, May 4, 1876–April 29, 1963
John Sr., May 1, 1875–November 20, 1962
John Jr., October 16, 1905–April 9, 1946
Lawrence Sr., July 28, 1912–July 22, 1938
Sarah, 1902–August 5, 1982
Thomas, November 3, 1888–July 26, 1980
Vernetta, February 20, 1949–November 24, 1977
William (Hamp), 1901–April 22, 1984

Also buried at Maryfield are **Cornelia Grant**, March 15, 1895–March 10, 1981, a midwife; and **Louvenia (Blossom) Robinson**, June 10, 1897–January 12, 1982. Robinson was one of the main characters in Pat Conroy's book *The Water Is Wide*.

A few names were recalled by a group of Daufuskie residents, who, over the years, were questioned every time they caught a ride on Billie Burn's school bus—not just children were transported; anyone who needed a ride was welcome to climb on. No dates could be remembered: **Bentley:** Sally; **Demery:** Frank; **Grant:** Hester; **Graves:** Sylvia; **Haynes:** Joseph, Maggie (Mongin); **Hudson:** Chloe, William; **Johnson:** July, Lizzie; **Jenkins:** Abe; **Lock:** Betsy; **Loyd:** Sam, Susie; **Miller:** Aaron, Ben, Jesse, Kit, Liz, Marshall,

Mingo, Phoebe; **Mongin:** Bradley, John, Lillie; **Robinson:** Sippio Sr., Sippio Jr.; **Sanders:** Chance, Clara; **Smith:** Susie (Susie Smith was the lady who first began making deviled crab to sell in 1917, then taught others how to make them. She was also a midwife).

WEBB TRACT CEMETERY

The Webb Tract Plantation—also known as Newburgh Plantation—consists of 740 acres and, like many large homes in the area, was claimed by Union soldiers during the Civil War. It remained confiscated for unpaid taxes by the U.S. Direct Tax Commission for the District of South Carolina and was sold in December 1875 for $260. Webb Tract Cemetery seems to be the smallest of the black cemeteries. It is located just north of the present Hargray Telephone Company on Cooper River Road and east of the gate on Webb Tract that leads down to Rabbit Point. Two headstones are known to remain, but only one is inscribed:

> **Robert Bryan**
> Born July 18, 1892
> Died July 1, 1960

Following are the names of a few of the people known to be buried here, with no dates: **Bacon:** William; **Bentley:** Amelia; **Bryan:** Ben, Katie, Matilda; **Jenkins:** Virginia; **McGraw:** Hagar; **Mordeci:** Robert; **White:** Andrew, Daffney, Katie.

Hilton Head Island, South Carolina

Hilton Head Island, occupied by Native American peoples since 1200 B.C., was visited by the Spanish in the 1520s and explored by William Hilton, its namesake, in 1663. Settlement began by the British, who finally drove the local Yamassee Indians out of South Carolina in 1718. About that time, settler John Bayley began to sell the property claimed by his family and the settlement of Hilton Head Island began. At forty-two miles square—twelve miles long and five miles at its widest—Hilton Head is the largest of the Sea Islands between New Jersey and Florida. By 1766, there were at least twenty-five families on the island; most were engaged in producing indigo, a plant valued for its deep blue color. After the Civil War, the island, largely isolated from the mainland and other sea islands, was occupied by black farmers. By the 1890s, however, there was increasing pressure to sell island property to wealthy northerners looking for hunting and recreational preserves.

By the 1930s Hilton Head Island's black population had dropped from three thousand to a mere three hundred. The island maintains its beauty today, but has undergone an incredible growth in both residential and commercial development. Bordering one of the few remaining unpolluted marine

LAY DOWN BODY

estuaries on the East Coast, its development as a resort island was begun in the 1950s. The shoe-shaped island's remaining black population includes native islanders, retirees, and part-time residents. Black families from California, Illinois, and Michigan predominate, but many other states are represented.

Charles L. Blockson, a renowned historian, professor at Temple University, and director of the Charles L. Blockson Afro-American Collection–William Penn Foundation, points out that African American island tradition places great importance on burials taking place on "home ground." Native islanders will pay all their lives on insurance policies designed to ensure an island funeral costing many thousands of dollars. Many who once lived on the islands believed that a person is composed of three parts—body, soul, and spirit. When the body dies, the soul departs, but the spirit remains behind and is capable of doing good or mischief to the living. As in West Africa, graves in the sea islands traditionally have been adorned with belongings of the departed and with charms designated to contain or placate the spirit of the person buried there. Real or imagined threats to graveyards are, therefore, a cause of disquiet.

The cemeteries of Hilton Head Island included here are Amelia White, Braddock Point (also known as Harbortown), Pinefield, Talbot, Spanish Wells, Simmons Memorial Gardens, Jenkins Island, Union, Joe Pope, Elliott, and Lawton.

Hilton Head Plantation, a region on Hilton Head Island, contains Talbot and Elliott cemeteries.

Historic Sites on Hilton Head Island

The Museum of Hilton Head Island sponsors walking tours of many of the island's historic sites. Barbara B. Lothrop, executive director of the museum, has "found that many of the visitors to Hilton Head are not golfers or tennis players—they are vitally interested in the history, ecology, and culture of this area. This is why our historical and nature walks and tours have been so successful. . . . The museum was doing ecotourism before the word 'ecotourism' came into use." Among the sites included on museum tours are:

Fort Mitchel (Hilton Head Plantation): An earthwork fortification constructed in 1862 as part of a larger system of defense that stretched from Fort Sherman (Port Royal Plantation) to Skull Creek.

Fort Howell (Beach City Road): A large earthwork built in 1864 to strengthen the defense of Mitchelville. This fort was never manned, and probably never armed.

Fish Haul Plantation (off Beach City Road near the county baseball complex): First established as a plantation in 1717 by Colonel John Barnwell. By the time of the Civil War, Fish Haul was owned by Thomas F. Drayton, who commanded the Confederate forces on Hilton Head Island. Only chimneys remain from the "slave street," but a recent description states that "no plantation on the island had more comfortable or substantial Negro quarters."

continued on next page

While space on the island is limited, in the 1800s many of the black communities had their own churches and cemeteries nearby. Braddock Point and Lawton cemeteries, for example, are located on Sea Pines Plantation, while Talbot and Elliott cemeteries lie on Hilton Head Plantation at the other end of the island. Other cemeteries are in areas where some of the land is still black-owned. Most Hilton Head cemeteries are church-related or family-owned. In some instances, however, an extended family may find its loved ones buried in three or four different locations due to marriages, etc.

All the cemeteries of Hilton Head Island are all on prime waterfront property. Some families feel confident that their land is safe; others keep a watchful eye. Island land is now a scarce but valuable commodity; the city is flexing its muscle and both Pinefield and Jenkins Island cemeteries are in danger of being lost to developers. Indeed, growing numbers of blacks with loved ones interred on the island have experienced a sense of disquiet and frustration in recent years. Often there have been continuous battles to fight off developers seeking rights to as much of this prime property as possible. In areas where the struggle has been particularly fierce, only the diligence of various families has saved the land.

As the community of Hilton Head grows into the year 2000, a cross-island highway designed to relieve the congestion of U.S. Highway 278 is under construction. This new roadway, while adjacent to both Pinefield and Spanish Wells cemeteries, has not encroached on either burial ground. Even so, Perry White, owner of the Gullah Market on Highway 278 and an official of the NAACP, has encouraged business owners to become involved with local politics and advocacy. Others native islanders such as Doris Grant, Juan Byars, Moses Grant, and Michael Cohen have also expressed interest and concern; to a certain extent they each feel that the legacy of these cemeteries is in danger of being lost through developers' hands.

L A Y   D O W N   B O D Y

Because of the warmth and beauty of the islands of Hilton Head, African American visitors often pose the hypothetical question to native islanders: "And where could I be buried if I so chose?" The silence is often deafening. All of the islands are racially integrated in business ownership, public and private schools, and in recreation activities and country club memberships. However, the churches and cemeteries are primarily limited to *a single race;* and space within these black burial grounds is increasingly threatened with extinction.

Most of the black cemeteries on Hilton Head Island do not display names. If a cemetery sign is missing, however, a query to any native islander will result in directions to any of the cemetery sites.

AMELIA WHITE CEMETERY

Amelia White Cemetery, founded in the 1800s by the family of Amelia White, can be reached from Squire Pope Road, and is located behind the offices of Davis Landscape Company. Doris Grant, a Hilton Head resident and native islander, whose grandmother and other relatives are buried there, spearheads much of the one-family cemetery's maintenance and cleanup.

One family member, Bobbie Green, sold his portion of the property—about three acres—to a white church, the Church of God, in 1989. A survey done during the sale caused a dispute concerning the site's boundary; the surveyor thought that the land contained two different, but adjacent, cemeteries. The circa-1800 grave site of a White family member, Ms. Raleeh, in the center of the property, helped to clarify the situation.

The area purchased by the Church of God was eventually determined to be protected by the state due to the location within the grounds of the

continued from previous page

Mitchelville (east of Fort Howell): The first town developed specifically for freed slaves was laid out here on Fish Haul Plantation in 1862.

Zion Chapel of Ease (on Highway 278 at Matthews Drive): A chapel was built on this site in 1786 for members of the Episcopal Church in Beaufort; hence the name "Chapel of Ease." The church was destroyed in 1868, but the communion silver is still in use today.

Stoney-Baynard Ruins (Sea Pines Plantation): The ruins of a plantation house and outbuildings built circa 1790–1800 by James Stoney, a successful cotton planter. A thriving cotton plantation until the Civil War, the site was occupied by Union forces until 1865.

Fort Sherman (Port Royal Plantation): Fort Sherman, one of the largest earthwork forts ever constructed, was built by the Union during the Civil War as a landside fortification for Fort Walker. This site is now accessible only through the Museum of Hilton Head Island tour.

Fort Walker (Port Royal Plantation): Fort Walker was first built by the Confederate Army, but was captured by Union troops in the Battle of Port Royal on November 7, 1861—the largest amphibious assault on the shores of the continental United States in history. Fort Walker was renamed Fort Welles in honor of Gideon Welles, secretary of the navy to President Abraham Lincoln, but it is commonly referred to as Fort Walker. A large complex and town emerged adjacent to the fort when the Union Army made Hilton Head their Department of the South headquarters. This fort is also accessible only through the Museum of Hilton Head Island tour.

somewhat mysterious "green shells." Too late the church found it was prohibited from building on the land, primarily because the site had been declared a state landmark after it was discovered that these valuable shells dated back to the time of slavery. It became a memorial to the Indians and the enslaved who once inhabited the area.

Church of God pastor Reverend Carr eventually sold the land to the town of Hilton Head Island and the South Carolina Department of Natural Resources, and ended up deeding two-tenths of an acre back to the Amelia White Cemetery Preservation Society. A local museum now sponsors visits to the Green's Shell Enclosure (named after Bobbie Green), one of only two known sites of its kind in the Low Country. Not to be confused with the Indian Shell Ring on another part of Hilton Head, the historical Green's Shell Enclosure sits off Squire Pope Road, abutting the Amelia White Cemetery.

Amid its lush setting, the cemetery often becomes thick and overgrown, making it difficult to walk through. Grant sets aside each Mother's Day as the time to clean up the burial grounds. "As long as I have breath in my body," she declares, "this cemetery will be clean." During a visit to the Amelia White Cemetery, it is easy to see Grant's personal touch. She has provided seating, "so different members of the family can come here and sit as long as they like. My father said, 'God's out here,'" she adds. Grant has planned additional projects to enhance her family burial ground. "I'm going to plant one purple and one white lilac bush and when they bloom they will add beauty to the grounds." Other related family members buried in Amelia White Cemetery include Draytons, Owenses, and Greens. There is no charge for burial.

BRADDOCK POINT (HARBORTOWN) CEMETERY

Braddock Point Cemetery, also known as Harbortown Cemetery, was founded in the 1800s by a distant ancestor of island resident Juan Byars. The cemetery is located in the section of Hilton Head Island where Byars's family once lived. Once known as the Harbortown area of the original plantation, it now lies near Harbortown Golf Course. Byars is a sixth-generation islander; among his related family members who, together, own this beautiful site are the Williamses, Campbells, Bryants, Fraziers, and Chisholms.

Byars's ancestors moved from the Harbortown area to another part of Hilton Head during the last century because of the frequency of strong storms. In the 1950s a young Harvard graduate named Charles E. Frazier conceived the idea of a resort in the area and bought the five thousand acres of land known as Sea Pines.

Green's Shell Enclosure

Green's Shell Enclosure is a unique archaeological site on the north end of Hilton Head Island. It consists of a three-acre tract of land between Squire Pope Road and Skull Creek that currently houses a prehistoric "structure" of oyster shells. The site was excavated by archaeologists in 1968, and again in 1994. Archaeological experts maintain that the four-foot-high, twenty- to thirty-foot-wide semicircular ring of oyster shells was originally the substructure of a palisade wall that protected a Native American village dating back to 1335 A.D.

The site is currently preserved and maintained as a nature park by the town of Hilton Head in conjunction with South Carolina's Heritage Trust program, part of the South Carolina Department of Natural Resources. The Museum of Hilton Head Island sponsors walking tours while being careful to tread lightly near an old family burial ground, the Amelia White Cemetery, which is adjacent to the shell enclosure. Although at a distance the enclosure appears to be "just a mound in the woods," closer inspection reveals a boundary constructed in the formation of an irregular circle enclosing almost two acres of land. In contrast to the shell enclosure, the neighboring cemetery is clearly defined, housing a handful of graves that are adorned with fresh flowers by Doris Grant, a local woman dedicated to maintaining the graves of her ancestors.

Now called Sea Pines Plantation, this large tract of island property currently houses some of the island's most luxurious homes. The area has several golf clubs and courses, tennis courts, marina shops, restaurants, a lighthouse, and a dock for the ferries that provide shuttle-service to nearby Daufuskie Island. Around-the-clock security guards stop each car entering the area; unless a sticker of residency is displayed a $3 entry pass is required.

Although family members connected to the Braddock Point Cemetery are allowed entry, it is painful for some, many of whose close relatives are buried at the cemetery, when they try to enter the Sea Pines gates. "I'd like to

Braddock Point Cemetery was founded in the 1800s by a distant ancestor of island resident Juan Byars, shown here speaking with Dr. Charles Wright.

put a 'blood cuff' on them," Byars exclaims, "to measure their pressure as they approach this gate." Although Byars and his relatives have a personal connection to this portion of the island, because they are not residents of Sea Pines Plantation they are asked to pay for the visitor pass.

As one approaches the cemetery at the far end of Sea Pines, the reality of it all is shocking and frightening. A luxury condo has been built in a position to block its residents' view of the graves; marked and unmarked burial sites lay right outside its walls. Byars sometimes imagines the affect of a funeral taking place during the time of the resort's Heritage Golf Classic—the course's eighteenth hole is practically on cemetery grounds. "I put in a request to the good Lord," he chuckles, "for good timing on my death."

From within the cemetery itself, villas now block the vista of Calibogue Sound that the original founders had planned as the view "over to Africa"—across the water—as a comfort for lonely souls. Byars explains that African Americans once believed their spirits would more easily make the trip across the water to return to Africa if they were buried near the water. "There is a strong spiritual feeling. . . . Daufuskie Island is directly across the water—and ostensibly, so is Sierra Leone, Africa."

"In order to get a grave," Byers explains, "you mark the spot you want. It's understood as family that you do that. The funeral home handles the

L A Y   D O W N   B O D Y

digging. The family cleans the cemetery. One sad feature," he adds, "is that we had people who were buried and couldn't afford headstones. I've a grandaunt who is buried here. She's buried outside this area that the developers fenced in and designated as the cemetery." He explains that the developers filled in the cemetery land bordering their property to make room for the eighteenth hole of Plantation golf course. "My great[-great] uncle showed us the real boundaries of the cemetery. They built right over some graves that were not marked."

A tour of the graveyard reveals some interesting local customs. Byars explains the tradition of attaching plates to the headstones of departed loved ones. "When they would bury the head of the household, [they] would show respect by taking his plate and have it pressed into the headstone. The father, the head of the household, had the plate. It was too costly for others to have a plate; they ate out of a pan or whatever."

Byars has been approached by the township regarding the possibility of making Braddock Point Cemetery a historic site, but he questions whether this is an attempt to halt burials. "We plan to keep burying here," he states. The cemetery contains about a hundred clearly marked graves, with many more now lost to view. Some grave sites marked with small artifacts have been lost through time. Others have disappeared due to the construction of Sea Pines Plantations' condos and villas and golf course. Of all the cemeter-

The lovely Braddock Point Cemetery has been beset by modern woes: Villas now block the view across Calibogue Sound. This view was important to African Americans, who believed their spirits would more easily return to Africa if they were buried near the water.

65

ies on Hilton Head Island, Braddock Point is, perhaps, the saddest to visit. One of the oldest graves here is that of **Susan Brown Williams**, born in 1861. Now surrounded by some of the most expensive and valuable property in South Carolina, one has to wonder how much longer she will be allowed to rest at the edge of the sea.

PINEFIELD CEMETERY

This large expanse of land is beautiful beyond description. But, wildly overgrown with shrubs and the undergrowth born of the varied forest that shelters it, Pinefield Cemetery is difficult to explore. A construction company working nearby adds to the confusion by dumping materials in an area adjacent to the burial ground, which was founded in the late 1700s. Unfortunately, such a situation is all too common in this region, as commercial overindustrialization eats away at many of the historical lands and special properties.

Pinefield Cemetery lies at Broad Creek; it can be reached by turning off Highway 278 onto Matthews Drive, and proceeding to Marshlands Road. While recorded in the records of the state of South Carolina as Otter Hole Cemetery, it is known under the name given to it by Hilton Head residents many years before.

Some graves are marked with homemade concrete tombstones, names and dates scratched carefully onto each surface. Others are discernible only as depressions in the sandy earth. One marker reads:

Sandy Stafford
Died April 14, 1883, at the age of 98.

Residents Joseph Mitchell and Doris Grant and a local boy scout troop have tried to mark off the property and do some minimal cleaning. Recent rumors have indicated that developers are attempting to take over this valuable, marshlands-bordered property. The construction that moves ever closer would tend to confirm these reports.

TALBOT CEMETERY

Talbot Cemetery, less than ten acres in size, is on Skull Creek Road on Hilton Head Plantation. It is heavily wooded and dates back to the 1800s, when blacks farmed the land and made the island their home. Although today only the cemetery remains amid streets lined with plush homes, a country club, and well-manicured golf courses, one can see that area developers made a clean sweep of only the old houses and churches, and left burial

LAY DOWN BODY

grounds like Talbot Cemetery somewhat intact. Markers at Talbot show such inscriptions as:

Edward Landson
Born December 1840
Died December 26, 1904

Katie Miller
Born December 14, 1854
Died April 15, 1935

Although it would be wonderful to be able to discover all the others who have been laid to rest here over the years, many markers are unreadable. Today, Talbot Cemetery seems but the skeletal remains of what was once a prominent burial ground.

SPANISH WELLS CEMETERY

Some of the extended family of island native Juan Byars are buried in this small cemetery located off Spanish Wells Road; Chisholm and Campbell family members also have ties to this spot. Spanish Wells Cemetery can be reached from the road that bears its name, not far from the bridge at the entrance to the island. The Oak Marsh subdivision is adjacent to the cemetery, which also borders on a large expanse of marsh. Like some of the other island burial grounds, an overgrowth of bushes and grass competes with the burial sites and marshes. Although little is known about when the cemetery was founded, and native islanders can recall little information about its heritage, an off-the-beaten-track cemetery such as Spanish Wells can provide useful information to the African American seeking his or her roots. Spanish Wells is one of a number of cemeteries that has a family lineage attached to it; it is precisely these types of cemeteries that the investigative genealogist or curious family member is sure to appreciate. If nothing else, it's interesting to see how some of these cemeteries become almost transparent amid the natural beauty that surrounds them.

SIMMONS MEMORIAL GARDENS

In 1927, Charlie Simmons Sr. provided a welcome service to island residents when he purchased a boat. He made trips from Hilton Head to nearby

Savannah and Daufuskie Island three times a week, picking up passengers and freight. His cargo included produce, oysters, pecans, chickens, and other staples. Business was so good that Simmons purchased a larger boat, and then another. He traveled the route for many years but halted deliveries to Hilton Head in the 1950s after a motor bridge to the island was built. However, he continued to assist Daufuskie residents crossing to Hilton Head Island until 1986. The Simmons family also ran the first bus transportation service on the island. Charles Jr. had a store and barbershop at the entrance to the island.

The Simmons Memorial Gardens was established in June 1968 by Simmons. His mother, **Estella**, was the first to be buried in the cemetery. The son of Rosa and Charles Simmons Jr., **Charles E. Simmons III**, and their grandson **Charles E. Simmons IV**, are also buried in the garden.

JENKINS ISLAND CEMETERY

This beautiful, wooded cemetery, founded in the 1700s, is just off Highway 278, not far from the Hilton Head bridge. It cannot be seen from the highway, and must be approached by a narrow path that leads through brush and trees to this oasis. Even though hidden, it faces the increasing threat of development. Michael Cohen, a native islander, whose family is buried alongside members of the Gadson family in Jenkins Island Cemetery, explains that the site is being watched carefully. Thus far, developers have staked the property right up to the cemetery line. Local residents report rumors of a possible expansion of the marine base that lies adjacent to the site. "All of the black cemeteries in Hilton Head are 'on water,' except Union Cemetery," Cohen says, discouraged that the desire for resort living increasingly threatens the peaceful repose of the dead.

UNION CEMETERY

Union Cemetery, on Union Cemetery Road just off Highway 278, is nestled near one of Hilton Head's popular golf courses. Among the cemetery owners is the Benjamin White family. Nathanial White explained that the nearby St. James Baptist Church, at the intersection of Dillon and Beach City Roads, helps to maintain the grounds. He is undecided about the rumors that the site once served as a Civil War battleground, a speculation that prompted the name of both the street and the cemetery.

Frank Shelton, a writer for the *Island Packet,* asked sixty-nine-year-old island native Gene Wiley about his love for Union Cemetery: "That's my uncle right there," Wiley pointed out on a walk through the grounds, "and that one over there is my father. Half the people in here are related to me." Wiley, owner of the Golden Rose Restaurant on Beach City Road, has lamented the area's development: Companies purchased tracts of land around the cemetery and turned it into a private, fenced-in community called Port Royal Plantation. Wiley speculates that developers "took advantage of the landowners." According to Shelton, the situation reflects the days when whites "us[ed] their [blacks'] lack of education against them as they purchased land acre by acre for prices that could barely buy a meal on the island today. . . . Wiley said his grandmother, Sarah Polite, once sold twenty-five acres near Union Cemetery Road for $50 in 1939."

Among the families buried here are the Wiley and Hay families.

JOE POPE CEMETERY

The Queen Chapel holds the deed to this valuable property, a practice the cemeteries try to adhere to for safekeeping. Joe Pope is in an unusual location; its surroundings are far different than they were in the 1800s, or even as late as the early 1900s. The front of the cemetery faces Hilton Head's only

cross-island road, busy Highway 278. The grounds cover approximately five acres and are heavily blanketed with bushes and trees. The foliage is so thick, in fact, that it allows only the truly inquisitive to see the many tombstones. On one side of the cemetery—from the highway to the rear marsh—is the driveway for the local Piggly Wiggly supermarket. With no fence surrounding it, one can park at the grocery store and walk through this beautiful property, being careful, of course, not to disturb those areas where freshly laid flowers have been placed. Buried in Joe Pope are members of the Christopher, Grant, Day, Bryan, and Mitchell families.

ELLIOTT CEMETERY

Elliott Cemetery, located on the grounds of Hilton Head Plantation, is on the beautiful, expansive Port Royal Sound. Densely wooded, it is fre-

quented by deer who sleep among the graves. Founded in the 1830s, Elliott Cemetery is now bordered on one side by a golf course. That and the water, which forms its other boundary, makes parking most difficult for the regularly used cemetery. It is necessary to circle through and around a surrounding neighborhood of palatial homes and leave one's car in a small park before walking through the woods to the cemetery site. One has to wonder how a funeral procession can manage the trip; the only clear ground is the golf course bordering the wooded area. After parking, the coffin would have to be carried anywhere from twenty-five to one hundred yards. Among the islanders buried in this beautiful isolated cemetery are members of the Barnwell family.

LAWTON CEMETERY

Lawton Cemetery is one of the oldest burial sites on Hilton Head Island. It lies inside Sea Pines Plantation at the corner of Oyster Landing Road and Oyster Landing Lane, on a tiny finger of Broad Creek. The site is heavily wooded; only four markers, all professionally made, are visible through the brush, and some yards away stand elegant condos with showcase lawns and gardens. The headstones stand firmly, singularly, and solemnly, but almost comically in the thick ground cover—comically because it is doubtful that any of the residents of Oyster Landing Road or Oyster Landing Lane have the slightest idea that, as they idle their cars daily at the corner, they stand less than twelve yards from an early 1800s African American burial ground.

The near-forgotten cemetery is no longer used for burials, possibly because there are no heirs living. Buried in Lawton is **Rosetta Frazier,** great-aunt of Walter Green, a Hilton Head native. Her stone bears the inscription, "born December 25, 1847 and died March 21, 1936." Frazier is buried next to **Thomas Frazier,** whose grave is marked with a Civil War–era federal tombstone.

Beaufort, South Carolina

The delightful town of Beaufort, South Carolina, is, ostensibly, also an island. The Bay Street area is home to quaint shops and restaurants, while the beautiful waterfront is the scene of the city's air and water shows, art and market festivals, and a busy docking area. The drawbridge from Bay Street over Port Royal Sound to Ladys Island responds regularly to boats whose masts are too tall to pass under it. The bridge turns slowly and gracefully as drivers on both sides idle their cars' engines restively, waiting for the water traffic to glide by.

First discovered by Spanish explorers in 1514–1515, early attempts to settle the area were unsuccessful. The town was almost destroyed by Native Americans in 1715, then captured by the British during the American Revolution. Beaufort flourished as a shipping port for rice and cotton grown on its many plantations, then was captured and evacuated by northern troops during the Civil War. Rebuilt slowly after the war, it has become a lovely community whose main businesses are tourism and the military.

Theaters and strip malls and other businesses line Boundary Street at the far end of the city. Also along Boundary Street are located several cemeteries, including Beaufort National and Sixteen Gate. Farther into the city, near where the large plantation houses of yesteryear still stand, are several historic churches and cemeteries. Among them is the Tabernacle Baptist Church, resting place of Civil War hero Robert Smalls.

Other black cemeteries in the Beaufort area are Citizens, Mercy, and Wesley United Methodist. In the surrounding county are Bonny Hall Plantation River Cemetery (Yamassee) and Hope Bunny Cemetery. In the town of Burton, on Highway 21 just outside of Beaufort, is the South Carolina Marine Corps Air Station, built on and around New Hope Christian Church, Pilgrim, and Rose Hill cemeteries.

While all but Beaufort's National Cemetery are similar in appearance, each cemetery in Burton and Beaufort is distinct in some way. Burton's ceme-

Civil War hero Robert Smalls is buried at Baptist Tabernacle Church in Beaufort, where a monument now stands in his honor.

teries tend to be smaller and all are church-owned. Sixteen Gate Cemetery in Beaufort is owned by a group of businessmen. Beaufort National Cemetery is, of course, federally owned.

Traveling to the area from the north on Highway 21, the town of Burton is the first stop. At its traffic light, on the left, three air corps planes stand on display, marking the entrance to the Marine Corps Air Station. Quite near this entrance is New Hope Christian Church Cemetery; just past it is Pilgrim Cemetery.

A busy intersection a few miles down marks Burton's downtown, the theaters, restaurants, a bank, and small shops all bustling with small-town activity. At this point, Highway 21 changes its name to Boundary; a mile further down stands the sign welcoming travelers to Beaufort.

Proceeding down Boundary on the right is Sixteen Gate Cemetery, just before the corner of Ribaut Street, where stands the Beaufort County government complex. Turning onto Ribaut takes travelers to Port Royal and the United States Naval Hospital. It was on the grounds of the naval hospital that the first public reading of the Emancipation Proclamation took place, on January 1, 1863, and where the first black South Carolina volunteers were mustered into the Union army. The Michigan Support Group, in conjunction with Penn Center, continues to hold annual reenactments at that site. The January 1, 1996, unveiling of a plaque awarded by the South Carolina Department of Archives and History and the U.S. Department of the Interior represents the pinnacle of their efforts.

A few miles further down Boundary is the pristine and starkly mysterious Veterans Cemetery. Boundary then becomes Cateret and follows the beautiful Beaufort River. The University of South Carolina's Beaufort Campus is located on Cateret.

The Sea Island area has become important to Hollywood: the motion pictures *Conrack* and *Prince of Tides* were filmed in Beaufort, *Forrest Gump* in Beaufort and Savannah, and *Daughters of the Dust* on St. Helena and Hunting islands.

BEAUFORT NATIONAL CEMETERY

A brick wall surrounds the grounds of the Beaufort National Cemetery. Laid out in the shape of a half wheel, the cemetery's oyster-shelled roads form the "spokes," and the large iron gates are set at the "hub." The grounds are serenely landscaped with numerous shrubs and large trees, predominantly magnolia, live oak, and palmetto.

Beaufort was one of the first national cemeteries designated by President Abraham Lincoln, who personally authorized its establishment in a letter dated February 10, 1863. The commanding general of Federal Occupation troops bought the twenty-nine-acre tract known as Jolly's Grove for $75 at a tax sale on March 11, 1863. It became the final resting place for soldiers who gave their lives during the war between the states.

The cemetery is the resting place for veterans from every military conflict involving U.S. troops since the Civil War, including the remains of Union troops that were moved from eastern Florida, Savannah, Charleston, Morris Island, Hilton Head Island, and other islands near Beaufort. About twenty-eight hundred remains were removed from Millen, Georgia, and reinterred in Beaufort National Cemetery.

There are more than seventy-five hundred Civil War veterans interred here, including 4,019 unknown Union soldiers and 117 known Confederates. Many of the troops fell on battlefields in Georgia, Florida, and South Carolina. In addition, there are presently more than five thousand veterans of the Spanish-American War, World War I, World War II, Korean War, and Vietnam War who have joined their comrades in final peace here.

"Pass the *Planter!*"

Robert Smalls was born in Beaufort, South Carolina, of an enslaved family. He moved to Charleston at an early age to work. There, at the age of seventeen, he married fellow slave Hannah Jones. The year was 1856.

Five years later the Civil War began. Smalls was secretly on the side of the North, where black people were free. However, he was drafted into the Confederate navy and forced to work as a wheelsman on the gunboat *Planter*. Captain Relyea of the *Planter* and his two mates were white, the rest of the crew enslaved blacks. Smalls worried about his freedom; buying freedom for himself, his wife, and two kids was expensive. He decided to escape by sea and risk the threat of discovery from three forts that had their guns trained on the harbor, looking for enemy ships venturing north.

Why couldn't he capture the *Planter*, Smalls thought, and sail her right past those guns? The northern fleet was anchored seven miles outside the harbor. Freedom was only seven miles away.

Smalls discussed his plan with the slave crew and all were eager to join him. If anything went wrong, they would blow up the ship and die rather than be captured. On May 16, 1862, Smalls and his followers made their move. Eight family members were hidden aboard a second ship, anchored in the Cooper River, with the cooperation of that ship's steward, a fellow slave. They would be taken aboard the *Planter* after Smalls took command.

continued on next page

Boundary Street hums with the activity of ships, businesses, and nearby residences. The charming historic churches and refurbished plantation houses bordering the river are in proximity to Bay Street, with its boutiques, restaurants, antique shops, parks, and boat docks. On most days, tourists can enjoy carriage rides around the historic district. The beautiful "swing" bridge, from Bay Street across the river to Cat Island, Ladys Island, and St. Helena, Hunting, Harbour, and Fripp islands, regularly opens to allow tall pleasure boats to pass. The other bridge to the islands starts just below Parris Island in Port Royal.

continued from previous page

That night, after the captain and his mates went ashore, Smalls took over and readied the ship for action. Firemen Jackson, Alston, and Tarno shoveled fuel into the furnaces. John, the engineer, checked the instruments. Jebel raised the Confederate flag, while Alfred cast off the ship's lines.

At the wheel, Smalls—wearing the captain's broad-brimmed hat—steered the *Planter* away from the dock. The desperate trip had begun. As he neared the second ship, he sent a rowboat for the five women and three children. The steward also came aboard, increasing to sixteen the *Planter's* total number of enslaved passengers.

Smalls headed the ship upstream. He did everything he had seen Captain Relyea do. As the *Planter* approached Fort Jackson, he pulled the cord on the steam whistle and gave the proper salute. As the *Planter* often steamed upriver before dawn, there was no reason for the sentry on shore to think its passage unusual; he yelled: "Pass the *Planter*."

Passing Fort Moultrie was the next challenge. Smalls repeated the whistle salute and again they passed safely. But the most dangerous part was yet to come. It was now near dawn and Smalls could make out the menacing cannons of Fort Sumter. Would the sentry be able to see that he was not Captain Relyea beneath the broad-brimmed hat, but a slave?

continued on next page

Beaufort National Cemetery, located on Boundary, occupies many acres of walled-in property. Although its gate is almost flush with the sidewalk, cemetery grounds are almost invisible to motor traffic. But, as with any national cemetery, a clear view of the immensity of the site graphically illustrates the horror of war. The absolute beauty of the grounds stands in clear contradiction to the reality and purpose of its existence. Row upon row of stately white crosses stand in silent testimony to the courage of those who fought and died for their country.

Beaufort's story has not ended with the interment of casualties from the Vietnam War, however. On May 29, 1989, thanks to the efforts of the local community, members of the Civil War's all-black 55th Massachusetts Regiment were buried, with pride, honor, and dignity, within its walls. Organized in Readville, Massachusetts, on June 22, 1863, the regiment was stationed at New Bern, North Carolina, before being transferred to Folly Island, South Carolina. There, about fifteen miles southeast of Charleston, it participated in operations against Charleston and Johns Island, five miles due west of Charleston. It was in this area that many perished, their bodies dumped in the brigade cemetery on Folly Island. It is from this cemetery that archaeologists excavated their remains in 1987.

Members of a Union reenactment unit reinterred the soldiers of the 55th Massachusetts in black wooden caskets during a ceremony prescribed by 1863 military codes. Dirt brought from Massachusetts was sprinkled over some of the graves, and the ceremony was led by the then-governor of Massachusetts, Michael S. Dukakis, and his wife. Twin historic monuments now overlook the rows of small marble markers in Section 56 of the cemetery, each bearing only a number to identify each of the unknown soldiers. The all-black 54th Massachusetts Regiment was the "sister" regiment to the 55th. On July 18, 1863, the 54th Regiment attacked Confederate Fort Wayne, at Morris Island in the Charleston, South Carolina, harbor. At day's end, one

L A Y   D O W N   B O D Y

half of the 54th was either wounded, missing in action, taken prisoner, dead, or dying. The soldiers of the 54th—along with those of the 55th Massachusetts— were buried at the National Cemetery in Beaufort. Their heroism and valor was movingly illustrated in the movie *Glory,* released in 1989.

The following black defenders of the Civil War and late soldiers of the 54th Massachusetts Regiment answered the command of God Almighty during the period 1863–1865 and assumed the position of "at ease" in peaceful rest:

NAME; COMPANY;
DATE OF BIRTH
Private Anderson Lewis; G;
     August 7, 1863
Private John Bancroft; A;
     July 29, 1863
1st Lieutenant William Biggs;
     E; July 21, 1863
Private Charles Cane; A;
     August 15, 1863
Private Charles Clark II; G;
     July 21, 1863
Private Thomas F. Cooper; E;
     March 1, 1864
Private Anthony Davis; G;
     March 25, 1864
Sergeant William Ellis; G;
     August 10, 1863
Private Emanuel Williams; F;
     October 28, 1863
Private Elia Franklin; C;
     July 31, 1863
Private John H. Freeman; I;
     February 1, 1864
Private Martin Gilmore; D; July 27, 1863
Private Alex Green; D; March 19, 1864
Private Charles Green; C; April 10, 1864
Private Adrastus Hazzard; F; July 7, 1865
Private George Holmes; F; August 14, 1863
Private Franklin Jackson; K; April 11, 1864
Private Sanford Jackson; A; September 13, 1863
Corporal Charles H. Johnson; F; September 18, 1863
Corporal Joseph Johnson; I; July 27, 1863

continued from previous page

Smalls leaned on the windowsill of the pilot house. He folded his arms across his chest as he had seen the captain do. Jebel pulled the signal cord. Smalls waved to the sentry on shore. The sentry did not answer. Smalls prayed silently. "Let us through safely."

Finally he heard the sentry yell: "Pass the *Planter.* Pass the *Planter!*" They were not going to be blown out of the water! They were saved! Smalls piloted the ship past the Fort's huge guns and out to the open sea. By the time the sentry realized something was wrong and fired, the *Planter* was out of range.

The crew and their families crowded to the rail. They had gambled with death and won. Smalls and Hannah looked at each other and at their children. They were free. No longer would they have to call any man "Master." Jebel pulled down the Confederate flag and raised the white flag of truce. When they reached the ships of the Northern Fleet, Robert turned the *Planter* over to the fleet captain.

After the North won the war, Captain Smalls, as he was now called, returned to Beaufort with his family. He was eventually elected to Congress, where he served five terms, championing the cause of equal rights for his people. He was buried at Baptist Tabernacle Church in Beaufort, where a monument now stands in his honor; his home is a National Historic Landmark, though not open to the public. Smalls is remembered today as a true hero. As a boy, he had only dreamed of freedom; as a man, he had risked all he had to win it.

Corporal Alex Jones; D; July 7, 1864
Private Robert Jones; D; May 10, 1865
Sergeant George F. Merriman; B; August 1, 186
Private John Nettle; A; August 8, 1863
Private James Nelson; F; December 27, 1863
Private George Parker; E; March 2, 1863
Corporal Henry T. Peal; F; January 24, 1864
Private Gallahill Porter; I; June 23, 1863
Private Samuel E. Price; I; August 28, 1863
Private Charles R. Reason; E; July 27, 1863
Private Charles Rideout; I; February 16, 1865
Private Albert Scott; H; February 29, 1864
Private George Streets; D; July 22, 1863
Private Ezra Tobias; K; June 15, 1865
Private George Washington; E; August 3, 1863

THESE HALLOWED GROUNDS HOLD THE
REMAINS OF AT LEAST NINETEEN BLACK
UNION SOLDIERS, 55TH MASSACHUSETTS
INFANTRY REGIMENT, WHO LOST THEIR
LIVES ON FOLLY ISLAND IN THE SIEGE
OF CHARLESTON, DURING THE WINTER
ENCAMPMENT OF NOV 1863 - FEB 1864,
CIVIL WAR.

THEIR EARTHLY REMAINS LAY LONG
FORGOTTEN UNTIL REDISCOVERED IN
MAY 1987. THEY WERE REBURIED AT
THIS SITE BY THE COMMUNITY OF
BEAUFORT, MAY 29, 1989.

Private William Wells; E; May 29, 1864
Private Nathan Young; C; July 19, 1863

This is one of two plaques that overlook the Section 56 of Beaufort National Cemetery, commemorating members of the 54th and 55th Massachusetts infantry regiments. These soldiers' heroism during the Civil War was illustrated in the 1989 movie Glory.

SIXTEEN GATE CEMETERY

Sixteen Gate Cemetery is located on the south side of Boundary Street; the cemetery's southern boundary is the marshes of Battery Creek. Although just a few steps from a busy thoroughfare, as one enters the grounds one is transported from the present. Although the cemetery is very much in use, the aura and solemnity of the past are most intense. Walking through and around, and unfortunately sometimes on, the graves brings to mind questions: "who?," "what?," "when?," "why?" Many of the inscriptions on the tombstones have faded with the passing years and the small stories are not legible.

Lois Jenkins and her son, Edward J. Allen, are Beaufort residents and descendants of former owners of Sixteen Gate. Part of the current corporate ownership, they are understandably proud of the beautiful cemetery. Gerhard Spieler, Beaufort County historian and columnist for the *Beaufort Gazette,* writes of the many stories behind the cemetery's name. One version is that in the 1880s, sixteen black social and fraternal organizations united in establishing a cemetery for their members. However, the most likely story is that Sixteen Gate refers to a military post, or gate, that stood on the Old Shell

Road during Civil War times. An old plot shows a proposed black village named Higginsonville and lists XVIII, XIX, and XX streets. It is assumed there may have been a XVI street, giving its name to the cemetery.

The cemetery had its beginning on March 8, 1888, when Annie M. Bartlett and her husband, both from New York City, sold the land to Edward Wallace for $100. A declaration, dated a month later and attached to the deed, stated that Wallace was holding the land for the benefit of the Beaufort Memorial Burial Association. In 1966, Gilbert Walker and William Pegler, trustees of the unincorporated Beaufort Memorial Burial Association, transferred the deed to Sixteen Gate Cemetery, duly incorporated in August 22, 1966.

Among those buried at Sixteen Gate are **George Moody**, and his sons **George Jr.**, **Alvin**, and **Bennie**.

NEW HOPE CHRISTIAN CHURCH CEMETERY

This cemetery, owned by New Hope Christian Church, Disciples of Christ, is approximately seventy-three years old. It faces Highway 21 and extends for more than four acres, bounded on its remaining sides by the Marine Corps Air Station. The cemetery is beautifully maintained.

The church and cemetery were established in 1924, at a time when the entire area was farmland or wooded. The church was separated from the cemetery by five or six miles; while that meant nothing to the original residents, today it seems a longer distance because of busy Highway 21. Buried at New Hope are members of the well-known **Rivers** family: **Bennie**, the eldest, **Josie**, and **Hector Rivers**.

New Hope and Pilgrim cemeteries both lie near the Marine Corps Air Station.

PILGRIM CEMETERY

What remains of the once-vast Pilgrim Cemetery fronts Highway 21, a few hundred yards from the main entrance to the Marine Corps Air Station. The cemetery was once called Donaldson Cemetery after the family that was buried there.

The cemetery was founded in the early 1800s by members of the now defunct Pilgrim Baptist Church. In 1899, three prominent families within

the church, the Donaldsons, Grays, and Griffens, split from the congregation to form the Pine Grove Baptist Church. The new church was built a few miles down the road from Pilgrim Baptist Church, next to a tall cedar tree that Pierce Gray, one of the new congregation's leaders, had dreamt about months earlier.

Eventually almost the entire congregation of Pilgrim Church migrated to the new church and Pilgrim Church ceased to exist. The Pine Grove congregation eventually took over caretaking duties of the cemetery.

At present there are less than forty graves in the Pilgrim Cemetery and only a handful of headstones have survived. Most of the cemetery was lost with the construction of Highway 21; those whose graves were disrupted were reburied at other cemeteries in the area. Among the prominent local African American residents buried at Pilgrim Cemetery are descendants of the same three families who once abandoned the church after which it is named.

RED HOUSE CEMETERY

The 1800s-era Red House Cemetery, just over an acre in size, is still in use. The cemetery is located on property that was formerly known as the Edgely Plantation, home to many black families. When the air base property was

LAY DOWN BODY

purchased, these families were forced to move. Although technically on the air base property, the cemetery is owned by Second Jordan Baptist Church of Burton.

Red House Cemetery is accessible only by entering the grounds of the Marine Corps Air Station, which gives immediate consent to all interested parties. However, it is only natural that families are unhappy about having to weave their way around barracks and buildings to reach the grave sides of family members. The cemetery itself has been fenced off and is protected by a gate, but it is difficult to get to for maintenance; the lush foliage seems to reclaim the grounds almost immediately after it is cut back. Buried at Red House are longtime Burton residents **Victoria Frazier, Betty Frazier, Nell Frazier, Rose Bryan,** and **Barney Bryan.**

St. Helena Island, South Carolina

St. Helena Island, as described in the historical text *Tombee: Portrait of a Cotton Planter* by Theodore Rosengarten, is situated off the Atlantic coast, about fifty miles southwest of Charleston, South Carolina, and forty miles northeast of Savannah, Georgia. About fifteen miles long and three to five miles wide, St. Helena belongs to a fertile chain of islands separated from each other and from the mainland by rivers and creeks. Many of these streams might better be described as "arms of the sea," because they bring the salt water inland to a pine belt and carry it out again without meeting significant sources of fresh water.

Twice each lunar day, the tide flows toward the land, then ebbs seaward. When the moon is in the first and third quarters, the tides rise six to eight feet around St. Helena. At the new moon and the full moon, the waters rise eight to ten feet. As the tides ebb, the islands appear to draw closer together. The flats exposed at low tide are mud-filled moats, friendly only to oyster catchers and armies of hungry crabs. St. Helena is larger than the neighboring islands of Ladys and Port Royal—located west along Port Royal River.

In the 1800s there were no farms on St. Helena Island worked by free labor, and no cotton that was not produced by slaves. Plantations usually bore the names of their owners, who by 1795 were sowing seeds of a new, long-staple cotton plant in beds where indigo had grown before demand for it collapsed. The planter's family lived in a plain, low house with a sprawl of rooms that had been added over the years. A porchless front facade looked out on an irregular row of Negro houses, stables, and provision grounds, including a piece set aside for a house garden.

Fifteen years later, fattened by the high prices paid for his cotton, the typical planter had moved into a mansion, or "Big House," on the creek-

side of his plantation. Today these homes line the banks of the island, reminding visitors of the past: the stately mansions standing arrogantly before the windowless cabins and shacks of the enslaved. Tombee House and Coffin Point House, are two of the largest and most popular of the old island mansions.

St. Helena is practically the only sea island that retains vestiges of a style of life commonplace on the islands during the early 1900s. Traveling to Jekyll, Hilton Head, Kiawah, or some of the other islands stretching from Florida to the Carolinas, one is awed by the trappings of an increasingly more affluent society. St. Helena, on the other hand, counts among her significant landmarks the live oak trees draped with Spanish moss, the beautiful marshes, the small homes and family-owned businesses of her warm and friendly people—though the islanders are cautious of outsiders. There are no traffic

lights or supermarkets; the island boasts only a single motel and three restaurants. Luxury homes border the ocean, while at St. Helena Sound, numerous shrimp boats rev up their motors "at day clean" as they set out to cast their nets for the day's catch.

Penn Center dominates life on the island. Emerging from Penn School in the mid-1950s—after Beaufort County took over the responsibility of educating African Americans on St. Helena and the surrounding islands—it sits on fifty acres dotted by groves of towering oak trees heavy with moss. In 1863 Penn School teacher and diarist Charlotte Forten described the trees as breathtakingly beautiful. They still are. The campus consists of approximately sixteen buildings, all recently remodeled and refurbished, but retaining the charm and distinctiveness of the original buildings of a century ago. Along with its campus, the Center's activities and programs have grown

through the years, and the extent of its involvement with and effect on the island is immeasurable.

Penn's current mission, under executive director and Hilton Head native Emory Campbell, is to preserve Sea Island history, culture, and environment. The center serves as a local, national, and international educational resource center and acts as a catalyst for the development of programs for self-sufficiency. Penn's three main service programs are History and Cultural Affairs, Land and Environmental Education, and the Program for Academic and Cultural Enrichment.

The difference between church and community cemeteries on St. Helena, as elsewhere, is minimal. Church cemeteries are usually located at the side or rear of the edifice, and they tend to have "older" burials, some dating back to the post–Civil War era. All the church cemeteries are well cared for and do not have the problem of encroaching undergrowth that some of the community cemeteries face. Longtime parishioners and church officials are most often interred in church cemeteries.

Community cemeteries tend to be in more secluded, natural areas. Most are maintained by residents of the community who take pride in maintaining them. Some, however, receive a bit more "tender, loving care" than others. The history and heritage of the island can be "read" in the cemeteries, part of the wonderful charm of St. Helena Island.

Dr. Patricia Guthrie, a professor in the Department of Women's Studies at California State University at Hayward, wrote about St. Helena and has surveyed the island's black churches. Those marked with an asterisk have a cemetery at their location: Adams Street Baptist Church; Brick Baptist Church*; Ebenezer Baptist Church*; Faith Memorial Baptist Church*; First African Baptist Church (the church uses Coffin Point and Fripp cemeteries); Grace Truth Bible Chapel; Jehova Holiness; Oaks Holiness; Orange Grove Baptist Church*; Scott Holiness; Scottsville Baptist Church; Seven Day Adventist; St. James Baptist Church; St. Joseph Baptist Church*.

Most of the churches on St. Helena still actively serve the black community. There are also Jehovah's Witness and Black Muslim congregations on the island; most white residents attend St. Helena Baptist Church and Holy Cross Catholic Church, both located off the island in Beaufort.

A close relationship exists between the island's communities and churches and its praise houses. Historically, slaves did not find true pleasure or spiritual expression at church. They depended on the weekly talks and shouts at the praise house that could be found on every plantation. Sometimes the plantation owner erected a little praise house for the express purpose of giving his slaves a place of their own to worship; if not, a family would declare its cabin the plantation praise house.

Praise houses (or "prays houses") were devised by farmers to provide slaves with a spiritual outlet that wouldn't take their servants and field workers off the plantation for religious services. They were often used for midweek services when distances to established black churches were too great to travel. Praise houses also served as centers for social and political activity. It was at the praise house that blacks found their spiritual release in song, prayer, and dance. Although plantation owners sanctioned praise house meetings, they were often frightened and disturbed by the sounds. Shouts would often last well into the night, and the monotonous thud of feet prevented sleep up to half a mile away.

Members of the praise house would often oversee funerals and assume the role of unofficial keepers of the burial plots scattered throughout the plantations. Funerals would often take place at the praise house or in the

The Penn School of St. Helena

In 1861, at the start of the Civil War, some twenty thousand Union troops landed on Hilton Head Island, just across from St. Helena. The Union forces moved onward, seizing control of other nearby islands, including St. Helena, and freeing ten thousand slaves. Defeated, the former plantation owners fled to the mainland.

The Philadelphia Port Royal Commission was formed to send superintendents to St. Helena as quickly as possible to continue operation of the plantations. In addition, it enlisted teachers to go to St. Helena to teach the newly freed blacks. Thus, with the Civil War still in its infancy, President Abraham Lincoln rose to the challenge of equality, believing that former slaves could and would work the fields, attend school, and learn to read and write. He overthrew the fundamental Slave Code of 1790, which had prohibited the teaching of reading and writing to slaves.

Penn School was established at St. Helena's Oak Plantation in April 1862 as one of the first schools for blacks in the South. Its first two teachers, Laura M. Towne and Ellen Murray, traveled to St. Helena from Philadelphia; Towne, who had some limited medical training, was frequently referred to as a physician. Before long, the school outgrew its space at the plantation and classes were moved a short distance away, to the Brick Baptist Church.

continued on next page

yards of the deceased. "One of their key functions was to provide a proper burial service for the dead," says Lula Holmes, a longtime resident and historian for St. Helena Island.

Most praise houses eventually vanished as mainstream black churches expanded into the area following the abolition of slavery. However, there are at least four praise houses still operating on St. Helena Island: Coffin Point Community Praise House, on SC Road 77, one-third mile northeast of US 21; Croft Community Praise House, on SC Road 74, 1.3 miles north of US 21; Eddys Point Community Praise House, on SC Road 183, one-tenth of a mile north of DC Road 73; and Mary Jenkins Community Praise House, on SC Road 74, 2.1 miles north of US 21. The Moving Star Hall is located on neighboring Johns Island, on SC River Road, about six miles south of Charleston.

In Guthrie's *Catching Sense: The Meaning of Plantation Membership among Blacks on St. Helena Island, S.C.* is an interesting discussion of praise houses on the island:

After the slave laws discouraged the gathering of slaves away from their own plantation, masters allowed their people to worship in plantation groups, usually at the house of one of the older people, sometimes in a special praise house. The "leaders" of these plantation groups were persons of considerable authority in spiritual matters. They have been referred to as the lineal descendants of the African medicine man, and they were the forerunners of the present African American ministers. They presided over meetings, gave spiritual advice, and in some cases officiated at weddings and funerals.

With the breakdown of the antebellum plantation and the shifting of the freed population, praise houses disappeared from most sections, to be supplanted by churches. In the sea islands, churches were organized, but were merely superimposed upon the praise house system.

LAY DOWN BODY

Holmes recalls stories of a time when islanders congregated at praise houses two or three times a week; the houses also provided accommodation for the infirm and the elderly. "They were close to the plantations and much more accessible than some of the churches. For those who attended, they could also hear the community happenings and announcements that were part of the regular program. Some praise houses even had Sunday school classes for the children." Two praise houses, Mary Jenkins and Eddys Point, still have fairly regular bimonthly meetings. Both are located near Penn Center and are led by Deacon Henderson and Deacon James Smalls.

Today, on St. Helena, praise house leaders no longer officiate at weddings and funerals. They do, however, continue to preside over meetings and give spiritual advice, though any links with "African medicine men" have long since been severed. The twentieth-century praise house, far different from those of earlier centuries, serves as a sanctuary to reflect, "shout," and pray in a wonderful historic setting. Like area cemeteries, praise houses offer a rare glimpse into African American history and provide an opportunity for those walking the area to supplement their historical knowledge and satisfy their curiosity of what once was.

continued from previous page

In October 1862 Towne and Murray were joined by Charlotte Forten, a black teacher who had taught school in Salem, Massachusetts, and in Philadelphia. Forten, like her father and grandfather, had been active in abolitionist movements in Pennsylvania, New York, and Massachusetts.

Towne supervised the instruction and traveled to and fro in her carriage, traversing St. Helena's dirt roads and thick woods on her "doctoring expeditions." Murray and Forten spent most of their time with the children. Even in its new location, the school soon became overcrowded, and the restlessness of the students—especially the very young—made teaching difficult. Forten's beautiful singing voice helped charm and interest the students as she taught them a variety of songs.

In March 1864, little more than a year after President Lincoln issued the Emancipation Proclamation, the Philadelphia Commission began efforts to secure a building for a new school. In 1905, the need for industrial education led to the establishment of trade courses in carpentry, blacksmithing, wheelwrighting, basket weaving, harness making, cobbling, and mechanics. Students and community people also took agricultural courses and teacher training, and the school became known as Penn Normal, Industrial, and Agricultural School.

continued on next page

Dr. Guthrie's survey has also included the plantations—now called communities—located on St. Helena Island. Those with an asterisk have cemeteries at their location: Brisbane; Pope; Capers*; Tom Fripp*; Pritchard; Cedar Grove*; Frogmore*; Saxtonville Memorial Gardens* (Brick Church owns the cemetery); Fuller*; Scott Farm; Cherry Hill; Club Bridge; Hopes*; Coffin Point*; Indian Hill*; Corner (Major)*; Mary Jenkins*; Tombee and Cuffy*; Croft*; Lands End*; Wallace*; McTureous*; Warsaw*; Dataw; Mulberry Hill; Dr. White*; Oakland*; Eddings Point*; Oaks*; Fripp Point*; Orange Grove*; Ann Fripp*; Pollywanna*.

Membership in the community is essential to burial in its cemetery. As Dr. Guthrie writes:

continued from previous page

Until 1948 the school continued to serve children and adults of the area. It was, in fact, the major source of formal educational training for African Americans on St. Helena Island and the surrounding regions. In the late 1930s, the South Carolina State Board of Education and the General Education Board used Penn School to host an experiment in elementary school teacher training for the South Carolina State College at Orangeburg. Rosa B. Cooley and Grace B. House succeeded Towne and Murray as principal and assistant principal; Forten, because of ill health, had left the school much earlier.

In 1948, the South Carolina public school system was extended to St. Helena. All island schools operated concurrently until the Penn class of 1953 had graduated. The school was then reformed as Penn Community Service; a further name change dubbed it Penn Center, and the center initiated new programs such as Penn Nursery School and the Rosa B. Cooley Health Clinic.

Penn Center was the facility where biracial groups in South Carolina could meet during the 1950s and early 1960s, and it became a major retreat for civil rights groups. From 1961 to 1967, Dr. Martin Luther King Jr., the Hon. Andrew Young, and their staffs met often at the center to formulate strategies for social change in the South and throughout the rest of the country. The historic March on Washington, D.C., was, in part, planned on Penn's campus.

Members of a plantation, regardless of their residence at the time of their death, have the right to burial in the graveyard of the plantation where they hold membership. It is not at all uncommon for people to ship the bodies of deceased plantation members back to the island for burial. Spouses of plantation members may be buried alongside their mates, if they so desire, even when they hold membership elsewhere. If, however, a person had multiple spouses during his/her lifetime, only one pair of mates will be laid to rest in the same graveyard. This is the only right that accrues to plantation members who are not residents on the plantation where they are members. Plantation members who reside on the plantation where they belong are eligible for the office of leader, may seek land use rights for a dwelling site, and also have the right to burial in their plantation's graveyard.

Individuals who reside on St. Helena but do not hold membership in a plantation lack access to the rights of plantation members. Specifically, non-members of a plantation are not eligible for the office of praise house leader, they are not buried in the plantation graveyard and, except under unusual circumstances, they are not eligible to seek use rights in land for the purpose of establishing a dwelling.

Each of the essential ingredients of personhood accrue to every person who is a member of a plantation on St. Helena Island regardless of his/her affiliation. In the context of this discussion, bear in mind that the rights of full personhood, that is, access to the office of praise house leader, the right to seek land use rights, and the right to burial in the plantation graveyard, come into existence when persons attain plantation membership.

Although Guthrie's comments were written several years ago, much is still true. However, as with many customs and mores, changes have occurred over time. St. Helena's changes are small but, nevertheless, they would likely shock the elders of previous generations who formulated some of the island's strict burial rules and procedures.

BRICK BAPTIST CHURCH CEMETERY

Brick Baptist Church Cemetery, which extends from the front of the "yard" to the rear, elegantly epitomizes a historic countryside cemetery. The two tall monuments overlooking the road are dedicated to Penn's first two teachers, Laura Towne and Ellen Murray. Popular tourist attractions, they date back to the early 1900s.

A few of the family graves in the cemetery are ringed by tabby walls—sturdy oyster shell constructions that have withstood the passing of time—that represent the kind of structures common during that early period. Scattered among the cemetery's older markers stand headstones conspicuous in their newness. These headstones mark the burial place of those more recently interred.

The Brick Baptist Church was built in 1855, using the labor of the enslaved. After it was completed, whites sat on the first level while blacks were remanded to the balcony or sat outside under a nearby grove of live oaks. Under the trees on a Sunday morning would be tied every conceivable combination of horse and vehicle: from six-seated carriages with fine northern horses to one-seated sulkies and mules saddled with cotton bags. But horses were a luxury to many, including those of color whose possessions numbered

Oyster shell walls dating back to the 1800s ring some of Brick Baptist Church Cemetery's family graves.

A granite memorial honoring Charlotte Forten, the first African American teacher at Penn School, was erected in 1992.

few. Some men would carry their shoes in their hands on the walk to the service, putting them on only when they got to church; many more owned no shoes at all. By mid-century there were still relatively few whites on the island.

After the start of the Civil War in 1861, the Brick Baptist Church doubled as the local schoolhouse. In December 1992, the Michigan Support Group for Penn Center presented the church with a granite memorial honoring Charlotte Forten, the first African American teacher at Penn School. It now stands at the doorway nearest the walkway leading from the cemetery. Like Forten, the school's first two white teachers, Laura Towne and Ellen Murray, are buried in Pennsylvania.

After the war, Brick Baptist became a black church. Inside its plain white interior, its galleries and central hall filled with black people who stood at the doors, near the windows, and in the aisles. The "elders" were seated under the pulpit and in the front seats. They were all well dressed—a few in gaudy toggery, hoopskirts, and shabby bonnets, but most in simple "head handkerchers." The service has remained essentially unchanged to the present day. Parishioners begin each service with song. There are no hymnals; when it's time to sing, someone leads off with a song and everyone seems to know all the words. It's a wonderful service, led today by the Reverend Ervin Greene, a member of the committee that recently completed the Gullah translation of the Book of Luke.

Among the many Penn School graduates buried at Brick Baptist Church Cemetery are **York W. Bailey**, M.D.; his nephew, **David Chisholm**, M.D.; and **Celia Chisholm**, David's mother and Dr. Bailey's sister. Dr. Bailey became St. Helena Island's only resident doctor in 1906, in a community where islanders regularly utilized nature's medications and there was widespread practice of superstitious beliefs. A graduate of Penn School, Bailey furthered his studies at Hampton Institute in Virginia and Howard University in Washington, D.C. Before retiring in 1956, he served for half a century, providing proper medical care to the island's black community. During his early years of practice, island residents had no money to pay him; he was compensated with corn, peas, chickens, ducks, or turkeys, which he sold in Beaufort.

Also buried at Brick are **George Brown**, father of current resident **Leroy Browne** (who changed the spelling of his surname), and **A. J. Brown**, another Penn student who taught shoemaking at the school. Brown was one of four singers who comprised the renowned St. Helena Quartet.

Today, the live oak trees on both sides of Lands End Road (now called Martin Luther King Drive in acknowledgment of King's involvement with the local Penn Center), form a breathtakingly beautiful canopy to the approach of the church. With its great history and heritage, the Brick Baptist Church,

standing regal and charming atop a slight hill, attracts visitors who enjoy roaming the surrounding grounds and cemetery, hopefully getting the chance to see the church interior. Like a living thing, the church once extended its arms outward to masses of recently freed blacks; today it embraces an equally loyal congregation. The church recently purchased a large tract of land about three to five miles down Lands End Road, in Saxtonville. Destined to be the church's new cemetery, it is called Memorial Gardens.

ORANGE GROVE BAPTIST CHURCH CEMETERY

Orange Grove Baptist Church Cemetery is about two acres in size and lies to the side and rear of the church. Both were founded in 1917. The church is a spin-off of Brick Baptist Church. Its first pastor was Reverend Handy Johnson; Reverend William H. Carpenter, the present pastor, has been at the church over twelve years. It is situated in a beautiful grove of trees and, as with other church cemeteries, is maintained by church employees and members. Buried in the church cemetery are **Rebecca Mitchell Daise** (March 1986), **Gibbs Daise**

Kathleen Singleton and

many more St. Helena

islanders are buried at the

two-acre Orange Grove

Baptist Church Cemetery.

(December 1994), the Freeman family, the Johnson family, **Kathleen Singleton**, and many more islanders.

EBENEZER BAPTIST CHURCH CEMETERY

Ebenezer Baptist Church Cemetery runs the width of the church grounds and lies to the rear of the edifice. Its markers date back to the 1800s and the cemetery, like the church, is quite large. Walking through the cemetery one cannot help but feel the nostalgia of the past; real and artificial flowers reflect the constant visits and other expressions of caring for departed loved ones.

After the Reverend Kit Green, pastor of the Brick Baptist Church, died in 1881, some members of the congregation left to form a new church, which they organized and named the Ebenezer Baptist Church. The building was constructed in 1883–1884 at a site just half a mile down Lands End Road from Brick Baptist. Through the years, the church has enjoyed a succession of pastors. The longest years of service were given by the Reverend D. C. Washington, who served as pastor from 1895 to 1934. A native St. Helena islander and Penn School graduate, Washington was descended from a line of ministers and was loved and respected far and near. Ebenezer is the largest

church on St. Helena, both in space and membership. The original building burned in 1938; it was rebuilt in 1940.

ST. JOSEPH BAPTIST CHURCH CEMETERY

St. Joseph opened in October 1937 as a spin-off from the nearby Ebenezer Baptist Church. Its quaint, well-cared-for cemetery dates back to the 1950s. St. Joseph's first pastor, Reverend Joseph Heyward, is buried there.

St. Joseph's Baptist Church Cemetery tends to be a smaller and more structured burial ground, with tombstones more patterned and specially placed. Pastor Kenneth C. Doe has been with the church for almost twenty years. The Kiwanis Club of Beaufort named him 1995 Clergyman of the Year

Corner Cemetery, also known as Major Cemetery, holds the grave sites of local African American families such as the Majors and the Dudleys.

due to his contributions to the civic, moral, cultural, and educational welfare and betterment of the community. Particularly cited were his Young Men's Academy at the church and his ministry at the Beaufort Detention Center.

St. Joseph, Ebenezer, and Brick Baptist churches are less than half a mile apart. On any given Sunday, Lands End Road and their parking lots are full to capacity.

FAITH MEMORIAL BAPTIST CHURCH CEMETERY

Founded in 1955, Faith Memorial Baptist Church and Cemetery are located on Lands End Road, just a few miles from Penn Center. The cemetery at the side of the church is approximately one-half acre in size and has about fourteen graves. Faith Memorial Baptist Church was an offspring of Brick Baptist Church, created when some of the members of Brick decided they wanted to form a "less historic" church, in a "less historic" building.

The church's first pastor, **Reverend Johnson**, died after only two years in service. He is buried in the church cemetery, as are longtime island residents **Mazie Greene** and **Florence Parkes**. Reverend Horace Williams, the present pastor, has been at Faith for twelve years. An ambitious and active churchman and educator, he has developed a strong youth ministry, along with other significant programs for the church.

CORNER (MAJOR) CEMETERY

The small private road to Penn Center's Retreat House leads to a right-hand turn and the hidden Corner Cemetery. A visit to the small burial grounds reveals various small objects and artifacts left by loved ones, in memoriam. Although the area is widely overgrown with bushes and ground cover, recent markers confirm the continued use of the cemetery. Situated in a hidden and unexpected location, the site is both lovely and lonely. The Dudley and Major families and other African American families from the community are buried here.

CUFFY CEMETERY

Cuffy Cemetery is located down Seaside Road, just past a large commercial farm, and not far from the marsh and the Atlantic Ocean. It is almost one-half acre in size and is well cared for. Buried in Cuffy are longtime island residents **Liza Johnson** and **Colleen Jefferson**. More recently buried here was **Becker Johnson**. When the 1994 purchase of Tombee Place House denied Tombee community residents access to their cemetery, they joined Cuffy

Cemetery, which is located nearby. Resident George Alston said, "The community does an excellent job caring for our cemetery. We are proud of it and enjoy keeping it beautiful."

ADAMS STREET BAPTIST CHURCH CEMETERY

Adams Street Baptist Church is situated far down Lands End Road past a few miles of beautiful trees near large tomato and other agricultural farms. The church is fairly new, and the cemetery at the rear of the church suggests that burials began in the 1980s. The grounds are high and treeless, and the granite markers—some with intimate inscriptions—are rather more elaborate than those of the other small cemeteries. The name **I. H. Middleton**, significantly engraved on the church entrance, tells the story of his prominence as the first pastor. His tombstone toward the front of the cemetery is dated 1987. Others interred are **Nancy Rivers Wrotten** (1980), **Catherine Pearl Mack** (1987), **Ezekiel Paul** (1990), and **Pheobe G. Green** (1987). These, among about twenty others, comprise the small attractive cemetery.

Coffin Point Cemetery stands on a lovely, oak-lined street leading directly from Coffin Point House.

COFFIN POINT CEMETERY

Founded in the 1800s as a burial ground for the enslaved, Coffin Point Cemetery stands on a lovely, oak-lined street leading directly from Coffin Point House. The cemetery, about eight acres in size, while rustic in appearance, is neither overgrown or unkempt. It is frequently used by residents of the Coffin Point community, as well as native islanders who have lots in the cemetery and who previously lived—or had a family living—in the area. It is open and bright and has its own distinct character as a pleasant, peaceful resting place.

Only a small amount of St. Helena Island history is recorded in books and diaries. In *Letters from Port Royal, 1862–1868*, a letter from Harriet Ware, a white Gideonite from Boston, written June 9, 1862, reveals her negative reaction to the ways of the recently freed blacks and sheds some light on the black burial practices of the time.

Gideonites comprised a sect of professionals, businessmen, and a few ladies from New York and Boston who were sympathetic abolitionists. At the call of Edward Pierce (selected by President Abraham Lincoln to lead the challenge), they banded together in the mold of the fighting prophets of the Old Testament. Although the desire to travel to Port Royal to strike a blow for freedom was compelling, there were underlying inducements—such as adventure, and the semi-tropical climate—that made such philanthropy especially attractive. Ware writes:

Just after dinner, we saw the people assembling at their burying place. This burying place was an unfenced quarter of an acre of perfectly wild,

tangled woodland in the midst of the cotton field, halfway between here (Coffins Point manor) and the quarters. Nothing ever marks the graves, but the place is entirely devoted to them. . . .

Uncle Sam followed us, book in hand and spectacles on nose, reading as he walked. As we drew near to the grave, we heard all the children singing their ABCs through and through again, as they stood waiting round the grave for the rest to assemble and for Uncle Sam to begin. Each child had his schoolbook or picture book that Mr. Gannett [a do-gooder who came from Boston to work with the newly freed slaves] had given him in his hand, another proof that they consider their lessons as some sort of religious exercise.

We were joined at once by Mr. Edward S. Philbrick [who came to the island from Boston when President Lincoln started the Port Royal Experiment] and stood uncovered with the rest about the grave, at the mouth of which rested the coffin, a rough board one, but well shaped and closed. Uncle Sam took off his hat, tied a red handkerchief round his head, and, adjusting his glasses, read the hymn through, and then deaconed out two lines at a time for the people to sing. He repeated the process with a second hymn, when Abel made a prayer; then Uncle Sam read from the Burial Service and began his exordium apologizing for his inability to speak much on account of a sore throat, but holding forth for about half an hour upon the necessity for all to prepare for "dis bed," filling his discourse with Scripture illustrations and quotations aptly and with force, using the story of "Antoninus and Suffirus" as a proof that God would not have any "half religions"—that if anybody had "hid his Lord's money in de eart' he must grabble for it before 'twas too late."

He read from the service again, one of the men throwing on earth at the usual place. When they came to cover up the grave, the men constantly changed hoes with those who had not handled them before, that each might aid, women and old men stopping to throw in a handful. Abel made another prayer, they sang again and dispersed.

It was of this scene that W. C. Gannett of Boston wrote the following lines, also included in *Letters from Port Royal*:

The Negro Burying-ground

'Mid the sunny flat of the cotton field
Lies an acre of forest-tangle still;
A cloister dim, where the grey moss waves
And the live oaks lock their arms at will.

Here in the shadows the slaves would hide
As they dropped the hoe at death's release,
And leave no sign but a sinking mound
To show when they passed on their way to peace.

This was the gate—there was none but this
To a Happy Land where men were men;
And the dusky fugitives one by one,
Stole in from the bruise of the prison pen.

When lo! in the distance boomed the guns
The bruise was over, and "Massa" had fled!
But Death is the "Massa" that never flees
And still to the oaks they bore the dead.

'Twas at set of sun; a tattered troop
Of children circled a little grave.
Chanting an anthem rich in its peace
As ever pealed in cathedral-nave.

The A, B, C, that the lips below
Had learnt with them in the school to shout.
Over and over they sung it slow
Crooning a mystic meaning out.

A, B, C, D, E, F, G,
Down solemn alphabets they swept;
The oaks leaned close, the moss swung low,
What strange new sound among them crept?

The holiest hymn that the children knew!
'Twas dreams come real, and heaven come near;
'Twas light, and liberty, and joy.
And "white folks" sense—and God right here!

Over and over; they dimly felt
This was the charm could make Black white,
This was the secret of "Massa's pride,"
And this, unknown made the negro's night.

What could they sing of braver cheer
To speed on his unseen way the friend?
The children were facing the mystery Death
With the deepest prayer that their hearts could send.

Children, too, and the mysteries last!
We are but comrades with them there,
Stammering over a meaning vast,
Crooning our guesses of how and where.

But the children were right with their A, B, C;
In our stammering guess so much we say!
The singers were happy, and so are we:
Deep as our wants are the prayers we pray.

The Coffin Point Cemetery, as it exists today, differs from Mrs. Ware's cryptic description. It is well kept and lovely, signs of the work of the elder Leroy Jenkins, who for many years has tended the grounds. Many family members of native islander Marie Gadson are buried here, including **Julia Smalls Holmes**, **Lula Jenkins**, and **York Smalls**. The land for the cemetery was given to the people of the area by the late Senator Campbell, owner of the plantation during the 1800s.

Low Bottom, South Carolina

It is not known if the name Low Bottom was taken from the designation "Low Country," a name that local residents love with a passion that is both fierce and possessive. The area is low and flat and is dotted by numerous wetlands and marshes. Consequently, a drive from "here to there" is always spectacular in beauty. Since the area is unbuildable, there is the assurance of trees and more trees, birds, and wildlife to be enjoyed for generations to come. Low Bottom Cemetery, which is actually on a slight hill, sits alone on a road that would see no traffic were it not for the Callawassie Golf and Country Club, a few hundred yards away.

The area is sparsely populated. No homes line the road leading from the highway to the cemetery, though at one corner and a few yards down stands a small community of houses.

LAY DOWN BODY

LOW BOTTOM CEMETERY

The road from St. Helena Island to Hilton Head Island directs motorists past a guarded entrance to the Parris Island Marine Corps Recruiting Base, across the wide expanse of beautiful Broad River, over the smaller Chechessee River, to a corner where sits the little, white, country-style St. Luke's Church. Highway signs encourage travelers to turn left, toward the sales office of the residential and golf resort, Callawassie Golf and Country Club.

Following the half-mile drive to view the manicured, flower-lined entrance to the resort, a quarter-mile down, an unexpected sign attracts the eye. "Low Bottom Cemetery—Going Home to Rest," it says. The first surprise is to see the cemetery name posted. A second surprise is to see the cemetery, sitting in still solitude—the tombstones in unstructured patterns throughout its few acres—in this particular location. Interred here are **Wright Young** (buried just after the Civil War), the **Rev. Bolden** and his family, the Austin family, the Jenkins family, and **Deacon Gaston.** Beyond the cemetery are live oaks, flowers, landscaped gardens, and the security gates leading to the beautiful country club.

Low Bottom Cemetery is two acres in size, and although the ground is covered with fallen leaves it is splendid in appearance and presentation. However, it comes to mind that the cemetery founders encountered a far dif-

It is unusual to find signs

for such small cemeteries

as Low Bottom.

ferent setting. No doubt this was once a secluded field, a fitting location for church and cemetery. Perhaps, particularly after the Civil War, scattered cabins graced the landscape and freedmen plowed their crops. Several inquiries to residents in the area reveal that the cemetery is owned by St. Luke Baptist Church, which sits on nearby Highway 802, between Hilton Head Island and Parris Island, in proximity of the beautiful Broad River.

A visit to the church on a Sunday morning reveals a closely knit, upbeat congregation led by the Rev. Luther Jones and Deacon Joseph Young Jr. Recently, the congregation has been approached by developers; as one parishoner said, describing a visitor one hot August day in 1995, "The man has come from one of those big companies to buy our property." The little white church, once on a country corner, now finds itself on land that is extremely valuable.

Charleston, South Carolina

Charleston is, beyond a doubt, one of the South's most fascinating cities. It exudes charm and creates in one's mind imagined memories—both good and bad—of life in the Old South. Though African Americans might be mesmerized by the beauty of the place, one cannot help but remember those whose backs were bent and broken while they toiled under the threat of the master's whip to help build the beauty that now surrounds visitors to this grand old city.

Nevertheless, Charleston is truly an elegant city. Stately, white-columned mansions overlook the great park and the ocean. A plethora of carriages, the clump of their horses' hooves sounding through the brick streets, lead tourists to the tall, balconied building where, in the 1700s, former Africans waited to be sold and enslaved. From this building, now part of the Charleston market, a colorful array of goods and products extend like tendrils down several streets. The aisles are saturated with jewelry, sweet grass baskets, dolls, rugs, perfumes, paintings, clothes, books, teas, hot sauces, and other assorted items. Weaving through the market is a not-soon-to-be-forgotten experience.

In Charleston County, at the end of the 1700s, 775 free "colored people" resided. They included skilled artisans and businessmen of considerable intelligence who had accumulated considerable property. The "community-active" St. Phillips Church rector suggested to some of his parishioners that they organize a society for mutual benefit along the lines of similar groups organized by white people. The parishioners proceeded with the undertaking at once and, in 1790, formed the Brown Fellowship Society. One of the first steps taken by the five founding members was the purchase of a burial lot for the dead. Within a few years other societies were formed; the period between

1790 and 1820 seems to have been one of great prosperity for these people, though not for other blacks.

By 1820 there began to be a marked change. The great national struggle over carrying slavery into new states had begun and the abolition movement was making itself felt. South Carolina was alarmed. Then, in the spring of 1822, a planned Negro insurrection orchestrated by Denmark Vesey was discovered. Vesey was a Negro who had purchased his liberty by working after-hours for his master, a sea captain with whom he sailed to many ports. After his emancipation, Vesey settled in Charleston as a carpenter and put his mind to the problem of emancipating all slaves. When his conspiracy was uncovered, he and thirty-four associates were tried, convicted, and hanged.

These events put free colored people in a very delicate position. Formerly able to travel freely, they were now watched closely and with

Burial of the Drowned Among the Gullah Negroes (1958)

The Gullah Coast of South Carolina extends from Murrell's Inlet in Georgetown County southward to the Savannah River, a rural region except for the metropolitan area about Charleston near its midpoint. . . .

Most of the cemeteries at Hilton Head are situated near the water's edge, for if a Negro drowns he must be buried so that the water, at night from the high spring tides, will wash over his grave. If this is not done it is said that another member of his family will drown within the year. This appealing custom is accounted for on the grounds that "you must give back to the sea what belongs to the sea."

There are, however, several island graveyards on Hilton Head. If the body of a drowned man is interred in one of them, members of the family will be spared misfortune provided they "pay the water," a fee which consists of casting a few coins into the sea, pennies or perhaps a silver half dollar. But "paying the water" is not exclusively a mortuary ritual. A coin dropped into the sea before a hazardous voyage will insure

continued on following page

suspicion. Laws were enacted to forbid meetings of more than several blacks. The societies were able to survive, however, with help from some of the more noble-minded and Christian white members of the community. Vesey's home in Charleston is now a National Historic Landmark, though it is not open to the public.

In the 1860s Charleston had an ancient, quaint, and almost foreign appearance. It contained several public buildings and churches of pleasing architecture. About half of the city's forty thousand inhabitants were white. Within close proximity to each other in the city's downtown area were the public buildings, leading churches, law offices, merchants, railroads, steamboats, and telegraph agents. Virtually all of the buying, selling, and hiring of slaves that was transacted was done in this section of the city. From the colonial period through the mid-nineteenth century, hundreds and even thousands of slaves were sold annually to the highest bidder.

Many of the cemeteries and burial sites from the 1700s still exist. Among the cemeteries of beautiful, historic Charleston are Brown Fellowship Society, Brotherly, Old Bethel United Methodist, Friendly Union, and Unity and Friendship Society cemeteries. Brown Fellowship Cemetery was moved to the downtown area from another part of the city.

BROWN FELLOWSHIP SOCIETY CEMETERY

When Brown Fellowship Society was founded in 1790, one of their first steps was to purchase a burial lot for their dead. The society had an interest in maintaining schools for colored children, promoting "social purity," protecting family life, and befriending orphans. The organization proved so successful that it inspired a number of others that were later started on a similar plan. The Humane and Friendly Society was started in 1802 and the Friendly Union in 1813, followed by the Friendly Moralist, Brotherly Association, and the Unity and Friendship group. Each of these had its own burial lot and its system of mutual benefit.

Brown Fellowship Society Cemetery was originally laid out on land bordering Pitt Street, near the College of Charleston. In the 1940s a private Catholic school named Bishop England bought the cemetery. By 1957 the school needed more space for a parking lot and purchased some more land. When the Brown Fellowship Society moved its cemetery to a new location near 88 Smith Street, it left behind several unidentified, broken tombstones in a pile near a historic home called Blacklock House.

Brown Fellowship Society Cemetery is currently maintained by perpetual care funds—funds obtained through the sale of some property. In October 1995, Brown Fellowship celebrated its 205th anniversary. Among those buried at Brown are the Craft and Holloway families.

continued from previous page

a safe return; and sometimes when a fisherman is drowned, his death is attributed to failure to pay the water. This way of propitiation has numerous parallels. An Abenaki Indian informant states that "we used to go down the river in our canoes to burrow for cranberries in the autumn, and . . . we always threw tobacco into the water as an offering, so that we might have a calm time going and returning." The sacrifice of the hapless Iphigenia at Luis and the espousal of the Doge of Venice to the Adriatic on Ascension Day are examples which immediately come to mind.

Jacob Benjamin Green, a Hilton Head Negro born in 1874, denies any harmful results from failure to bury the drowned in the accustomed manner or to pay the water. He explains that the tradition is maintained because his people like to "follow the same thing" that their ancestors have done. The rite has been performed as long as Green can remember, or in his own words, "ever since I had sense."

—HENNIG COHEN, *Southern Folklore Quarterly, 1958*

BROTHERLY, OLD BETHEL UNITED METHODIST CHURCH, FRIENDLY UNION, AND UNITY AND FRIENDSHIP CEMETERIES

Nearby the Brown Fellowship Society Cemetery, behind and to the left of 88 Smith Street, lie four cemeteries. They all share the same block, running from one street to the next, separated from each other by a fence. Together they create a spectacular picture, with their various sizes and styles of tombstones and markers.

The founder of Brotherly Cemetery, Thomas Smalls, was a wealthy man with over $7,800 in real estate assets, but he was dark-complected and didn't qualify for the Brown Fellowship Society. In 1843, he established the Brotherly Cemetery in an effort to have a society where he would be welcomed.

Brotherly and Friendly Union cemeteries flank Brown Fellowship and are larger in size. The Friendly Union Cemetery was founded in 1813 by the Friendly Union Society, which still meets occasionally. Philip La Roche's fam-

Septima Clark is among those buried at Old Bethel United Methodist Church Cemetery.

ily is buried here, as is **Joseph Irvine Hoffman,** father of Michigan resident Norma Davis, who died in August of 1988.

Old Bethel United Methodist Church Cemetery was started in 1807. **Septima Clark,** a dear friend of Martin Luther King Jr., and very active in the civil rights movement, is buried here.

Unity and Friendship Cemetery is also located within the montage of cemeteries just off Meeting Road. As with the others, its grounds are well cared for and the appearance of the cemetery is good. The Unity and Friendship Society meets annually and collects dues to offset the cost of maintaining the grounds. Buried here are well-known Charlestonians **Lelia Hoffman Drayton** (1947); **Hubert Drayton** (1969); and **Eva Dawson Hoffman** (1953). The society was founded in the early 1800s, as was the cemetery.

Columbia, South Carolina

On December 17, 1860, a convention assembled in Columbia's First Baptist Church and drew up the Ordinance of Secession, setting off a chain of events that culminated in General William T. Sherman's troops occupying the city. Scarcely more than five years later, the city was reduced to ashes. A total area of eighty-four blocks, housing 1,386 buildings, was destroyed. From those ashes, the present city has risen.

Columbia, the capital of South Carolina, which lies just north of the Low Country and Sea Islands, similarly possesses unlimited stories of the struggles and the valor of its black residents. Although it is relaxed, beautiful, and historic, as a capital city Columbia is busier and more formal than its sister cities. Besides containing the capitol building and offices for U.S. lawmakers, it has more of everything: more shops, more restaurants, more local museums than any of its neighboring cities. Columbia also houses the State Department of Archives and History, the South Carolina State Museum, and an abundance of schools and colleges in or near its boundaries. Its residential neighborhoods are diverse and beautifully maintained. From its position in the center of the state, Columbia is the city of choice for those who want to reside at the hub of activity.

RANDOLPH CEMETERY

Randolph Cemetery is two blocks west of Elmwood Avenue at Interstate 126. In 1871 nineteen black men founded the cemetery as a memorial to fellow African American **Benjamin F. Randolph.** Randolph Cemetery has been under the spotlight in recent years due to the efforts of a group of Columbians fighting to preserve the wealth of black history that it represents.

L A Y   D O W N   B O D Y

Benjamin Randolph was a Methodist minister and Reconstruction-era Republican legislator. Ernest L. Wiggins, staff writer for Columbia newspaper *The State,* writes that in the outlying areas of South Carolina in 1868, resentful whites began gunning for blacks who attempted to campaign for public office. While seeking reelection, Randolph was warned to stay out of Abbeville County; as a former Union Army chaplain he was no stranger to conflict, so he bravely—or recklessly—rode the rails into Abbeville on October 16, 1868. As he emerged from the train in Hodges Depot, he was ambushed by three white men and killed. They were never tried for the assassination; a witness to the shooting was mysteriously murdered a few days after Randolph's death.

Historians say that Randolph fought for the rights of all children to an education. A stone obelisk memorializing his life as both pastor and politician marks his death at the cemetery that now bears his name. In 1992, members of the Columbia chapter of Delta Sigma Theta Sorority and the Committee for the Restoration and Beautification of Randolph Cemetery together honored Randolph by laying a wreath to commemorate his life and the lives of those buried at this three-acre site just west of Elmwood Cemetery.

Elaine Nichols, curator of African American History and Culture for the South Carolina State Museum and member of Delta Sigma Theta, states that Randolph Cemetery is a historical and cultural treasure of national significance because it holds the remains of nine black legislators from the Reconstruction Era. In addition to Randolph, buried here are **Charles M. Wilder,** the first black postmaster in Columbia; **Henry Cardozo; Fabriel Myers; William B. Nash; R. J. Palmer; William H. Simons; Samuel Thompson;** and **Lucius Wimbush.** Also interred here are Columbia's first black physician, several presidents of Allen University, and veterans of America's wars abroad.

Randolph Cemetery Is Showcased

In 1989 the South Carolina State Museum sponsored an exhibit, "The Last Miles of the Way: African American Homegoing Traditions, 1890–Present," that showcased Columbia's Randolph Cemetery.

Elaine Nichols, then guest curator for the museum, led a research team that included professors, archaeologists, archeology students, museum curators, individuals donating or loaning artifacts, and scholars and researchers from area colleges in a massive effort to make this a one-of-a-kind exhibit. The catalog accompanying the exhibit, edited by Nichols, documents many of the material expressions of traditional West African concepts, as well as information about funerals and burial procedures:

"Today, one of the most visible manifestations of West African religious thought in the New World can be found in the black cemeteries of the South, where many meaningful and seemingly unusual objects adorn individual graves. Ranging from bed frames and bathroom tiles to car parts and Christmas tinsel, these decorations reveal artistic and philosophical roots in the ancient Kongo civilization of central Africa. . . .

"At an A.M. Zion church in Bladen County, North Carolina, an inverted coffee cup marks the site of one woman's grave. Next to it is a grave decorated with a candy jar and an inverted plastic bowl. A black Baptist church in the same county contains graves marked by jugs, pitchers, ceramic figurines, and an upside down bowl.

continued on next page

continued from previous page

"When a man's or woman's spouse died, the surviving partner sometimes carried the bed of the deceased into a stream and broke it apart, letting the pieces float away with the current. Thus, the bed was symbolically `killed' in order that its spirit might be free to travel, via water, to its owner in the other world. In other cases, the bed remained intact as a grave marker. Metal bed frames have been observed in a black cemetery on the island of St. Thomas and in two separate black graveyards in Hale County, Alabama.

"Although rapidly disappearing from black graveyards, the practice of decorating graves with pottery, housewares, and possessions of the deceased was once widespread in the South Carolina low country and in other southern states. These objects were placed on graves to satisfy any wants and needs of the deceased person. Toys, broken glass, cups, and banks containing a few coins were placed on children's graves."

Time and vandals have toppled many of the markers. Urban development has obscured the cemetery from view; I-126 runs along and above the road leading to the burial grounds. Though there is no significant count, between three and four hundred burial plots lie in Randolph Cemetery. Families continue to lay their dead in its red clay soil.

The difficult job of preservation and maintenance continues in this beautiful and very popular cemetery. While many of the markers are beautifully inscribed and are surrounded by a wrought iron fence that enhances the beauty of the grounds, time is taking its toll. The cemetery's restoration committee plans the construction of a wrought iron gate to dissuade vandals, erection of a sign to aid visitors, and repair of damaged and uprooted gravestones. Hard at work here, the national office of Delta Sigma Theta is promoting the preservation of black Americans' monuments and sites in other states as well.

Winnsboro, South Carolina

Accessible from Highway 77 on County Road 20, Winnsboro is approximately a half-hour's drive north of Columbia. Now the Fairfield County seat, Winnsboro had one of the highest concentrations of black slaves in South Carolina before the Civil War.

The area was first settled in the 1740s by white English farmers. Blacks first entered the region a decade later, when settlers along the Broad River began importing slaves to grow indigo. However, the first large-scale plantations didn't appear until early in the 1820s.

According to a local census dating back to 1830, black slaves in Winnsboro and the surrounding county already outnumbered the white population. By 1860 black slaves outnumbered whites by two to one. Today, African Americans make up more than sixty percent of Winnsboro's 3,475 residents.

General Sherman and fifty-eight thousand Yankee troops briefly made Winnsboro their headquarters during the general's "Carolinas Campaign" in 1865. However, they later pillaged and burned the prosperous town—a blow from which, many local residents claim, Winnsboro never fully recovered.

LAY DOWN BODY

Among Winnsboro's most famous residents are Sergeant **Webster Anderson**, South Carolina's second African American son to earn the Congressional Medal of Honor during the Vietnam War, and a former dean of Howard University, Professor **Kelly Miller**, who died in 1939.

To this day there are scores of unmarked African American grave sites scattered throughout Winnsboro's farmland.

CAMP WELFARE CEMETERY

The eleven acres of the campground are owned by the African Methodist Episcopal Church (A.M.E.), although people of all denominations are welcomed. Lying twelve miles from the city of Winnsboro, the camp is nestled in a grove of oaks and pines, a circle of "tents" surrounding an open arbor containing benches for the worshippers. The original tents—built of boughs and brush—gave way to log cabins, pine board cabins, and small buildings made of cinder-block.

Camp Welfare opened a few years after the Civil War, sometime between 1870 and 1878. Before the war Negroes attended camp meetings with their white "masters." When freedom came, it is said that one Charles Hall, who lived in nearby Mountain Gap, wrote to New York City's Old Zion Church, asking for a minister. Reverend James H. Jackson and three other persons were sent. As they traveled, they stopped for the night at this site. In the morning, when Reverend Jackson was asked how he slept, he answered, "I fared well." Hence the name.

Annually each August, after the "crops are laid by" and before the fall harvest, about four hundred people spend between a day to a full week at the camp; increasing numbers of participants tend to be businesspeople and other professionals, whose secular demands prohibit them from staying the entire week. Most who attend are descendants of persons who camped here in the 1870s. In years past, buggies and carriages lined the rocky, red clay roads, laden with supplies that included tallow candles, kerosene lamps, large iron pots, and live chickens. In more recent times, families bring prepared food, small refrigerators, and mattresses for the built-in beds. Although many of the campers are from the Carolinas, others come from New York, New Jersey, Pennsylvania—even as far as California—to join family members for this one-week religious celebration.

The Zion Church sits at the entrance to the campground and opening services are often held there. As more people arrive, services are moved to the open arbor. A different pastor is assigned to preach each night; the campers know that the sermons and the prayers will last well into the morning hours. Each preacher knows his Bible and gives it his all. The "choir" and the congregation raise their voices in wild abandonment and the air is filled with joyous singing to the Glory of God.

Each August about four hundred people spend time at Camp Welfare, most of them descendants of those who camped here in the 1870s.

On Sunday, the campers move out of their tents and silently steal away. By the next day the quiet in the campground has an eerie quality, as if it were "lying in wait" for the clamorous voices of next year's campers.

The Camp Welfare Cemetery, located at the end of the long row of tents, is where the descendants of slaves and campers are interred. Regular camping families and Fairfield County residents such as the Browns, the Gaithers, the Halls, and the Gladdens, have relatives there. Freeman Gladden, who was first taken to the camp by his parents when he was still a baby, says that his parents and his grandmother "sleep in the cemetery," which has bridged the gap down through the generations.

Savannah, Georgia

The city of Savannah, a stone's throw from both Hilton Head and Daufuskie Islands of South Carolina, is situated at the Georgia-South Carolina border. Much of Savannah's charm starts right at water's edge, where the city has smartly lined the cobblestone walkway with quaint shops and restaurants. A few yards in front, tug boats, freighters, and large, tourist-filled ships glide through the deep waters of the Savannah River. Up the cobblestone road, traversing a steep hill, sit a major hotel, inns, and vintage buildings such as the old courthouse and the famous cotton exchange.

L A Y   D O W N   B O D Y

In many ways, Savannah rivals Charleston, South Carolina, which lies approximately ninety miles to the north. Both have histories that reflect the heritage and the struggles of the South. Both cities also manage to retain significant replicas of the past. In days past, Charleston boasted expansive plantations, each with a sizable slave population. Savannah, on the other hand, was a fast-paced riverboat city where slaves busily worked the docks. Both cities, however, possessed a significant cadre of wealthy, mint julep-sipping landowners, and both can lay claim to the fact that many of their buildings were built by the enslaved.

For those who have toured old Savannah and walked the busy, shop-lined Savannah River waterfront, no description of this town is necessary. For those who have not, there is no easy way to do justice to the city. Perhaps a day spent with city expert W. W. Law, former president of the King-Tisdell

Cottage Foundation for the study of African American culture, and president of the Savannah branch of the Association for the Study of African American Life and History, is the best solution. A griot in the true sense of the word, he leaves his audience spellbound.

In search of information about the city's cemeteries, another source is retired army major Frank Bynes, owner of Bynes-Royal Funeral Home on Hall Street in Savannah. His funeral home is, reportedly, the oldest continually operated Negro business in the state of Georgia. Law and Bynes alternately relate the history of burial practices in Savannah:

> The funeral business originated in 1876 as a result of a yellow fever epidemic that broke out in Savannah and lasted for two years, from 1876–1878. During that period, the dead were piling up all over Savannah. The city's limits ended at Gaston Street, the boundary when the city of Savannah was laid out.

> When General James Oglethorpe, the founder of Georgia, came over, he brought the blueprint and plans with him from London, England. The Savannah River was the north boundary and the very first street south of the Savannah River was called North Broad Street. The eastern boundary was called East Broad Street; it's still East Broad today. The south boundary is called South Broad Street, now known as Oglethorpe Avenue. The west boundary was West Broad Street, which is now known as Martin Luther King Boulevard.

> West Broad Street was the black business and commercial street of Savannah. Following the end of the yellow fever epidemic, there was one white funeral business, a combination of a funeral home, a furniture company, and what they called a hair treatment company. In other words, it was a barber shop combined with casket sales and furniture sales and it was owned by two brothers, the Henderson brothers. They were white Northerners. There was no system of embalming. All of the dead were taken care of by this white funeral home. With the epidemic, with people dying all over the city and county, Henderson needed some help. So he got a man, who happened to be literate and black, by the name of William H. Royal.

> Mr. Royal was literate because he came from a background where training and education were permitted. Those people were trained in order that they might be the tools for training white children; but they were convicted if they were caught teaching black children to read and write. Mr. Royal was a man who could be trained to handle the dead. At the end of the yellow fever epidemic, there was no other way to dispose of contaminated equipment except to burn it. Rather than burn it, Mr. Royal wanted it.

Now, Mr. Royal had something else going for him as well; the burial of the dead involved transportation. Royal was already equipped with a transportation system. His main line of duty was as a drayman [one who used a wagon to carry rocks, etc.]. If you go down the Savannah River, you'll find that those ramps leading up to the street levels are paved with big cobblestones, ranging in diameter from four to fifteen inches. You had to have very strong draft animals, like mules, to pull a 600-pound bale of cotton up those ramps. That's the way he earned his living. Mr. Royal was listed, in 1876, as a drayman and as a caretaker of the Henderson Bros. Coffin & Casket Co., at 22-1/2 Whitker Street.

Royal's high adaptability rendered him quite successful to come in and take over all of this contaminated equipment that they gave to him, without charge. Thus, at the end of the two-year yellow fever epidemic, he was equipped with experience and know-how, and he had the keys to get in and out of the one gate leading into Laurel Grove Cemetery.

Spending time with Law and Bynes—not only hearing the stories of the cemeteries but trying to keep them "on track"—is no easy task. Both men are totally consumed with fascinating stories about Savannah. There is constant interplay and chiding over minor historical incidents and dates. Both men have superior knowledge of national as well as local history, and the city is blessed to have them as residents. Through such individuals, African American history is being recorded for posterity.

LAUREL GROVE CEMETERY

Laurel Grove Cemetery, founded in the 1700s, is said to be one of the largest cemeteries still in use in the entire area of Savannah. It can be reached by entering on West 37th Street, which actually ends at the cemetery gate. From early times, there was a dividing line between burial sections for blacks and those for whites; the south end of the cemetery was referred to as the "colored section." Mr. Royal was in charge of this operation and he kept records and issued deeds in the city's name for lots sold. Royal became active manager of the black section of Laurel Grove. Law and Bynes relate their knowledge of the history of Laurel Grove Cemetery:

One of Mr. Royal's employees or co-workers was Ernest Johnson. Ernest Johnson was actually the first man that the city put on record as the official caretaker of the colored section of Laurel Grove Cemetery. Johnson started a little funeral business with a man named Fields, called Johnson & Fields. After four years, William Royal bought them out and absorbed it into his business, Royal Funeral Business. He continued until about 1905, when he died.

MY EPITAPH

I AM NO BETTER THAN THE BIRDS THAT SING,

SO, WHEN I DIE DO NOT BRING ME FLOWERS,

DIG NO GRAVE, ERECT NO MONUMENT;

BUT LAY ME HIGH UPON A LONELY HILL

CLOSE TO GOD'S WINDOW-SILL CALLED HEAVEN.

LET BIRDS OF PREY COME FEAST UPON MY BODY

AND WHEN MY BONES OF FLESH ARE EMPTY QUITE,

LET THEM REMAIN TILL TIME HAS PLAYED ITS PART.

THE SUN AND WIND AND RAIN AND TIME, ALAS,

SHALL DWINDLE THEM TO NOTHING BUT WHITE DUST.

THEN LET THIS DUST COMMINGLE WITH THE HILL,

AND DRIFT DOWNWARD INTO SOME HUNGRY STREAM,

THERE TO BE LOST FOREVER TO MEN'S SIGHT.

I NEED NO GRAVE, I NEED NO MONUMENT.

LET ME BUT BE REMEMBERED THROUGH MY SONG.

—LEWIS GRANDISON ALEXANDER

People did most of what they called "random burying" at Laurel Grove Cemetery. It was close to 1900 when the city actually surveyed it off and began to lay out lots with definable lines. The average burial lot down there is about fourteen feet by twenty-eight feet. They are set up in nine grave lots. You can put almost twice that many graves on a lot. They allowed three-and-a-half feet by nine feet per grave, for grave space. The cemetery has approximately 255 acres.

Because many lots are abandoned or unaccounted for (because deeds cannot be found, families have moved away or descendants have forgotten), ownership to some lots remains confusing. There is no way to account for all those sales at Laurel Grove and even some burials. It is better now, of course. The exact location of every grave is registered, as required by law.

General Oglethorpe called the land Colonial Cemetery when he laid it out and designed it. Records do show that Buttin Gwinett and Lyman Hall, signers of the Declaration of Independence, are buried there.

According to friends, Law has worked tirelessly and diligently to improve the cemetery in every way that a determined individual can. He has been described as a one-person stampede, naming the streets in the cemetery and posting a map in the cemetery office with arrows showing burial locations of many of Savannah's prominent blacks. And, thanks to Law, the grave of Andrew Bryant, one of the founders of the county's first organized black Baptist church, is buried at Laurel Grove. Law took it upon himself—with no help from any organization—to have Bryant's remains moved from a deserted area outside the city and properly marked and memorialized in Laurel Grove Cemetery, where he could be laid to rest with other members of his family. He also had street markers and signs put up in the cemetery to lead visitors to this historical plot.

Bynes spoke of the Mutual Benevolence Burial Society and his role as chairman of the 100th anniversary celebration. Unlike other lodges and societies, the Mutual Benevolent Society (MBS) was not organized as a burial

LAY DOWN BODY

society. Founded in Savannah in 1876, the blacks who formulated this group were so-called elite Savannahians—most had never been enslaved. In the fall of 1875, after the Civil War ended, a group of men formed a nucleus of leadership in Chatham County, Savannah's Negro community, and strove for political, fraternal, economic, industrial, social, and spiritual progress. Edwin Belcher, who had organized the MBS in Macon, Athens, and Augusta, Georgia, had planted the seed from which this organization soon sprang. (His grand niece, Eursaline Belcher Ingersol Law, now lives in Savannah.)

"The society was, in reality, an answer to the Ku Klux Klan which the civilian white community invented as its own bureau for reconstruction," explains Bynes. "Thousands of illiterate, destitute, unskilled, and socially disoriented ex-slaves poured into the city from the plantations of South Carolina and numerous Georgia counties. The Freedmen's Bureau was in shambles, the northern troops had withdrawn and the local constabulary forces were under white southern command."

A few members of the MBS, all of whom were buried in Laurel Grove Cemetery in the late 1800s or early 1900s, are **James M. Simms, James Porter, John H. DeVeaux, Anthony K. DesVerney,** and **Andrew Monroe.**

James H. Simms was one of the most dynamic of the group. His mother, a mulatto, purchased his freedom when he was nine. Simms was buried in Laurel Grove Cemetery in 1912. The only member of the Mutual Benevolent Society who was born a slave, he was an educator, politician, orator, carpenter, musician, publisher, and fraternal organizer. In 1867, Simms published a newspaper called the *Southern Radical*, the first Savannah newspaper to be published by a black. He served a term in the Georgia House of Representatives, representing Chatham County from 1872 to 1874. Prior to the Civil War, he was repeatedly caught violating the law by teaching blacks to read and write. Upon his second conviction, he was given thirty-nine lashes at the public whipping post and chased out of town.

The Eugenia Cemetery Settles In

Edna Luten, secretary of the Eugenia Cemetery Society, is a trailblazer in Savannah. For decades, Luten and other relatives of those interred in Eugenia Cemetery cared for the graves and grounds under the assumption that the property was theirs. She tells this story:

"During the period of slavery when Negroes were held in bondage, the area about which I am describing was set aside for the burial of slaves. . . .

"This area was located at a slave plantation, located now on the Old Montgomery Cross Road. The plantation was the home of the slave master and his slaves or field hands. According to history, the owner's name was a Mr. Hugunin but the emancipated slaves spelled it the way they heard and interpreted his name. When it ceased to be a slave plantation, the owner or descendants sold it to the Chatham County commissioners for a prison for inmates, who lived and raised all of the foodstuff they ate. . . . It stipulated in the deed that the Negro cemetery must remain a burial ground.

continued on next page

continued from previous page

"Down through the years, the families did not know that the county owned the cemetery, and we continued to bury ex-slaves and descendants there. In the year 1953, we realized the importance of keeping the graveyard clean for burials. Approximately ten or twelve persons from the community churches began to hold monthly meetings, paying ten cents per meeting to encourage community people to become interested in the graves of their relatives. . . . We raised enough money by selling fish and chicken dinners to pay a lawyer, Harry N. Ginsberg, fifty dollars to research what he could find relative to the plot.

"Mr. Ginsberg found that, sure enough, a deed was recorded in the Chatham County Courthouse, and that the cemetery was owned by the county. In the early years of the 1980s, we learned that the Department of Transportation was widening Montgomery Cross Road and there was a probability of moving the dead and relocating them elsewhere. Since it was county property, we faced the commissioners at several of their meetings. In June 1986, the commissioners agreed to take forty-five feet of the cemetery, which would have reduced the cemetery to nothing. This was done to keep from interfering with white homes on the other side.

continued on next page

In the fall of 1862, Simms headed back to Savannah, stopping in Richmond long enough to pick up a pre-release copy of the proclamation that Lincoln was planning to issue on January 1, 1863. Simms brought the advance copy with him and filed a report on behalf of himself and two others for permission to have a New Year's Eve party. The city granted the request and on New Year's Eve, 1862, the first emancipation celebration took place—before the document had been officially signed into law. Simms died on July 9, 1912.

James Porter was laid to rest in Laurel Grove Cemetery in 1895. Born in Charleston, South Carolina in 1826, he was an educator, musician, tailor, politician, fraternal organizer, military officer, preacher, lecturer, linguist (German, French, and Spanish), and a Christian gentleman. Porter went to Savannah in 1854; from 1870 to 1872, he served a term in the Georgia House of Representatives from Chatham County. From 1876 to 1878, he served as U.S. Collector of Customs at the Port of Savannah. In 1868 he became the first person ever hired by the Savannah Chatham Board of Education to teach blacks to read and write. Porter was made principal of Broad Street Church where, in 1879, he was ordained as a minister. His Methodist itinerary took him to many states before he died in New York City on September 26, 1895.

John H. DeVeaux was buried in Laurel Grove Cemetery in 1909. He was born in Savannah on May 10, 1848. In 1866, the governor of Georgia awarded him a life commission as a colonel in the Georgia militia. In 1875, DeVeaux was one of the organizers of the Republican party of Georgia and a founder of the Wage Earners Bank. From 1868 to 1869, and again in 1896, he was U.S. Collector of Customs at the Port of Savannah. In his later appointment as Collector of Customs, he operated the port single-handedly through an epidemic of yellow fever while both the city and the port lay under quarantine. For his efficiency, DeVeaux was cited by the U.S. Department of Commerce and the Coast Guard for valor beyond the call of duty. He died at his home on June 7, 1909.

Anthony K. DesVerney was buried in Laurel Grove Cemetery in 1892. Born in Charleston, South Carolina, in October 1831, he came to Savannah at the age of twenty-six. In 1864, DesVerney served as captain and commanding officer of an infantry company known as the Colquet Blues; in 1866 he became a cotton shipping agent and buyer, and, later, a bookkeeper and cotton buyer in the firm of C. A. Shearson. He subsequently became an independent cotton buyer, which was comparable to a seat on the Savannah Cotton Exchange. At his death, DesVerney was claimed to have been the wealthiest Negro in Chatham County.

Buried in Laurel Grove Cemetery in 1920, Andrew Monroe had the distinction of being the first black to be entombed in a mausoleum in the city of Savannah. Monroe was a Savannah native and operated an ice cream parlor in the city for many years. Electric refrigeration had not been invented and when closing time arrived each night, fellow society members would bring their children to his parlor to eat up all the ice cream that had not been sold during the day. In 1891 Monroe became a bank porter in the Georgia Railroad Bank and in 1910 he established the Monroe Funeral Home. He was a member of the Second Baptist Church. The church pipe organ was his donated by Monroe prior to his death.

Although Laurel Grove Cemetery is now city-owned, there are numerous other cemeteries throughout Savannah that are black-owned or designated as black cemeteries. These are basically small and owned by individuals or by funeral homes.

continued from previous page

"Again, we faced the commissioners and came to an agreement to take fifteen feet from each side. On the fifteen feet taken were graves of slaves unknown and recent graves, so it was finally agreed to relocate these deceased on the back side of the cemetery, with markers. Finally, the county put a brick fence around the cemetery and agreed to deed the cemetery, taken from the 1889 map, to the organized board of directors—and got out of the cemetery business.

"Before we received the deed we had to organize and present to the board a list of officers, trustees, and meeting dates. We received from the county's law office a letter informing us to be present at the courthouse after four weeks of legal advertisement for the sale of the property. I, along with the president, members, and trustees met on June 1, 1992, and bid one dollar for the land.

"The cemetery is still located on Montgomery Cross Road between Sally Mood Street and Kent Drive. The county chairman, Robert McKorkle, gave the deed to us. I think we got a good deal."

LINCOLN MEMORIAL CEMETERY

Lincoln Memorial is presently owned by Frank Bynes. Both the city of Savannah and the U.S. Army have vied for the land on which the cemetery is located; each has been successful in nipping off some of this valuable property. In 1940, when the country was about to enter World War II and air traffic was becoming increasingly popular, the city made a deal with Walter Scott, the cemetery's former owner, to buy some of the property for landing strips. At the same time, the military negotiated with the city for much-needed air space. Some of the Lincoln cemetery land the city had just purchased was sold, in turn, to the federal government; the army then fenced in the cemetery.

Bynes recalls former President Bush's visit to Savannah in 1991: To thank the 24th Infantry troops for going to Saudi Arabia, the presidential entourage found itself occupying the air base surrounding the cemetery. Everybody was put on tight security, and only dignitaries and media that were clearly identified could come through the gate. The military extended Bynes the courtesy of calling to inform him that if there were any funerals planned, a conference would be necessary with the provost marshal. Since no funerals were scheduled for that day, the conference was unnecessary.

Lincoln Memorial Cemetery is now down to nineteen and six-tenths acres, with access from White Bluff Road or from Montgomery Street (open 7 a.m.–5 p.m.) through military police gates. A beautifully upkept burial ground, it is definitely worth a visit.

EVERGREEN CEMETERY

Evergreen Cemetery is located on the west side of Savannah, on Atlantic Coastline Boulevard. A newer cemetery started in 1936, it is owned and operated by Jones Funeral Home, and was purchased as a result of problems with harassment by both the city of Savannah at Laurel Grove and by the former owners of Lincoln Memorial. Evergreen is one of the few cemeteries with room for expansion.

Evergreen is about twenty acres in size and is well-maintained amid some areas of dense undergrowth. The funeral home handles the cemetery's management and maintenance. Buried here are **Norman Rivers**, a longtime city firefighter, and members of the Rickenbacher family, longtime residents of Savannah.

WOODVILLE CEMETERY

Most other community or individually owned cemeteries in Savannah date back to Reconstruction or pre-Reconstruction days, and Woodville is no exception. Like Woodville, most were started by plantation owners for burials of their blacks.

Over the years Woodville's acreage has diminished. At one point, the city's Board of Education needed land on which to build a school and the

LAY DOWN BODY

cemetery's underdeveloped land was purchased, although the dates are sketchy regarding exactly when the transaction took place. Today, the cemetery, which is located on the west side of the city, can be reached from West Bay. The burial ground is operated by the Woodville Community Association, and is used primarily by members of the community. Woodville is a quaint cemetery and a colorful addition to the rich tapestry of African American history.

OAK GROVE CEMETERY

Originally called Skidaway Island, Oak Grove Cemetery, on the grounds of Wilmington Baptist Church, is located on Skidaway at 52nd Street. The church pastor is Reverend Lewis Stell, and the manager of the cemetery is Joseph Williams. The Bolton family bought the ten-acre plot of land for use as a burial ground for their plantation people. Later it was deeded it to the Oak Grove Community Association as a black cemetery for the burial of black people.

CHEROKEE HILL CEMETERY

Cherokee Hill Cemetery, owned by Clifton Baptist Church, 100 Big Hill Road, is about five miles northwest of downtown Savannah. The community, in older times referred to as "Five-Mile Bend," is now known as the Garden City community.

Many of the older graves have no headstones. More recently, since the 1950s, more headstones have been erected, and today the cemetery remains very much in use. Cherokee Hill is about two miles from the church. Not plotted well, the grounds have become somewhat overrun with trees and shrubs. Members of the church, along with the Reverend Claud Cobb, are planning an extensive study of the old cemetery. Buried here are members of the Russell, Williams, and Wiley families.

WOOD GROVE, SANDFLY, LAKE MAYERS, EAST SAVANNAH, ZION WHITE BLUFF, AND LAUREL GROVE SOUTH CEMETERIES

These cemeteries are also Reconstruction- and pre-Reconstruction-era burial grounds that were originally part of plantation properties. Wood Grove Cemetery is owned by the Wood Grove Community Association. Sandfly Cemetery, located at the intersection of Ferguson Avenue and Skidaway, is owned by the Stiles family. Only families who have existing lots can use this pre-Reconstruction cemetery. Less than one hundred fifty feet away is Lake

Mayers Cemetery, at Montgomery Cross Road and Eisenhower Drive. It is bounded on the east by Skidaway and on the west by Sally Mood Road. East Savannah Cemetery, also closed to new sales, is owned by the East Savannah Community Association. It borders a little creek running off the Savannah River and is at the end of Gwinnet Road. Zion White Bluff Cemetery is located just off newly named Hodge Memorial Drive. The cemetery, now bounded by a newly built subdivision, is named after the Hodge family, philanthropists who constructed the first "old folks home" for blacks in Savannah in the 1920s.

In December 1991 Daniel Ellsberry, who as director of cemeteries managed the city's four cemeteries, wrote a brief statement of their histories. Of the four—Laurel Grove North and South, Bonaventure, and Greenwich— Laurel Grove was founded in 1852, and was the city's second public burial grounds. At the time, fifteen acres were set aside for the burial of "free persons of color and slaves." This section of the cemetery was later to become known as Laurel Grove South; Laurel Grove North was reserved for the burial of white citizens.

Laurel Grove South was placed on the National Register of Historic Places in 1978. This cemetery holds a significant record of black history in the Savannah area and documents various aspects of black social history in the nineteenth century. Interred in the cemetery are the bodies of slaves as well as the largest number of free blacks of any cemetery in Georgia. Laurel Grove South is an important landmark in Savannah's black community because its stones and grave markers are in many cases the only visible memorial and record of many of the important blacks in the city's history.

L A Y D O W N B O D Y

WHEN I AM COLD AND BURIED DEEP AWAY,

AND HAVE NO ZEST TO LIVE OR TO RETURN,

COME TO MY GRAVE AND FLOWER-STREW THE CLAY,

AND DANCE AND SING, BUT NEVER WEEP OR MOURN.

—EDYTHE MAE GORDON

Like the burial grounds of the Sea Islands, cemeteries in other parts of the United States vary in size, structure, and ownership. It is, of course, not possible to include all of the black-owned or predominantly black cemeteries in the United States. Nor is it possible to give a count—or even an estimate—of the number that exist. Besides the large, well-established urban cemeteries, thousands of African American burial grounds lie scattered in churchyards and neighborhoods all across the country. Those in urban areas are more likely to be state-regulated; they are required to maintain a perpetual care fund, which is the setting aside of money for care and maintenance of the cemetery in perpetuity. Although regulation assures at least a minimum level of maintenance, cemeteries vary in their presentation to the public.

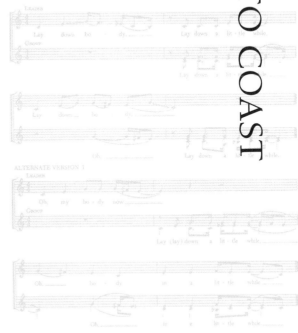

Cemeteries in the Civil War regions of the South are especially distinctive for their rich history. Those in larger cities often have facilities for care and maintenance, while most smaller cemeteries are cared for by the families of the deceased. Large facilities in cities like Atlanta, Georgia, as well as select smaller cemeteries, have adequate funding. But, in general, there are very few exceptions to the continual struggle against time and the encroachment of "progress."

Several cemeteries with unique, fascinating, and sometimes quite troubled histories exist. Among them is Geer Cemetery in Durham, North Carolina, where focused, loving effort was expended towards making it a showcase property, a goal that was not achieved. And Mount Ararat, in Nashville, Tennessee, with its great heritage, showed a promising beginning but a sad ending—until its rescue.

There are fewer African American–owned cemeteries in the North than in the South; most burial grounds of the Northeast are integrated. Throughout this historic region stories of struggle and hope abound. Helen Y. Davis, a Boston funeral director, tells of a cemetery in nearby Nantucket that was traditionally a black cemetery, but which is now overseen by the Nantucket County office. Lucille Barbour, a licensed mortician in New Jersey, explains that burials are not permitted in Atlantic City because it is actually an island. The nearest cemetery on the "mainland" is seven miles away in

LAY DOWN BODY

Pleasantville, and it is not black-owned. "Many years ago," she writes, "there was a black-owned cemetery called Lincoln Memorial Park, located in Mays Landing, New Jersey, about fifteen miles from Atlantic City. Mr. Rice, the owner, died, and the cemetery was sold to whites."

Burial grounds located in the less temperate regions like the Northeast and northern Midwest face additional maintenance problems. The ability to keep driveways and paths clear for processions in wintertime, and to open and close graves during freezing weather, takes on added dimensions of difficulty. Even during the warmer months, groundskeeping must also be more aggressive. Unlike the heavily wooded Sea Island cemeteries, which have little or no grass, lawn upkeep becomes a regular chore in other locations. Cemeteries that adhere to the "memorial park plan" forbid upright markers on the graves; maintenance is somewhat easier when markers are flush with the ground.

There are also few exclusively black cemeteries in the Middle and Far West. Most cemeteries are not owned by African Americans and most are reportedly integrated. The cemeteries of the central states have special histories and traditions, as do those of the South. In general, however, they are owned and managed by boards of directors. However, the board of Detroit's Memorial Park Cemetery is still comprised of "family"; most members are related to the founders of 1925. In the West, California has several black-owned cemeteries, including Angeles Abbey Memorial Park, which is owned by active cemeterian Jean Sanders.

Canada, too, has some quaint "family style" burial grounds, a reflection of the major role that she played in the lives and struggles of those escaping bondage prior to the Civil War. Canadian cemeteries like the Fugitive Slave Cemetery in Puce, Ontario, and the North Buxton Cemetery serve primarily family and extended family.

Atlanta, Georgia

The beautiful city of Atlanta was, in 1860, one of the newest jewels in Georgia's crown. Its white population numbered 7,615 and its colored, 1,939—nearly all of whom were slaves. In comparison with Augusta and Macon, Atlanta was not a convenient location for the buying and selling of slaves, but it was never without a few dealers regularly engaged in the trade.

More than almost any other southern city, Atlanta has begun to break away from the traditional mold of the "Old South." The city has grown by leaps and bounds, and although the hectic pace and noise level is less than in Chicago and New York, a big-city atmosphere predominates. Even before the advent of the 1996 Olympic Games, construction in the "peach tree" city was at an all-time high.

Southview Cemetery in Atlanta, Georgia, was established in 1886 when several black, church-related organizations purchased twenty-five acres of land on Jonesboro Road.

Atlanta history abounds with stories of the enslaved, freedmen, and the progress of blacks throughout the years. The embodiment of the Old South in its grandest manner, Atlanta was always a busy, bustling community. Today it is a good example of a megalopolis. Expressways and highways intersect its center and extend like spokes to connect with major suburban cities. It is a favorite meeting and conference site: Its tall hotels flank and overlook restaurants, churches, libraries, government buildings, medical facilities, and the Underground, where a variety of shops cater to thousands of tourists daily. There are several sizable black-owned eating establishments and areas of black residences ranging from "just adequate" to residences that surpass the mansions of many other cities. The famed Martin Luther King Jr. Center for Non-Violent Social Change, the Apex Museum, and other history-related sites welcome their share of tourists as well. However, the pride and joy of Atlanta must most certainly be its black colleges. Spelman, Morehouse, Morris Brown, Clark, and Atlanta University form an educational conglomerate that has achieved national recognition.

Atlanta is home to several cemeteries, including those that follow.

SOUTHVIEW CEMETERY

This cemetery was established on April 21, 1886, when several black, church-related organizations purchased twenty-five acres of land on Jonesboro Road.

LAY DOWN BODY

The Friendship Baptist Church, Sister's Union, the Youth Society, the Daughters of Bethel, Brother's Society, and the Mutual Aid Society of Atlanta and Thomasville worked together to provide a form of burial insurance for blacks who could not get such support from white insurance companies.

Before 1886 some blacks were buried at Westview Cemetery, located on the west side of the city. Westview, which opened to the public in the late 1880s, required that blacks be buried in the most undeveloped portions of the cemetery and that they use the back gates as an entrance for funerals and visiting. The white caretakers of Westview suggested that area blacks purchase their own cemetery. These caretakers were instrumental in helping blacks locate the Southview property and assisting with initial arrangements for the land purchase. Additional acquisitions of land have brought Southview cemetery grounds to over 125 acres.

The gravestones of this famous, chartered, black cemetery read like a "Who's Who" of city history. Albert Watts, Southview Cemetery's third-generation caretaker, is a source of pertinent information about the over seventy-five thousand persons interred here, many of whom are also memorialized in names of city streets or schools. Among them are **Dr. H. Moss**, one of the first black doctors in the city, and his brother, the first black postmaster of south Atlanta; **Alonzo F. Herndon**, founder of Atlanta Life Insurance Company and namesake of the Herndon Homes public housing project; **Bishop Bowen**, a Methodist minister associated with Gammon Seminary; and Bowen's son. The Bowen Homes Housing project is named for Bishop Bowen.

The **Reverend Martin Luther King Sr.** ("Daddy King"; 1899–1984); his wife, **Alberta Williams King** (1904–1974); and **Benjamin Mays** (1894–1984) beautify the grounds with their elegant and elaborate tombs. A mathematics teacher, president of Morehouse College, chairman of the Atlanta Board of Education, a preacher and church historian, and an advisor to the Southern Christian Leadership Council, Mays was dean of Harvard University's School of Religion early in his career. By the time of his death he had earned forty-three honorary degrees.

Benjamin E. Mays, Morehouse College president and adviser to the Southern Christian Leadership Council, lies among the many prestigious African Americans buried at Southview Cemetery.

HISTORIC OAKLAND CEMETERY

Historic Oakland Cemetery, Atlanta's oldest, was established in 1850 as a Victorian-style burial ground at 248 Oakland Avenue, S.E. The layout, as well as the monuments themselves, speak to the history of the period through their symbolic interpretation. Oakland boasts early founders of the city—including seven Georgia governors and five Confederate generals—as well as author Margaret Mitchell among the Atlanta residents buried here. Some of the city's earliest African Americans were laid to rest in Oakland Cemetery; until Westview opened in 1884, Oakland was the only burial ground available. The following are among the many enslaved who became notable citizens:

Dr. Roderick D. Badger was a prominent black dentist. He learned dentistry while enslaved and grew in popularity in Atlanta among both black and white patients.

Dr. Henry Butler was a well-known physician. In 1964 his wife, Selena Sloan Butler, founded the National Congress of Colored Parents and Teachers, which merged with the National P.T.A. A portrait of Mrs. Butler hangs in the Georgia Capitol

Mary Combs was the first black to actually own property in Atlanta. Oakland Cemetery shows a Mary Combs buried on April 4, 1877, but indicates her age at death to be thirty years. While this could be an error, Oakland is not entirely sure it is the same woman.

William Finch, a tailor by trade and an ordained minister, served on the city council in 1870, one of two black councilmen that year. George Graham was the other.

Bishop Wesley J. Gaines was the second pastor of Big Bethel and bishop of the African Methodist Episcopal Church. He founded Morris Brown College and was president of its board.

Antoine Graves was a widely known black real estate broker esteemed throughout his fifty-five-year career for his integrity.

Georgia Harris was one of two documented cases of black interments in the white sections of the cemetery. The Boyd family received permission for this interment from city officials and neighboring lot owners.

Dougherty Hutchins owned a barber shop and in the early 1880s employed **Alonzo Herndon** as a journeyman barber. Within six months Hutchins and Herndon were partners. Herndon became the wealthiest black in Atlanta.

Carrie Steel Logan was a former slave who started the first black orphanage in Atlanta. The Carrie Steele-Pitts Home is still in operation today.

Ransom Montgomery was a former slave whose courage in rescuing passengers from a train caught on a burning Chattahoochee River bridge won him the purchase of his freedom by the State of Georgia. His "freedom," such as it was, thus moved from private ownership to ownership by the state.

Reverend Frank Quarles organized Friendship Baptist Church. He supported the Atlanta Baptist Female Seminary, now Spelman College, which was founded in the basement of the church.

LAY DOWN BODY

Henry A. Rucker was president of Georgia Real Estate Loan and Trust Co.—one of two black financial institutions of his day—and served as internal revenue collector for Atlanta from 1897–1910.

Dr. Thomas H. Slater, a popular physician, opened the first black-owned and -operated drug store with Dr. Henry Butler.

James Tate Sr. began the first black business in Atlanta in 1866—a grocery store—with six dollars' worth of inventory. He also opened and taught in the first school for black children in the city.

Augustus Thompson, a master blacksmith by trade, was active in the politics of the city and ran for a council position in 1880.

Reverend Joseph A. Wood was the first pastor of Big Bethel A.M.E. Church.

Augusta, Georgia

Located on the banks of the Savannah River, Augusta was founded in 1735 and was named after the mother of King George III of England. Augusta was the second city in Georgia, established as a trading post. Tobacco became the dominant agricultural product of the region until cotton took over with the invention of the cotton gin in 1793. Today, Augusta is a thriving industrial and transportation center.

The Reverend A. C. Redd of Augusta, prominent citizen and member of the board of directors of Penn Center on St. Helena Island, provided a wealth of information on Augusta's black-owned or black-only cemeteries. Hillcrest Memorial Park, a large, well-landscaped cemetery with an impressive mausoleum is open to all races.

SUMMERVILLE CEMETERY

Summerville, located at 2700 Fetten Street, was chartered in 1906, and is owned by twelve men. The city of Augusta helps maintain the grounds. Summerville Cemetery is in a more wooded setting than other Augusta cemeteries; burial plots are divided into square sections and lined with bricks to designate family plots.

CEDAR GROVE

Cedar Grove was organized by Springfield Baptist Church in the early nineteenth century; Morehouse College was started in this same church. The

Burial plots in Summerville Cemetery are divided into square sections and lined with bricks to designated family plots.

cemetery, now owned and maintained by the city of Augusta, is located at Watkins Street and East Boundary, and occupies forty-five acres. Called the "crown jewel" because so many of Augusta's distinguished citizens are buried here, Cedar Grove was named after the giant cedar trees that grace the cemetery's entrance. **Judson Lyons**, a black registrar for the U.S. Treasurer buried at Cedar Grove, was later exhumed and moved to Arlington National Cemetery. Also buried at Cedar Grove is **Colonel Wimberly**, a customs collector for Savannah, Augusta, and Charleston, South Carolina.

WALKER MEMORIAL PARK

Walker Memorial was developed in the 1960s. Land for the cemetery was purchased and developed by a group of business and professional men to honor the memory of Dr. C. T. Walker. It is located at the lower end of Laney Street at Walker Boulevard.

SOUTHVIEW CEMETERY

The land for Southview was purchased in the late 1930s. It was developed as a cemetery by the late John H. Strother and is located off 15th Street in the

southern section of the city, at 1225 D'Antignac Street. It is a wide open, beautifully landscaped cemetery.

MT. OLIVE MEMORIAL PARK

Mt. Olive was developed in the early 1970s. Dr. Paul Weston and his wife purchased the land and built the cemetery. This well-developed site is located on Highway #1, near Fort Gordon, south of Augusta.

Durham, North Carolina

Durham, located outside the Low Country but still in the Southeast, was left with fewer than one hundred residents after the Civil War. Within a few years, however, business began to grow, tobacco farming grew profitable, and Durham became a busy manufacturing town. The city's mild climate and the beauty of the nearby Great Smoky Mountains have made it an increasingly popular city to which northerners choose to migrate.

African Americans have achieved significant financial success in Durham's business community. North Carolina Mutual Life Insurance Company, established in 1898, grosses more than one billion dollars annually. Its home office was declared a National Historic Site in 1975.

GEER CEMETERY

Geer Cemetery is located on Camden Street at Colonial Street in Durham. For years there was talk that the city of Durham was considering renovating this all-black burial ground, which had been closed in 1939 and abandoned to time, overgrowth, and vandals. In 1990, the newly formed Durham Service Corps, a nonprofit organization promoting young adults' employability, approached the city and secured a contract for the Corps' first work project—the clearing of Geer Cemetery. Corps members began working in the cemetery the following April, cutting down trees, hacking back vines, clearing heavy brush, and removing old mattresses and other debris that had been dumped there over the years.

In 1995, Denise Rowson of the Durham Service Corps regretfully reported that the cemetery had reverted back to its original condition. "It's the same as before and it is most disheartening," she said. The money awarded to the service corps, it appears, was a one-time grant. The funds were not sufficient to complete the improvements or build a fence. The Service Corps requested a second grant, noting the very pressing need for additional cleanup and a fence to enclose the property, but the request was denied.

The only available written material about the cemetery is a document written by Kelly Bryant Jr., a well-known historian of black Durham. The Service Corps members learned the area's history from Bryant's writings and from oral histories they conducted. In 1876, they learned, an eleven-year-old black farm hand of Jesse B. Geer was accidentally killed after being dragged by a horse on the Geer plantation. With no cemetery for blacks in the area, Geer entrusted this two-acre piece of land to the other black sharecroppers to be used as a burial ground. On March 28, 1877, Geer sold the land for fifty dollars to three men: Willie Moore, John Daniels, and Nelson Mitchell. The deed they drew, signed by Geer and his wife, Polly, stated that the land was to be used for burials and that the heirs of Moore, Daniels, and Mitchell were to be responsible for the property.

The cemetery was closed in 1939 after the health department inspected the cemetery and found that it was overcrowded. Nothing more was done for the site's upkeep until 1991, when the Durham Service Corps took on the cemetery as a work project.

Two of the Corps members toured the cemetery to read tombstones that came to light after the brush was cleared. They discovered approximately 117 names. After comparing birth and death dates, corps members wondered why so many infants and children were buried at Geer Cemetery. This led them to discover, through oral histories and information from the city health department, that an epidemic of influenza occurred in Durham in the early 1900s and probably caused many of these children's deaths.

The following oral history was given by Mr. Willis G. Carpenter, a seventy-five-year-old gentleman who lived near Geer Cemetery and has distinct memories of it. The following excerpts are from Lacretia Wilkerson and Isaac Johnson's interview as related in Durham Service Corps' pamphlet, *Reclaiming Yesterday—The Geer Cemetery Project.*

Interviewer: *Mr. Carpenter, where were you born and what is your connection with the Geer Cemetery?*

Carpenter: I was born in Durham in 1917 and my family is originally from Durham County. We lived right adjacent to the cemetery. I lived on the corner of what is now Colonial and McGill. A fellow, Cal Rush in the 1920s, he had some pretty white horses, mainly used for horse and buggy. He worked for my father. I was only about six or seven years old. I would help Cal carry wood around on those two horses.

Do you know anyone buried here?

Cal was buried up there. We went up there to the grave. I can carry you right exactly where it is now. All the young 'uns were crazy about Cal. They got flowers and throwed them on the grave after the funeral was over.

What were some of the practices when they buried people? Were they the same as today?

Most of them were buried in wooden boxes. They since decayed and that's reason why there's all those sunken places. Y'all saw them up there didn't you? They buried so many up there that they filled the graveyard up. And then they started burying where graves was. I saw them digging up out there and they dug up a skeleton.

So they started burying people on top of each other?

That's when the health department come out there and told them they couldn't bury no more if they didn't have no more spaces. That was probably in the early 30s or something like that.

Is that around the time the cemetery started to deteriorate?

Well, after they quit burying them up there, a few people came out there but then all of the people's relatives in there is dead and it just went down to nothing. Until y'all started doing something it just went down to nothing. I talked to a woman at the public library. I went to a session on genealogy. There was a lady trying to find out something about that. I got to talking about it to her and she got real interested about it. I told her that I wish someone would get a hold of it and clean it up. It was a shame to have all those people laying up there and no record of them or nothing. I don't know whether she did anything or not. You all were the next to do something about it.

Were there any black funeral homes in the area?

That one on Dowd Street, not Scarborough.

Fisher?

Edison, that's it.

That one was in business at that time?

Probably some of his ancestors was around. They had some big funerals out there. There was as many people walking as in cars. There are several preachers out there. A Reverend Joyner is out there. He's close to the front.

We found his gravestone.

Those stones were up just like any other cemetery. Some vandals come out there and push those stones over. I don't know what fun they get out of that.

During the time the cemetery was being used, what was the race of most of the residents who lived out there?

It was mostly whites out there but it was just about all of that land, there was only two houses out there, but the rest was farmland. I used to farm back there. All out there where the telephone company is and out near the creek to the railroad, I farmed every bit of that land. And then went behind those two houses near Camden Avenue. Let me tell you something funny. I was plowing right along the side of the cemetery. That street wasn't there then. I stopped about twelve o'clock until it got cool in the evening when I could go back. Well in the meantime, I was eating my dinner and they had a funeral out there. Well I didn't know it. I went back over there to plow where I had left off that morning and all of a sudden that horse jerked that plow out of my hand like that and hit the [inaudible].

This boy was working out on the farm. They bought a new mule. He wasn't but eleven years old. He wanted to plow the new mule. So they let him plow one thing. We told him to ride it but don't get on his back. And when you get ready to come home just leave him. So he went ahead and plowed. And he got ready to eat dinner, he said I'm gonna ride that mule anyhow. He hopped up on his back. That mule started kicking and he didn't take the harness off of him. He left the harness on him and somehow or other it got around his ankle and when it did, the mule just took off to the house like that and started dragging him and when he got to the house his head had hit every rock on the way and the whole back of his head was off.

LAY DOWN BODY

Old man Geer, he owned the place, said we got to bury him some-where, so he buried him up under that old tree. Someone else came along later and wanted to bury someone. So old man Geer said I'm gonna let y'all have this for a graveyard. I ain't gonna charge nobody nothing to be buried here. And that's why its the Geer graveyard. They didn't have no place in town to bury them so everybody started com-ing out there. As far as I know, there's all blacks in there—no whites, no Indians, no nothing else in there.

What did it look like?

It looked nice out there. It had a fence going around it. It had a big gate with an arch on it. Back in the '20s it was a nice place out there. Everybody kept it just as clean. Folks would drive buggies out there and work on the graveyard. When the old people died off, it started to go down. Some people said the city should do something, but the city said it was private property, it ain't ours.

Who kept the deed to the place?

I don't know. The church didn't pay no taxes or keep no deeds or nothing else. So nobody could do anything with it. That's the reason it went down.

Do you know anyone who might have pictures of the graveyard?

No, everyone who was around in those days is just about dead; 1920 to 1990. That's seventy years. Most of the people then were fifty or sixty years old or so; 70 and 60 is 130 years old and no one is that old. I don't think they kept records of the city cemetery until way after that.

Rowson remains hopeful that in time, funds will be made available so that they can renew their efforts and complete their plans for maintenance and fencing of this important historic site.

Nashville, Tennessee, and Neighboring Kentucky

Nashville, the capital of Tennessee, is an active and vibrant city that serves as the home of the country music industry and numerous publishing companies. The historic Grand Old Opry, considered the "Mother Church" of country music, makes its home in a part of the city's renovated downtown area. For some time, however, Nashville, like many other U.S. cities, was enmeshed in struggles against blighted housing, poverty, and the destruc-tion of neighborhoods by highway construction. The city's recent revitaliza-tion has been encouraging. Among Nashville's jewels are its many colleges and

A Tribute to Tennessee's Black Civil War Soldiers

Contrary to the falsification by many white historians, whites did not give blacks their freedom on a silver platter. Black Americans fought gallantly and died bravely for their liberty and the emancipation of the slaves. Many of Tennessee's United States Colored Troops (USCT) veterans are interred in the national cemeteries at Chattanooga (103 bodies), Cumberland River (12 bodies), Knoxville (663 bodies), Memphis (4,208 bodies), and Nashville (1,909 bodies). The Memphis National Cemetery . . . includes a "Fort Pillow Section" for the USCT murdered during the April 1864 massacre by General Nathan B. Forrest and his Confederate troops. When walking through the national cemeteries, one easily can identify the [graves of] black Union army soldiers . . . by the initials USCT at the top of the headstones. Each December [during the anniversary of the Battle of Nashville], a group of black Nashvillians participate in a commemorative ceremony in the Nashville National Cemetery and place a wreath on selected USCT's graves.

—Tennessee Tribune, **February 1993**

universities, three of which are historic black colleges. Fisk University was founded in 1866, Tennessee State in 1866, and Meharry Medical College in 1867.

The two large black-owned cemeteries in Nashville are Greenwood and Mt. Ararat. The latter, now known as Greenwood-West, was founded in the 1860s and served as a showcase property for many years; many of Nashville's most prominent citizens are buried at Mt. Ararat. Tragically, the cemetery suffered years of neglect because lack of money prevented the owners from maintaining the grounds and preventing vandalism. Fortunately, in 1982 neighboring Greenwood Cemetery assumed management of its thirty-nine acres of grounds. Since the beginning of restoration efforts by Greenwood, several acres have been restored and hundreds of new grave spaces created.

Nashville stood in the midst of heavy conflict during the Civil War. The city had been under federal control since February 1862 and had been a haven for freed men and women throughout the war. During the winter of 1865–1866, Nashville's muddy streets were crowded with hundreds of impoverished former slaves who had settled there. To accommodate those who had no means, several small cities bearing the local names of "By-Town," "Hell's Half-Acre," and "Black Center" sprang up within the larger one. Newspaper editorial columns carried stories of assaults, starvation in the open streets, widespread illness, and people freezing to death on a daily basis.

In time, secular benevolent societies and auxiliaries began to send volunteers to aid the freed people of the South. In Tennessee the most active were the American Freedmen's Union Commission, the Western Freedmen's Union Commission, and the Western Sanitary Commission. The Interdenominational American Missionary Association, which also founded Fisk University, and the Freedmen's Aid Society of the Methodist Episcopal Church, which founded many black colleges, were the leading church-sponsored relief agencies.

In May 1865, President Andrew Johnson organized the Freedmen's Bureau and appointed Major General Oliver Otis Howard commissioner.

Brigadier General Clinton B. Fisk was appointed assistant commissioner for the district comprising Kentucky and Tennessee, with Nashville as his headquarters. Fisk, through persistent work, persuaded many blacks who had crowded into Nashville to return to the countryside and resume farming. In Howard's view, the most urgent need of the freed people was education; his bureau made a strong commitment to providing instruction to freed blacks and their children. The bureau's educational work was carried on in close cooperation with benevolent societies from the North. Meharry Medical College drew its sustenance from both the Methodist church and the benevolent societies of the time. As Nashville's educational community grew, its business, professional, and religious communities also flourished.

Nashville remains proud of its strong educational heritage. Among all the cities with black colleges, it attracts the greatest number of former students back to alumni meetings. Meharry Medical College, long recognized as the largest predominantly black medical school in the country, continues to graduate a substantial number of the nation's black physicians and dentists.

GREENWOOD CEMETERY AND MOUNT ARARAT (GREENWOOD CEMETERY–WEST)

In February 1992 Tammy Smith, staff writer for the *Tennessean,* wrote of the memorial service inaugurating Black History Month: "The service was held at the old Mount Ararat Cemetery off Elm Hill Pike in honor of Dr. Robert Fulton Boyd. Ironically, Sam Cameron, who helped plan the service, was memorialized along with Dr. Boyd."

Sam Cameron, a Meharry Medical College archivist, was gunned down a month prior to the service by an assailant during an apparent robbery attempt. It was Cameron who had discovered the location of Mount Ararat Cemetery several decades earlier during research on a paper about Dr. Boyd. And with his energy and enthusiasm, efforts to restore the cemetery were undertaken. A Meharry student speaking of Cameron stated, "His enthusiasm and love of history should always encourage us to keep the dream alive." Dr. Richard Garvin, a personal friend of Cameron's, stated, "For Sam, the restoration of Mount Ararat was the implementation of a historic venture. For Sam, each one of the stones represented history."

Greenwood Cemetery, located a few miles from downtown Nashville at 1428 Elm Hill Pike, celebrated its 100th anniversary a few years before Cameron's tragic death. The thirty-seven-acre cemetery, with its impressive entrance, seven monumental sections, and six memorial gardens, appears well groomed and cared for. Greenwood's purchase of the newly discovered Mount Ararat Cemetery, and its scheduled long-range improvements, have made it a point of pride within the community.

Greenwood Cemetery, founded in 1888, lies a few miles from downtown Nashville.

Elder Preston Taylor, founder of the cemetery, was one of many Nashville residents who became a distinguished and courageous citizen in the post–Civil War period. Born of slave parents in Shreveport, Louisiana, in 1849, he heard God's word and, even in early childhood, expressed a desire to become a minister. This ambition directed his entire life; Taylor studied with a white preacher and undertaker and learned the ministry as well as the undertaking business. In 1888 he established Greenwood Cemetery and served as its chief executive officer for forty years.

Elder Taylor was a Christian church minister and Nashville's first black funeral director. He sponsored an amusement park for black families and children and in 1903 helped found Citizen's Bank, which continues to be one of the major black-owned and -controlled banks in the South. Preston Taylor died in 1931 and is buried near the front entrance of the historic burial ground.

Greenwood Cemetery and Mount Ararat Cemetery are now owned and operated by the National Christian Missionary Convention. Greenwood assumed management of Mt. Ararat in 1982, and four years later renamed it Greenwood Cemetery–West. In February 1992, plans to sell the new acquisition to the neighboring Cummings Sign Company for a parking lot were stalled when archaeologists discovered there may be five to six hundred graves in a part of the cemetery then thought to be unused. Officials were mystified since no records existed on that part of the cemetery. "That area

had been abandoned for thirty or forty years," said Robert Moseley Jr., manager of Greenwood Cemeteries. "It looked like it would not be of any use for further burials. We initially thought there were less than a dozen graves there." The 1.17 acre lot bounding the site's northern edge had always been badly overgrown and was prone to flooding.

Billy Earley, a columnist for the *Tennessean,* writes of some of the distinguished black citizens who are buried at Greenwood Cemetery:

Dr. Robert Fulton Boyd (1858–1912), a pioneering Nashville physician and dentist, was memorialized in 1992 during Black History Month. Dr. Boyd ran for Mayor of Nashville in 1893, and later was cofounder and first president of the National Medical Association, which celebrated its 100th anniversary in July 1995. Boyd was a graduate of Meharry Medical College and, like a third of all early Meharry graduates, was trained in both medicine and dentistry because patients at that time did not have that many sources of medical care available to them.

Reverend R. H. Boyd, one of the founders of Citizen's Bank, is buried fairly close to cofounder Preston Taylor. Boyd, who also founded the National Baptist Publishing Board, died in 1922. The Publishing Board continues to publish Sunday School literature and other similar church

Dr. Robert Fulton Boyd, a pioneering Nashville physician and dentist, was memorialized at Greenwood Cemetery in 1992 during Black History Month.

books and materials for affiliates of the six-million-member National Baptist Convention.

Benjamin F. Cox (1874–1952), a well-known and respected educator is buried at Greenwood Cemetery alongside his wife, Jeannette Keeble Cox (1876–1956), and her father, Sampson W. Keeble (1833–1887). Keeble was the first Negro representative of the Tennessee state legislature.

Z. Alexander Looby (1899–1971) is among many prominent Nashville citizens buried in Greenwood Cemetery. Looby, a West Indian native, arrived in the United States in 1926. Tom Norman of the *Banner* wrote, "The local civil rights climate would never be the same after Looby's arrival. Looby, civil rights advocate, attorney, retired city councilman, was the one black middle Tennessean who made the greatest contribution to the development and culture of American life." As Looby told a reporter in 1972, "Things have changed from the time I first came here. I feel the major change is in the attitude of the people—there is less hate based solely on color."

J. C. Napier was another of Citizen's Bank's founders. He served as registrar of the United States Treasury under Presidents Taft and Wilson. Napier, an attorney, lived to be almost ninety-five years old.

Dr. Charles Spurgeon Johnson (1893–1956), the sixth president of Fisk University, is buried at Greenwood. He served Fisk from 1946–1956 and wrote several books, including *The Negro in American Civilization* (1930), *The Economic Status of the Negro* (1933), *The Negro College Graduate* (1936), and *Education and the Cultural Crisis* (1951).

William B. Reed. Billy Eisley, writer for the *Tennessean*, stated that "Greenwood Cemetery holds the bodies of some black citizens who left big footprints in Nashville history—and it contains the remains of others not so well known. But all of them, the well known and the little known, were once special to someone—many of them special to a lot of people. A rail car wheel was made into a headstone at the grave of William B. (Uncle Billy) Reed. His marker reads: Born December 26, 1849; joined the church July 2, 1866; went to work for NC and St L on March 3, 1883; honor roll, June 1, 1901; died August 26, 1934; His creed for life: I love my Lord. I love my family. I love my job." A grave close by has the name D. W. B. Reed (1890–1961), probably the son of the railroader.

Dr. Harold D. West Sr. was buried here in 1974. His monument identifies him as the first black president of Meharry Medical College, serving from 1952–1966. From the time of its founding until 1952, Meharry's presidents were white doctors even though nearly all the school's students were black.

Others buried at Greenwood and Mount Ararat include **Cornelia Shepherd** and two fellow members of the original Fisk Jubilee Singers; civil rights leaders **Dr. Kelly Miller Smith** and **Alfred C. Galloway;** former Tennessee State University head football coach **John Merritt**, remembered as one of college football's winningest coaches; Grand Ole Opry legend **DeFord Bailey**, the first black performer to appear at the Ryman Auditorium; and **Dennis Comer Washington**, a former Baptist Sunday School Publishing Board executive director.

RIVERSIDE CEMETERY

"Here sleep the founders of Jackson" are the words carved on a plaque at the entrance to this historic and beautiful cemetery in southwest Jackson, Tennessee. Today, not only the founders sleep here; many families have also purchased lots and individual graves.

The site has undergone several name changes. Prior to 1820 the site was known as Pioneer Graveyard. Those buried there were reinterred in the 1820s, after local resident Tom Shannon gave an acre to the city of Jackson for a cemetery. Some records dating to around 1928 call the cemetery Lancaster Graveyard, and in 1878 the name was changed to Jackson Graveyard. Immediately afterwards, a newspaper notice requested readers to help select a new name for the burial ground. The name "Riverside" was submitted by Benjamin Davidson, a cotton buyer from Jackson whose grave, along with his wife's, can now be found in the cemetery.

Research and study by the Mid-West Genealogical Society has shown that through the years slaves and whites were buried side by side in the ten-acre Riverside Cemetery. The first burial, that of Mary Jane Butler, occurred on September 12, 1824. Also interred here is her father, Dr. William Butler, who was called "the father of Jackson." A veteran of the War of 1812, he married a niece of President Andrew Jackson.

The recent research of Jackson resident Jonathan Smith has revealed that many previously believed facts about Riverside Cemetery may need revision. It appears that the bodies moved from Pioneer Graveyard were reinterred without identification, so that it is impossible to compile a complete listing. However, there was an area of the new cemetery where the enslaved and free Negroes were buried. During slavery, some family plots contained the nuclear family and the slaves. Blacks buried at Riverside include **Bishop Isaac Lane** (1937), for whom Jackson's prominent black college, Lane College, is named. Also buried here are members of the Lane family: **Francis B. Lane**, a World War I veteran (1899–1956), and **Joshua Lane** (1869–1949).

The cemetery is the final resting place for veterans of all the wars, including Confederate and Union soldiers of the Civil War and servicemen from World Wars I and II. Also buried here are several prominent Jackson cit-

izens, including attorney **Milton Brown.** Brown defended John Morrell, a land pirate accused of murder and of stealing slaves. While Brown successfully argued against the murder conviction, his client, Morrell, went to prison for robbery. Brown subsequently became a judge and railroad executive. As a congressman he submitted the bill for the annexation of the state of Texas. He was buried in Riverside in 1830.

THE ALEX HALEY STATE HISTORIC SITE AND MUSEUM

This site, established in the mid-1980s, contains the grave of author **Alex Haley.** It is the first state-owned historic site in western Tennessee and the first devoted to an African American in Tennessee. The boyhood home of Alex Haley, it was historically known as the Palmer House. The ten-room, bungalow-style home is located at 200 South Church Street and Haley Avenue in the small incorporated town of Henning, Tennessee, about forty-five miles north of Memphis. The museum is open year-round and annually attracts thousands of visitors from all over the world, many of whom follow the museum's tour map to the town's historic homes and churches. One spot on the tour is the Bethlehem Cemetery, where Haley ancestor Chicken George is buried in the Haley family plot.

Henning, a picturesque town of Victorian houses and turn-of-the-century storefronts, was founded in 1873, close to the tracks of the Illinois Central Railroad. The city developed industries based on the sawmill, grist mill, and cotton gin.

Will E. Palmer, grandfather of Haley and a well-known businessman and community leader, had the Palmer House constructed in 1918. Currently the house is being restored to the period of Haley's youth, when he would sit on its front porch listening to his grandmother, Cynthia Palmer, aunts Liz, Plus, Viney, and Till, and cousin Georgia tell stories about the family's history.

They spoke of Africa, and of the Mandingo youth Kunte Kinte, who was seized by four slave catchers near his village of Juffure on the Kamby Balongo in West Africa. Just sixteen years old, he was dragged aboard the slave ship *Lord Ligonier* and carried to Annapolis, Maryland, where he was sold into human bondage. These *griots* traced the lineage of Kunte Kinte, called "Toby" by his owner, John Waller; to Kinte's daughter, Kizzy; to her son "Chicken George," a game-cock trainer who won his freedom even before the Emancipation Proclamation; to his son, Tom Murray; to Murray's daughter, Cynthia, who married Will Palmer; to Will and Cynthia Palmer's daughter, Bertha, who married Simon Alexander Haley; and finally to Alex Haley.

Haley's relatives related the saga of how their ancestors were led from Alamance, North Carolina, to the western Tennessee settlement of Henning, by Haley's great-great-grandfather, nicknamed Chicken George. The six women conversed about how the families who arrived in "Rockaways" established themselves and became productive citizens in their new-found "Promise Land." After the families built their homes, barns, sheds, and fences, they turned their energies to building a house of worship, the New Hope Colored Methodist Church, in which they placed a stained glass window purchased from Sears and Roebuck. It was in this church that Tom and Irene Murray's daughter, Cynthia, married Will Palmer in 1893.

Palmer was a highly motivated and ambitious young man. For several years he managed the local lumber mill for its owner, Mr. James. James suffered from alcoholism, which caused him to declare bankruptcy in 1893. After he became insolvent, ten white businessmen consigned a note to reopen the mill under Palmer's proprietorship. Palmer continued to operate and manage the mill in a very astute and businesslike manner, becoming esteemed in circles of commerce and a leader in the Negro community.

As Palmer's business acumen bore fruit, he built the ten-room, electric, bungalow-style Palmer House. In 1921, Simon and Bertha returned to Henning and presented Will and Cynthia with a grandson, Alex Haley. Young Alex and his mother remained with the Palmers while Simon returned to New York to continue his graduate studies. Simon later returned to Henning and, after the death of Will Palmer in 1926, operated the family

business. In 1929 Simon Haley began a teaching career, and the family moved. Two years after they relocated his wife died in Normal, Alabama.

Alex and his brothers spent every summer in Henning. The stories Alex heard as a youth in the 1920s and 1930s prompted his exploration of his ancestry during the 1960s. Twelve years of research culminated in the publication of *Roots*, for which he received the Pulitzer Prize in 1977. *Roots* was significant not only because it documented the history of a single family, but because it also characterized the trials and tribulations experienced by African Americans in a manner meaningful to readers of all backgrounds. Haley accomplished what was considered an impossible task: tracing his ancestry back over seven generations—more than two hundred years—to a small village in West Africa. *Roots* inspired many to explore their family histories and helped many African Americans realize that they had a heritage of which to be proud.

Twelve years of research culminated in the publication of *Roots*, for which Alex Haley received the Pulitzer Prize in 1977.

BETHLEHEM CEMETERY

"Chicken George," great-great-grandfather of *Roots* author Alex Haley, is buried in Henning, Tennessee, in this cemetery that contains the Haley family plot. Bethlehem Cemetery is one mile east of Henning, on Durhamville Road. This gently rolling land was given to the Bethlehem Methodist Church by the Currie family at a time when the area was known as Stonewall, a little settlement of few families. A log building was made from hand-hewn logs cut from the forest that once stood on this land. A few years later, the log building was used as a school, the Stonewall Academy, and a larger frame building was erected for a church.

Church members gradually began to bury their dead at the east end of the property, and their servants on the northern boundary. The Haley family plot, where Chicken George is buried, is in this northern section of the cemetery. After the battle of Fort Pillow, during the Civil War, the doors of the church were opened to the wounded and suffering. Those who died were buried here. Bethlehem Cemetery, one of the oldest in Lauderdale County, continues to serve the community in the present as it did in the past.

CANFIELD CEMETERY

In Ripley, Lauderdale County, Tennessee, a story circulates that dates back to 1893. Realizing the necessity for a common burial ground for black residents, members of four churches—Holly Grove Baptist Church, Miles Chapel Methodist Church, and Morning Star Baptist, all of Ripley, and Nelson Chapel, of the neighboring town of Flippen—met and appointed two members from each to form a committee to find land for a cemetery. On February 18, 1893, Isaac Russell, Elias Clay, Phil Lee, Gilbert Parker, Charles Henning, and Calvin Dupree, acting as trustees of the Canfield Cemetery Association, purchased land from H. H. Glass and his wife.

Canfield is hallowed ground to members of the black community. It was through the hard work and dedication of their forefathers that money was raised to purchase land for the burial of blacks in this common burial ground. Through the years, many have given both their time and money to carefully maintain the ten-acre cemetery. In years past, Memorial Day was considered a special day to gather to pay tribute to the deceased, clean up and beautify the grounds, and collect donations for the maintenance of the cemetery. Through the years, this practice has slowly disappeared.

Located about fifty miles north of Memphis and about six miles from Henning, Canfield is a place of consolation for the friends and families who visit the grave sites of loved ones. While it is heartening to realize they are resting in peaceful surroundings, many improvements are still needed, included year-round maintenance. Among those buried here are **Dennis Holcomb**, a member of Holly Grove Baptist Church, and **Ralph Anderson**, of New Hope C.M.E.

ZION CEMETERY

Zion Cemetery is located on Range Road and Hickory Hill Road, about five miles from Memphis, Tennessee. The C.M.E. Church was founded in 1888, and the one-acre cemetery that was started around that same time is still in use. The last owner, a descendent of the Sons and Daughters of Zion who once owned the land, left the burial grounds to the C.M.E. Church.

Several members of the church congregation are concerned about the condition of the cemetery and are hopeful that a massive effort will be launched to make the grounds beautiful again. C.M.E. members buried in the cemetery include **Sam Walker**, superintendent of the Sunday School who died in 1949; **Porter Tuggle**, a former chairman of the board of the church; **Della Walker** (died 1938); **Alice Jones; Cora Calhoun; Betty** and **Polk Brown,** who owned considerable land in the area; and **Roxy Brown,** sister of Polk Brown.

Zion Cemetery, in the heart of the black community, is also the site of the graves of three black men who were lynched in 1892. **Thomas Moss, Calvin McDowell,** and **Henry Will Stewart** had opened People's Grocery Company on a Memphis streetcorner in what was primarily a black neighborhood. Nearby, however, was a grocery store owned and operated by a white man, and he saw People's as unwanted competition.

Constant fighting and harassment soon broke out, eventually resulting in the jailing of the black three men. One night, while they lay in their cells, a group of men were admitted to the jail; they took Moss, McDowell and Stewart to a switch engine behind the jail building and shot them to death. A mob destroyed the store and the murderers were never apprehended.

Whitney Young Jr., buried at Greenwood Cemetery in 1971, was a longtime president of the National Urban League and earned the nation's highest civilian award, the Medal of Freedom, in 1969.

GREENWOOD (CO-HAVEN) CEMETERY

Kentucky's fifteen-acre Greenwood Cemetery, sometimes also called the African Cemetery #1 and officially named Co-Haven since 1987, is located on Lexington's West End, or Georgetown, neighborhood. Constructed in 1907, it abuts the Lexington Cemetery, which was built in 1849 to serve white Kentuckians. The original owners and board members of this fifteen-acre burial site have all passed away, and with them, much of the cemetery's history.

Whitney Young Jr. was buried at Greenwood on March 11, 1971. Young was prominent nationally; in 1961 he was elected president of the National Urban League, and during the next ten years the League grew from sixty-three to ninety-eight affiliates. Young served on numerous commissions and advisory committees and was elected by President Lyndon Johnson to receive the Medal of Freedom, the nation's highest civilian award, in 1969. Young died two years later, while attending a conference in Africa.

The folklore surrounding Young's burial is muddled. It seems that local residents wanted him to be buried in Kentucky, the state where he was born and raised. They proceeded to plan for this with a good deal of fanfare, arranging for his burial in Lexington, near the graves of his parents. President Richard Nixon and other dignitaries attended the funeral. After the ceremony, however, Young's wife had his body moved to New York so that "he would be near her."

Young's father, **Whitney Young Sr.**, was buried at Greenwood Cemetery on August 21, 1935; his mother **Sally** was buried in November 1951.

THE AFRICAN CEMETERY #2

Lexington, Kentucky's oldest cemetery, the African Cemetery #2, is located in the city's East End. Two to three acres in size and bordered on the east by 7th Street, the cemetery was renovated during the mid-1980s with block grant funds. African Cemetery #2 is run by a private, nonprofit group, the members of which are selected by the mayor. Although no burials have taken place here since 1865 and all heirs have apparently moved away or are deceased, the city of Lexington continues to maintain the historic cemetery.

Fort Lauderdale, Florida, and Area

Fort Lauderdale, Florida, is often called "the Venice of America" with its twenty-three miles of Atlantic Ocean beaches and a myriad of rivers, inlets, and man-made canals. The city was named for Major William Lauderdale, who built a fort there in 1838 during the Seminole War. It is in close proximity to the larger, more metropolitan Miami, also in southern Florida.

During the past few years, a growing public awareness has developed concerning the importance of early graveyards and cemeteries. At the same time this appreciation has emerged, however, the sites themselves have been rapidly deteriorating and disappearing from the landscape. This is especially true for the state of Florida. Still, while touring the state's burial sites, the amateur genealogist is sure to uncover some remarkable history about African Americans, many of whom heroically laid down their lives in the name of freedom.

Despite the fact that Florida's Bureau of Historic Preservation, assisted by the Historic Preservation Advisory Council, has provided grant support for preservation planning, surveying, and restoration of many of the state's cemeteries, some sites have—both literally and figuratively—fallen by the wayside.

Legislation that affects both the preservation and protection of Florida's historic cemeteries and graveyards has been passed in recent years, an indication of the concern and seriousness of the state in protecting these properties. The Florida statutes, chapter 872, called "Offenses Concerning Dead Bodies and Graves," were made effective October 1, 1987. The two pertinent amendments concern: (1) Injuring or removing tomb or monument, or disturbing contents of grave or tomb; penalties are either misdemeanor of the first degree or felony of the third degree; and (2) Unmarked human burials; equal treatment and respect must be accorded, and respect common to human dignity.

Tallahassee's Old City Cemetery

Tallahassee's Old City Cemetery was officially established in 1829, five years after the town was founded as the capital of Florida Territory. A cross-section of early Tallahassee's population—slaves, planters, governors, yellow fever victims, soldiers killed in battle, and the many other citizens who were part of "everyday life"—are buried there. Because it is the final resting place of so many of the men and women who contributed to the history of Florida during its territorial and antebellum periods, the cemetery is of statewide significance. All Floridians have a vested interest in its remarkable history and in its preservation.

City commission meetings minutes reveal how Old City Cemetery and other city cemeteries reflected Tallahassee's social and political climate. In 1936 and 1937, efforts began to close the city's public cemeteries to Negro burials.

continued on next page

WOODLAWN CEMETERY

Woodlawn Cemetery, on Northwest Ninth Street and 19th Avenue in Fort Lauderdale, was founded in the 1920s to provide blacks a place to bury friends and family members. Segregation followed them even in death; blacks were not accepted in the city's main cemeteries. Until Woodlawn's creation, relatives were forced to bury their dead in the woods. Although burying in the woods was often done, it was a heart-wrenching, unacceptable alternative for African Americans to endure. Knowing the customs, tradi-

continued from previous page

Tallahassee's earliest burying ground allowed burials of all races, although in segregated areas, as decreed by city ordinance in 1841. The minutes of the January 12, 1937, city commission meeting show that the city sexton recommended to the city commissioners that the Negro section of the old cemetery be closed. The commissioner directed the city attorney to draw up an ordinance "requiring that that part of the old cemetery devoted to the burial of Negros be closed unless they can show title to family lots in the said cemetery."

On January 26, 1937, the ordinance was introduced: "An ordinance closing that part of the city cemetery heretofore designated as the public burying ground for the purpose of the burial of the dead bodies of colored persons and prohibiting the further burial of the dead bodies of colored persons in said cemetery."

On February 9, 1937, the members of the city commission voted upon and passed the ordinance. This action resulted in the establishment of the Greenwood Cemetery Company in 1937, a private corporation that purchased land to be developed as a burying ground for the city's black population.

—SHARON THOMPSON,
Florida's Historic Cemeteries: A Preservation Handbook

tions, and care exercised at death, particularly in the early 1900s when life itself was so difficult, it was a gross disservice to blacks to be refused burials at private and city-owned cemeteries.

A story in Fort Lauderdale's *Sun Sentinel* tells of the plight of high school teacher Mary Foster, who went to Woodlawn Cemetery in 1991 to bury her aunt and was shocked to tears. Instead of a peaceful, manicured resting place, the grass was knee-high and weeds had overtaken the tombstones. Buzzing swarms of insects that hovered nearby were drowned out by the rush of traffic on Interstate 95. The graves of Broward County's black pioneers—and all the history resting with them—were lost in a tangle of overgrowth.

"It hurt to leave my aunt there." Foster said, recalling the pain she felt laying her beloved aunt to rest in a field of rubble. On that hot June day in 1991, Foster decided that her aunt—and all those buried in Woodlawn—had the right to rest in dignity, a fitting honor for all they had accomplished in life.

Foster organized the Woodlawn Revitalization Committee, a group committed to transforming Woodlawn into a beautiful burial ground worthy of its historic promise. "Many of the pioneers of Broward and Fort Lauderdale now rest there," notes Roosevelt Walters, president of the Fort Lauderdale branch of the NAACP. "These are people who made or caused dramatic changes for black people in our area."

Buried there are people like **Raleigh P. Moore**, publisher of Fort Lauderdale's *Colored Bulletin,* the city's first black newspaper. Moore ran a candy store, fixed cars, and was deeply involved in church activities. Widowed, he raised three daughters by himself. "He was very concerned about the black community," remembers Ceaniel Ford, Moore's daughter. "He felt the black community should have its own newspaper . . . and the newspaper did really well. He was a great man. Woodlawn is important to me because of him."

L A Y   D O W N   B O D Y

Foster is determined that Woodlawn be known for its pioneers—not for its shoddy condition and neglect. Her committee plans to immortalize the cemetery's history by publishing a book about the pioneers buried there. "It won't be easy," she is quick to admit, "because . . . accurate burial records were never kept and the cemetery is filled with unmarked tombstones." Her committee hopes to discover the names of those buried underneath the fallen and crumbling tombstones by interviewing relatives of the fifteen families known to be interred in the cemetery. Such efforts at research, which include plans to comb newspapers and other archives, will be the second project undertaken by Foster and her associates. In August of 1991 the committee encouraged the community to spend several weekends cleaning the cemetery. They cut weeds, washed tombstones, and attempted to reorganize the chaos. "Our dream is to leave a legacy to the children," Foster said.

That legacy includes pioneering school reformer **Reverend O. W. Wells,** buried in Woodlawn in the 1960s, who led the fight to repeal the law shortening the school year to allow students to work longer in the fields. Modern-day activists like Roosevelt Walters see the value in handing down that legacy. "It is important that the children know where they come from, so that they can decide where they should be heading," he says.

The Woodlawn Revitalization Committee also hopes to build a monument inscribed with the names of the interred, pave the roads in the cemetery, and install a sprinkler system. "Everything requires a lot of time, planning, and dedication—from not only the African American community, but from the entire Fort Lauderdale community—to make our dreams a reality," Foster realizes. Walters agrees. "It must be the entire community's goal to bring the cemetery and its history the honor they deserve," he says. "Most people now don't want folks buried there because they feel it's degrading. It should be the reverse. It should be a great honor to rest with such great people."

LINCOLN MEMORIAL CEMETERY

One of several historic Florida cemeteries in Dade County is the Lincoln Memorial Cemetery in Brownsville. It, along with so many other of the nation's black historic burial grounds, has suffered from vandalism and maintenance problems through the years. Recently, however, the Metro-Dade Historic Preservation Board approved a historic designation for the site. Says Lincoln's present manager Ellen Johnson, "This is good because it will help perpetuate the history of black people in Dade County."

Also, $50,000 from the U.S. Department of Housing and Urban Development, administered through Dade's Department of Community Development, has helped the cemetery reverse the toll of time, lack of funds, and vandalism. This grant was the fruit of efforts by residents, the Community Action Agency, Dade's Preservation Office, and Johnson.

Lincoln Memorial Park Cemetery was purchased in 1929 by **Kelsey Pharr**, funeral director, philanthropist, and Liberian consul. Pharr, who died in 1964, is buried in the cemetery.

At the urging of Johnson, Lincoln was designated as a local historic site in 1991. The cemetery, which now operates under the legal name of Lincoln-Evergreen, is twenty acres in size and in good condition. Located on 46th Street in Miami, the cemetery has many above-ground interments; some caskets are even encased in concrete, a holdover from the era when a high water table prevented traditional burials.

Others buried at Lincoln include **Dr. D. A. Dorsey**, Miami's first black millionaire, who donated land to the Miami school board to build the junior high school that bears his name; **Arthur** and **Polly Mays**, residents of nearby Homestead who, in the 1930s, arranged to transport African American children to a Miami high school when that facility did not exist in Brownsville; **Dr. William Sawyer**, founder of Christian Hospital, and, with his wife, **Alberta Sawyer**, the Mary Elizabeth Hotel, the first overnight accommodation in the area for blacks.

Many other prominent blacks are buried there. Among them are **E. S. Reeves**, founder of the *Miami Times;* **Artemus Brown**, Miami's first blacksmith; and **Julia Baylor**, who established the first YMCA for black women.

EVERGREEN MEMORIAL PARK CEMETERY

Evergreen Memorial Park Cemetery has been owned alternately by blacks and whites through the years. The most recent owner, Garth Reeves, is an African American who purchased it from a white family in 1991. That same year, Lincoln Memorial Park manager Ellen Johnson worked to get Evergreen designated as a local historic site. Approximately fifteen acres in size, Evergreen is one of many cemeteries that could benefit with more upkeep.

James E. Scott was buried at Evergreen in May 1995. He was a Tuskegee airman; the area's first government-sponsored low-rent housing development was named after him. Scott's very well attended funeral included an honor guard.

PUBLIC CEMETERY

The Union soldiers buried in Tallahassee's Public Cemetery lost their lives in the battle of Natural Bridge. Their graves are situated in the southwest corner

LAY DOWN BODY

of the cemetery. In 1936 and for many years after, efforts were made to close Public, as well as the city's other public cemeteries, to Negro burials.

Birmingham, Alabama

Alabama seems to have always been a battleground. French, British, and Spanish explorers fought here for both land and control of the New World. It served as the site of perhaps the single most bloody battle between European settlers and Native Americans, which occurred in 1540. Many Civil War skirmishes took place here. In the 1860s, Alabama's slave population accounted for nearly half its total, a fact essential to illustrating the thriving agricultural economy of the time. After Reconstruction, the state became more industrialized. Steel became an important industry, inspiring the state's nickname of "the Pittsburgh of the South."

Despite the victories of Union troops, the outcome of the Civil War did little to erase the conflict in Alabama's atmosphere. A century later, Birmingham was targeted by the South Christian Leadership Conference to be the site of demonstrations and rallies for desegregation. The bombing of the Sixteenth Street Baptist Church and the subsequent rioting focused the nation's attention on the issue, and the civil rights movement gained momentum. In his "Letter from Birmingham Jail," Dr. Martin Luther King Jr. wrote, "One day the South will know that when these disinherited children of God sat down at lunch counters, they were in reality standing up for what is best in the American dream."

Today, Birmingham is the largest city in the state of Alabama. A leading financial, industrial, and educational center, this city has much to be admired. Watched over by a statue of Vulcan, blacksmith to the gods, it remains a busy, sophisticated, and now peaceful city that has retained much of its southern charm.

NEW GRACE HILL CEMETERY AND ZION MEMORIAL GARDENS

New Grace Hill Cemetery is about 150 acres in size, and is very well maintained. It is located in Mason City, a black community within the city of Birmingham. Informally known as Mason City Cemetery, New Grace Hill is the burial place of many prominent families, such as the Lees and the Montgomerys.

The original directors were Dr. A. G. Gaston, president/treasurer; Louis J. Willie, executive vice-president; and P. L. Butler, secretary. An impression-

149

George Washington Carver is buried near his friend Booker T. Washington in the small cemetery on the Tuskegee grounds.

George Washington Carver

George Washington Carver (1864–1943) was a scientist, agronomist, and educator who revolutionized the southern agricultural economy by demonstrating that a single food—like the peanut or sweet potato—could be translated into hundreds of different products. By 1938, the once lowly peanut had grown to become a $200-million industry and one of the chief products of the state of Alabama. For this and other contributions to the economic welfare of the South, Carver was memorialized by a federal monument, the first black scientist to be so honored in the United States. In 1953 the George Washington Carver National Monument was erected on his birth site near Diamond, Missouri; it was dedicated July 17, 1960.

continued on next page

able youth of eighteen when he read Booker T. Washington's *Up from Slavery,* Gaston heard the legendary Washington speak at a black church in Birmingham. "He held me transfixed," Gaston wrote fifty years later, then enjoying his status as the state's most successful black businessman. He and the other directors of New Grace Hill have now been replaced; the new directors include president/treasurer Louis J. Willie, executive vice-president K. R. Balton, and secretary James Johnson.

New Grace Hill Cemetery purchased the fifty-six-acre Zion Memorial Gardens, located about eighteen miles away, in 1972. One of the busiest black cemeteries in the area, Zion Memorial Gardens handles over four hundred interments a year; construction began on a mausoleum in 1979. Buried at Zion are famous blues harmonica player **Sonny Terry**, who, along with his many performances with fellow musician Brownie McGee, appeared in the film *The Color Purple,* and the Woods family.

All the property encompassing the present New Grace Hill complex was at one time owned by Dr. Gaston. Eventually the property was transferred to the employee ewnership stock plan at the Booker T. Washington Insurance Company, which means that employees now own both their company and the two cemeteries, which are both beautifully maintained. Both cemeteries sell pre-need and at-need service. While there are, at present, no perpetual care laws in Alabama, the cemetery association, funeral homes, and suppliers are lobbying for the passage of some legislation.

TUSKEGEE CEMETERY

A student at Tuskegee University was overheard asking a teacher, "Where is the cemetery where Booker T. Washington is buried?" She was told it was the place she walked by everyday, the unassuming cemetery where markers stuck up out of the ground. Located near the University Chapel and next to a parking lot, Tuskegee Cemetery is not a "formal" cemetery; it is overshadowed by a historic building that once served as the school's creamery.

LAY DOWN BODY

Booker Taliaferro Washington was laid to rest on the campus of his beloved college, Tuskegee Normal and Industrial Institute, now known as Tuskegee University, after his death on November 14, 1915. A monument to his honor on the campus, attracting students as well as visitors, is stately in its dominance. Washington, born in Virginia in 1856 into an enslaved family, learned the value of both labor and discipline at an early age. He graduated from Hampton Institute after an early life of poverty and struggle. Washington later moved to Alabama, where he dreamed of building a school for black students in Tuskegee. Traveling for four weeks through rural Alabama to observe the people and assess their needs, the poverty and despair he witnessed reinforced his determination to model Tuskegee after Hampton Institute. Washington contacted a coalition of Alabama legislators and several northern philanthropists to gain the funding needed to build his school.

George Washington Carver, who died on January 5, 1943, was buried beside his dear friend, Booker T. Washington, in the small cemetery on the grounds of Tuskegee University. In addition to Washington and Carver, **Frederick Douglas Patterson**, who served as president of the university for twenty-five years and was laid to rest in 1988, and president emeritus **Luther Hilton Foster Jr.,** who died in 1994, are among all former Tuskegee University presidents save one who are buried here.

For many years, historic Tuskegee University was famous for offering vocational opportunities. In the 1950s, however, emphasis began to shift more towards a liberal arts curriculum. Tuskegee University, located at 339 Old Montgomery Road, stands today as the pride and joy of Alabama.

continued from previous page

Carver was born into an enslaved family; his mother was "owned" by Moses Carver. In 1894, he became the first black to graduate from Iowa State College, where he received a master's degree. He joined the faculty of Tuskegee Institute—"on a scientific basis"—in 1896 at the invitation of Booker T. Washington. There Carver developed a program of research in soil conservation and crop development, among other accomplishments during his forty-seven-year tenure. Originally planning to be an artist—he continued to paint throughout his lifetime—Carver turned his creativity to science; emphasizing materials at hand, he devised hundreds of uses of and products from the most ordinary sources. In 1938 he used his savings to establish the George Washington Carver Foundation to continue his work for the benefit of humankind.

The Orientation Center and Carver Museum on the Tuskegee University campus are dedicated to the work of this incredible man, and to the contributions of both Carver and Booker T. Washington.

Hattiesburg, Mississippi

Hattiesburg, a city of approximately forty thousand people, is now famous because of its beautiful gambling casinos. It stands today a far cry from its former incarnation, a gritty industrial town on the confluence of the Bowie and Leaf Rivers about seventy-two miles from Biloxi, Mississippi. Before the Civil War, Hattiesburg had one of the

The Tuskegee Study

James H. Jones's book *Bad Blood* tells a strange story set in the city of Tuskegee, Alabama. It describes a study—held in the early part of the twentieth century but not revealed until 1972—wherein for forty years the U.S. Public Health Service (PHS) followed the effects of untreated syphilis on black male residents of Macon County, of which Tuskegee is the county seat. The Tuskegee Study involved a substantial number of men: 399 who had syphilis, and an additional 201, free of the disease, who were chosen to serve as controls. All of the syphilitic men were in the later stages of the disease when the study began.

Both Jones and Fred Gray, the attorney for the families of many of the men involved in the experiment, were questioned about the burial sites of these men. Both men indicated that those involved in the study were buried in various churchyard and family cemeteries and that no specific burial site was required for participants.

Bad Blood offers vivid details of the study's need to "bring them to autopsy." The need to perform autopsies on study subjects introduced a significant twist to experiment protocol. The study's nurse director informed the doctors overseeing the study that families were hesitant to allow the autopsies because of the resultant disfigurement. Because the idea of autopsy was distasteful to both the nurse director and to the relatives of those in the study group who died, a compromise had to be made.

continued on next page

smallest black slave populations in the South. Copiah County, of which Hattiesburg is part, was one of the last holdouts against the state of Mississippi joining the Confederacy.

The railroad lines that pulsed through Hattiesburg were a key lifeline for Confederate troops—and thus a frequent target of Union raiders based out of New Orleans. The first black regiment formed by Union forces in New Orleans used the area near Hattiesburg as a base for guerrilla raids against the rail lines.

Once the slaves were freed, many African Americans used the Southern Homestead Act to open small farms. Today, several families remain that still work land obtained through the Homestead Act in the 1860s. As the timber industry boomed and the railroads expanded, land prices quickly rose above the ten-cent-per-acre price blacks paid under the Homestead Act, creating a strong, black middle class in Hattiesburg. It was this middle class that played an active role in politics during the Reconstruction era and beyond.

John Roy Lynch, the first black to represent Mississippi in the U.S. Congress (1873), represented a district that included Hattiesburg. Another of the city's famous African American sons was **Jesse Brown,** winner of the Distinguished Flying Cross and the first black to become a U.S. Navy pilot. Brown was also the first black naval officer to be killed in the Korean War. In another honor, the christening of *USS Jesse L. Brown,* a destroyer escort, in 1973 made him the first black man to have a naval vessel named after him. Hattiesburg now has an African American military museum; a memorial to Brown stands at the corner of Country Club Road and Jesse Brown Drive.

PINERIDGE CEMETERY–HATTIESBURG

Pineridge Cemetery, owned by the Mt. Olive Church, is located on church grounds on Country Club Road. It is approximately seven acres in size, and

L A Y   D O W N   B O D Y

members of the church and the community are buried here. The current pastor is the Reverend Arthur Siggers. Hattiesburg residents **Alice Barnett, Ella Williams,** and **Cozy Hudson** are among those that lie buried here.

SCOTT STREET CEMETERY

This cemetery, used by the city's African American residents, is approximately ten acres in size. Buried here are **Mack Nunley, Camel Jackson, Mrs. Olivia Allen,** and **Joshua Harris,** who drowned at age ten in the city's Leaf River on June 8, 1995.

RIVERVIEW CEMETERY

Riverview is an African American burial ground that has fallen into extreme neglect over the years. A local newspaper, the *Hattiesburg American,* described it thusly: "The tracks of small animals are visible in the sand and dirt near some of the sunken grave sites at Riverview Cemetery. Jagged holes in the earth reveal vaults at two sites. High mounds of untidy red sand hide some graves from view. Some markers slant at strange angles, following the sunken contour of the ground. The years of neglect are evident." The city of Hattiesburg closed Riverview Cemetery in 1994.

continued from previous page

Beginning in 1935, the PHS began offering burial stipends in exchange for permission to perform autopsies. The idea seemed to have originated in a request for a cash payment from the widow of the first subject on whom an autopsy was performed. According to the nurse, the woman asked "for a hundred and fifty dollars for her husband's body as we performed an autopsy." This request was politely refused, but in October 1934, the PHS submitted a formal request to the Rosenwald Fund for $500, with the understanding that the application would be renewed every year for the next ten years in order to provide ten burial stipends annually, each of $50.

The Rosenwald Fund refused, but in May 1935 the Milbank Memorial Fund, a New York medical foundation, awarded $500 to the PHS to pay the burial expenses of the men whose families consented to autopsies. Later, one of the doctors reported that the $50 that had been set aside for each death had been "insufficient to meet both the cost of burial and incidental expenses connected to the autopsy," and asked that the fund "continue to support this study to the extent of providing for a maximum of ten autopsies per year." The request was approved. The fund renewed the grant every year for nearly four decades, increasing the amount of its annual appropriations as necessary to keep up with rising costs.

continued on next page

SHADY GROVE MISSIONARY BAPTIST CHURCH CEMETERY

Still in use in Hattiesburg is this cemetery, located on Church Road at the point where Monroe ends. The white Providence Church deacons founded Shady Grove for their African American neighbors. In turn, the members of Shady Grove helped organize the other African American churches in and around Hattiesburg.

continued from previous page

The nurse director viewed these burial stipends as a godsend for many participants and their immediate families, who could not afford decent funerals. The cash payment also provided protection against losing the opportunity to autopsy subjects who died away from the hospital. "They would not let me know when somebody died," she observed. "[But] in those early days, fifty dollars was a whole heap of money for a funeral." Most of the families accepted the offer without hesitation, considering themselves fortunate to receive aid. The nurse director's interest in the families didn't end after permission for the autopsies had been granted. She attended every funeral service and often sat with the relatives of the deceased.

Shady Grove, which covers about ten acres, is the burial place of civil rights activist **Vernon Dahmer**. Dahmer was an ardent worker for voting rights for blacks. "If you don't vote . . . you don't count," he repeated just before his violent death at the age of fifty-eight.

One January night in 1966, three carloads of Klansmen in white hoods circled Dahmer's front yard, shooting rifles and tossing gasoline bombs through the windows of his home. Dahmer helped his terrified wife, Ellie, and their three children escape out the back before braving the flames and attempting to fight off the attackers. He died the next day of third degree burns.

Besides the Dahmer family, buried at Shady Grove are members of the Mott, Kelly, Craft, and Eaton families, the **Reverend W. Holloman**, and other church members.

St. Francisville, Louisiana, and Area

Visitors to New Orleans are usually fascinated by the strange, picturesque appearances of its cemeteries, so different from the grass-carpeted, tree-lined vistas and the marble and granite monuments of conventional cemeteries in other parts of the country. In most of the cemeteries in the area, the dead are buried above the ground in tombs resembling small, windowless houses, built close together, row upon row. The tombs are usually made of brick, plastered and whitewashed. Many are protected by iron fences with gates. The reason for constructing cemeteries in this fashion is the city's low, swampy soil and the climate, which boasts a rainfall of about sixty-four inches annually.

St. Francisville, also in northern Louisiana, up the Mississippi River from New Orleans and Baton Rouge, sprang up around a 1720 French fort. The parish encompassing it, Feliciana, is often referred to as English Louisiana due to its history of heavy English settlement.

L A Y   D O W N   B O D Y

ROSEDOWN BAPTIST CHURCH CEMETERY

An anonymous donor bought the Rosedown Baptist Church and its cemetery and donated them to the church members, all African American families. The new owners had to negotiate with their neighbors, however, to create access from the main road to the church. It was also necessary to move the baptismal font and rearrange parking. Church members are buried in the cemetery, including the Reverend Lafayette Veal, former pastor of Rosedown Baptist. In a February 10, 1994 *New York Times* article, Peter Applebome wrote:

> On the surface, the majestic Rosedown plantation house, perhaps the most famous antebellum home in Louisiana, and the tiny Rosedown Baptist Church, most of whose 90 members are descended from the slaves who built the house, don't share much more than a name and some common soil.

> But often the surface does not tell very much about life in a place like St. Francisville, which is about as Old South as it gets. Just ask the out-of-town businessman who bought the plantation and is now trying to evict the church, bringing down the wrath of an unlikely alliance whose most visible members are black parishioners and white dowagers.

> "This is heinous, it's dastardly, it's so unkind and reprehensible I don't know what else to say," fumed Elisabeth Dart, president of the West Feliciana Historical Society. "It's morally indefensible to attack a church, and a small church at that. White, black, green, purple, it doesn't matter."

> Since Rosedown was built, the plantation had belonged to only two families until last month [January 1994], when it was sold to Gene Slivka, a businessman from Townsend, Ga. He made an immediate impact, telling members of Rosedown Baptist, which sits on a tiny slice of the 2,000-acre plantation well away from the main house, that they would have to move. They had six months to demolish the church building and put a black fence around its adjacent cemetery, which they could no longer use.

> "He came and told us the church is the people, not the building, and we would do just as well elsewhere," said the Reverend Lafayette Veal, Jr., pastor of Rosedown Baptist and son of its previous pastor. The current building dates from 1972, but the congregation dates to before the Civil War.

> Blacks and whites have now joined in a petition drive, imploring Mr. Slivka to leave the church alone. There has also been much frosty public comment. Mamie Austin Rouzan, an elderly white woman, wrote the St. Francisville newspaper, for example, calling Mr. Slivka's action "a cruel blunder that even the veriest Scrooge would shrink from making."

When the dispute became public last month, Mr. Slivka told the *Morning Advocate* in Baton Rouge that the community should "appreciate that a sensitive owner has bought Rosedown." But he would not say why he wanted the church to go nor what he intended to do with the land. He has since stopped talking to the press.

Unlike many other black churches founded on plantation grounds, Rosedown Baptist was never given title to the land and has no lease. It is considering both legal action against Mr. Slivka and the possibility of trying to buy the land.

Some people here believe that racial amity coexists with white paternalism and that it is only Mr. Slivka's move against the church that has united whites and blacks in the same cause.

Many individuals and events have contributed to the heritage of New Orleans since its founding in the early 1700s. This heritage will be forever perpetuated in the city's cemeteries—lasting monuments to the men and women who, in the words of Henry Wadsworth Longfellow, "have left behind them / footprints on the sands of time."

MOUNT OLIVET CEMETERY

Established in March of 1918, Mount Olivet is located at 4000 Norman Mayer Avenue in New Orleans. According to the booklet *Preserving Black Heritage for Future Generations,* it is one New Orleans cemetery where "an afternoon's stroll past a number of picturesque, stately tombs and copings, and through contemporary mausoleum corridors provides insight into the city's black heritage. Throughout the years, many prominent individuals have chosen Mount Olivet Cemetery as their final resting place. Whether in the arts or business, education, medicine, or religion, these individuals have made their mark not only on New Orleans, but in their chosen fields, as well."

Following is a list of individuals that provides a sense of the breadth and scope of the contributions made by the black citizens of New Orleans:

Oscar "Papa" Celestin died December 15, 1954. In a city renowned for its jazz heritage, he was one of the greatest New Orleans jazz musicians ever to rise from the ranks. Affectionately dubbed "Papa" by Louis Armstrong, Celestin's musical talents as a cornetist and trumpeter surfaced around the turn of the twentieth century when he played with the Algiers Brass Band. He went on to establish the Original Tuxedo Orchestra in 1910 and the Tuxedo Brass Band in 1911.

Joseph A. "Cle" Frazier Sr. died January 10, 1985. Since a teenager in the early 1920s, Josiah "Cle" Frazier Sr. enjoyed playing the drums. Having begun when traditional New Orleans jazz was still in its forma-

tive years, Frazier's career as a jazz drummer spanned more than six decades. He started playing professionally around 1921 with Lawrence Marrero and, in 1923, was a member of the Young Tuxedo Brass Band. Frazier worked in the ERA and WPA bands during the mid-1930s, and performed, at one time or another, with all the leading brass bands of his day.

Alphonse Picou, a renowned jazz clarinetist, is best remembered as the creator of a celebrated chorus in the musical "High Society." He adapted a written piccolo variation of "High Society" for the clarinet. During the 1930s Picou took up the trade of tinsmithing—working with sheet metal. It was not until the late 1940s that he was seen with the Celestin Band or, more frequently, working in the Paddock on Bourbon Street. He died February 4, 1961, and it is said that Picou's funeral, held during Mardi Gras, was one of the biggest in New Orleans' history.

Herman J. Roth, who died April 8, 1988, was a native New Orleanian whose rise to fame was as a baseball athlete. His career began when he was fourteen years old, playing semipro baseball with the Grand Dukes. Roth made his professional debut as a catcher with the Caulfield Ads, which represented New Orleans in the Negro Southern League. In 1923 he was called up to the Negro Major League, joining the Chicago American Giants through the 1925 season. For the next four years Roth was back with the Caulfield Ads in the Negro Southern League where, as catcher and team captain, he lead the team to its first Southern League championship. In 1979, Roth was elected to the Greater New Orleans Sports Hall of Fame.

Dorothy Doretha Lawless, a lifelong resident of New Orleans and founder of the Dorothy Lawless Mortuary, was active in the Progressive Baptist Church, New Zion Baptist Church, NAACP, and the Ladies Tammany Social Aid and Pleasure Club.

Avery "Kid" Howard, best known for his interpretation of spirituals, was a trumpeter and cornetist who played in both his own and many other bands from the 1920s through the 1960s.

Emmanuel V. Gregoire was a public school teacher, principal, and newspaper columnist.

Octave Lilly Jr., a businessman prominent in the insurance industry, was a recognized writer whose works included the collection *Cathedral in the Ghetto, and Other Poems,* published in 1970.

Archibal E. Perkins, a civic leader and educator, served as principal of the R. T. Danneel School for twenty years. He also authored *A Brief History of the Negro in Louisiana* and regularly contributed articles to the *Journal of Negro History.*

Theodore L. Miller was a pharmacist who eventually used his pharmaceutical background to create face creams and soaps, which he developed into a very successful nationwide business.

Thomas H. Mims, M.D., though not a native of the city, lived almost seventy-five years in New Orleans as a practicing physician and active community leader.

Louis Reimonenq, founder and pastor of New Orleans's Calvary Spiritual Church, was a New Orleans native very active in the community, and a veteran of World War II.

Lillian D. Loeb was a Grand Worthy Matron Emeritus of Martha Chapter O.E.S., and Royal Grand Matron of the Masons.

St. Louis, Missouri

Black men and women have been a strong part of the St. Louis fabric since the year of the city's founding. St. Louisians prided themselves then, as now, on the efforts of blacks striving to bring about major changes in education, housing, and other facets of life.

A brief glimpse into the city's colorful history shows one such effort: the establishment of Freedom School in 1847. That same year, out of fear of a slave uprising like the Nat Turner Rebellion, the Missouri General Assembly passed one of the harshest laws against blacks: one prohibiting Negroes or mulattos from learning to read or write.

This did not discourage the **Reverend John Berry Meachum**. He defied the laws of Missouri by building a steamboat and anchoring it in the middle of the river—federal territory outside the jurisdiction of the Missouri authorities. Each morning Meachum picked up his students from the riverbank and took them to his "boat school" to learn reading, writing, and arithmetic. At the end of each day he returned them to the bank. Meachum's floating school became famous throughout the nation. During the 1840s and 1850s, hundreds of black children learned their "three Rs" in the middle of the Mississippi River.

The construction of the old courthouse in St. Louis, an interesting architectural example of government structures of its era, began in 1839. Its great historical significance extends back four years to 1847, the same year the Freedom School was established. During that year, a slave named **Dred Scott** appeared in one of the building's courtrooms to bring suit for his freedom. The Dred Scott case was in the state and federal courts for ten years. It became a raging political and social issue throughout the country and made Dred Scott the most famous enslaved person of his time.

LAY DOWN BODY

The chief issue of the case was whether Scott was, in fact, a slave. His master had taken him into Illinois, where slavery was forbidden by the state constitution, and to the Wisconsin Territory, where it was banned under the Missouri Compromise. Ultimately, the case went to the U.S. Supreme Court. Chief Justice Taney ruled that slaves could not become free by escaping or being taken into free territory, and blacks could not become citizens. The decision started a furor that continued until passage of the Fourteenth Amendment at the close of the Civil War. By that time, it made no difference to Dred Scott; his owner had liberated him as soon as the case was settled and Scott died a year later, in 1858.

St. Louis lives up to its reputation as a city in the "Show Me" state. It is aggressive and innovative in its attack on the status quo. Improvements and beautification programs continue to make a difference. The Gateway Arch stands regally over a city that prides itself on being equally accessible to all parts of the country.

IF WINTER COMES

THE FROST HAS KISSED THE FLOWERS—

NOT WITH THE CRUEL TOUCH OF UTTER DESOLATION,

BUT WITH THE CALM CARESS OF TENDER LOVE.

HAVE THEY NOT DONE THEIR WORK?

SHOULD THEY NOT SLEEP A SPACE

AND WAKE WITH SPRING TO FULLER LIFE?

DEATH COMES AND TOUCHES ALL—

NOT IN AN ANGRY MOOD THAT BRINGS OBLIVION,

BUT IN A REVERENT HUSH THAT QUIETS PAIN.

FOR AS THE NIGHT DRAWS ON,

SHOULD WE NOT REST A WHILE

UNTIL THE TRIUMPH OF A BRIGHTER DAWN?

—EDNA GULLINS, *Negro Voices*

MOSES DICKSON CEMETERY

Moses Dickson Cemetery is named in honor of the founder of the Knights of Liberty. Dickson was born a free black man in 1824, in Cincinnati, Ohio. According to the records of the Knights's exploits, his was "a gigantic, desperate movement. We expected to arrive at Atlanta, Georgia, with at least 150,000 well-armed men. Dickson advised his men to wait when the Civil War began. The Knights of Liberty fought with the Union forces. There were many casualties but Moses Dickson survived. After the war, Dickson became an ordained minister of the African Methodist Episcopal Church. He joined the successful effort to get the Missouri legislature to adopt the `separate but equal' doctrine that made black schools possible in the state. Moses Dickson, along with **James Milton Turner**, the country's first black diplomat, is buried in the cemetery."

BELLEFONTAINE CEMETERY

Bellefontaine Cemetery is located on the city's northwest side, at 4947 West Florissant. In the old Baptist church lot of the cemetery lie buried the two spiritual advisors of Dred Scott: **John Berry Meachum** and Scott's pastor, **John Richard Anderson** of the Second African Baptist Church.

JEFFERSON BARRACKS AND NATIONAL CEMETERY

There stands a marker on grave number 15009 in Section 57 of the Jefferson Barracks burial ground that recalls a hazard of nineteenth-century warfare even more costly than bullets. It is dedicated "to the memory of 175 non-commissioned officers and privates of the 56th U.S. Colored Infantry who died of cholera, in August 1866." The remains of these soldiers were brought here from Quarantine Station, Missouri. The probability is that these men were sent there from Helena, Arkansas, where their unit was stationed from March 1864 to September 1866, and where they most likely contracted the epidemic. Much of their service was in garrison duty, although they saw action at other points in Arkansas and Mississippi on several occasions. During two-and-a-half years of service, the 56th Infantry lost 674 men: twenty-five were killed or mortally wounded in action, and 649 died from disease.

NEW COLD WATER BURYING GROUND

New Cold Water Burying Ground is located on Old Halls Ferry Road, adjacent to Paddock Golf Course. The cemetery was created in 1866 by five trustees who purchased the one-half acre for $50. The deed specified that the land was to be used "as a graveyard or burying ground under the name of New Cold Water Burying Ground." The 1878 atlas showing a colored school and church already located across the street from the cemetery is a further reflection of the close-knit community that created these institutions. The 1909 atlas shows "African church and school" still in this location. Subsequently, they disappeared. Not much information can be had regarding who is buried at New Cold Water, but a walk through the grounds reveals old markers juxtaposed with the new.

ST. CHARLES BORROMEO CHURCH CEMETERY

St. Charles Borromeo Church Cemetery is located on West Randolph Street between South Wheaton Drive and Mission Court. It was to this location that the remains of **Jean-Baptiste Point Du Sable** were moved in 1854. Unfortunately, his tombstone was broken and lost during one of the two cemetery relocations as the town grew. The first non–Native American settler in the region and considered the founder of Chicago, Illinois, Du Sable was born to a French mariner father and an African-born "slave mother." His date of birth is unknown; his place of birth has variously been reported as Santo

Domingo, Haiti, and French Canada. After his mother's death, Du Sable's father sent him to Paris to be educated. Later, he worked as a seaman on his father's ship. After the ship wrecked, he came to St. Louis by way of New Orleans, with a French companion by the name of Jacques Clamorgan. The two started a trading business in the late 1760s. From St. Louis, Du Sable went on to Peoria and then to Chicago, where he became the first non-Indian to establish a permanent settlement in the area. In 1800, Du Sable sold his real estate holdings and moved in with one of his children in St. Charles, Missouri. He died a pauper; a priest at St. Charles Borromeo Church recorded his death as August 28, 1818.

Indianapolis, Indiana

Indianapolis prides itself on being a renaissance city. Famous as the home of the Indianapolis Motor Speedway, it is also an industrial and manufacturing center. The largest city in Indiana and a leading agricultural center, its downtown—as well as many of its neighborhoods—has seen extensive rebuilding and beautification. There are numerous African American "treasures" in the city, including the Madame Walker Urban Life Center and Theatre. **Madame C. J. Walker,** the first African American woman millionaire in the United States, moved to Indianapolis in the early 1900s and established numerous beauty shops and an entire line of cosmetics.

SUTHERLAND PARK CEMETERY

Sutherland Park Cemetery, the only black-owned cemetery in Indianapolis, is located at 4141 North Tacoma Avenue. It was founded in the mid-1930s and is just under ten acres in size. The owner of the cemetery is Melvin D. Thompson.

The cemetery management began a refurbishing program in 1993, which thus far has resulted in the addition of a wrought iron fence around its grounds, new columns adorning its entrance, a beautiful sign, and extensive landscaping and cleanup.

Presently, the cemetery is used by families who purchased grave space from previous owners of the cemetery. There are very few new grave purchases, but the present owner has begun to increase sales. Prices of the graves vary, depending upon location within the cemetery. Among the families buried at Sutherland are the Hollins family, longtime Indianapolis residents, and the Southgate family, interred here in the 1950s.

Also buried here are **Charles Horn** (1938), **Susan Horn** (1939), **Alphonse Petition** (1937), **John McGreevy** (1939), and **Ella McGreevy** (1954).

Nicodemus, Kansas

Nicodemus, a small, Midwestern farming community, lies approximately two hundred miles from Topeka on the dry, arid, light-brown land of the high plains of northern Kansas. The town is a cluster of small and unassuming buildings, just off Kansas Highway 24. It is the welcome sign erected by the Kansas State Historical Society at the highway rest stop that gives visitors an idea of the uniqueness of this little village.

Nicodemus is the earliest Midwestern black settlement associated with the massive westward migration of former slaves out of the South during Reconstruction. Deliberately begun as a commercial venture, Nicodemus capitalized on the anxieties and desires of southern blacks for freedom, land, and opportunity. By segregating themselves on the great expansiveness of the High Plains, black settlers hoped to gain opportunities that the South simply would not allow.

The first residents of Nicodemus were largely Kentucky-born, although a wide mix of home states was present. Despite their origins, the settlers were united in their common experience as slaves.

After years of trials and tribulations that included intense racial problems with neighboring white farmers, Nicodemus today remains committed to preserving its proud history. In July 1994 the town celebrated its 116th annual "Emancipation Day" homecoming.

Although the town has few residents, the celebration drew some five hundred former Nicodemites, including businessmen and philanthropists, farmers and athletes, writers, nurses, and others. Children enjoyed attending the reunions and hearing stories about the black pioneers, four and five generations back, who arrived here in covered wagons.

The Nicodemus town company was formed April 8, 1877, by one white and six black residents of Kansas. By 1878 the town boasted nearly seven hundred residents. Its prominence was short-lived, however, when the railroad bypassed the community ten years later. A majority of the businesses relocated to nearby communities and the town slowly withered. About fifty descendants of the town's original immigrants still reside in the area and some historic structures remain.

Angela Bates, a Nicodemus native and historian, is president of the Nicodemus Historical Society. She is working diligently to have this National Historic Landmark designated as a National Historic Site so it can become part of the National Park Service.

The honor that the first settlers warrant is exhibited in the town's three cemeteries. The grave markers are visual reminders of the community founders. All three cemeteries are small, rural burial grounds, each with its own colorfully lettered sign.

NICODEMUS CEMETERY

Nicodemus Cemetery, founded in 1877, is the largest of the town's three cemeteries. In 1983, the National Park Service prepared maps and rosters for both Nicodemus and neighboring Mount Olivet cemetery, to help visitors locate areas of the cemetery that might be of interest. Nicodemus has several ornamental cedar trees and decorative plantings. The oldest known marker is that of **Junior** and **Vergie Vaughn**, who died in 1880. Members of the Alexander and Williams families are buried here.

MOUNT OLIVET CEMETERY

Also founded in the 1800s, Mount Olivet is one-half mile north and half a mile west of Kansas Highway 24, on County Road 183. The cemetery is on the former site of the Mount Olivet Sanctuary, begun by the Reverend Daniel Hickman. Hickman's first church, the Mount Olivet Church of Stamping Ground, was in Scott County, Kentucky. It was at this church that W. R. Hill visited and gave his most important sales pitch; three hundred families at the area relocated to Nicodemus as a result. When Hickman arrived, he started a church under the same name as his church in Kentucky.

The oldest marker on the site is that of **Norma Thomas**, who died in 1885. The Bates, Jones, and Moore families traditionally have used the Mount Olivet Cemetery to bury their dead.

SAMUELS CEMETERY

The Samuels Cemetery, a few miles south of Wildhorse Township Cemetery in Bogue, is on land donated by John and Lee Anna Samuels, two early Nicodemus settlers. Historically, the Garland, Napue, Samuels, and Scruggs families of Nicodemus have been buried in this cemetery. The oldest grave marker is that of **William Napue**, who died in 1890. The cemetery is on a rolling, hilly stretch of grazing land, just southwest of the Nicodemus town site. It has few decorative plantings and no trees.

Chicago, Illinois, and Area

Chicago, a busy metropolis, was built in and around the Chicago River and along the shore of beautiful Lake Michigan. It is one of the country's most commercially successful cities. Its first permanent non–Native American settler was **Jean-Baptiste Point Du Sable**, an African American who arrived in the 1700s and is commemorated in the city's Du Sable Museum of African American History, established in 1961 by Dr. Margaret Goss Burroughs.

Many persons of renown
are buried at Chicago's Burr
Oak Cemetery.

Dr. Burroughs, a writer, educator, museologist, organizer, and cultural leader, is a distinguished artist in her own right. She is the author of several books and the recipient of many citations for her poetry. The Du Sable Museum, the oldest African American history museum in the United States, was first opened as the Ebony Museum in her home. In 1973, after a successful community-based campaign, the museum moved to its present location in Washington Park on the city's South Side. A twenty-five-thousand-square-foot wing named for Chicago Mayor Harold Washington allowed the museum to expand its extensive permanent collection of artifacts, books, and photographs. Among the holdings are original slave documents and civil rights memorabilia.

BURR OAK CEMETERY

Burr Oak Cemetery is located in Alsip, Illinois, approximately twenty minutes by car from downtown Chicago. Because of this, the cemetery services families from all sections and neighborhoods of Chicago. Unlike numerous other cities, Chicago allows funeral processions to drive on Chicago freeways and expressways. Cemetery vice-president Delores Johnson indicated that many funeral directors nevertheless prefer the surface streets because of safety factors. She also explained that five or six years ago the city ordinance was changed, prohibiting funeral cars from driving through red lights. The only exception is when written permission is requested and received from the proper authority.

Burr Oak Cemetery is approximately 120 acres in size. A small back portion of the grounds is designated as a nonperpetual care section. The costs for burial in this section are considerably lower than for other, more attractive, parts of the cemetery.

Burr Oak was purchased by a group of five or six black men in the early 1930s. It was operated as a memorial park with its markers at ground level. Although all of the original members are dead, certain members of the cemetery's current eighteen-person board have served for many years. The board chairman, John H. Johnson, is the publisher of *Jet* and *Ebony* magazines.

Dinah Washington was acclaimed by blues, jazz, gospel, pop, and R&B audiences alike.

Many persons of both little and great renown are buried at Burr Oak. Among the more well known interred here are **Dinah Washington, Ezzard Charles,** and **Emmett Till.**

Dinah Washington (née Ruth Jones), whose singing style helped lay the groundwork for numerous rhythm-and-blues and jazz artists, died on December 14, 1963, at the age of thirty-nine, in her home in Detroit. She was buried at Burr Oak after a large funeral in Chicago, where she'd started her career singing gospel at St. Luke's Baptist Church on the South Side. With composer and critic Leonard Feather, Washington later gained legendary status with songs like "What a Difference a Day Makes" and "Unforgettable," and she proved to be such a versatile artist that she was acclaimed by blues, jazz, gospel, pop, and rhythm-and-blues audiences alike.

Emmett Till was a young resident of Chicago's South Side. In the forty years since World War I began, Chicago's black population had grown from some forty thousand to half a million. Many blacks had moved up from the South, seeking jobs and a better way of life. Fourteen-year-old Emmett Till was part of this immigrant community. On August 20, 1955, he was in the delta town of Money, Mississippi, population fifty-five, to visit relatives still living on his family's home place.

Till was accused of saying, "Bye baby" to a white woman in a candy store; a few nights later he was taken from his uncle's house and killed, his body later found in the Tallahatchie River. His mother, Mamie Till, wanting the world to see her son's mutilated corpse, brought his body back to Chicago. The black press was outraged about the killing. *Jet* magazine ran a photograph of the corpse. The *Chicago Defender,* one of the country's largest national black weeklies, gave the Till case and the open-casket funeral prominent coverage. Till's body was buried in Burr Oak Cemetery.

Emmett Till's murder at the age of fourteen provoked outrage within Chicago and across the country.

MILLER GROVE CEMETERY

Miller Grove Cemetery, while located near the Macedonia Free Will Baptist Church in Golconda, is far less accessible than the church. Even in dry weather it is recommended to come by truck or have a good pair of hiking boots. The old Miller Grove Cemetery is the last remaining vestige of what once was an early African American settlement. Some burials date back as far as 1865.

Some claim that this area was the first all-black community in Illinois, established before the Civil War. Free families came to the area as early as the 1830s. All, however, had departed by 1925.

FREE FRANK McWORTER BURIAL SITE

The cemetery of the McWorter family is located less than twenty miles from the Mississippi River across from Hannibal, Missouri. This cemetery is one of only three Illinois sites listed on the National Register of Historic Places.

Dr. Juliet E. K. Walker, great-great-granddaughter of Free Frank and a professor of history at the University of Illinois at Urbana, notes in her biography of Free Frank that he was "an ex-slave who purchased his own freedom and that of fifteen of his family members at a total cost of about $15,000."

Frank McWorter was born in 1777 and came to Illinois from South Carolina, via Kentucky, making the six-hundred-mile journey in a covered wagon. McWorter, a saltpeter manufacturer, small land speculator, commercial farmer, and town founder, died in 1854.

Though no longer in existence, New Philadelphia, the town Free Frank founded in 1836, was, until the 1880s, a thriving frontier community that served as a way station for travelers heading west on Illinois roads. The site of the station is commemorated by a marker.

Detroit, Michigan, and Area

Founded in 1701 in the name of Louis XIV of France at *le place du détroit* (the place of the strait), this was a quiet city—until the automobile changed it forever.

Falling into decay after the racial tumult of the 1960s dislodged its formerly close neighborhoods, by the mid-1990s Detroit, Michigan, has become a city once again on the move. The beauty of this motor-car capital, bordered on one side by the magnificent Detroit River and neighboring Canada, is slowly being revived by a caring mayor, Dennis Archer, and concerned citizens. Detroit's cultural center is home to some twenty cultural institutions, including the Museum of African American History, the Detroit Institute of Arts, the Science Museum, and Wayne State University. Among its other jewels are the Motown Museum, the New Center area, and some magnificent residential areas such as Rosedale Park, Sherwood Forest, and to the east, Indian Village.

The beautiful grounds of Detroit Memorial Park, East and West, are among the jewels of the city. Detroit Memorial Park is the oldest African American–owned corporation in Michigan.

DETROIT MEMORIAL PARK CEMETERY, EAST AND WEST

Detroit Memorial Park is presently occupying two sites: The East branch is located on eighty-five acres at 4280 East 13 Mile Road in nearby Warren, and a recently purchased sixty-two-acre site at 25200 Plymouth Road in Redford serves as Detroit Memorial Park West.

Prior to 1925, blacks in Detroit suffered unspeakable indignities because of the white-operated cemeteries. A few of these cemeteries allowed burials of blacks but only on certain designated days and at inconvenient burial hours, and most often the funeral entourage was directed to a side entrance. Added to this were the exorbitant fees charged for the burial of a black person.

This embarrassment and degradation inspired a small group of business and professional men, under the leadership of funeral director Charles C. Diggs Sr., to purchase land for a cemetery of their own. When Diggs announced the idea of the sale of stock for the purchase of land, many local businessmen responded, recommending investment in the cemetery to their friends and clients and writing newspaper articles of endorsement. The other real "angels" in this venture were the ministers. They advised their congregations to invest in a corporation that would grow and repay them, someday, and a place where they could lay loved ones to rest with full dignity and complete satisfaction. The Detroit Memorial Park Association was incorporated in July 1925, with thirteen persons selected as the first board of directors.

During the spring of 1926, special meetings were held to consider methods of raising the money necessary to pay for the property in full. Since Michigan cemetery laws required that land available for human burial could not be encumbered by a mortgage, the organizers were forced to borrow money, on faith and credit. The only lending institution willing to extend credit to the corporation was the newly organized Michigan Mutual Savings Bank, which insisted that association investors make deposits in its bank.

Board members and stockholders faced a monumental task: secure the $25,000 loan they required with an equal amount of cash deposits in the bank. Amazingly, they succeeded.

The cemetery was designed in accordance with the "Memorial Park Plan," meaning there would be no upright monuments or grave markers. A Perpetual Care Fund was to be set aside from each burial or lot sale, its interest to be used to keep the cemetery beautiful forever.

With the money in hand, the company purchased a total of eight-five acres of farmland in what was then Warren Township. Although the Warren community had agreed to sell to black investors, soon after the land was sold, some within the community pressed the members to give up the land. The

L A Y   D O W N   B O D Y

board hastily agreed that in order to prevent a legally successful reacquisition, a burial or interment had to be made on the property. On the night of October 30, 1926, two morticians unceremoniously buried a stillborn baby, **Emma L. Brown,** on the grounds, thus evaporating any opposition to their intended use of the land.

The grounds are divided into sections and in some areas, into gardens, each with its distinctive feature or marker, bearing names such as "Garden of the Cross," "Garden of Love," and "Garden of Prayer." There are also sections for burial of children and a veterans' section.

In the 1940s and 1950s the board began studying the process of double burials and of the construction of a mausoleum; a forty-eight tomb mausoleum was completed in 1971. The need for double burials became acute by

Elijah McCoy, interred at Detroit Memorial Park, invented the "drip cup" that helped perfect lubrication systems.

the 1970s. After meeting with state officials, it was determined that double interments—using a large container box holding the casket of one family member and reserving space for another—were legal.

The first serious attempt to seek additional land occurred in 1978, but it was ten years before a suitable location for expansion could be found. In 1988 the board purchased National Memorial Gardens; the closing of Detroit Memorial Park–West's sale took place on June 25, 1988.

Detroit Memorial Park was a child of necessity created by the city's black community in its pursuit of racial pride and human dignity. As a result of the efforts of founders, shareholders, and supporters, the cemetery has been able to provide dignified burials for all. In addition, the cemetery association has returned significant portions of its earnings to the community through wages, donations to numerous organizations, and, during a period of economic depression, extended loans to residents. This attention to the needs of the community have produced one of the oldest and most profitable African American businesses in the state. The book *Detroit Memorial Park: The Evolution of an African American Corporation* by Roberta Wright relates the complete story of the cemetery, from its inception in 1925 to the present time. The story's interest lies not only in its description of the cemetery, but also as a chronicle of an African American corporation in the United States.

The Detroit area has a rich heritage of black-owned funeral homes. They are distinctive in setting, but universal in maintaining high standards and good business practices. On Memorial Day, May 31, 1976, a historic marker was installed on the cemetery ground by the State of Michigan designating Detroit Memorial as an official historic site.

Among those interred at this historic burial ground is **Elijah McCoy.** Born in Canada, McCoy studied in Scotland and moved to Ypsilanti, Michigan, after the Civil War. Interested in science, McCoy acquired some fifty-seven patents for his inventions, devices primarily connected with the automatic lubricator he designed for moving machinery. One of McCoy's most important and valuable efforts was the "drip cup," a small container filled with oil that flowed to the moving parts of heavy-duty machinery. This device for perfecting overall lubrication systems continues to be used in large industry today. McCoy was buried in Detroit Memorial Park Cemetery in 1929.

WESTLAWN CEMETERY (WAYNE AND YPSILANTI)

Westlawn Cemetery, located at 31472 Michigan Avenue between Merriman Road and Gloria Street in Wayne, was founded in 1920 by the Clearview Association, a group of prominent local undertakers. The association purchased eighty acres of land from the Merriman family to set up a predominantly Lutheran cemetery. The burial ground has been open to all races since

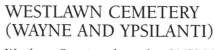

its inception. Singer **Jackie Wilson** is buried there, as are some members of the Gordy family. An additional location is in Ypsilanti, at 9470 Ford Road.

METROPOLITAN MEMORIAL GARDENS

Metropolitan Memorial Gardens is located at 48300 Willow Road in Belleville, Michigan, a few miles west of Detroit's Metropolitan Airport near Lake Belleville. The cemetery was founded in 1958 by businessman Sid Frunkin and is currently owned by the Reverend J. Herbert Hinkle of Detroit's Cathedral Center of Faith, who purchased the land in 1985.

The cemetery is about seventy acres in size, and is well cared for. An impressive chapel graces the grounds, which include several plots owned by Detroit's Wayne State University Medical School to bury the remains of human anatomy specimens donated for research. The plots' inscriptions read: "These people died so others could live."

Among the prominent African Americans buried at Metropolitan Memorial are **Florence Ballard**, one of the original Supremes who left the group in 1967 after the Supremes recorded twenty hits that made the rock record charts; the **Reverend J. J. Worth**, founder of Detroit's First Baptist Church; the **Reverend Ray Jackson**, founder of Detroit's Church of God and Christ; Deacon **Henderson Hendricks**, **Zula Hendricks**, and **Donald L. Smith Jr.**

ELMWOOD CEMETERY

Elmwood Cemetery stands in Detroit's Lower East Side and was founded in the 1700s. It is the final resting place for twenty-seven Detroit mayors, six governors, the builder of the first and third cars driven in Detroit, many figures from the American Civil War, and numerous others prominent in Michigan history. This beautiful cemetery sits along the banks of historic Bloody Run Creek, the site of the Pontiac uprising against the British. Like Historic Oakland Cemetery in Atlanta, Georgia, Elmwood is a beautiful historic landmark. Although the cemetery is white-owned, throughout the years many of Detroit's early black families selected Elmwood. A Black Heritage Tour, outlined by the cemetery, highlights black civil rights workers and leaders who are buried there:

Cora Brown, the first black woman in the nation to be elected to state senate in 1953.

Amos Burgess, an early civil rights leader.

Albert Burgess, son of Amos, and the first black child to graduate from Detroit High School.

Reverend Supply Chase, pastor of Second Baptist Church from 1861–1874.

Lomax B. Cook, considered by many to be the best barber in Detroit during the late 1800s and known throughout the Midwest as an unbeatable checkers player.

George DeBaptiste, White House steward and close personal friend of President Harrison prior to his residency in Detroit. He became a successful merchant and used his ships to transport runaway slaves to Canada.

Dr. Joseph Ferguson, a physician, community leader, and abolitionist. One of Michigan's first black doctors, he was a practicing licensed physician as a "freed man" in Richmond, Virginia, before coming to Detroit.

William Ferguson, the first black child admitted to Detroit's public schools in 1871. He became Michigan's first black legislator in 1893 and, in a landmark civil rights case, argued successfully as plaintiff attorney before the Michigan Supreme Court in 1890.

Elizabeth D. Forth, one of the first black landowners in Detroit and Pontiac. An ex-slave who fled to Canada with the help of Colonel Elijah Brush in 1807, she worked for John Biddle, mayor of Detroit, for over thirty years. Money from her estate was used to build St. James Episcopal Church on Grosse Ile.

William Lambert, a community leader for almost fifty years. An important agent for the Underground Railroad and organizer of the "African Mysteries," Lambert owned a successful tailoring business.

Robert Millender Sr., an attorney and campaign manager for Mayor Coleman Young. Millender died in 1978. Detroit's Millender Center is named after him.

Benjamin and Robert Pelham, brothers who helped found the *Detroit Plaindealer* in 1883, the first successful black newspaper in Detroit. It was located at Shelby and State Streets.

Curtis Randolph, Detroit's first black firefighter to die in action. Randolph was killed in 1977.

Fannie Richards, the first black schoolteacher to teach in the Detroit public school system in 1871. She taught kindergarten and Sunday school and helped found the Phyllis Wheatley Home for destitute and aged black women in 1897.

John D. Richards, a businessman and supporter of the Underground Railroad. The brother of Fannie Richards, he was instrumental in organizing the 102nd U.S. Colored Infantry during the Civil War.

James Robinson, who fought in the American Revolution and War of 1812. Robinson was personally awarded the gold medal of valor by General Lafayette. The oldest person buried in Elmwood, he died in 1868 at the age of 115.

D. Augustus Straker, known as the "black Irish lawyer." The brother-in-law of Fannie and John Richards, he was the attorney in *Ferguson v. Gies* (1890) and served as Michigan's first black judge.

Charles Stone, a famous orchestra leader in the early 1900s. His Stone Family Orchestra played on the Put-in-Bay ferries and, later, at Fairlane Manor in Dearborn. He was Henry Ford's favorite musician for social gatherings.

William Webb, an attorney, community leader, and abolitionist.

Lorenzo C. Wright, who won the Olympic gold medal in the 480-meter relay in London in 1948.

Members of the 102nd U.S. Colored Infantry, formed entirely of volunteers from 1863–1865. The First Michigan Colored Regiment was organized at Camp Ward, which once stood on the present day Duffield School grounds. The regiment saw service in South Carolina, Georgia, and Florida. More than fourteen hundred men served in the regiment; ten percent gave their lives in battle. The regiment disbanded in October 1865. Among those Michigan soldiers fallen in battle and interred in Elmwood Cemetery are: **William H. Carter, London Floyd, Charles Gilbert, George H. Griggs, Greenbury Hodge, Albert J. Ratliff, George A. Holmes, Frank Robinson, William Riley, Augustus Stewart, Robert K. Russell, Henry Smith, William Shorter, Berry Thomas, Robert Thomas, Henry Williams,** and **Daniel B. Walker.** Although these names are not easily recognizable to most, their prominence in the cemetery forms a vital link to African American heritage.

Philadelphia, Pennsylvania, and Area

Although many of the cemeteries in the East, as in the western United States, are integrated, stories of African American burials still need to be told. Northeastern cemeteries, particularly in the Philadelphia area, tend to be on a larger scale than in the South. However, the same struggle exists; the same fight for equality in life and death dominates the stories of those who rest there.

Evidence suggests that African Americans arrived here as early as 1639. In 1694, three years after the first Quaker settlers arrived, 154 enslaved

Africans were brought to Philadelphia on the ship *Isabella*. Many prominent area merchants, religious people, and political figures were involved in the trade of African men, women, and children, including William Penn and other members of the Society of Friends. A short distance from where the Liberty Bell now stands, enslaved Africans were once sold.

Where were they buried? As in New York City, Dallas, Texas, and other cities, burial grounds exist beneath many of the buildings. During the existence and legal acceptance of slavery in the "City of Brotherly Love," Philadelphia once contained the largest free African American community in the United States. As a result, pioneering black leaders and abolitionists created local institutions for the purpose of collectively challenging slavery and racism and championing the cause for the universal application of "life, liberty, and the pursuit of happiness."

Today, as in the past, Philadelphia boasts a diversity that provides a sources of strength and stability to the African American community. Although there are presently no black-owned cemeteries in use within the city of Philadelphia and the surrounding Philadelphia County, some burial sites in the close environs are black-owned, and most white-owned cemeteries in the city are now burying blacks. One such cemetery is Mount Peace on Lehigh Avenue.

MORRIS CEMETERY

Historic Morris Cemetery was established in 1867 at 428 Nutt Road, Phoenixville, Pennsylvania. Located on the property is the chapel, which is also a historical landmark, as well as a Civil War monument erected in 1868. The monument marks the town's highest elevation in Phoenixville. Morris Cemetery is owned by John Walker, an African American who has been in the cemetery business for fifteen years and plays an active role in the community. With a diverse background in speaking, theater, and production, Walker worked at several other cemeteries before purchasing Morris Cemetery.

Morris is one of the first cemeteries in the area that allowed both blacks and whites to be interred together. It is also one of the few cemeteries in the area to offer a choice of markers or a mausoleum. Among those buried in Morris Cemetery are former governor **Penny Packer** and **Samuel Whitaker**, famous for his role with the American Legion.

EDEN CEMETERY

Eden Cemetery was chartered on June 20, 1902, as Eden Cemetery Company. Jerome Bacon, founder and organizer, was a teacher for the Institute of

Colored Youth, later named Cheyney State College, as well as an employee of Philadelphia's Millbourne Flour Company. In his determination to establish Eden, Bacon motivated J. C. Asbury, Daniel W. Parvis, Martin Lehman, and Charles W. Jones to join him.

Eden Cemetery Company began with horse and wagon; today it has the latest equipment to perform all of its functions. While continuing to be black-administered, it has never been discriminatory and has all races reposing in the facility.

Remains from the First African Baptist Church Cemetery—also of Delaware County—dating from 1824–1842 were transferred to Eden when that church's cemetery was excavated during the mid-1980s. Also reinterred at Eden are bodies from the Olive, Lebanon, and Home cemeteries, which were moved when those cemeteries were condemned. Eden, comprised of fifty-three beautiful rolling acres, had, as of 1990, more than eighty thousand bodies reposing in its confines.

Some of the outstanding citizens interred in Eden since the cemetery's first burial on August 12, 1902, are **Stephen Smith**, founder and benefactor of Stephen Smith Home; **Col. John McGee**, black millionaire; **Amos Scott**, first magistrate for Philadelphia; **Ed Henry**, magistrate for Philadelphia; **Chris J. Perry**, founder of the *Philadelphia Tribune;* **William and Letitia Still**, authors of *The Underground Railroad;* **Dr. Caroline Anderson**, Philadelphia's first black female physician; **Dr. Rebecca Cole**, another female physician; **William Cole**, an ambitexter; **Caroline Lecount**, principal of O. V. Catto School; and **Henriette S. Duterte**, first black female undertaker.

The Reverends **John Bunyan Reave, Charles Tindley, J. Campbell Beckett, Wesley Parks, William Creditt, Father McDuffy, Father Bright**, and **Bishop Ida Robinson** are also interred in Eden.

Several organizations acted upon their belief in Eden Cemetery's worth and purchased lots for their members, including the British Great War Veterans, Veterans of Both Wars, House of Refuge, the Association for Colored Orphans of Philadelphia, Home for Destitute Colored Children, the Prince Hall Masons, the IBPOE, Odd Fellows, the Cyrenes, African Presbyterian Church, Lombard Central Presbyterian Church, Wesley A.M.E. Church, Grace Union A.M.E. Church, Church of God and Saints of Christ, St. Thomas P.E. Church, St. Mark P.E. Church, Church of the Crucifixion, St. Mary P.E. Church, St. Simon the Cyrenian Church, and Union Baptist Church.

MERION MEMORIAL PARK

Historic Merion Memorial Park, in Bala Cynwyd, Pennsylvania, was founded in the late 1880s and is the final resting place of many prominent blacks.

The cemetery is in good condition, and the families whose loved ones are interred here are pleased. The new management has erected a sign, built a new fence, and made road repairs, and it has begun selling memorials.

The Merion Memorial Park was originally owned by James Smart. It was sold to John and Katie Laird in 1894, who immediately sold it to the Merion Cemetery Company. From the start, people of all colors and religions were buried at Merion. In the 1940s, Hobson Reynolds became the cemetery's first black owner; in 1947 he sold it to C. Percy White. Ownership then passed to his son, Donald White, who was succeeded by his wife, Rita White, the present owner.

In 1951, Asian associations began buying sections of the cemetery. Presently, five sections of the cemetery are owned by the Philadelphia Chinese community. They, like the African Americans, have had difficulty finding a cemetery willing to accept their business.

Of eight black sections, most are named for prominent personalities in black history. Among them is the Benjamin Banneker section, which honors the black scientist who served on the commission that planned Washington, D.C., and who, for ten years, edited a popular almanac published in Philadelphia.

The Charles Sumner section is named for the Massachusetts senator who, from 1851 to 1874, fought for desegregated schools and championed equal suffrage for blacks. Thaddeus Stevens, Pennsylvania congressman in 1848 and 1858, is remembered in another section. He was a chief anti-slavery and pro-equal suffrage spokesperson.

There is an Abraham Lincoln section and another named after George H. White, the North Carolina congressman who, in 1900, introduced a bill to make lynching a federal offense.

Among those buried here is **Robert Mara Adger** (1837–1910). Born in Charleston, South Carolina, Adger was one of thirteen children. In 1848 he moved to Philadelphia with his family and developed business skills working with his father. Later becoming director of the Philadelphia Building and Loan Association, one of the first African American mortgage companies, Adger joined the Black Enlistment Committee to help recruit black soldiers for the Union army.

In 1865 Adger served as a delegate to the first state conference in Harrisburg to discuss the creation of a Pennsylvania Equal Rights League. He later organized the Afro-American Historical Society, which contained his personal collection of rare books and pamphlets of black history and the anti-slavery movement. He died of a heart attack on June 10, 1910.

LAY DOWN BODY

Not far from "Bishops Row"—resting place of six A.M.E. bishops—is the burial site of composer **James A. Bland.** Born on Long Island in 1854, he studied at Howard University and became a prolific songwriter and minstrel, living in London for twenty years. He authored "Oh Dem Golden Slippers" and "Carry Me Back to Old Virginny," which became Virginia's state song thirty years after Bland's death. He traveled widely, but died in obscurity at Philadelphia in 1911. Bland's grave is in the Catto section of the cemetery.

Also buried here are **Nehemiah James**, jazz musician; **Walter P. Hall**, largest wholesaler of meat and game, who employed many and paid them all the same as he paid himself; and **Skip James**, a well-known Mississippi blues man whose popular biography is titled *I'd Rather Be the Devil*. Old and stately monuments give tribute to the Allen family. Two black Philadelphia physicians, **Dr. William Warrick** (1900–1979) and **Orlando B. Taylor** (1904–1986), are also buried at Merion, as is the first black Philadelphia caterer of the Trower family.

Newport, Rhode Island

Founded as a shipbuilding center and port in 1639, Newport rivaled New York and Boston in importance in the seventeenth and eighteenth centuries; during the Civil War the U.S. Naval Academy was located here. The city's African American community was large and diverse and included a large number of professionals and skilled artisans. Newport's clergy was at the center of the abolitionist movement prior to the Civil War. Black clergymen in the city were prominent in the African colonization movement during the early nineteenth century, as well as the counter-reaction espoused by integrationists.

Slavery was abolished in Rhode Island in 1784, and for years following, Quakers and other abolitionists developed stations for the Underground Railroad. Portsmouth, Providence, and Newport have, through the years, built many cultural centers to highlight the accomplishments of these early refugees. The museum in Providence holds periodic displays of local history and also sponsors discovery tours of black roots in Rhode Island.

Today Newport is a thriving resort town and is home of the Naval Underwater Systems Center. Historic downtown Newport is a bustling tourist attraction. The city lies on a beautiful harbor, the setting for many resort hotels and shopping facilities. Tours to the classic Newport mansions and the numerous museums are not to be missed. More details about the role of African Americans in the community can be found in the book *African Americans in Newport: An Introduction to the Heritage of African Americans in Newport, Rhode Island, 1700-1945,* by Richard C. Youngken.

"GOD'S LITTLE ACRE" COMMON BURIAL GROUND

In early times, this was apparently a large section of what was then called the Common Burial Ground in Newport, Rhode Island. Several of the markers in the cemetery include the words Negro, black, and servant. There is some indication that, possibly prior to 1865, some siblings—who had the same parents but different masters—had different surnames. Each adopted the name of the family for which he or she labored.

Portsmouth (Truxton), Virginia, and Area

Portsmouth, part of the Hampton Roads port, is known for its commercial shipping and shipbuilding. It is connected to Norfolk by two bridge tunnels and a pedestrian ferry that crosses the Elizabeth River. Truxton, a planned neighborhood of Portsmouth, Virginia, is unique in that it was built especially for workers in the nearby Norfolk Naval Shipyard, the largest naval shipyard in the world. The forty-three-acre community, designated for black families, was built around 1919 by the U.S. Housing Corporation. The 253 houses were surrounded by a church, school, grocery, and drug store. The Truxton houses were later sold to two black businessmen who, in turn, sold them to some of the original tenants.

In 1995, the Portsmouth mayor declared May as "Truxton Month," and more than three hundred families joined the parade and celebration that followed. Longtime residents, remembering the past, encouraged their children to take pride in the community. Catherine Harris Bowser and Lucy Overton are two of the residents who actively promote the community.

LINCOLN CEMETERY

Black-owned Lincoln Cemetery, on Deep Creek Road, has eleven acres and is currently in use. It is owned by Vernon Wimbrough of Wimbrough & Sons Funeral Home. Lincoln was originally owned by the Smith "box container" family, but in 1925 its ownership reverted to the American National Bank. In 1935 Wimbrough began management and soon purchased the cemetery. Families maintain the cemetery, which displays a good appearance. Several prominent local persons are buried in Lincoln, including the Hall family.

CEDAR GROVE, OAK GROVE, AND MOUNT OLIVE CEMETERIES

Cedar Grove, which opened during the Spanish-American War, has only a few acres and is not currently in use. Oak Grove, which opened in 1910, has

LAY DOWN BODY

a section at the front of the cemetery set aside for black soldiers buried during World War I. Before World War I, the cemetery was divided into four parts, each owned by a separate black family. Two of the owners were undertakers. Mount Olive has twenty-five acres and was opened less than thirty years ago.

ELMWOOD CEMETERY

It is estimated that there were seventy thousand former slaves in Norfolk, Virginia, at the end of the Civil War. However, in May 1862 the city's fall before Union forces terminated its allegiance to the Confederacy. The city became a focal point for black refugees.

After the U.S. Army agreed to accept blacks into service, many were recruited from Norfolk. Elmwood Cemetery, located on Princess Ann Road in Norfolk, has on its grounds a memorial to the many black soldiers of the Civil War who are buried here. Elmwood also serves as the burial place for black veterans of the Spanish-American War.

Famed banker Maggie L. Walker, who had been buried at Woodland, is now interred at Evergreen Cemetery in Richmond, Virginia.

WOODLAND AND EVERGREEN CEMETERIES

Until the about 1970, blacks could not be buried in city-operated cemeteries in Richmond, Virginia, so their only choices were privately owned Woodland, located just outside of Richmond in Henrico County, and Evergreen, a private black cemetery in Richmond. Unfortunately, maintenance of both properties had been neglected, and one citizen of Richmond reports that Evergreen had become so overgrown it had to be closed.

The death of world renowned tennis player Arthur Ashe in 1993 prompted Richmond City Council member Roy O. West to complain to city officials, who, with the help of the state, cleaned up Woodland in preparation for Ashe's burial next to his mother. Also buried at Woodland was Maggie L. Walker, the first woman to organize a U.S. bank. Her remains were later moved to Evergreen Cemetery in Richmond.

New York, New York, and Area

The African American presence both within New York City and throughout New York state has been most significant. The history of African Americans in New York City dates from the time of the Dutch settlement; the stories highlight the gross injustices, poor education facilities, and extreme prejudices of the period. This, perhaps, is the reason that, even after the Civil War, blacks chose to live on farms or in rural areas of the state and why the countryside is flanked by numerous small cemeteries.

The African Burial Ground Project

The African Burial Ground Project involves the reconstruction and analysis of the skeletal remains of approximately 390 ancestral Africans who lived, labored, and died in colonial New York City. The results of this research will help give voice to African American ancestors who have been silenced for over two centuries. This research will also shed light on their origins in West Africa, as well as the stresses they faced while being oppressed on these shores.

Faculty, students, staff, and the general public are invited to tour the laboratory facility housing these projects. Visitors can observe lab activities, from reconstructing skeletal remains and determining the age and sex of individuals to discussions about the stresses faced by African American ancestors. Howard University in Washington, D.C., continues to analyze the human remains excavated from the lower Manhattan site.

The African Burial Ground Project is committed to the national and international recognition and preservation of the heritage of Africans and their descendants in the Americas. They are presently launching a national campaign to have the U.S. Postal Service issue an African Burial Ground commemorative stamp. Their goal is to collect one million signatures to submit to the U.S. Postmaster General by the end of 1995.

continued on next page

HUDSON-MOHAWK RIVER CEMETERIES

Cemeteries along the Hudson-Mohawk rivers and in the Champlain Valley contain the remains of many black soldiers. Some chose to join up with the 54th Massachusetts. Others stayed with the New York troops, becoming part of the 20th, 26th, and 31st U.S. Colored Troops. A small graveyard atop Cedar Hill holds the remains of two blacks, **John W. H. Atkins** of Company B, 20th Regiment, and **William Henry Jefferson** of the 8th Pennsylvania Regiment, who died on July 14, 1864, at Yellow Bluff, Virginia. The remains of two brothers who served with the 31st New York Colored Troops, **Charles** and **George King**, are buried in nearby Beekman Precinct. The remains of the **Freeman** brothers—**Agustus**, **John**, and **Perry**—lie in Union Vale Cemetery, also in Dutchess County. They served in the New York 20th Regiment of Colored Soldiers.

JOHN BROWN CEMETERY

The John Brown Farm in Lake Placid, New York, is where the famous nineteenth-century radical abolitionist is buried. Fellow abolitionist Gerrit Smith deeded the land to Brown in 1849, and Brown lived there for a short time. Restless, he left in the mid-1850s to fight in "Bleeding Kansas" and in 1856, Brown and his followers won a victory over a large number of Missourians.

Brown was for many years busily engaged in anti-slavery activities and crusades. Famous in the annals of American history is his seizure of Harpers Ferry, Virginia. He was caught and executed on December 2, 1859, for his role as leader of the raid. After his death, Brown's remains were brought back to the Adirondacks. He, his two sons, and the ten followers who also died at Harpers Ferry are buried some two hundred feet east of his farmhouse. The John Brown Farm Historic Site is currently operated as a museum and historic site by the New York State Historic Trust.

L A Y   D O W N   B O D Y

FORT HILL CEMETERY

Harriet Tubman, one of the most illustrious persons whom historians have ever studied, was buried in Fort Hill Cemetery in Auburn, New York. She died at the age of ninety-three and was buried in March of 1913. The cemetery is just three blocks from Thompson Memorial A.M.E. Zion Church, where she was a member. Born circa 1820–1821 in Maryland, Tubman, sometimes called "the Moses of her people," was enslaved and suffered harsh punishment. In 1848 she escaped to the North, but as a free woman she made plans to assist others. For the next ten years she made nineteen trips back into the South and rescued more than three hundred slaves. A reward of $40,000 was posted for her capture.

Tubman met and aided John Brown in recruiting soldiers for his raid on Harpers Ferry. She spent time in Canada and in South Carolina, where she was valuable to the army as a scout. Tubman's birthplace has been awarded a historical marker. The plantation, near Bucktown, Maryland, is eight miles south of Cambridge. Her home in Auburn, New York, is also on exhibition. It has been restored to its appearance during her lifetime and contains some of her possessions.

continued from previous page

The sites were excavated in 1991 and 1992, as the U.S. General Services Administration began construction of a new federal office building at 290 Broadway and a new federal courthouse building at 500 Pearl Street, in lower Manhattan. The African Burial Ground site is now a national historic landmark, located within a city-designated historic district on the corners of Elk and Duane Streets near Broadway.

Headed by urban anthropologist Dr. Sherrill D. Wilson, the Office of Public Education and Interpretation of the African Burial Ground (OPEI; formerly known as the Liaison Office of the African Burial Ground and Five Points Archeological Projects) was established in 1993 to meet the increasing interest and requests for updated information and education in the form of public presentations and written materials on the early history of Africans in New York. OPEI has reached more than eighteen thousand individuals in the tri-state area through educational tours and materials. The OPEI offers public educators available for slide presentations, tours of the Foley Square Archeological Laboratory, educational resource materials, film screenings, and internships and volunteer opportunities.

Los Angeles, California

Los Angeles and its surrounding area have beckoned African American settlers since the early 1900s. The largest influx of black settlers, however, began just after World War II. Many were families of military men who were assigned to the Army and Air Force bases of the West. Often the entire family became enamored of the semi-tropical beauty and the pleasant, all-year climate—a big change for those used to the hot, humid conditions of the South.

Los Angeles is home to the popular and frequently visited California Afro-American Museum. The museum regularly sponsors exhibits about the history, art, and culture of African Americans.

ANGELES ABBEY MEMORIAL PARK

Angeles Abbey Memorial Park is a beautiful resting place for the families of Compton, California, and other surrounding communities. It is convenient- ly located in the hub of Los Angeles County, only seventeen minutes outside of Los Angeles. The peaceful grounds are sequestered amidst Moorish, Byzantine mausoleums.

Within a ten-acre area, the owners built their first mausoleum, the famous Abbey of the Angeles, whose name arose from the magnificent stained glass window of the famed Millet painting "The Angelus," which overlooks the Cathedral chapel. The cemetery's mausoleums have won praise from visitors from around the world, who are awed by both their fine art and architecture.

Angeles Abbey Memorial Park is a composite of the finest old-world artistry and the enduring steel-laced construction of today. In 1933, during a most devastating earthquake, not a stone, tile, or panel of glass in the mau- soleum was damaged, a testament to its construction. Angeles Abbey Crematory is equipped with modern, automatic "all-industrial" and "American" retorts. The park has an endowment care trust fund for future care of the cemetery.

David Reid, in *Sex, Death and God in Los Angeles,* tells this story: "It was- n't too long ago that finding a plot of soil to bury a black body posed a prob- lem in Los Angeles. In some areas, private charters blocked these interments as late as 1966. African American families, in black veils and ash-gray suits, loaded caskets onto streetcars and rode to Evergreen Cemetery in East L.A. That is where three generations of the family of Jean Sanders are interred."

Ms. Sanders has watched this neighborhood change three times—pre- dominantly white, predominantly black after Watts went up in flames in 1965, and then mainly Latino. Angeles Abbey has adjusted well to the com- munity's changing face, welcoming the Gypsies, for example, who throw noisy feasts and roast pigs in honor of the newly departed, and the Vietnamese, who fill caskets with the loved one's earthy possessions, then decorate the grounds with ripe fruit and flora. The gang funerals, Sanders explained, despite what is reported in the dailies, have been low key and uneventful. "They come in, do their thing, and then they leave."

"These kids are more afraid of the known than the unknown," Sanders states. "They live with the known everyday. Live with a father on crack or a mother on welfare, maybe a brother in the gangs. They take their hostility out on buildings—mark it up with graffiti, break windows. They take their hostility out on people. They take human lives. I had a lot of babies coming in recently. A lot of babies. Young adults with gunshot wounds—victims of violent crimes."

L A Y   D O W N   B O D Y

EVERGREEN CEMETERY

This sixteen-acre cemetery located in the Boyle Heights section of Los Angeles was founded in 1877, and is one of the oldest privately owned cemeteries in the Los Angeles area. Evergreen was unusual at the time because its burial plots were open to all races and grave sites were not segregated by race. Among the most famous African Americans buried at Evergreen are:

Biddy Mason, a freed Mississippi slave, nurse, midwife, and philanthropist who later became one of Los Angeles's more wealthy property owners before her death in 1891. She was the first black woman to own land in Los Angeles after she purchased a home on Spring Street in the heart of downtown Los Angeles in 1866. She parlayed that $250 purchase into a sizable property empire. Her grave remained unmarked for nearly a century before Los Angeles Mayor Tom Bradley and members of the First African Methodist Episcopal Church donated a memorial tombstone.

Reverend William Seymour, a driving force behind the Holiness religious movement at the turn of the twentieth century, led the Azusa Street Revival in Los Angeles and preached that speaking in tongues was evidence that one had received the baptism of the Holy Spirit. Thousands of believers continue to visit his grave annually.

Mathew Beard, an actor who played the role of Stymie in the *Little Rascals (Our Gang)* comedy series.

ANGELUS ROSEDALE CEMETERY

Angelus Rosedale Cemetery, one of the last cemeteries established in Los Angeles during the end of the nineteenth century, comprises sixty-five acres of land facing Washington Boulevard between Normandie Avenue and Walton and Catalina Streets. The cemetery was incorporated June 9, 1884, by the Rosedale Cemetary Association. The original stockholders included many prominent Los Angelians, like William Vickery and F. C. Howes.

Angelus Rosedale was one of the first cemeteries in the Los Angeles area open to people of all races and the first in Los Angeles to adopt the concept of a "memorial park" where the grounds were landscaped with decorative trees, shrubs, flowers, and works of art. It also housed the second crematory in the United States, built in 1887.

Among the prominent African Americans buried at Angelus Rosedale is **Hattie McDaniels**, known as Hi-Hat Hattie. She was a singer, songwriter, and actress who appeared in more than three hundred films during her career. McDaniels became the first black woman to sing on radio when she made her debut in 1915, singing with Professor George Morrison and his Negro

Orchestra in Denver, Colorado. McDaniels, who was best known for her role as Beulah (1947) on the nationally broadcast radio series of the same name, died in 1952.

PARADISE MEMORIAL PARK

In June 1995 the California State Cemetery Board took control of this once black-owned private cemetery, located in Santa Fe Springs about thirty miles east of Los Angeles, and shortly thereafter closed the cemetery. The takeover followed a scandal that involved the reselling of burial plots—a felony punishable by up to eight years in prison and a $5,000 fine per violation—and the alleged destruction of the remains of many of those interred there.

This small cemetery originally held about 2,700 graves, but it is almost impossible to determine just who lies where now. State officials have found dirt mounds scattered throughout the cemetery laden with disinterred remains, according to cemetery employees; one pile was reportedly seven feet high. According to *American Cemetery* magazine in August 1995, one mourner, Betty Campa, related her story to the *Los Angeles Times* in June 1995. Campa learned that the remains of her grandfather, who was buried in the cemetery in 1933, had been disinterred in 1992 and dumped in a pile. Six bodies were later buried in his grave. "Here I think I'm talking to my grandfather and I'm talking to someone else," she told the *Times*. "They said his bones were in that pile. It's too sacrilegious."

Among those buried at Paradise Cemetery is **Latasha Harlins**, a black teenager who was shot dead by a Korean grocer in Los Angeles in 1992, in an incident that triggered a sharp rise in racial tension between the two ethnic communities.

Ontario, Canada

Canada was viewed by African Americans as a land of hope and freedom for millions of enslaved people in the United States. With the assistance of Quakers and other abolitionist workers—both black and white—many thousands of slaves were able to make their escape from bondage.

What was termed the "Underground Railroad" was a changing system of "way stations" with "leaders" called conductors. In the ten years preceding the Civil War, this network of "freedom roads" led from every slave-holding state in the South to states such as Michigan, Ohio, Indiana, Pennsylvania, and New York. From these states many chose to secure their freedom by traveling into Canada. The Fugitive Slave Laws of 1793 and 1850 marked the beginning of this massive migration. Although slaves escaped into Canada along its entire border, one of the most highly concentrated areas was southwestern Ontario, particularly the Buxton and Elgin settlements.

From 1800 to 1861, it is estimated that approximately forty thousand fugitive slaves left the United States for freedom in Canada. Canada's Slavery Abolition Act of 1833 virtually cleared the way for the safety of the fugitives. As early as 1793, however, Ontario had already taken the first steps toward abolishing slavery and many fugitives had already made their way to freedom by following the North Star.

Some of the early families settling in Canada were the Watts, Shadd, Shreve, Rhue (assisted by Harriet Tubman), Carter, and Hatter families. The Timbers, Smith, and Robbins families were among the thousands of others that settled in places like Amherstburg and Dresden (as in *Uncle Tom's Cabin*) as well as North Buxton.

TOWNSHIP OF SANDWICH EAST CEMETERY

One of the oldest graveyards in the Windsor, Ontario, area lies just outside the city in the Township of Sandwich East, Concession No. 3, west of Banwell Road. Here in a section of Farm Lot 143 lie some of the oldest settlers of Windsor's colored community. There are many graves here; some are sunken and many have been overgrown by weeds. The stonework on many of these markers borders on art. Some that remain standing are those of **Eliza Bush**, born October 6, 1877 and died December 2. 1930; **Louis Smith**, who died December 10, 1922, at age 51; and **James H. Wray**, who was born in 1855 and died in 1931.

Other headstones are marked 1877, 1865, and 1870, but names are illegible. This was definitely a black graveyard, as Clarence Ouelette, the former clerk of Sandwich East, has verified.

NORTH BUXTON CEMETERY

Buxton was a settlement of woods and fields through which passed the "unseen" railroad. North Buxton is a unified community located about an hour's drive from Windsor, a few miles from Chatham, and about a two-hour drive from Toronto, Ontario. It prides itself on its Annual Homecoming and Labor Day Celebration; 1994's celebration marked its seventieth anniversary. James Ricci reminds us in a May 24, 1992, *Detroit Free Press* article that no place helps us link the past to the present like a graveyard: "There's no forgiving slavery; there's no forgetting it either." There are two small graveyards at North Buxton, near Chatham, Ontario. The village was once part of the Elgin Settlement, a community of freed and fugitive American slaves established on the tabletop-flat southwest Ontario landscape in 1849.

North Buxton Cemetery, built in the late 1770s, stands flush with North Buxton's main road. The annual homecoming celebration takes place in the school and church grounds that surround the cemetery and the Raleigh Township Centennial Museum. The lovely cemetery seems more like

A notable Canadian
family, the Shadds, lie
interred at Ontario's
North Buxton Cemetery.

a park; markers indicate the Shadd and Robbins family members. According to James Ricci's article:

> In its graveyards lie bones that are positively radioactive with the base element of the American dilemma. Buried there are men and women who knew racial division as the snap of the lash and the clang of neck irons, not merely the sanitized bigotry of office seekers in modern business suits.

> Stand, for example, at the graves of Dennis Robbins in the North Buxton cemetery. Contemplate his story, the details of which are on file at the nearby Raleigh Township Centennial Museum: originally named Dennis Calico. Given his freedom on condition that he marry his master's slave mistress, who'd borne several of the white man's children, and that he adopt the master's surname, Robbins. Dennis Calico (Robbins) died in 1871 at age 66.

> The wind vibrating the dandelions around his marker might bring the sound of clanking machinery from a farm on the other side of Centre Road. A stocky black man atop a huge John Deere tractor hitched to a discing machine might wave congenially. The name on the farmhouse mailbox is "Robbins." The 200 black Canadians who make up the present day North Buxton populace trace their roots to the Elgin settlers.

LAY DOWN BODY

Next, commune for a bit with Eliza Ann Parker (acquitted in the killing of a slavecatcher in Christiana, Pennsylvania, dead in 1899 at age 82) and Charles Watt (allowed to live free after saving his master's life during the Mexican War; dead in 1903, age 86.)

At the Elgin Settlement, people built and owned their houses, farmed their own land, set up prosperous businesses, forswore alcohol, raised churches, and emphasized religion. The school they established was so advanced, white farmers preferred to send their own children to it, rather than to the local public schools. Before the Civil War and Reconstruction drew many of the settlers back to the United States, the settlement's population peaked at 2000.

North Buxton's annual homecoming celebration takes place in the school and church grounds that surround the cemetery and the Raleigh Township Centennial Museum.

MORRIS-HATTER CEMETERY

About an acre in size, the Morris-Hatter Cemetery lies within a family farm in South Buxton, Ontario, fifty miles east of Windsor. Frances Belfon White cares for the cemetery, along with her sister, Letitia Belfon Bolden, and other family members who jointly own the property.

The cemetery was established in the late 1800s and named, in part, for **George** and **Mary Hatter** and their descendents, many of whom are buried in

Frank Morris, the youngest of James and Barbara Morris's thirteen children, stands in Morris-Hatter Cemetery in the early 1980s, about ten years before he died in Detroit at the age of 101.

the cemetery. George Hatter was nineteen years old when he sought freedom in Canada in 1837. He peddled goods along the roadside in Niagara Falls, Ontario, amassing a modest fortune. In 1844 Hatter married Mary Baker, who was born in Liverpool, England. Six years later, they moved with their five children to South Buxton, Ontario. One of their daughters, Barbara Hatter, married James Louis Morris, who lent his name to the Morris-Hatter Cemetery.

THE NORTH AMERICAN BLACK HISTORICAL MUSEUM AND CULTURAL CENTRE

Many slaves came across the Detroit River into Amherstburg because it was the narrowest point at which to cross. This made Amherstburg one of the Underground Railroad's largest terminals for coming into Canada.

L A Y   D O W N   B O D Y

In the summer many fugitives swam the river with their few belongings tied to their backs. During the winter months, many who saw snow and ice for the first time crossed the frozen river with great difficulty. Most brought with them new energy for developing prosperous farms and businesses, and focused their many skills into meaningful trades, like building churches, schools, and homes.

It was because of his deep concern for the past that Melvin Simpson founded a museum in Amherstburg in 1964. He wanted to uncover and preserve the record of the rich heritage of black people. In 1966 a major effort was undertaken to gather information and to establish appropriate research. The pastor and members of the Nazery A.M.E. Church raised money to build a hall adjacent to the church for the black museum. In 1971 five members of the A.M.E. Church purchased the adjacent property. A log house on the land later became part of the museum complex. The North American Black Historical Museum became incorporated on October 20, 1975. Melvin Simpson died on January 7, 1982.

John and Jane Freeman Walls, after their own harrowing escape from slavery, established the Fugitive Slave Cemetery in 1846.

FUGITIVE SLAVE CEMETERY

Located less than twenty-five miles from Windsor, the Fugitive Slave Cemetery in Puce, Ontario, can be reached from Windsor via the QEW Route

The Fugitive Slave Cemetery, which includes this covered bridge, log cabins, a museum, wooded "escape trails," and a cemetery, is exciting to both children and adults.

401. This fascinating site, which includes log cabins, a museum, wooded "escape trails," and the cemetery, is exciting to both children and adults.

John Freeman Walls and his wife, Jane—the former wife of a declared slaveholder—made their perilous way from Troublesome Creek, North Carolina, through the woodlands of Virginia, Tennessee, Kentucky, Ohio, and Michigan. There were stretches when the only food was raw squirrel. Surviving endless weeks of being tracked by search parties, bounty hunters, and even a pack of wolves that John had to ax to death, their travels ended on the flatlands of Puce, thirteen kilometers east of Windsor, where the Puce River makes it meandering way. The story of their lives, described in *The Road That Led to Somewhere,* by Dr. Bryan E. Walls, epitomizes the contrasting triumphs and tribulations such fugitive slaves experienced.

After some years in Canada, John and Jane purchased land in Puce, Ontario. John, whose father, Hannabal, was from Africa, had never owned land. John told his wife, "I want to leave some land to my heirs and then have a family cemetery on it that is never to be sold. I want as many of your and my descendants as you desire, resting there, in a family cemetery, when Judgment comes."

John lived to be ninety-six; Jane died at age eighty-eight. They were buried in the Walls's cemetery, beside the log cabin he built and which still

L A Y   D O W N   B O D Y

stands on the historic site. The Fugitive Slave Cemetery was built in 1846. Among the family persons buried in the cemetery are **John Freeman Walls** and **Jane Walls**, known by all in the area for her active involvement in numerous organizations, groups, and causes. Also buried here is **Stella May Butler**, born August 16, 1884, and died August 13, 1986, at the age of 102.

GENEALOGY FOR THE BEGINNER

Recently, a prominent Southerner was heard to remark, "If you don't give a whit about the past, how can you plan for the future?" In a way, he was paraphrasing those words written by Edmund Burke almost two hundred years ago: "People will not look forward to posterity who never look backward to their ancestors."

With this thought in mind, Evelyn M. Frazier writes in *A Guide for Amateur Genealogists* that an avid interest in ancestry is not always the "ancestor worship" that some would assume. More people in the United States than ever before are compiling family histories, or genealogies, as they are called by people specializing in this type of work.

Once you begin your own research into your family background, you too enter the field of the genealogist. Just as a writer must compile a multitude of facts about a certain period of time in researching a historical novel, the genealogist must be well-informed on all phases of life relating to the period he or she is researching. In uncovering family histories, you, as researcher, must look beyond mere dates and statistics. A creditable history of your family, if properly and creatively compiled, will be interesting reading as well as a *true* history.

For this process, cemetery records and tombstone markers are a primary source of information; they often yield interesting and reliable information. However, much more must be done before embarking upon a cemetery search. Those tracing the lives of African Americans are encouraged to determine what records—either at home or in repositories such as libraries, state or church archives, or historical societies—may be available for genealogical research in the regions where their ancestors once lived. Information also appears in records a family historian would normally expect: personal family records, like Bibles, letters, diaries, and photographs; census, church, court, military, naturalization, and vital records; passenger-ship lists; newspapers; and numerous other sources, both primary and secondary (like transcriptions or indexes of original records). City directories, social security files, and school and hospital records also act as excellent resources. The pages that follow discuss these and other records, the types of information that they contain, their location, and their strengths and limitations as they apply to African Americans. Also included is a brief survey of the types of charts and record keeping systems used by genealogists in their research, and a few peripheral charts to help you assimilate information for your own history-seeking process.

Charting and Record Keeping

Probably the most important part of any type of research is developing an efficient way to organize information. This is particularly true for genealogical research. Without a system for organizing information in place at the start of the project, as more data is uncovered it becomes increasingly difficult to locate each particular piece. A variety of methods for taking notes and organizing information exist; the key is to find one that works well for you.

Keeping good notes involves several factors. As simple as it may sound, a good researcher should be able to read his or her own handwriting later, when the notes may not be as fresh in the mind as when they were taken. Select the type and size of paper, note cards, or notebooks that will be most convenient for each particular type of note-taking. Notebooks, for example, can contain many notes and are easily accessible, particularly if there is a lot of information to be recorded at one place. Whenever possible, documents and other information should be copied verbatim, exactly as they appear in the original source, except when lengthy legal documents, such as deeds, would be more easily recorded and later understood as a brief summary or abstract.

The source containing the information and the location wherein the information was found should be completely cited. The name of the repository (such as the county courthouse), the source (name or title, volume and page numbers, copyright date), and the results (whether or not information was found, how reliable the data is) should be noted. For example, "Mobile County Courthouse, Mobile, Alabama, Recorder of Deeds office, Deed Book 1, page 10, January 12, 1850," should be included in your notes. You should be as specific as possible when identifying sources, primary or secondary. When citing information from a book, the author's name, title of the book, place of publication, publisher, publication date, and page should be listed. If nothing on the person or topic being researched was located in a specific source, you should still note that the book was examined to avoid examining it again later. Consult a style manual for more details on how to cite sources: Richard S. Lackey's *Cite Your Sources: A Manual for Documenting Family Histories and Genealogical Records* and *The Chicago Manual of Style* are among those available.

You may use a number of different charts to organize your research notes. Basic forms, such as a family group sheet, pedigree or ancestor chart, research log, and correspondence log are important tools that may be purchased from genealogical societies, the Church of Jesus Christ of Latter-day Saints (LDS) Family History Centers, or Everton Publishers in Utah.

You should complete a family group sheet with all the documented evidence on a particular family. The sheet may contain spaces for some or all of the following data: father's name; mother's name (including maiden name); dates and places for births, baptisms, marriages, deaths, and burials; occupations; religion; military service; names of other spouses. Information on children should include date and place of birth, marriage, death, and name of spouse. Each fact on the family sheet should be individually referenced by number to its source in the researcher's file. You, as the compiler, should be identified by name, address, and date. Appended to the group sheet should be a chronological summary of everything found to date on every person in raw note form, not as a narrative summary.

For example, if the husband of the person you're researching has been located in several census records, indicate the birthplace from each record on the group sheet, and use a number to indicate each specific source, such as "The federal census, population schedule, Cole County, Missouri, page 43." On a separate sheet, record the complete citation of the data with notes from the sources. This would include the names, dates, and other data found in the census, for example, on each family member. The complete citation would include the census year, schedule, county, page, dwelling and household numbers, and line numbers.

L A Y   D O W N   B O D Y

Pedigree or ancestor charts contain basic genealogical data: names; dates of birth and marriage for the person being researched; and similar data, along with dates of death, for the research subject's parents, grandparents, great-grandparents, and so on. These charts can provide a quick overview of one's family. Numbering individuals on these should refer researchers to the correct family group sheet and vice versa. For example, if Joe Smith is person 16 on pedigree chart 4, you would find his family group sheet numbered 4–16.

Other useful charts include a research calendar or log and a correspondence record. The former contains spaces for the ancestor's name; date of the research; location and/or call number of the source; description of the source, such as census or will book; time period searched, such as 1850–1900; and comments (names searched, purpose of each search, results, etc.).

A correspondence record may contain your ancestor's name, addressee, address, date sent, purpose of the letter, date replied, and results of the correspondence.

Before You Begin

"Who am I?" is a question most people ask at some point in their life. To find the answer you must be prepared to work hard, digging in dusty archives as an archaeologist might delve into the darkness of a newly discovered tomb. But the starting point is you. Unless you build a firm foundation with the facts surrounding your immediate past, the structure built of the lives of those you are researching will be weak. As you begin to record facts about yourself, plan a course of action that establishes a pattern you can easily follow for receiving and recording new information. A form like the example included at the end of this chapter can help you with this process. Your first form, about yourself, will help you shape the beginning of your research and, ultimately, your family tree if you choose to create one. The forms about your ancestors and other family members, which were adapted from Rosemary A. Chorzempa's *My Family Tree Workbook, Genealogy for Beginners,* can be studied and completed with information that you might already have at hand.

As a next step, approach your closest relative and ask for information on him or her, as well as other persons known to your relative who could be helpful. Make telephone calls, visit relatives, write letters, and practice your interviewing skills, using a tape recorder at times, if appropriate. Remember to remind the person you are interviewing to check Bibles, diaries, and files of old records and papers.

Even before you begin to use the resources outlined in this chapter, you should consider the possibility of using a computer to help with your search. There are numerous publications and computer programs that can aid in recording and structuring data. One in particular is *Family Treemaker* by Banner Blue Software Inc. Even if you choose not to use a computer, you can and will have fun playing detective, delving into nooks and crannies and pursuing all the possible leads that open before you.

However, before elaborating on the variety of primary sources available for investigation, you should be aware of certain caveats, which, if ignored, could extend the time you spend on research unnecessarily. They involve dates, note taking, and letter writing.

DATES

Be certain that you pay *close* attention to all dates you encounter. Upon close examination of dates in statements of fact, inconsistencies are often discovered. Does the date of the child's birth correspond with the age of the mother? Is the date of death recorded that of the actual death, or the date of the funeral or placing of a memorial? Were the months correctly transferred into roman numerals? Of course, these inconsistencies can only be discovered after you have gathered considerable information. But even in the early stages of research, it is easy to reverse numbers—and lengthen someone's life by nine years by transcribing a death date of "1878" as "1887"—or habitually record a Revolutionary War–era birth date as "*1957*" rather than "1757."

NOTE TAKING

There is no set rule on the type of paper to use; some prefer index cards, others notebooks. Whatever your chosen medium, be sure to record: (1) the topic; (2) the source of information (books, etc.), along with inclusive page numbers; (3) the city and institution where you found the source; and (4) the date you took the notes. Set aside separate cards or pages for each ancestor before transferring the information to your charts.

LETTER WRITING

During your research, you will often find it necessary to write letters to people you believe will be a source of needed information. Here are some suggestions:

- Make your request as clear as possible. Let him or her know the record you want, the *complete* name of the person who you are interested in, and the birth and death dates, if you have them.

- Keep your letter as short as possible. If you are asking for birth and death records, spell it out quickly and don't bury your purpose for writing in chatty prose.

- Enclose a self-addressed, stamped, business-size envelope with your request, so the person can respond quickly.

- If it seems appropriate, enclose a small amount of money and offer to pay for any additional expenses encountered.

- Enclose your phone number and ask that the person call collect if he or she has any questions.

- If you have access to a fax machine, include the number to which he or she can fax questions or responses to your request.

- Be sure to extend your thanks at the time; sending an additional thank you after the information is received is sometimes also appropriate.

Now you are ready to explore the primary sources of information.

Sources of Information

Searching for clues to your past begins at home, building basic genealogical skills by reviewing your own family records and interviewing members of your immediate family. To facilitate the search, you should examine family Bibles, letters, diaries, photographs, scrapbooks, legal documents such as deeds or wills, military discharges, tax receipts, birth or death certificates, obituaries, and any other personal or legal documents you can find at home that may contain information about the family. Family Bibles sometimes contain valuable data concerning marriages, births, and deaths—information that may not have been recorded in civil or church records. Personal letters may also contain clues to further research. Photographs, which may be inscribed with the names of those pictured, a date when the picture was taken, or the name and location of the photographer, provide direct glimpses into the past. Even with just the name and location of the photographer—usually obtainable from a city telephone directory—information may be ascertained regarding the approximate date of the picture. Clothes, buildings, or people in the picture might provide clues concerning the date of the photograph. Identifying the type of military dress worn by someone in the picture could help you locate the service records of that individual. A tax receipt might provide a street address, a clue for further research in deed records or city directories. The latter source may list that person's occupation, or other relatives who resided at the same address. Wills and estate settlements may contain the names and addresses of other family members.

Any record that contains information about the family, however minor it might seem, should not be overlooked as a potential clue to the question, "Who am I?" After you have extracted all the possible data from the people and things in your home, and organized all your notes, it is time to take your search to other locations.

A note of caution: Before using any published source, check through any introduction wherein the author may describe limitations to the work, criteria for inclusion, location of the records, or problems, such as legibility, that might undermine the integrity of the original records.

CENSUS RECORDS

There is perhaps no other source used more frequently by genealogists than census records. Beginning in 1790, and in every tenth year since, the federal government has taken a census, a count of the nation's population along geographic, demographic, and numerous other divisions. You should immediately note that federal census schedules less than seventy-two years old are restricted and are not made public. And the amount of information recorded in the census has changed over the years; earlier records are not as detailed as later ones, but they all are important sources for those tracing the ancestry of any ethnicity. Although pre-1850 censuses do not contain the names of every free member of the household in any racial category, they can at least confirm that a family resided at a certain place at a certain time and can reveal the age and sex composition of the household. Census records should be read carefully, as the data contained therein may not be accurate and may conflict with data from other sources.

Federal censuses from 1790 to 1840 contain only the names of the heads of households and are not "every name" censuses. Members of the household—white, nonwhite, slave, and free—were enumerated in age brackets by sex, with the age categories revised through the years. Unlike later censuses, information such as relationships, birthplaces, or other personal data, was not listed. The 1790–1810 censuses listed free nonwhites as "all other [free] persons" and did not specifically mention free people of color. The 1820–1840 record provided a separate listing for free people of color. For example, the Mobile, Alabama, household of Richard Field, a free man of color, contained two people, according to the 1830 U.S. census: a free woman of color between thirty-six and fifty-five years old, and Field, between fifty-five and one hundred years old. The household of John A. Collins in the same city, as outlined in the 1840 census, contained three free males of color, one between thirty-six and fifty-five years old, one between ten and twenty-four, and the third under ten years. It also contained five free women of color, one between thirty-six and fifty-five years old, one between twenty-four and thirty-six, and three under ten. One female slave aged between ten and twenty-four also resided with the Collins family. The household of John McDonald, a white male, contained two male slaves, two female slaves, and a free woman of color.

For all U.S. censuses between 1790 and 1849, it is important to note that the "other free" or "free persons of color" categories do not distinguish between individuals of African ancestry and those of Native American descent. No assumptions about ethnicity can be made from this data without evidence from other records.

A major change occurred with the 1850 census. For the first time, the population schedule listed the names of each free member, white and nonwhite, of the household. In addition, the enumerator was instructed to record each person's age, sex, color (white, black, or mulatto), profession or occupation of males over the age of fifteen, value of real estate owned, place of birth (state, territory, or county), whether married within the year, whether attending school within the year, whether able to read and write (if over twenty years of age), and whether deaf and dumb, blind, insane, idiotic, pauper, or a convict. For example, the same John Collins listed in the 1840 census was identified in 1850 as a fifty-year-old mulatto carpenter who resided with four other mulattos: Isabella, fifty; Virginia, seventeen; Emma, sixteen; and John, fifteen. Each member of the family was born in Alabama.

One additional column of information was added to the 1860 federal census: the value of personal property owned by the family. The household of the same Collins family that appeared in the 1840 and 1850 censuses included the same individuals, but the assessed value of personal property was added. As stated earlier, inaccuracies in censuses are not uncommon, and the entry of John A. Collins provides an excellent example. From the 1850 to the 1860 census, Collins did not age: both censuses listed him as fifty years. His wife aged seven years in that decade, Virginia nine, and John only five years.

The 1860 census is important, as it was the last federal census conducted prior to the Civil War. As such it can provide clues for nonwhites, who have traced their ancestry at least as far back as the 1870 census, as to whether a particular ancestor was a free black or slave prior to or during the war. This information can be uncovered by searching for ancestor surnames in the 1860 census within the same general area where they resided in 1870. One should also consider searching the 1860 census for the white neighbors so listed in 1870. Comparisons can also be made between 1870 census data and sources such as slave schedules, estate records, and bills of slave sales.

Beginning in 1870, population schedules of the federal census began to list the names of all nonwhites. Of particular interest to the researcher would be the place of birth for each person: state, U.S. territory, or foreign country. The additional information recorded for each person basically repeated that

Help with Your Family Tree

Here are nine quick-start ideas for researching your family tree. Keep your mind open to the information you hear and where you hear it. Try to cross-reference material whenever possible. Be creative in your research. You are sure to learn some surprising and interesting facts about your family.

Relatives. Interview relations both close and distant. Ask to see scrapbooks, Bibles, and photo albums. Ask permission for copies of pictures, etc., that you would like to include in your own album.

Public libraries—genealogy and local history departments. Libraries have a variety of reference documents (maps, newspapers, directories, etc.) available, and can often help with other sources to contact for additional assistance. Some even have genealogy sections.

continued on next page

continued from previous page

State bureaus of vital statistics. You can often obtain copies of birth and death certificates for a small fee. You'll find addresses for contacting the proper state bureau at the library.

Church records. Call first and explain what you are doing. Church records are private, but the pastor will often help if you are polite. Church records are often more accurate and informative than government records.

Cemetery records. If the records books have been carefully kept, the cemetery office can provide a wealth of information, especially if the graves do not have markers.

Federal census records. Every decade since 1790, a census has been undertaken, and it can provide much information. Many libraries have census records on microfilm (records up to the early 1900s are open to the public; those dating from the present to seventy-two years previous are closed to protect the privacy of those still living).

continued on next page

contained in the previous census: age, sex, color, occupation, values of personal and real estate, whether parents were of foreign birth, whether born or married within the year, and citizenship status for males twenty-one years of age or older. Following the same Collins family, the 1870 census indicated that John A. Collins was a seventy-one-year-old carpenter, Isabella was a sixty-year-old housewife, and that the household now contained Clara, twenty-one years old, and John, one year old. All were mulattos born in Alabama.

While conducting your research, you should note that none of the federal censuses considered up to this point state any relationship between members of a household. You may hypothesize that Isabella was the wife of John A. Collins; that Clara was their daughter; and that young John was Clara's son; but you must seek evidence supporting the hypothesis elsewhere.

The 1880 census provided even greater detail on family members. It was the first federal census to specifically state the relationship of each person to the head of the household. Also shown are marital status (single, married, widowed, or divorced), whether a person was sick or disabled, and the birthplace for each individual as well as his or her parents.

Thus, if the census recorded the names of a family consisting of a father, mother, their children, and grandparents, it may be possible to trace that family to another area, or perhaps to the previous census in the same state. Tracing the migration of a family would be possible if, for example, the children were born in a different state from their 1880 residence. If the entire family was born in the same state where they resided in 1880, then that state's 1870 census could be checked. For example, John Collins continued to reside in Mobile. He lived with Isabella, whom we now know to be his wife, and John A. Collins Jr., his grandson. Each was a mulatto born in Alabama, and each person's parents were born in Alabama. The identification of the grandson, John, supports the hypothesis drawn from the 1870 census suggesting that Clara of 1870 should be sought as the mother of the child John of 1880. Thus, the 1880 census contains valuable clues that previous censuses do not.

LAY DOWN BODY

Do not overlook the special schedule of so-called dependent, delinquent, and defective classes from the 1880 census. Many nonwhites may be found in them. People from prisons, jails, mental hospitals, or orphanages, for example, were enumerated like others in the 1880 population schedule, but because they were inmates of public institutions they were removed from the family unit and often from the counties—or even states—in which their families lived. The supplemental schedules may contain the person's home residence (city/town, county, and state), as well as other relevant data that varied from class to class. The schedule for homeless children included, for instance, whether the child was orphaned or abandoned and whether he or she was born in the institution where residing at the time of the census. For instance, in Florida the "insane" schedule shows that Leonard Basset, a nonwhite resident of Jacksonville, was afflicted at age twenty-eight, that he was sight and hearing impaired, and that he was a patient of an institution. Dolores Hull, a resident of a colored asylum, appears in the homeless children schedule as a resident of St. Augustine, Florida.

continued from previous page

County courthouses. You can do a search for vital records, such as land and naturalization records, by calling and arranging a visit to the county courthouse.

Historical and genealogical societies. Many localities have groups that collect and preserve information about their area's history. They will often sponsor lectures and workshops, and may have research materials available to help the amateur genealogist.

Church of Jesus Christ of Latter-day Saints (Mormon) library. The Mormon Church is very much involved in genealogy and the preservation of records. Their records are available on microfilm at some libraries, or you can arrange, for the cost of postage, for particular reels to be lent from the church to your branch library. For information, contact the Genealogy Department, Church of Jesus Christ of Latter-day Saints, 50 East North Temple Street, Salt Lake City, UT 84150.

Most of the 1890 federal census was destroyed by a fire in the Commerce Department building in 1921. The National Archives has prepared an index to the surviving schedules, available on two rolls of microfilm (National Archives microcopy No. M496). Partial listings exist for areas in Alabama, the District of Columbia, Georgia, Illinois, Minnesota, New Jersey, New York, North Carolina, Ohio, South Dakota, and Texas.

The 1890 special federal census of Union veterans, as well as widows of Union veterans, of the Civil War was one of two censuses that contained information about military personnel; the other was the 1840 census that listed pensioners for Revolutionary War service. Information provided in the 1890 special return may include the enumeration district, house and family number from schedule one of the same census, name, rank, company, regiment or vessel, dates of enlistment and discharge, length of service, post office address, disability incurred, and other remarks. For example, William Wiggens was a private in Company C of the United States Colored Troops who served from November 1863 to March 26, 1866. His address and length of service are also listed. With this information, the researcher could check

Civil War service and pension records. According to *The Researcher's Guide to American Genealogy* by Val D. Greenwood, the 1890 special censuses from "those fourteen states and territories alphabetically from 'A' through 'Kansas' and into part of `Kentucky' have been lost."

Several changes occurred with the 1900 census. The following items were included: dates of birth (year and month); number of years married; for mothers, the number of children born and number living; for immigrants, the year of arrival in the United States, number of years in the United States, and whether naturalized; whether one's house was owned or rented; and whether the house was mortgaged. The census form also contained other information. Some of this new information can be especially useful to the researcher since it may provide the only existing record of the number of children born to a slave mother, and whether those children were still living when the census was taken.

Data in the 1910 census are similar to that of 1900. For example, location; relationship to the head of the family; personal description (sex, color, age, marital status, and, if a mother, number of children, and number yet living); place of birth; place of birth of parents; year of immigration; whether naturalized; occupation; literacy; whether home was owned or rented and, if owned, whether mortgaged; whether a survivor of Union or Confederate army or navy; and other data. Unlike the previous census, the 1910 census did not provide the month and year of birth.

The 1920 census contains much of the same data as the 1910 census. Information on the 1920 form included address; name; relationship to head of household; whether home was owned or rented; personal description (sex, color or race, age); marital status; year of immigration; whether naturalized; year of naturalization; literacy; place of birth for both resident and parents; occupation; and other data.

Censuses for 1900–1920 are valuable to the researcher as one of the first sources of information usually checked outside the home. They are useful in verifying information gathered from family documents found in the home, other written documents, and oral histories. If the researcher has located family members in the 1920 enumeration, for example, a possible next step would be to trace the family backward through the censuses and other appropriate records.

In addition to the federal census, additional governmental agencies have required their own censuses. These include special enumerations taken by the federal government—such as the military censuses discussed above—and those taken by territories, states, counties, and cities. For example, some Missouri state censuses, which are incomplete, are available at the Missouri State Archives. Selected city and county of St. Louis censuses were taken in the antebellum period and are available at the Missouri Historical Society in St. Louis. Thus, thorough researchers should inquire about the availability of

non-federal censuses and how they may be obtained in the area in which he or she is conducting research.

African Americans trying to trace their enslaved ancestors need to first identify the slave-owner family. Freed slaves did not always take the name of former owners. According to *Ancestry's Guide to Research: Case Studies in American Genealogy:*

> Some slaves took surnames before the Civil War ended, while others waited until they began establishing themselves as free citizens. Many slaves took the surname of their last owner or their father who might have been a white slave owner or overseer, a deceased slave, or a slave sold to another owner several years prior to the Emancipation. Hundreds of slave families took the name of a prominent American, a local political figure, or the given name of the father of the family. It wasn't uncommon for freed slaves to be known by several surnames, making a final choice years after the Emancipation.

Slave schedules are a valuable source for the African American researcher attempting to bridge the gap between slavery and freedom. Compiled in 1850 and 1860, they typically contain the name of the owner and list the age, sex, and color of each slave, though not the name (although some exceptions exist). As noted in the article "To My Daughter and the Heirs of Her Body," by Curtis G. Brasfield, from the *National Genealogical Society Quarterly,* "When researchers identify a potential master through other sources, they can compare the age, sex, and color of each tallied slave against the data given for freedmen on later censuses; this process may strengthen or eliminate the possibility of a connection." While by itself this source of information can be inconclusive, by comparing such data with the information in deed books containing bills of sale, owner's records, etc., connections may be strengthened. Some free people of color owned slaves, and sources providing information on these people should not be overlooked by researchers looking for African Americans who were freed before 1865. Although not a typical slave owner for either race, a South Carolina free man of color in 1860 owned sixty-three slaves. In Alabama, a free nonwhite owned six slaves aged between one and twenty-eight years.

What if your pre–Civil War ancestors were enslaved and cannot be located easily by assuming that they took their former owners' surname? It may be necessary to check records on possible white families in the neighborhood where the black family was known to reside after Emancipation. This would entail examining antebellum documents, such as wills and bills of sale, and comparing data found in those records with the information contained in pre-war sources. Thus, when examining census records, you should attempt to identify slave owners' neighbors, whose records may provide sought-after answers to your questions.

In addition to the population and slave schedules, agricultural schedules of the federal census, 1850–1880, are available. These schedules provide data on farm size and value, number and type of livestock, livestock value, amount of crops produced, and other information. Though agricultural producers were not identified by race, and owning land was not a requisite to be listed, these schedules can provide more detail on ancestors already discovered elsewhere. In 1860, for example, Zeno Chastang Sr., one of the more prosperous free Negro farm owners in Mobile County, Alabama, owned eighty improved acres, 1,230 unimproved acres, and produced, among other items, twelve hundred bushels of corn. The value of his farm was $3,900.

Mortality schedules of the federal census are another valuable source for genealogists. These records cover the years 1850–1880 and contain the names of persons who died in the twelve months preceding the date of the census. Obviously, there are limitations to these schedules. For instance, they listed deaths for only every tenth year, and they were not complete. According to researchers, "It is estimated that in the mortality schedules for 1850, 1860, and 1870 only 60 percent of the actual deaths within those twelve-month periods were reported—that means that less than 8 percent of the actual deaths for this thirty-one year period are in the mortality schedules."

The 1850 and 1860 forms contained the same data for each person: name; age; sex; color; whether slave or free; marital status; place of birth; month of death; occupation; disease or cause of death; and number of days ill. Data in the 1870 schedule include the number of the family as given in the second column of schedule one (population); name; age; sex; color; whether parents of foreign birth; month of death; occupation; and cause of death. Data in the 1880 schedule include the number of the family as given in column two of schedule one (population); name; age; sex; color; marital status; place of birth; place of birth of the person's parents; occupation; month of death; disease or cause of death; length of residence in the county; and other data.

Several examples illustrate the value of this source. In March 1850 Tom Smith, a fifty-five-year-old free black born in Virginia, died in Dallas County, Alabama, of rheumatism. Harriet Smith, a forty-four-year-old free mulatto born in Georgia, died in the same county in June of unknown causes. In St. Louis, Joseph Dooley, a free black laborer born in Africa, died in June 1849 from cholera. In Howard County, Missouri, several slaves born in Kentucky were listed consecutively; each died in the same month from the same disease—cholera. Information in this source may not have been recorded in other records, especially for slaves. Obviously, for the researcher especially interested in tracing family medical history, these records have a special significance.

An example from the 1880 schedule provides greater clues. For example, if one checks the St. Louis schedule for the surname Washington, several entries are discovered in enumeration district 145. Betty and George L. Washington, two black children born in Missouri, whose father was born in Virginia and mother in Missouri, died in the same month and from the same

LAY DOWN BODY

disease. By examining the population schedule with the same enumeration district and knowing the family number from the mortality schedule, the researcher can locate the children's family. George L. Washington, his wife Hester, and their daughter Mollie are enumerated and information on them can now be extracted, such as the birthplaces of both the elder George and his wife.

You can obtain census records in several ways. Microfilm copies of agricultural, mortality, population, and slave schedules are available at many public, university, and genealogical libraries, as well as historical societies. If a local library does not have the needed census records, the interlibrary loan department may be able to order them from another library or rental program. For a nominal charge, you may also order films through the LDS Family History Library system. In addition, you can rent various microfilms, including census records, from the National Archives Microfilm Rental Program or the American Genealogical Lending Library. For a fee, these organizations lend microfilms and send them directly to individual researchers.

Printed indexes are generally available for pre-1880 censuses, as well as some indexes to the 1890 special federal census of Union veterans and widows of Union veterans. Information in most of these indexes is divided by state and listed alphabetically by surname. A special index, called the Soundex, is available for the 1880, 1900, and 1920 censuses. The key to the Soundex system lies in its name: According to researchers, census records "were alphabetically coded and filed by state under a system where all names sounding alike, regardless of spelling differences or errors (if they began with the same letter of the alphabet), would be interfiled."

The Soundex is comprised of index cards listing volume, enumeration district, sheet or page number, and line number, that direct the researcher to specific census records. Soundex cards also contain the name of the head of the household; that person's color, sex, age, birthplace, city and county of residence; and the names of all members of the household, their relationship to the head of household, ages, and birthplaces. The index to the 1910 census, called the Miracode, is similar to the Soundex but has indexed only twenty-one states.

Both the Soundex and Miracode indexes use complex coding systems, and both are limited in their ability to provide complete information. If you cannot locate a family, check variant spellings of the surname. Use your imagination with regard to the way an enumerator recorded a name; it was recorded as the enumerator heard it, and regional dialects of the period may have affected how the recorder spelled the name.

In the antebellum period, if a white man was the head of a free Negro family, his children may have been listed in censuses (and other records) under the name of either their white father or nonwhite mother. For example, in the 1840 population schedule for the city of Mobile, Mobile County,

Alabama, the household of Polite Collins, a free woman of color, included several other free Negroes and an adult white male. Ten years later, Collins resided with several nonwhites and four children assumed to be white because their race was left blank. All children went by the surname Collins. However, in 1860 Polite Collins resided with Roswell Swan, a white man, and several of their children who were identified as mulattos and who went by the surname Swan. (In other records, Swan acknowledged that he had children by this free woman of color.)

According to researcher Gary B. Mills, in addition to the problem of identifying offspring of an interracial union, "any assumption of ethnicity on the basis of census data from a single year (or any other single document) may err. Determining the ethnic identity of any family labeled *free people of color* (or *f.p.c.*) on any record invariably requires exhaustive research in the widest-possible variety of resources." For example, a twentieth-century white governor of Alabama, Braxton Bragg Comer, "appears as a child on the 1860 Federal Census, Population Schedule, of Barbour County, whereupon he and his entire family . . . were clearly identified as *black*," Mills notes. Lawrence Brue appears as white in the 1860 federal census, but in previous censuses and in other records he appears as a free person of color. In 1860, in census records for Natchitoches Parish, Louisiana, the ethnicity of seventy-six of the 1,614 families was misidentified.

Although such inaccuracies in census records are frustrating to novice genealogists, some enumerators recorded more specific data than their instructions required. They sometimes included detailed information concerning places of birth, marriage, or other subjects for both whites and nonwhites. For example, an apparently free black couple residing in Arkansas informed an enumerator of their exact year of marriage. A free woman of color in the 1860 census for St. Louis, Missouri, ward 2, page 802, indicated that she had been "freed by Benjamin Soulard," and that she was "married to slave John Harris." In addition, the name of John's owner and the couple's birthplace, St. Louis, were listed. A free woman of color, born in New Orleans, was "on visit" in St. Louis in the same area. In another instance, a female slave was listed last in the household of a white man who had hired her. Not only was her given name recorded but also the complete name of her owner. The value of such information cannot be overlooked as such "errors" provide clues for additional research.

Viewed as a whole, census records contain a variety of detailed information. Generally, each successive census includes more detailed information than its predecessor. As a researcher, you should follow an individual through the complete schedules of all censuses, from birth to death, and extract additional information about the area wherein that person resided. Although censuses contain errors, they are particularly valuable genealogical sources that you can rely on with a reasonable amount of caution.

L A Y   D O W N   B O D Y

CHURCH RECORDS

Religion has traditionally played an important role in the lives of African Americans, and the activities of various denominations are documented in both sacramental registers and business minutes. Most major denominations accepted both free nonwhites and slaves. In the antebellum era, for example, Roman Catholic and Protestant churches contained both white and nonwhite members. Many predominantly black churches were also in operation, each with their own set of records. Whenever separate registers for the races were kept, researchers are urged to check both, as some nonwhites appear in the "white" registers.

Sacramental registers provide a wealth of information, including baptisms (which may list birth data), marriages, and burials (which may list death data). Information from these registers may not be available in any other source, especially in the periods before the 1850 census and before the recording of such vital records became mandatory. Registers may also contain the dates of birth and death for a child who lived between census years. You should note that some owners freed their bondsmen or slaves at baptismal ceremonies. As was the case for free people, the names of slaves, approximate ages (sometimes exact dates), and often the mother's name were recorded.

Baptismal records also may contain a variety of other information: names of parents (when known), dates when parents (white or black) acknowledged paternity (if unacknowledged at birth), dates of birth and baptism, names of sponsors (who were often related to the individual being baptized), and, in the case of slaves, the name of the owner. For instance, baptisms of the children (and slaves) of a free nonwhite couple appear in the "colored" register ("Baptisma Nigrorum, 1806–1828") of the Parish of the Immaculate Conception located in the Mobile Church Archives, the Catholic

Maps Can Help Unearth Clues

Early maps often indicated locations of families, as well as geographic locations. You can find such maps, including the *Mill's Atlas* and *Ruddock's Map*, in most county libraries, as well as in state archives. However, just because a person's name is indicated, this does not necessarily mean that person was living at the date of publication, since the material may have been compiled some years previously.

In Fairfax, Virginia, a staff librarian named Brian A. Conley has spent years tracking down long-forgotten cemeteries, from well-known church sites to abandoned family burial grounds. Once tipped off about a possible location (he works with historians, residents, and archaeologists), he plots the approximate location on aerial and topographic maps, and then travels to that location to start his search. He has thus far recorded over three hundred cemeteries.

Conley's tips include looking for tall, mature trees, knowing that trees near grave sites were usually left standing even when the surrounding land was cleared; and looking for flowers that don't grow naturally in the area but were planted over graves. He uses a three-and-a-half-foot steel pole with a T-shaped top to feel down into the earth. Even centuries after a burial, the earth remains loosely packed. The pole slides effortlessly into the ground when it hits the right spot.

Conley documents the locations he has found and marks them on county zoning and tax maps, hoping they will be safe from future destruction. He says, "These cemeteries are a part of cultural heritage. Nobody can divorce themselves from their own past."

Center, Mobile, Alabama (entries 251, 352). The researcher should note all information, even if it appears irrelevant at the time.

Marriage records may contain the names of the bride and groom, date of marriage, witnesses, place of origin, ages, and names of slave owners. In some instances, priests or ministers may have recorded other information pertinent to the marriage, including the fact that a couple had applied for a civil license or even that a man had previously changed his name. In Alabama, the marriage of Zeno Chastang and Maria Teresa Bernoudy, both free people of color, appeared on page 108 in the "white" register of the Parish of the Immaculate Conception, "Marriage Records Book 1, 1726–1832." John Baker married Marie Denise (of French-African descent) on October 25, 1820, at Natchitoches, Louisiana. The Spanish priest identified the groom as aged thirty-two, a native of Broneston, Virginia, and the son of John Baker, a man of color, and Nancy, a white woman. The bride was fourteen and a half years old, and the daughter of Marianne Baden, a free Negro, according to Elizabeth Shown Mills, in *Natchitoches Church Marriages, 1818–1850: Translated Abstracts from the Registers of St. Francois des Natchitoches, Louisiana.* When slaves Charles and Marie were married at the Cathedral of St. Louis, Missouri, the priest also recorded the names of their owners in the "Register of Marriages, 1840–1849." This register is now held in the Basilica of St. Louis, the King, the Old Cathedral, St. Louis.

In the absence of civil death records, church burial records are especially important. Data in Catholic registers may include dates of death and burial, place of origin, age, and names of the deceased's parents. Again, all information in a source should be skimmed. In one case, when a priest recorded several slave burials, he only identified the owner, a free man of color, by his given name ("Burials for Coloured People," Parish of the Immaculate Conception, Mobile Church Archives). A different priest, however, recorded the same man's complete name. In the same volume, John Martin, a free man of color, native of Virginia and approximately twenty-seven years old, received the benefit of a Catholic burial, as did a nonwhite woman who was a native of St. Domingo (entries 2, 19). On November 18, 1805, in New Orleans, Carlos Brule, son of Carlos Brule, "captain of the mulatto militia of this city," according to Earl C. Woods in volume 8 of the *Archdiocese of New Orleans Sacramental Records,* and Maria Constanza Gaillard, age six, were buried.

Protestant church records in the form of either minutes or registers also contain valuable information. Some Episcopal registers (baptismal, marriage, burial, and confirmation) contain data concerning African Americans similar to that found in Catholic records, including origins or former residences. Ministers did not always identify free nonwhites as such; they may appear as colored, and not necessarily as free colored or free persons of color.

Several examples illustrate this type of data. A minister of the Church of the Good Shepherd in Mobile, Alabama, recorded the baptism of William A. Saxon, "free" son of Armstead and Mary Saxon, in the Parish Register bap-

LAY DOWN BODY

tisms dated July 15, 1855 (volume 2). The Second Presbyterian Church, Mobile, received John Burton and wife Mary Ann, free people of color, as members, according to the "Session Book," Volume 1, 1842–1855. They previously had been members of the Presbyterian church in Demopolis, Alabama. This same book, located at the Central Presbyterian Church Archives in Mobile, also states that "Francis Godfrey a coloured (sic) servant, having been examined as to her experimental knowledge of religion, was unanimously received to the communion and fellowship of this church." In 1835, the First Baptist Church of Christ (with records located at the First Baptist Church Archives in Mobile) "received into the fellowship as a member of the church coloured brother William Jones belonging to J. G. S. Walker, upon a letter of dismission from the Baptist Church in Augusta, Georgia" ("Minutes, 1835–1848"). On October 5, 1845, in the Second Baptist Church "Minutes" (1845–1875) located in the same archives, it is stated that, "at the waters edge a free woman of colour Sally Chamberlain, presented herself for membership when upon her Christian experience she was received for baptism." On May 16, 1847, the same church licensed four nonwhites (Charles Leavens, Tom Knight, Guiford Ward, and Cupid Redwood) to preach in its African branch. "Being of good character, orderly and consistent in their conduct," they were "licensed to preach or exhort according and in conformity with the laws of Alabama."

Church records may be located in many different places. You should first determine if the church or parish is still in operation: if so, a phone call or letter may be a first step toward the examination of the records. If the church has been closed, a church or archdiocesan archive may house the records. Sometimes, however, other churches may acquire the records of a closed church. Libraries, historical societies, and state archives hold church records, either originals or microfilm copies. The Family History Library in Salt Lake City has microfilmed many church records, which may be borrowed through Family History Centers around the country. Other records have been published, although those researchers finding information in published (secondary) sources are urged to examine the original records.

In addition to possible difficulties in locating a specific church's records, you may encounter other obstacles when using these sources. Not all identify nonwhites as such, especially records kept during the antebellum period. All records are not accessible to the public; each parish or church has its own guidelines concerning the use of its holdings. Records may have been kept in a language other than English. Not all records have been indexed. Finally, unlike public facilities that house government records and are open during regular hours, church archives may be open for limited periods of time.

COURT RECORDS

Many types of court and legislative records may be used to trace the lives of African Americans, including civil and criminal records, probate documents, deed or general record books, and acts of state legislatures. Different courts operate throughout the United States on both federal and state levels, including circuit, chancery, probate, city, land, (state) supreme, county, and mayor's, and each generates its own records. To begin studying these records, first examine city directories (usually available in local libraries) to ascertain which courts operate in a particular area. Court records may consist of loose paper files or record, minute, and docket books; examine all the different types. Some items of interest that might otherwise be missed may be located by reading the books page by page, often necessary if indexes are not available. As with other records, nonwhites may not have been identified as such.

Court records are usually located in county courthouses. However, some may be found in other repositories, such as city, state, or university archives or historical societies. Many have been microfilmed.

Throughout history, African Americans' legal rights varied considerably. "Free Negroes in the South (like most of their Northern counterparts) did not enjoy all rights of citizenship; the court systems represented one area in which these abridgments are most noticeable," states Gary B. Mills, author of *The Forgotten People.* For example, most free nonwhites in the North and South were not allowed to testify in court against whites. "They were, in fact, prohibited from even instituting a suit against a white in most states before the Civil War," Mills states. There were, of course, exceptions to this. Free people of color were involved in a variety of lawsuits against whites and others of their class, and a variety of illegal acts were ascribed to African Americans. Nonwhites were able to purchase and sell real and personal property. Also, divorce proceedings involving African Americans may be found among civil records.

Several examples illustrate the value of these records. In 1850, Peter Bolling appeared in a Mobile County, Alabama, circuit court and indicated that, in 1837, he had been a slave of Thomas Batte, a resident of Dayton, Marengo County, Alabama (University of South Alabama Archives, Mobile). In 1830, George Mulhollen, a free man of color, brought suit in Adams County, Mississippi, alleging that he had been born free in Easton, Pennsylvania, in 1798 or 1799, and that he was being illegally held in slavery by a white named Robert McCullough. The defendant demanded that Mulhollen present proof of his freedom. Despite the fact that Mulhollen could only offer his testimony, a jury of twelve whites granted him his freedom (Record of Judgment, May 1830–May 1831). In another case, Sarah, a free woman of color, indicated that she had been claimed as a slave by Louisa Higgins of Mobile County. Sarah stated that she was approximately twenty-one years old, was born in Montgomery County, Alabama, that she had been held by Higgins but that she was not claimed by her as a slave until 1853, that her mother was also a free-born woman, and that she had a child. A witness for Sarah indicated that he knew Sarah's mother, Delphi, when they were in Upson County, Georgia, about 1829 or 1830, that a Negro slave named John was Delphi's husband, and that "in the neighborhood where she lived in

Georgia, it was generally reputed and believed that she (Delphi) was the daughter of a white woman, by a black man. I have heard the same report in the neighborhood where she lived in this state." This information was culled from the "Final Record Book, 1852–1856," of the Mobile County, Alabama, Circuit Court (University of South Alabama Archives) and the "Loose Paper File Collection," Mobile County (same archives, Circuit Court Case 27493). Finally, according to records at the University of South Alabama Archives, the court ordered a free man of color to contribute to the "support and education of the bastard child" of a free woman of color since he was "the reputed father" ("Circuit Court Minutes, 1856–1858," Mobile County, Alabama).

Abstracts of files from superior court records that deal with slaves and free people of color have been published by Helen T. Catterall. But, as in other records, in court cases not all free people of color are identified as such. After you have located a case, you should also read the published state court records, available at law libraries, which contain greater details. In fact, you must check the state records to determine the county from which the case was appealed. Catterall lists the name of the case, the source (published state court records), the date, and an abstract of the case. For example, in *Stikes, Administrator* v. *Swanson*, 44 Ala. 633, June 1870, 44 represents the volume number, and 633 the page on which the case appears in *Reports of Cases Argued and Determined in the Supreme Court of Alabama, During the January and June Terms, 1870*. Legal librarians can help you find the volumes wherein the citation exists. Note that only appellate cases are recorded in casebooks.

These court records may contain genealogical data. In one Louisiana case, several nonwhites sued for their freedom. The names of a slave mother and her master, her two children, and several grandchildren are provided. Case records reveal that Cassius Swanson was formerly a slave in Florida where he was emancipated, and that he later moved to Mobile and had at least three sons by two slave mothers; his date of death is also recorded. Antebellum cases may contain data about the post-war lives of nonwhites. In *Donovan* v. *Pitcher et al.*, 53 Ala. 411, Dec. 1875, for example, William Pitcher was a man of color "who had been a slave, permitted by his master to go at large, retain and dispose of his earnings, to acquire property, make contracts, and in all respects to conduct himself as a free man." During the 1850s, Pitcher left Alabama on two different occasions and went to Ohio, where he eventually died. His wife, born a slave in North Carolina and the daughter of a free man of color who purchased her and brought her to Alabama, also went to Ohio to live with her husband.

Criminal Records

Don't overlook criminal records as a source for genealogical information. Some dockets may contain names, offenses, judgments, and other useful data. In Daviess County, Indiana, Charles Brown was arrested for grand larceny (for allegedly stealing a coat worth $7.00), convicted, fined $10.00, and sentenced to three years in the state prison, after which he would be disenfranchised for five years. Before the Civil War, one free woman of color was arrested for failure to post bond. The record provided data on her background: "It appears from the evidence in the case that the defendant is descended from a white woman, [and] she is discharged not being subject to the free Negro laws" (Daviess County, Indiana, "Circuit Court Book D"; City of Mobile, Alabama, City of Mobile Municipal Archives, "Guard House Docket, 1862–1863").

Other criminal records, such as those of the mayor's court, list names of the defendants and the alleged crimes (such as assault or disorderly conduct). Interesting information available in such records includes facts regarding a jury finding a nonwhite guilty of grand larceny and ordering him to be sent to the state penitentiary. Newspapers also contain information concerning criminal and civil cases.

Probate Court Records

Records of the probate court are among the most important to the beginning genealogist. They include wills, court minutes, administrator account books, loose paper files that may contain all transactions of an estate record, guardianships, and other miscellaneous books of the court. Indexes to individual books, estates, or perhaps a general index covering all records of the court are usually available. One such computerized index (Mobile County, Alabama) contains all references to a person's estate as recorded in the various court documents. Thus, instead of having to check the indexes to each court book, you would only have to check one index. Most county courts, however, do not have one general index, so you may have to examine several relevant indexes.

Wills contain a wealth of information; often they mention relationships. In 1805, for instance, Abraham Jones, a farmer in Anson County, North Carolina, manumitted (released from slavery) his wife Lydia and their seven children whom he named in his will. He also carefully detailed how his estate was to be divided (North Carolina State Archives). In another instance, Romeo Andry indicated that he was the "son of the late Simon Andry by a free woman of color named Jane or Jeanne" (Mobile County Courthouse, Alabama, "Will Book 3"). In a will filed in 1866 another nonwhite indicated that he had purchased land from his brother, and that he owned land jointly with his sister. He also named his father and son-in-law, and left property to his children. The names of each relative were provided. In St. Louis, a free woman of color not only identified her grandson but also mentioned his age. Although she indicated that she had purchased him, she did not state his owner. However, a witness to the signing of the will had the same surname as the woman's grandson, suggesting some connection between the two.

Wills can also document previous relationships and former residences. In 1857 one free man of color made several bequests. In addition to identifying his wife by her maiden name, he made special bequests to his sons born from a previous union. The mother of those children was also named. Similarly Regis Bernoudy, "a free man of color of the city of Mobile" (Mobile

LAY DOWN BODY

County Courthouse, Alabama, "Will Book 1"), left property to his three daughters, children of a free woman of color who predeceased him. He also left lots in Mobile and Pensacola. A free woman of color indicated the name of her father and his previous residence in a nearby county where she owned land. Cyrus Evans, a free man of color, acknowledged that his son was "born in the bonds of slavery and purchased by me for a fair consideration from Oregin Sibley of Baldwin County" (Mobile County Courthouse, Alabama, "Will Book 2"). Finally, in St. Louis, Elmira Hawken stated that she was the former slave of Mrs. Victoire Labadie. Hawken also identified her two children, who had a different surname. She also mentioned a man who previously had conveyed to her several lots in the city of St. Louis; his surname was the same as that of her children (St. Louis County, Missouri, Probate Court, "Will Book E," Civil Courts Building).

African Americans tracing their enslaved ancestors are urged to check probate records of both whites and nonwhites. If former slaves did not take the name of a former master, researchers are encouraged to check the records of whites (or other nonwhites) who resided in the same neighborhood as their ancestors in 1870.

Wills also may contain the names and ages of slaves. Among the slaves Zeno Chastang bequeathed to his wife were Margaret and her two children Tom and Frank (Mobile County Courthouse, Alabama, "Will Book 3"). Probate minute books also contain the names and ages of slaves and the names of those who inherited them.

Probate and deed records may also contain references to slave sales, manumissions, and free papers which may list previous residences or other relatives. (Free people of color often carried proof that they were free, and these documents were recorded in the courts. Newspapers sometimes published these lists.) George Rootes of the town of Fairfax, Culpeper County, Virginia, freed his "wife Sarah and her three children, Ellen, Sarah Ann, and James . . . all of whom I have lately purchased for the purpose of carrying with me to the state of Ohio whither I am about to move" ("Deed Book 20," 1830). A public notary residing in the city of New York certified that a black twenty-one-year-old seaman was a free person. The papers showed that he was born in Scoduc, Rensselaer County, New York.

Deed Books

Deed, conveyance, or general record books usually contain the buying and selling of real property between two or more people, and not between individuals and the government. Indexes, direct and indirect or grantor and grantee, are normally available; the amount of information they contain varies from county to county. For example, one commonly encountered printed index contains the name of the grantor, grantee, type of instrument (such as deed or power of attorney), date recorded, book name and number, page number, and description of the property. Nonwhites were not identified as such in the index. Thus, if whites and nonwhites with the same names purchased real property, data from other sources such as tax records may be needed to determine if a particular deed is relevant to the researcher. An index published by Oscar W. Collet, 1804–1854, for St. Louis County, Missouri, lists the grantor, grantee, book and page numbers, and some genealogical information. Researchers are urged to copy all information from such indexes and then seek out the original documents for additional detail.

The types of data in deed books varies considerably. In addition to references to real property sales, including slave sales, deed books may contain information on free papers, manumissions, deeds of gift or partition (and possibly a list of heirs), or leases. They may also contain records of slaves who purchased their own freedom. Even the most mundane books can provide information on prior residences, family cemeteries, or occupations.

Among the most common types of instruments recorded in these deed books were land sales. Nonwhites sold and purchased land from whites and other nonwhites. Deeds may contain names of the buyer and seller, date of the transaction, description or location of the property, references to previous sales of the same property, or some genealogical data such as the names of a spouse or children. For example, Magdalene, a free woman of color and widow of Etienne Fuselier, sold to her son Pierre S. Fuselier land in St. Landry Parish, Louisiana (St. Landry Parish Courthouse, Opelousas, Louisiana, "Conveyance Book E," April 15, 1820). In Greenville County, South Carolina, Samuel Taylor, a free Negro who had been emancipated by Arthur Taylor in 1806, bought 131 acres in 1812 and ninety acres in 1813. Five years later he sold two acres to the Baptist Society of Columbia, South Carolina ("Deed Book I"; "Deed Book K"). In 1852 William Dugger purchased a lot in the city of Mobile, Mobile County, Alabama, on the north side of St. Louis Street between Lawrence and Cedar Streets. The deed did not indicate that he was a free man of color, but tax and census records did ("Deed Book 4," new series; City of Mobile, Alabama, "Tax Book, 1856," ward 7, City of Mobile Municipal Archives; "1850 Population Schedule").

Slave sales and manumissions may also be found in deed books. Slave bills of sale cite the name of buyer and seller, counties of residence, date of sale, and the market value of the slave. Often the name, age, gender, and color of the slave is also listed. According to "Conveyance Book F-1," in St. Landry Parish, Louisiana, a free woman of color sold a male slave named Nicholas, aged about thirty-six years, to her daughter. A court approved Robert Taylor's request to manumit his slave Milly, a mulatto who was about forty-five years old, "for and in consideration of the long and faithful conduct and services." Jack, a free Negro and previously the slave of Charles Comeau, freed Letty who "lived with him many years as a wife" (St. Landry Parish, "Conveyance Book A").

Other valuable genealogical information may be contained in deed records. In 1854 for example, a nonwhite mentioned that part of his land contained a family cemetery. He also indicated that his father, who was not

LAY DOWN BODY

identified as such, was buried in said cemetery. In another deed record, the possible origin of a free woman of color was documented when a record indicated that, when a resident of Pensacola, Florida, she had purchased land in Alabama.

State Legislative Acts and Petitions

Two other important record groups are state legislative acts and petitions. Most state legislatures in the South ruled upon manumission attempts made by white or free Negro slave owners. Researchers should check house and senate journals for "unsuccessful attempts at manumission," according to Gary B. Mills in *Tracing Free People of Color*. The researcher may have to search these records page by page. In 1827 the Alabama legislature approved an act to emancipate Cyrus, slave of the free woman of color, China Evans, of Baldwin County (Acts Passed at the Ninth Annual Session of the General Assembly of the State of Alabama 1828). In 1836 the North Carolina legislature emancipated "Henry Howard, Fanny Howard and John Howard, children and slaves of Miles Howard, of Halifax County (Laws of the State of North Carolina, 1837)." Although some legislative acts required the freed person to leave the state, many continued to reside there in contravention of the law.

Thus, a variety of court records contain valuable genealogical information. Civil, criminal, probate, and deed records, as well as legislative acts and petitions, document the activities of nonwhites (and whites). African Americans seeking information concerning manumissions, land and slave sales, estate records, free papers, divorces, and patterns of migration are urged to examine these records. Although they have limitations—including the fact that many do not identify ethnicity—the records may serve as valuable primary or secondary sources, enabling researchers to flesh out the facts already obtained from other sources or provide clues as to how the investigation into the lives of their ancestors should proceed.

VITAL RECORDS

In a genealogical context, vital records refer to records of births, marriages, and deaths. Kept even prior to statewide requirements for the filing of such records, local and family records such as church registers and Bibles help fill the void for researchers. Not until the early twentieth century were national requirements passed for the filing of such records. Some cities and states, particularly in the South and in New England, did maintain them prior to 1900, but not all were complete. Laws for maintaining vital records varied. And, for slaves, the laws were more loosely applied, according to one author. For instance, slave marriages were seldom registered or legally recognized.

Vital records are maintained by city, county, or state government offices, such as health departments for birth and death certificates, and county courthouses or city halls for marriage records. Usually for a fee, clerks will check their files for a particular record over a specific time period, such as a five-year span. Some indexes and records have been published and may be available in public or genealogical libraries; many have been microfilmed and may be obtained from LDS Family History Centers. While some newspapers also listed births, marriages, and deaths, these records remain selective at best.

Birth Records

The content and availability of birth records vary, depending upon the time period. For example:

Virginia began to register births and deaths in 1853. Birth records contain the gender but not the names of the baby or the parents. The slave owner's name, however, was listed. For slave records, the name of the plantation may be listed as well as the area in which the child was born. These county registries have been microfilmed and are available at the LDS Family History Library.

Records from Fayette County, Pennsylvania, include a register of Negro births from 1788 to 1826. It shows the slave owner's name, birth dates, and names of the child and parents.

An act of the New York legislature providing for the gradual abolition of slavery stipulated that any child born of a slave after July 4, 1799, should be "deemed and adjudged to be born free," according to researcher Marcia J. Eisenberg in "Birth Registrations of Children of Slaves" in the *Journal of the Afro-American Historical and Genealogical Society*. Records from the town of Bath, Steuben County, New York (located in the New York State Archives in Albany), indicate that the elder Presley Thornton's slave Lucinda gave birth to Mima, born March 15, 1806.

New Jersey has birth records, which sometimes designate race, dating from June 1848 to 1878.

In Missouri records created mainly during the 1880s and early 1890s may contain the name of the child and parents, race, date and place of birth, nationality, occupation of father, maiden name of mother, and ages and residence of parents. A standard certificate may contain the date and place of birth (county, city, name of hospital); child's name; mother's place of residence; whether mother was married; data on parents (name, race, birthplace, age, occupation); and physician's name.

Marriage Records

Data in marriage records also vary. The names of the bride and groom, dates of the license and marriage, whether the license was returned and signed by the person who performed the ceremony (a justice of the peace or clergy member), and location of the wedding may be cited. If two slaves who had resided as husband and wife before the Civil War were legally married

LAY DOWN BODY

after 1865 and if they had children before the legalization of their marriage, the document may contain information on those children. If the clergy member's name was provided, but not the name of the church with which the cleric was affiliated, other sources, such as city directories, may provide this information. Church records can then be located to provide further details. Marriage records do not necessarily identify nonwhites as such, although some records were classified by race.

Indexes to marriage records, some of which have been published, are available. They may contain the names of the bride, groom, or both, and volume and page numbers of the marriage books wherein the record is located. Some indexes may contain separate sections for the races, and nonwhite entries may be located after the white ones (as was the case in antebellum St. Louis County, Missouri). Other indexes may signify nonwhite marriages by the letter *C*, to indicate that the marriage involved a "colored" couple. Still others did not identify individuals by race. Indexes before the Civil War may also contain references to slaves and free people of color.

The following examples obtained from city or county civil records illustrate the variety of data that exists. When Jane Deveraux married Arthur Donnelly in Hancock County, Georgia, in 1819 the record did not cite either party as nonwhite, although other records created throughout their lives refer to them as free people of color ("Marriages: February 1819," Ordinary's office). According to "Marriage Records," St. Louis County, Missouri, St. Louis City Hall, Joseph Labaddie, a free mulatto, and Mary Anne Price, whose ethnic background was not recorded, were married by a priest, as were two slaves at a different time (volume 1). Another record indicated that two "colored persons" were married by an assistant minister, but it did not mention whether they were slave or free. According to "Colored Marriages," Jefferson County Missouri, a microfilm located at the St. Louis County Public Library, Richard and Sarah E. Collier were married in Jefferson County, Missouri, in 1869 and the names of their six children were also recorded. In the same county, John Posten married Josephine Becket, and the minister certified that Posten had an eleven-year-old daughter named Lucy. Frank Marshall and Louisa Reno, both "colored" persons, were married in that same county at the residence of Archie Reno. Similarly, in Natchitoches Parish, Louisiana, when Marie Eloise Jones married Auguste Delphine on February 8, 1876, the civil record of the marriage did not state whether both parties and all three witnesses were former slaves or free people of color ("Marriage Book 5").

Death Records

Death records, like marriage records, may contain a wide range of information. Depending upon the year, they may provide any or all of the following: dates of birth and death, age, sex, race, cause of death, place of birth, names and birthplaces of parents, places of death and burial, whether slave or free, occupation, marital status, residence, and name and address of undertaker. If death records are not available, coroners' or sextons' records may be of some use. As is true for other records, information in death records may not be accurate, and researchers are encouraged to compare and verify information in other sources.

Several examples illustrate the value of this material. Published records from Rhode Island contain references to slaves and free Negroes. In 1847, the St. Louis coroner reported that Sarah, a slave aged eight years and two months, "came to her death by violence inflicted on her person while in the employment of Edwin Tanner" (St. Louis County, Missouri, "Coroner's Record of Inquests, 1838–1848," volume 1, entry 84, Missouri Historical Society). Mary Walker, who was identified as a free woman of color, was forty years old when she died on August 18, 1864, in Mobile. The record indicated that she was born in Alabama, that the cause of death was consumption, that she was buried in the New Grave Yard (Mobile), and that her color was "dark." (Mobile, Alabama, "Death Certificates," reel 56, entry 834, August 18, 1864).

The LDS Family History Centers have the United States Social Security Death Index in their extensive CD-ROM collection. It contains information on people who died as early as 1937, but the emphasis is on deaths reported to the Social Security Administration since 1962. Researchers may find birth and death dates (month and year only for death dates through 1987; after that, the day of death is also listed), last place of residence, Social Security number and the state of issuance, state of residence at death, and where death benefit was sent. The index does not contain data about the person's family or birthplace. In addition, the researcher can contact the Social Security Administration directly.

Some areas may have laws that restrict access to vital records. In St. Louis, for example, the general public does not have access to the index of birth and death records; professional researchers may check the index to the latter, but not the former. Family historians, however, may obtain copies of records once they prove their relationship to the person whose records are being sought.

MILITARY RECORDS

African Americans have served in U.S. military units since the colonial period, and numerous records document the contributions made by these troops. These resources are available at the National Archives, state archives, historical societies, and libraries. Many have been filmed and are available through one of the commercial lending programs. The contents of the records may vary depending on the time period during which the person served his country.

Revolutionary War

Several sources dealing with the Revolutionary War contain information relevant to genealogists tracing their African American ancestry. A

L A Y   D O W N   B O D Y

review of Military Service Records (National Archives Trust Fund Board) lists several sets of records in the National Archives. One of them is the *General Index to Compiled Military Service Records of Revolutionary War Soldiers.* Each index card in this file contains a serviceman's name and unit and possibly his rank, profession, or office. Compiled service records are also available; many such records and indexes have been microfilmed. Other groups of records are the *Revolutionary War Pension and Bounty Land Warrant Application Files,* and *Selected Records from Revolutionary War Pension and Bounty Land Warrant Application Files.* Applications may list an individual's former rank, unit, age or birth date, residence, birthplace, and the names and ages of his wife and children. Applications from a widow who sought pension or land warrants may provide her age, maiden name, place of residence, date and place of her marriage, date and place of her husband's death, or a copy of a marriage record. Another useful source is the National Genealogical Society's *Index of Revolutionary War Pension Applications in the National Archives.* The listings provide access to the pension and bounty land application records. "A simple check of entries, however, tells one that many more servicemen recorded in this source were black men than are so designated," advises genealogist Marcia J. Eisenberg in "Finding Your Revolutionary War Ancestor and His Family," from the *Journal of the Afro-American Historical and Genealogical Society.* Some nonwhites who participated in the war are listed in Debra L. Newman's *List of Black Servicemen Compiled from the War Department Collection of Revolutionary War Records.*

Records of the Continental and Confederation Congresses also provide information on nonwhites who served during the Revolutionary War. Lists of former slaves taken by the British when they evacuated New York in 1783 were created so that the American government could pay reparations to former owners. These "inspection rolls" may show the slave's name, sex, age, and physical description; the former owner's name and residence; and additional remarks. The records are held at the National Archives on roll 7 of *Miscellaneous Papers of the Continental Congress, 1774–1789,* [M332], and roll 66 of *Papers of the Continental Congress, 1774–1779,* [M247]. These records are available on microfilm through the National Archives or the American Genealogical Lending Library.

Civil War

During the Civil War, African Americans served in the Union army, navy, and marines. They also contributed to the Confederate cause. African Americans served in regiments of U.S. Colored Troops; the *Index to Compiled Service Records of Volunteer Union Solders Who Served with United States Colored Troops,* a group of records in the National Archives available on microfilm at various libraries, contains an alphabetical listing of their names. Index cards provide a soldier's name, rank, and the name of the unit in which he served. For various reasons, the names of volunteer Union soldiers may not appear in the index: the serviceman may have been in a state-level unit, served under a different name, or used a variation of his name; or his record may have been lost or destroyed.

Creative Projects for the Amateur Genealogist

Once you've started gathering data about your family, there are many things you can do with that information. You can build a more elaborate family tree, or write the history of your family. Here are a few ideas to get you started.

Autobiography. Write about your life in relation to your family. Ask others in your family to write one (or perhaps they already have).

Family photo album. Collect photos from other family members, making copies and returning the originals. Always label the photos with as much information as you know: who is in it, what is the event, the date, etc. Start a family photo album.

Family scrapbook. Collect newspaper articles about members of your family (weddings, awards, obituaries, favorite things), and start a family scrapbook. This could also be incorporated into the family photo album.

Ancestral country scrapbook. Collect information about your ancestors' countries of origin and compile a scrapbook.

continued on next page

After locating an ancestor in the index, you may check the compiled military records at the National Archives. These papers provide the unit in which a soldier served, his physical description (age, height, complexion, color of eyes and hair), place of birth, occupation, enlistment data (date, place, term), and other remarks. For example, Murray Egins (or Higgins or Eggins) was a twenty-three-year-old farmer in Company G of the 7th U.S. Colored Infantry, Maryland, with black complexion, black eyes, and curly hair, and was born in Calvert, Maryland. Among his papers were a deed of manumission and evidence of title that indicated how and when his last owner had acquired him (Civil War, Record Group 94).

Other Civil War materials for tracing nonwhites are housed at the National Archives. They include a group of records titled *Compiled Records Showing Service in Volunteer Union Organizations,* which provides historical data concerning volunteer organizations. There is also *Tabular Analysis of the Records of the U.S. Colored Troops and Their Predecessor Units in the National Archives of the United States* (Joseph B. Ross), Special List 33, which contains data on regimental records, correspondence, orders, descriptive books, and morning reports; and "Colored Troops Division Records," which include fifty-four volumes of lists of nonwhite volunteers who enlisted in Missouri in 1864. Indexes are available for the lists, showing each person's name, age, physical description, place of birth, occupation, and date of enlistment. Also, in some instances, masters' names for former slaves may be given. Some of these records have been microfilmed and are available at or through the National Archives (Record Group 94).

You may also find valuable information on African Americans in Civil War pension files. An index, which has been microfilmed and made available at various libraries, contains references primarily to Civil War service. Index cards contain the veteran's name, rank, unit, and term of service, names of dependents, filing date and place (state), and application and certificate numbers. Information in one such file contained a serviceman's death certificate (which listed a birth date); county of birth; dates of enlistment and discharge; name under which he enlisted; marriage data; and names and birth dates of children. Documents indicated that his first wife died, that he remarried, and that his widow applied for a pension. Her file also contains valuable genealogical information. Another file showed the maiden name of the pensioner's wife, date and place of his marriage, and the names and birth dates of his eleven children.

Four other Civil War collections at the National Archives deserve mention. They comprise part of the holdings of the Adjutant General's Office in Record Group Ninety-four. The "Records of Slave Claims Commissions, 1864–1866," includes claims registers of slave owners seeking reimbursement for slaves who served in the U.S. army in some capacity. Registers for Delaware, Kentucky, Maryland, Missouri, Tennessee, and West Virginia are extant. Data include the date, owner's name, and the former slave's name and address. Proceedings of some commissions are also provided. The "Register of Claims of United States Colored Troops, 1864–1867," comprises three volumes and contains claims by slave owners from Kentucky, Maryland, and Tennessee. The register includes the name and residence of claimant, name and date of enlistment of slave, organization of the individual, and amount of owner's claim. The files are arranged by state, and then alphabetically by owner's name. Third, "Registers of Officers of United States Colored Troops, 1863–1865," comprises six volumes and indicates the officer's name, rank, birthplace, place of appointment, and remarks. This collection is "arranged by arm of service, thereunder by regiment, and thereunder by officers' name entered according to rank" according to Lucille H. Pendell and Elizabeth Bethel in *Preliminary Inventory of the Records of the Adjutant General's Office*. And "Descriptive Lists of Colored Volunteers, 1864," consisting of fifty-four volumes, records nonwhite volunteers from Missouri. The record lists the volunteer's name, age, eye and hair color, complexion, height, birthplace, occupation, date of enlistment, and (if a former slave) owner's name. The numerous volumes are indexed and arranged chronologically.

continued from previous page

Gravestone rubbings or photographs. Tape a large piece of strong paper to the gravestone and rub black crayon over the surface. You will get an image of the raised design, many of which are quite beautiful. Or, start a collection of photographs of your family gravestones.

Autograph album. Start an album and ask your relatives to write a few lines and sign their name. This could also be incorporated into the photo album.

Photos of old homes. Take pictures of homes your family has lived in, and ask relatives to come along and tell you any stories. Include photos of schools and places of worship members of your family have attended.

Pen pal. Ask family members if there are relatives or friends living in the "old country," and write to them. This is especially fun for children or relatives that are about the same age.

Newspapers from the day you were born. At the library you can look up newspapers from the day you were born. If it is possible, photocopy the headline and any other sections you find interesting, and include them in your scrapbook or album.

Similar records that detail the work of nonwhites during the war are located in at least one other repository. After the Union army took control of Nashville in 1862, fugitive slaves sought protection and basic necessities; the Army responded by impressing them for service on the railroad. Impressment rolls, which offer the slave's name, age, and height, and the slave owner's name and residence, are located in the Tennessee State Library and Archives. Nearly ninety percent of the slave surnames were the same as their owners, suggesting, perhaps, that military personnel may have chosen the surnames.

If an ancestor appears in U.S. Army records, the researcher should not assume that he was a free Negro before the Civil War. A number of enslaved blacks also joined the Union army. Arlene Eakle and Johni Cerny state in *The Source: A Guidebook of American Genealogy,* "Whenever a black citizen disappears from the records of an area in which he previously appeared, the possibility that he was a slave prior to that time should be considered."

Slaves and free Negroes also served in the Confederate military. Records of their involvement are located in the War Department Collection of Confederate Records, Record Group 109, at the National Archives: "Record of Details [unit assignments] of Free Negroes, Camp of Instruction at Richmond, 1864," records the date of detail, name of Negro, to whom detailed, date detail expired, and remarks. Entries are arranged chronologically. The "Register of Free Negroes Enrolled and Assigned, Virginia, 1864–1865," includes the Negro's name; age; color of eyes, hair, and complexion; height; birthplace; occupation; date and place of enlistment; by whom enlisted; assignment and date of assignment; and remarks. Entries are arranged alphabetically by name. The "Register of Slaves Impressed, 1864–1865," cites the slave's name, date of impressment, description, market value, and owner's name. References, which seem to include only those in Mississippi, are listed by county, and an index appears in the beginning of the volume.

The names of slaves also appear in Confederate payroll records. "Slave Payrolls, 1861–1865," contains information about slaves who worked on military defenses and includes length and place of service, slave owner's name, and slave's name and occupation. The "Index to Slave and Other Payrolls, 1861–1865," lists the name of owner and individual who signed the payrolls.

Other records at the National Archives generated in the aftermath of the Civil War include those of various claims commissions. The French and American Claims Commission and the Mixed Commission of British and American Claims were created to help French and British citizens in the United States regain property lost at the hands of the Union army. The government handled similar claims through the Southern Claims Commission from residents of the former Confederate states who professed to have been loyal to the Union. The files contain testimony from whites and nonwhites, including slaves and free people of color. According to Gary B. Mills, "Indeed, the claimants before the Southern commission included not only free

L A Y   D O W N   B O D Y

Negroes but also the quasi-free and slaves whose masters allowed them to accumulate property."

One example from the Southern commission illustrates the type of information you may find in the files. Details in one claim indicated that one man was born a slave, worked as a barber, and borrowed $2,500 to purchase his freedom. Because he married a slave who was not for sale, he bought another slave woman, lived with her during the Civil War, and later legally married her. The file contains other information about the man, his family, and the witnesses who testified on behalf of his family.

The names of claimants appearing before these commissions have been indexed, but only two of the indexes—the Southern and British—have been published in Donna Rachel Mills's *Civil War Claims;* and Gary B. Mills's *Southern Loyalists in the Civil War.* An unpublished index to the French commission (Record Group 76) is available at the National Archives. Even if an ancestor did not file a claim, it is possible that he or she testified on behalf of a relative or friend. So searching for the names of any of his or her acquaintances in the indexes may lead to information on your ancestor.

After 1865 African Americans served in the regular army. Several units were organized, and published works detail their involvement. Among these are William H. Leckie's *The Buffalo Soldiers,* Arlen L. Fowler's *The Black Infantry in the West,* and Marvin Fletcher's *The Black Soldier and Officer in the United States Army.* Frank N. Shubert's *On the Trail of the Buffalo Soldier* contains biographical data on thousands of nonwhites, including dates and places of birth, and military service.

World War I

World War I Selective Service records are available at the National Archives, Southeast Region, in Atlanta. This facility has more than twenty-four million World War I registration cards filed by state and draft boards. To access a particular file, you'll need the full name and city and/or county at time of registration. A home street address or other specific location (such as ward) is required for certain cities, such as Chicago or Los Angeles; if necessary, you can often glean this information from city directories. The records contain the serviceman's date and place of birth, age, race, and father's birthplace.

Other World War I records may be located in various repositories, including state archives or historical societies. Examples include:

The Missouri State Archives, which has some certificate-of-war service documents containing the serviceman's name, residence, place and date of induction, place of birth, age or date of birth, the organization in which he served (with dates of assignments), and other related information.

The Missouri Historical Society, which has several records from the State of Missouri Adjutant General's Office containing genealogical information. The records, however, are not complete.

Selective Service System records at the National Archives, Central Plains Region in Kansas City, Missouri, which contain lists of men ordered to report to local boards for induction, and docket books of the local boards in Iowa, Kansas, Missouri, and Nebraska. Some of the records may show the county of residence, address, marital status, number of dependents, citizenship, and remarks pertaining to discharge or alien status.

Other Military Records

Other twentieth-century military records may be located at the National Personnel Records Center in St. Louis. For example, certain records for army, air force, navy, and coast guard officers and enlisted personnel can be found here. However, a fire destroyed many records in 1973, and access may be limited. Records such as the "Separation and Qualification Record" and the "Enlisted Record and Report of Separation Honorable Discharge" may provide Social Security number; permanent mailing address; dates of birth, entry into active service, and separation; military and civilian occupational history; military and civilian education; physical description; decorations and citations; place of separation; race; and marital and citizenship status.

LDS Family History Centers have two military indexes available on CD-ROM that show American military personnel who died in Korea or Vietnam (Southeast Asia) from 1950 to 1975. The indexes may contain dates of birth and death, place of enlistment, country of death, and race. They do not contain information about the person's family or birthplace.

CEMETERY RECORDS AND TOMBSTONE INSCRIPTIONS

The information offered by cemetery records and tombstone inscriptions varies, and many records have since been published. Whenever possible, however, you are encouraged to examine the original registers or visit the cemetery to verify the information provided in these sources. In addition, locating the correct section and lot in the cemetery (a task that may present some difficulties, even in large cemeteries where maps are available) may introduce you to other ancestors.

If the stone is no longer readable, however, or if it has been destroyed, published accounts can help fill the void. Published cemetery and tombstone inscriptions may be found in libraries, state archives, and historical societies. Cemeteries or churches sometimes retain their own records. If a cemetery or church no longer exists or is small, records may be housed at nearby libraries, genealogical or historical societies, or at a particular denomination's archives. These sources of information are particularly important for time periods preceding the nationwide requirements for filing of death records. In St. Louis, for example, the books of several smaller Catholic cemeteries have been consolidated and are held in two different places.

Some years ago, members of the Church of the Latter-day Saints went about the country collecting cemetery records, which are now available at their archives in Salt Lake City, Utah. These are accessible to historical and genealogical groups, and to any individual seeking information. In *How to Trace Your Family Tree,* the American Genealogical Research Institute staff provide the following useful information:

> [When treating] gravestones as a source of genealogical data . . . we are dealing with what a researcher calls primary, original, or raw material. For the time being we can forget about libraries, records, and files, and take a trip outdoors to do research. Cemeteries are, in fact, storehouses of genealogical and historical information and for generations have created a genealogical pastime. They are particularly valuable sources of information when municipal death records or church burial records have been destroyed.

While some people may hesitate at the thought of visiting a graveyard, its value to genealogists cannot be ignored and it certainly need not be an unpleasant experience. Graves are marked so than an individual, in his or her death, can be remembered by the living; a visit to a cemetery can activate this remembrance. It is interesting to note that several cities across the nation are planning to make several large cemeteries into park areas, not in disrespect to the dead, but in mutual respect for the deceased, for the land, and for the living.

ELEGY: FOR HARRIET TUBMAN AND FREDERICK DOUGLASS

I LAY DOWN IN MY GRAVE
AND WATCH MY CHILDREN
GROW
PROUD BLOOMS
ABOVE THE WEEDS OF DEATH.
THEIR PETALS WAVE
AND STILL NOBODY
KNOWS THE SOFT BLACK
DIRT THAT IS MY WINDING
SHEET. THE WORMS, MY FRIENDS,
YET TUNNEL HOLES IN
BONES AND THROUGH THOSE
APERTURES I SEE THE RAIN.
THE SUNFELT WARMTH
NOW JABS
WITHIN MY SPACE AND
BRINGS ME ROOTS OF MY
CHILDREN BORN.
THEIR SEEDS MUST FALL
AND PRESS BENEATH
THIS EARTH,
AND FIND ME WHERE I
WAIT. MY ONLY NEED TO
FERTILIZE THEIR BIRTH.
I LAY DOWN IN MY GRAVE
AND WATCH MY CHILDREN
GROW.

—MAYA ANGELOU

Many old, private cemeteries have been neglected because families of the deceased have moved to other parts of the country. But in early

America, when people were less mobile and one family lived in the same locale for several generations, whole families were buried together, often on their own land. This fact is particularly valuable to the genealogist who, in searching for records of one particular ancestor, may discover the gravestones of other related individuals. The first step in approaching this type of research is to determine the approximate death date and place of your subject. Most local historical societies will then be able to tell you which cemeteries were in use at that time. Note should be taken to check cemeteries of neighboring towns as well, since the boundary lines have probably altered somewhat from the original survey lines. You might eliminate some choices by starting with a cemetery affiliated with the religious denomination of your subject.

When you visit a cemetery, go equipped to tackle the weathering effects of time on a gravestone. In other words, stones may need to be cleared of moss and underbrush before they can be read. If you plan to photograph a headstone, bring chalk to trace over the lettering so that it will show up clearly in your picture. If you wish to make a rubbing of the stone, for the best results bring wrapping paper and either a marking crayon or a soft lead pencil.

Headstones can be difficult to read, usually because of the effects of age or because of the style in which the inscriptions were made. If read incorrectly, confusion will abound, so special effort should be made to be as accurate as possible. Always copy the stone exactly as it is written—letter for letter, word for word—including all punctuation. These precautions should be taken to narrow or eliminate the margin for error. If parts of the inscription are illegible, indicate this on your transcript.

Gravestones of the late 1700s were hand chiseled in roman letters on a dark slate. While this lettering was easy to read, the stones were easily split and weathered. In the early 1800s a harder, grayish-blue slate was used, but the change to a very difficult to read italic script has rendered many of these stones illegible. In the 1840s hard marble was used and in the later 1800s granite was employed. More recent gravestones have sandblasted inscriptions, which survive the longest by far.

The basic information provided on a gravestone—death date and approximate age—has been consistently retained through the years, but stated or worded differently, so that it can at times lead to confusion. The age statement is not always exact: "died in her seventeenth year." If you are not given or cannot figure out the exact age of your subject, it is almost always possible to approximate that age. Occasionally, you may discover a stone that gives not only the year, month, and day of your subject's death, but also the hour. In the case of a child, the gravestone usually mentions the names of the child's parents (and the child's grave is usually situated close to the parents' graves). In the case of a married woman, her husband's name is generally given.

L A Y   D O W N   B O D Y

In studying headstones, always view them in association with surrounding gravestones and never assume too much from one marker; chances for error enter if the stone is difficult to read and if the original marker has at one time been replaced by a newer one. In addition, because of the expense involved in having a stone inscribed and erected, occasionally blatant errors in the inscription are left unaltered. You should also search the sexton's records. These files often indicate who purchased the lot, who pays for its upkeep, and who currently owns the lot. These files also have complete records of all burials in the cemetery and the locations of all graves. Records of now defunct cemeteries are usually held by a local historical society.

While the typical gravestone reveals few personal characteristics of your subject beyond their age, date of death, and possibly the name of a relative, frequently you will find short or even lengthy inscriptions which provide a clue to their personality. A visit to a cemetery can help you to verify facts you already have, or present new ones. And in judging the simplicity or the splendor of the stone, you often gain an insight into the lives of an entire family.

Consulting a combination of resources can offer the researcher an interesting range of data: place of birth, birth and death dates, age, whether free or slave, race, spouse's name, marital status, cause of death, parents' names, or occupation. In addition, legal descriptions (section, township, range) providing the location of a rural cemetery may be included. If the cemetery is no longer in operation or cannot be readily found, cemetery records may still be extant which describe the location where it once stood.

These records may be organized in several ways. Published accounts may be arranged chronologically and/or alphabetically. Others may list names alphabetically and then by section/lot numbers. For example, if a name is located in an alphabetical list, and section/lot reports are available, you should check those reports for further details. The section/lot accounts indicate who else was buried in the same lot with the ancestor. Thus, additional family members may be located. Other documents may be arranged by section and lot only. In such instances, one should check an index to locate all individuals with the same surname as the one being researched.

As with any other source, cemetery and tombstone materials have their shortcomings. Race may not be noted. Information on tombstones may not be accurate, meaning you'll have to compare the information you find with that of other sources. In *Amite County, Mississippi, African American Cemeteries*, author Marva F. Peavy cautions users of one published account that "names were copied as found. Many spellings of names in current usage have evolved over the years from different spellings in one or more steps. The index should be checked for these."

Examples of the types of data found—as well as the problems associated with cemetery records and inscriptions—demonstrate their value:

Published cemetery records for Amite County, Mississippi, provide the location (legal description) of one rural cemetery, list the names alphabetically, and copy dates as they appear on the stone. For example, records of the nonwhite Big Antioch Cemetery in Amite County indicate that four individuals with the surname Butler were buried there between 1957 and 1975. Names were listed alphabetically and do not appear in any section/lot format. Thus, researchers would not know the names of other individuals who were buried in the same area as their ancestors, according to Peavy.

In St. Louis, sexton's records of the period 1862–1863 were used to reconstruct the names of burials at the City Cemetery. These documents distinguished between slave and free nonwhites. For example, the free man of color, Israel Dyson, born in North Carolina, was fifty-five years old when he died in May 1863. John Alfred, a slave, died in the fall of 1862; his age was not listed according to the St. Louis Genealogical Society's *Old Cemeteries, St. Louis County, Mo.*

Registers for Oakland Cemetery in St. Paul, Minnesota, show names, burial dates, location in the cemetery, place of birth, and date and cause of death. Sharon Bruckner, project coordinator for *Oakland Cemetery Records, Volume 2* notes, for instance, that the records indicate that Amanda Wilkinson was a free woman, that she was "colored," that she was born in Missouri, that she was eighteen when she died on March 29, 1868, and that the cause of death was consumption. Minerva Lewis, "formerly a slave," was from Alabama and died in 1868.

In South Carolina, the inscription on the stone of William Ellison, a socially prominent, free man of color who was buried in the family cemetery, included the phrase "In God we trust," according to *Black Masters: A Free Family of Color in the Old South* by Michael P. Johnson and James L. Roark.

In Mobile, the tombstone inscription for Constance Hugon indicated that she was born in New Orleans and died on October 16, 1845. Her race was not identified, but other sources indicated that she was a free woman of color. Church records, however, list a different date of death, according to Col. and Mrs. Soren Nelson in "Burials for Colored People, 1828–1877," from the Church of Mobile, Alabama Archives, The Catholic Center.

NEWSPAPER ADS AND COLUMNS

Newspapers are a useful source for genealogical research. Births, marriages, deaths, legal notices (probate court proceedings, civil or criminal court cases, etc.), runaway slave notices, advertisements for businesses or lost relatives, tax lists, city or state laws, manumissions, and registrations of free people of color are some examples of the type of information that has appeared in newspapers over the years. If public records have been destroyed or lost, researching newspaper archives may be the only means available to retrieve

LAY DOWN BODY

this information. And newspapers from the relevant period and region are an excellent way to learn about affairs in the community where one's ancestors resided, as well as national events of the time.

Finding newspapers of past centuries may be a difficult task. However, directories, guides, or county histories may indicate where they are housed. The Library of Congress publication *Newspapers in Microform* contains names of newspapers arranged by state and thereunder by town or city, their location, and dates available. Another source is K. G. Saur's *Microfilms in Print.* After you identify pertinent papers, you may be able to order microfilmed copies through the interlibrary loan department of a public or university library. *American Newspapers, 1821–1936: A Union List of Files Available in the United States and Canada* by Winifred Gregory, which lists titles and repositories of extant papers, and Clarence S. Brigham's *History and Bibliography of American Newspapers, 1690–1820,* are other sources you can find in the reference departments of public or university libraries. In addition, some published abstracts specialize in certain types of information gleaned from newspapers, such as marriage or death notices.

Runaway Slave Notices

Runaway slave notices contain a variety of information. The advertisements may mention the slave's name, age, physical description, residence, former owner, and any unusual characteristics that could be useful in identifying the slave, such as the type of work the slave performed. Slave owners placed notices in newspapers circulating in the geographic areas in which they lived or, if necessary, places to which they thought their slaves may have run. Sheriffs also published accounts that indicated when a nonwhite had been committed to jail as a runaway slave. In some cases these nonwhites claimed to be free.

Some examples illustrate the nature of runaway slave notices: In Illinois, a "Negro man, who calls his name Jack," reported that he belonged to Duncan Steward who was "of or near New Orleans," writes Helen Cox Tregillis in *River Roads to Freedom: Fugitive Slave Notices and Sheriff Notices Found in Illinois Sources.* In 1810 James Norris offered a reward for the return of his bondsman James, aged thirty-five years, who had run away from Smith County, Tennessee. The slave was "African by birth," and his wife was named Rachael, according to Sherida K. Eddleman's *Genealogical Abstracts from Tennessee Newspapers.* In 1781, two Negroes, Paris and Anthony, fled from their master in Charleston. Their owner indicated that they had been seen in the town of Savannah, Georgia, where they hired themselves out and passed for free. The advertisements also provided physical descriptions of each man, according to *Runaway Slave Advertisements: A Documentary History from the 1730s to 1790* by Lathan A. Windley. In Albemarle County, Virginia, Philip Thurmond Sr., feared that his slave Ben, formerly owned by George Thomas of Hanover County, had either returned to that county or boarded a vessel. Lovick Jones of North Carolina advertised that his slave Sam, previously owned by Henry Chew, "may attempt to get to Virginia or Maryland, as he has Sisters and Brothers there." Jones also described Sam and the clothes he wore when he left, writes Windley. Cyrus, a slave belonging to John Lloyd of present-day Connecticut, ran away in 1761. Lloyd described the slave and the clothes he took with him, and reported that Cyrus was a butcher who spoke English and some French, according to researchers Billy G. Smith and Richard Wojtowicz in *Blacks Who Stole Themselves: Advertisements in the Pennsylvania Gazette*.

Registrations of Free People of Color

Registrations of free people of color were sometimes published in newspapers. The lists may show the individual's name, age, height, racial composition, place of birth, and length of residence in the area. Pre-1850 lists are especially important as they may contain the type of information that would not appear in census records before 1850 for persons of any race. In 1819, for instance, John Coleman, a thirty-five-year-old carpenter from Virginia who resided in Augusta, Georgia, had been in the state for six years, writes Chris Nordmann in the article "Georgia Registrations of Free People of Color" published in the *National Genealogical Society Quarterly*. In 1830, John Williams, a forty-three-year-old mulatto born in Virginia, was a thirteen-year resident of Mobile (*Mobile Commercial Register*, May 15, 1830).

Legal Notices

Take time to glance through the many columns of legal notices that appear in newspapers. Legal newspapers are also available which carry similar information. These columns may contain data pertaining to land sales, probate, divorce proceedings; tax lists; names of property holders (with descriptions and locations of the property) who did not pay their taxes; or other legal items. One note: Editors did not always identify people by race.

In 1830 the names of a free Negro's estate executors appeared in one notice that also listed the man's date of death. Letters of administration for the estate of another free nonwhite were granted by the judge of the probate court although the notice did not contain any other genealogical information. The executors representing the estate of another free man of color notified the public that his real property would be sold. The location of the property was listed.

Advertisements

Nonwhites placed advertisements to help locate displaced family members or even missing or stolen property. Advertisements in *The Colored Tennessean*, a newspaper run by African Americans that was published for only two years (1865–1867), may show the missing person's name and location of a former master, last known residence, age, or other relevant information. For instance, in 1865 Levy Done of Nashville was looking for his mother, Kissy Done, whom he last saw in 1862. Samuel Dove of Utica, New York, wanted to locate his mother, three sisters, and a brother. George Dove, their former owner, resided in Rockingham County, Shenandoah Valley,

Virginia. Samuel Williams of Nashville desired to find his mother, Sylvia Williams. Their former owner was James Maxwell, a resident of Augusta, Georgia. Previous to Maxwell, Sylvia had been the property of a Dr. DeGarr. As noted by Sandra G. Craighead in "Abstracts from *The Colored Tennessean,* 1865–1867: Want Ads for Lost Relatives," in the *Journal of the Afro-American Historical and Genealogical Society,* the notice also indicated that Henry Williams, father of Samuel, resided in Liberia. In Mobile, a free nonwhite offered a reward not only for the return of his mule but also for the apprehension of the thief.

Advertising one's business was another way African Americans used local newspapers. In South Carolina, a prominent free man of color began to advertise his cotton gin firm in 1817 and most likely continued to do so until the outbreak of the Civil War. However, none of the notices ever mentioned his racial background.

Lists of Letters

Newspapers published lists of letters left in the post office. Among the names appearing in such lists in Mobile papers were nonwhites who were sometimes identified as such. In the *Mobile Commercial Register,* for instance, one list contained the name Addison Lewis, "colored man." Under the heading "French Letters" appeared Zenon Chastang, although his ethnic background was not given (October 3, 1826). Several issues carried the name of Registe Bernody, another free nonwhite (April 7, 1823; January 6, 1826; June 3, 1829; March 5, 1830). These two men are probably the same two men (with variations in the spelling of their names) discussed earlier in "Court Records."

Vital Listings

Lists of marriages, births, and deaths were also published by the press. For older newspapers, a page-by-page search is recommended as these lists may appear in any part of the paper. After a certain time, editors generally placed the notices in the same location or section. Searching for obituaries by examining the column heading may be misleading unless the complete article is read. The amount of data in an obituary or death notice may vary. Look for an obituary, for example, several days or even weeks after the date of death. Society columns may also contain information on births, deaths, weddings, and the like.

Examples illustrate the type of information that has appeared in the press. In 1858 an Illinois newspaper reported that a marriage license had been issued to the "colored" couple Charley Weathers and Van King. On July 24, 1841, Sophia, daughter of John Thomas of Sumter County, Alabama, married J. D. Pollard of Mobile, both free people of color (*Mobile Daily Register and Patriot,* August 1841). In 1850 Henry Brooks and Catherine Stassbury, both "colored," were married by Edmond Douglass at St. Michael Street Church (*Mobile Daily Advertiser,* August 8, 1850). "Grandma Coleman," who died in Macomb, Illinois, was buried in the city cemetery of Macon, Missouri, where her son James Coleman resided, according to Phyllis E. Mears in *Macon County, Missouri: Obituaries*. Mears also notes that Mrs. Nellie Houston, believed to be over one hundred years old, died at her home in Macon where she was a member of the Colored Baptist Church. She was survived by several children, including Babe Houston of Macon. A Mobile editor reported the death of Pierre Chastang, a former slave who was "so remarkable a man in many respects, that a brief sketch of his life, will, we are sure, interest many of our readers, and, perhaps, have a beneficial influence upon his own caste" (*Alabama Planter,* August 8, 1848). The notice listed the names of his former owners as well as his accomplishments. "No person in this community, white or black," the editor opined, "was ever more highly esteemed and respected, and no one in his sphere has been a more conspicuous, honest, benevolent and upright man."

Crimes

Crimes committed by and against nonwhites also received the attention of local newspapers. In Maryland a mulatto named Roger was executed for "breaking open the store of James Weems, senior," notes Karen Mauer Green in *The Maryland Gazette, 1727–1761, Genealogical and Historical Abstracts*. Ursin August, a free man of color in St. Landry Parish, Louisiana, was sentenced to two years for stealing hogs (*Opeloussa Courier,* December 12, 1857). In Mobile, the court released a white woman who allegedly struck a free woman of color, and the mayor fined a white man for abusing a free nonwhite woman.

PASSENGER SHIP LISTS

Several types of records document the arrival of passengers at American ports. Those which might be useful for African American study include customs passenger lists and immigration passenger lists, many of which are available at the National Archives. The records are either original lists, copies, abstracts, or transcripts. Many of the records have been microfilmed and are available through commercial lending programs or at large public libraries housing a genealogical collection.

There are limitations to the files. The majority of passenger-arrival records cover the period between 1820 and 1945, and those before 1819 are mainly cargo manifests or baggage lists that also offer passengers' names. Most of the registers pertain to Atlantic or Gulf ports, and the National Archives does not have lists for every possible port where an individual may have disembarked. As with any other record, the handwriting may be difficult to read.

Indexes to many of the passenger lists are available. Such indexes may contain the name of the passenger, age, nationality, last permanent residence, destination, port of entry, name of vessel, date, occupation, sex, and

other relevant genealogical information. The indexes, however, are not complete and transcription errors are possible. To facilitate the search, some naturalization records, especially those of the twentieth century, may show the name of the port, the date of arrival, and the ship's name.

Customs passenger documents may be in the form of original lists, copies and abstracts, or transcripts from the U.S. Department of State. Original registers are available for only a few ports, and some have been microfilmed. The lists generally cover the period from 1820 to 1902. These papers were prepared aboard ship, and they may show, for example, the name of the vessel, master, port of embarkation and arrival, and the passenger's name, occupation, age, and country of origin. Passengers may have included immigrants, U.S. citizens, or tourists. Copies and abstracts of original lists date from 1820 to 1905 and were made by the customs collectors. Copies and abstracts contain information similar to that found in the original lists. Transcripts from the State Department were evidently compiled from copies or abstracts sent to them by customs collectors. Some of the same categories of information found in the other forms also appear in the transcripts.

The National Archives has microfilm copies of immigration passenger lists that begin in 1883 for the port of Philadelphia. The records of the remaining thirty-five U.S. ports of call date to the 1940s.

By 1893 federal forms may have included the names of master, vessel, and ports of arrival and embarkation; and the passenger's name, age, occupation, marital status, last residence, and nationality. If the individual was joining a family member already in the U.S., that relative's name and address would be listed, as well as his or her relationship to the individual. From 1903–1907, several revisions were made to the form, including the designation of one's race. The records contain names of immigrants, visitors, and American citizens coming home from abroad. The documents are arranged by port and therein chronologically. Microfilmed card-indexes are available for some of them. There is a restriction period of fifty years before the indexes and records of a specific year are available for inspection by the general public.

A few examples illustrate the content of index records and passenger lists. One index card from the *Index to New Orleans Passenger Lists* (Series T618, Roll 4, 1900–1952) shows that John Brown, whose race was marked as African, arrived in that port in 1913. His birthplace (Kingston, Jamaica), last permanent residence (Celon, Panama), age (nineteen years), and destination (New Orleans) was recorded. He was to join Mary Brown in New Orleans, but their relationship was not explained. John's height and hair and eye colors were also listed. In 1920, according to the same index, another John Brown arrived in New Orleans. His age (twenty-seven years), occupation (marine fireman), race (African, black), nationality (Barbados, British West Indies), last permanent residence (Bridgetown, Barbados), destination (New Orleans), complexion (black), and color of hair and eyes (black, brown) were shown on the card. On September 23, 1900, several nonwhites arrived at the port of

New York from Barbados on board the ship *Hevelius,* including Joseph Dummett, a blacksmith, who was going to join his brother. His age (twenty-five years), marital status (single), final destination (New York), brother's name (William Dummett), and address (1455 Broadway) were also listed. This was the first time that Joseph had been in the United States. Other details are provided (*List of Alien Immigrants, Passenger and Crew Lists of Vessels Arriving at New York, New York, 1897–1942,* Series T715, Roll 150).

It would appear that for the majority of researchers tracing the lives of African Americans (especially those transported as slaves), passenger lists would not be as useful as other standard genealogical records, such as censuses. At the turn of this century relatively few blacks in the United States could claim that one or both parents were of foreign birth.

NATURALIZATION RECORDS

Naturalization occurs when one is allowed to become a citizen of a country. With the passage of the Fourteenth Amendment in 1868, black Americans legally secured rights of citizenship. As late as 1910, relatively few African Americans were foreign born, and thus, few at that time could have been naturalized. In that year, about one half of one percent of the total African American population in the United States was foreign born. The total black population for the same year was about 9.8 million, so only about forty thousand people were born outside the United States. Seventy percent of that number resided in the North, about 25 percent in the South. Thus, even in 1910 relatively few nonwhites would have been naturalized (or probably could have appeared in passenger lists). Unless a researcher of African American ancestry had good reason to believe that a family member was foreign born and still living in 1868, time might be better spent checking other sources. However, these records do contain some references to nonwhites.

The naturalization process has undergone several changes. Before 1906, an individual could be naturalized in any court of record. Naturalization papers have been filed in local, county, state, and federal courts; historical societies; state archives; even the National Archives. It is wise to check with the courts or archives in the area where an ancestors resided. Some of these records have been microfilmed and are available through the Family History Library in Salt Lake City. Others have been published by various compilers. In 1906 Congress established the Bureau of Immigration and Naturalization to help regulate the naturalization process; in 1933 its name was changed to the Immigration and Naturalization Service. Thus, records created since 1906 may be located in federal courthouses, the National Archives, or its own regional archives.

Naturalization records may consist of declarations of intention or intent and petitions as well as records of naturalization. Intent papers show that an applicant renounced allegiance to a foreign government and intended to become a U.S. citizen. Prior to 1906, these intent files may show the date, and the applicant's name, country of origin, and residence. The amount of information varies by location. After 1906 the form provided more details, offering the applicant's name, date and place of birth, occupation, residence, marital status, names and birthplaces of children, and ports of embarkation and arrival. In some instances, as in St. Louis, the Works Progress Administration prepared a card-file index to records that appeared in various St. Louis courts prior to 1906. In other locations, the researcher should check indexes that may appear at the front or back of court books.

In addition to the declaration of intent, people applying for citizenship filed a petition of naturalization. Before 1906 petitions may contain a person's name, occupation, residence, dates of birth and arrival in the United States, and port of entry. After 1906, an individual's name, occupation, date and place of birth, marital status; names and birthplaces of children; ports of embarkation and arrival; and other information was most likely noted. Naturalization depositions are statements by witnesses who supported an applicant's petition. The files show the applicant's length of residence in a certain place, and other information pertinent to the case.

Documents showing the granting of citizenship are records of naturalization and oaths of allegiance. Court minute books contain many early naturalizations. Certificates were used later and are arranged chronologically in bound volumes that have surname indexes.

In 1868, for example, ten nonwhites filed declarations of intention to become naturalized citizens. In addition to listing their place of origin, Africa, the records also listed their ages and length of residence in the United States. Among those who expressed their desire to become naturalized were Cudjo Lewis and Ossa Kibbe, both twenty-one years of age and both ten-year residents of the United States. Eight of the ten had arrived in 1858 aboard the slave ship *Clotilde,* and later resided near Mobile (Mobile, Alabama Circuit Court Records, "City Court Minute Book, No. 8, 1868–1871," University of South Alabama Archives; King and Barlow 1986).

Searching for an ancestor's homeland is not an easy task. Locating a document that identifies the place of origin is something that researchers of all races hope to accomplish. Naturalization records can provide that information. To facilitate the search, other sources, such as the census, can be used to determine whether an ancestor was naturalized. When and where an ancestor arrived in the country may help determine the location of naturalization.

OTHER TYPES OF RECORDS

Numerous other sources may contain information on African Americans. These include, but are not limited to, records of private organizations, orphanages and asylums, banks, and schools; voter lists; city directories; local histories; employment and Social Security records; *Who's Who* publications; oral histories; hospital registers; tax lists; and coroner's inquests. In some instances, these files may be used to trace people who may have been in an area for a limited time and may not be located in censuses. Also, in the absence of 1890 census records, some other records from 1890 to 1900 may help locate individuals.

Some of these records may be indexed. Others are simply lists of names (with associated data) arranged alphabetically or chronologically. Not all sources identify individuals by race. These documents may be located in archives, libraries, historical societies, museums, government buildings, or in the agencies that generated them. Some organizations or institutions may have been exclusively for nonwhites, and city directories may help determine during what particular period of time they were operating.

Hospital Records

Some hospital records are available to the public; others are confidential. Among those that you might have access to are registers that may show a patient's name, age, race, place of birth, marital status, occupation, date of admission, diagnosis, place of residence, length of residence in the city, and date of death. For instance, according to the "Register of Patients, City Hospital #1, Female Hospital, St. Louis, Missouri, April 1, 1886–March 31, 1983," register numbers 1638 and 1642, Code Y 3240, Cabinet T, Drawer 6, Row 5 at the City of St. Louis Archival Library, St. Louis City Hall, on January 17, 1893, Julia Porter, a twenty-four-year-old nonwhite servant from Mississippi, was admitted to the Female Hospital in St. Louis suffering from phthisis pulmonalis. She was married and had been in the city for only one year. She died two days later. Porter resided at 1545 South 2nd Street. City directories could be searched for the name of her husband, and newspapers could be searched for an obituary. On January 19, 1893, Matty Williams, a forty-four-year-old African American "washwoman" from Mississippi, was admitted to the same hospital. She was a widow, had been in the city for three years, and was treated for malaria and released on February 11, 1893. A different register ("Index to Patients' Registers and Register, 1927–1929 and Mortuary Records, Female Hospital, 1900–1912, St. Louis Hospital #1" Code Y 3270, Cabinet T, Drawer 7, Row 2) from the same institution contained death records that provided the deceased's name, date of death, date and place of birth, cause of death, date and place of burial, and the birthplace of both parents. In Mobile, Alabama, "Hospital Reports, 1843" show that "Cheeseman," a free nonwhite, was a forty-five-year-old shoemaker. The document also provided a clue as to his economic status in the community: His name appeared under the heading "list of paupers or vagrants" (City of Mobile Municipal Archives, Box 5, Envelope 7, Folder 4, Documents).

School Records

School records document the educational activities of African Americans. School board minutes may describe the administrative affairs of

LAY DOWN BODY

nonwhite schools and mention specific individuals associated with the schools. Such was the case in Mobile with the school established for Creoles of color. In St. Louis County, an enumeration was taken in 1876 for whites and nonwhites; it showed names and ages, with each race in a separate section. For instance, William, John, Gibson, Joseph, and Nelson Taylor, ranging in age from eight to nineteen, and Jane, Mary, Eliza, and Annie Switzler, ranging in age from seven to sixteen, were recorded, as noted in *School Enumeration Records for Sub-District No. 2, Township No. 45, Range No. 7 East, County of St. Louis, and State of Missouri,* by Oliver Adams. From September 1928, to June 1932, Harold Washington, African American and former mayor of Chicago, attended St. Benedict the Moor School in Milwaukee, Wisconsin. St. Benedict's records provided his address, date of birth, general health, and parents' names and address. The Milwaukee school also showed that he had previously attended a public school in Chicago, according to Curtis G. Brasfield in *The Ancestry of Mayor Harold Washington.* Yearbooks and alumni directories are other possible sources of information.

Biographical Sources

Biographical sources contain genealogical information. Biographical directories for African Americans began in 1915 with *Who's Who of the Colored Race,* by Frank Lincoln Mather. Names are listed alphabetically. Sample entries: William C. Chance, born on November 14, 1880, in Martin County, North Carolina, the son of William V. Chance, was reared by his grandparents, Bryant and Pennie Chance. The names of the schools that he attended are also listed. On May 28, 1914, he married Evelyn Darlin Payton of Washington, North Carolina. The next year Chance was president of Parmele Industrial Institute in Parmele, North Carolina. His political and religious affiliations are also shown. *Who's Who among African Americans,* by Shirelle Phelps, provides similar information. You may also want to consult *Black Biographical Dictionaries, 1790–1950; Black Biography, 1790–1950,* by Randall K. Burkett, Nancy Hall Burkett, and Henry Louis Gates; *Black Biographical Sources: An Annotated Bibliography* by Barbara L. Bell; *Who's Who in Colored America; Biography and Genealogy Master Index* by Barbara McNeil; and *Black Women in America: An Historical Encyclopedia* by Darlene Clark Hine.

Employment Records

Employment records can also be useful to novice historians. The records of the Social Security Administration, which began in 1934, are restricted, but applications for Social Security account numbers may show the person's address, date and place of birth; parents' names; employer's name and address when the applicant applied for the number; and signature. To obtain a copy of application form SS-5, you must provide proof of death (death certificate) and a Social Security number. A Social Security Death Index is available on CD-ROM through the LDS Family History Library, as well as at many local Social Security offices. The index gives basic data including name, place and date of death, and Social Security number. Several different types of railroad employee records, such as those of the Railroad

Retirement Board (the Board, located in Chicago, houses records of anyone who received a pension from a railroad) and those maintained by the particular railroads, contain genealogical information. Some of the latter documents may be located in museums or historical societies, including those of the Brotherhood of Sleeping Car Porters, which are housed at the Chicago Historical Society. Before the Civil War some free nonwhites found employment in maritime trade and navigation while others apprenticed themselves to learn trades, such as blacksmithing. County court records often contain apprenticeship contracts.

Civic, Social, and Fraternal Organizations

Such organizations were formed by free nonwhites, especially in the South. In Charleston, for example, the Brown Fellowship Society, which was restricted to mulattos, limited its membership to fifty. The Humane Brotherhood was formed by free black men, and membership was limited to thirty-five. Both clubs assisted their own members, who, for example, were too ill to work or could not afford to pay funeral and burial expenses. In Mobile, Creoles of color operated a fire company. Their activities were documented in club minutes, the local press, and city government records.

Orphanages

Orphanages were established to help orphaned or abandoned children and were run by state and local governments, religious organizations, or private groups. Officials may have recorded the name of the child, age at the time of commitment, dates of commitment and release, reason for the commitment, disposition of the child after being released, and miscellaneous remarks. Locating the records may present a problem, but you may check historical societies, archives, or agencies that currently operate such institutions. Perhaps, as in St. Louis, writes Peggy Greenwood in "Beyond the Orphanage" from the *Saint Louis Genealogical Society Quarterly,* someone has eased the task and published an account in a local genealogical journal that provides the location of the records. City directories usually list names of orphanages or asylums.

In St. Louis, for example, on August 3, 1854, Thomas Jefferson, "colored," age fourteen years, was committed to the House of Refuge for incorrigibility. He was released the same day and sent to the city workhouse. On September 28, 1855, William Johnson, also "colored," age thirteen years, entered the same institution, but for a different reason: larceny. Johnson was released a week later, on October 4, and also transferred to the city workhouse. The journal did not indicate whether they were free or slaves. In 1888 the St. Louis Colored Orphan's Home was organized to help orphaned and neglected black children. In 1946, it was renamed the Annie Malone Children's Home. At least one other asylum served St. Louis's African American community. Other communities had similar homes for nonwhites.

City or County Directories

Local directories are another valuable source of information, especially for the period around 1890 when most federal census records are not avail-

LAY DOWN BODY

able. The books, located in libraries or historical societies, provide the names of individuals, organizations, institutions, churches, or cemeteries. The directories also contain advertisements and useful information concerning the community. Check all possible variations in the spelling of a name to find an ancestor. It is best to search directories for several years beyond the last located entry, as names sometimes were not listed every year. Information may include the person's name, address, race, occupation, employer's name, and marital status. A list of abbreviations is usually included at the front of the book, which should help you interpret the data. Inclusion of nonwhites in city directories was often erratic. Property owners or boarders with a trade were more likely to be included. The higher up the socioeconomic ladder an African American was, the more likely it was that he or she would appear in a directory.

City directories may be used in conjunction with other sources. For instance, if census indexes are not available, or if, as in the case of the 1880 Soundex, not all families were entered, data in city directories may help locate the appropriate household in census records. Locate the address in a directory closest to the census year and then determine the ward number for that address. Some books provide maps with ward boundaries, while others include street directories that help pinpoint the ward number. If you have ascertained the ward number, you can then check census records for the same ward. City directories may be used to determine an approximate year of death. For example, a man's name may have been located in one year, but the following year his wife's name may include the designation *widow*. These volumes are also helpful in determining the location of church records. For instance, civil marriage records may provide the name of the clergy member but not the name of the church. City directories may show the names of the clergy member and the church where the ceremony was performed. You can then check church records for further details.

Several examples illustrate the type of information the directories provide: In St. Joseph, Missouri, in 1898, Louis Ellsworth, a barber, resided at 1702 Howard; Robert Ellis worked at the Columbia Foundry and Machine Company; and Mary Emery, a "domestic," lived at 1020 Charles, according to the *1898 Directory of St. Joseph*. In Quincy, Illinois, John J. Gunn, a cook who worked at Ellis Restaurant, resided with his family at 711 North Ninth; and Mrs. Anna Steele, widow of Samuel Steele, resided with her family at 818 North Eighth. The individuals in St. Joseph and Quincy were identified as "colored," as noted in *Stone's Quincy, Illinois City Directory* from 1898. In Mobile, free Negro barbers advertised their services. Elam Page, a barber, informed readers that he was a "hair cutter, wig dresser, hair curler & shaver." In addition, he offered for sale numerous items, including "soaps of various kinds, razors, and razor straps," says the *Mobile Directory of Strangers' Guide* from 1839. The guide also features a full page advertisement: George McBride indicated that he could accommodate his customers "all hours, day or night, either at his shop or their private residences."

Voting Rolls

Voting rolls should not be ignored. In Louisiana free people of color did vote "when politically expedient," and in North Carolina and Tennessee they were allowed to vote until the 1830s, notes author Gary B. Mills. Efforts to disfranchise nonwhites after the Civil War have been well documented and need not be mentioned here. Some canceled voter affidavits are available and may show, for instance, the individual's name, race, address, occupation, and date of birth. In 1938, Robert James Johnson, a colored laborer born on September 3, 1907, resided in St. Louis on LaBaume Street (City of St. Louis, Missouri, "Cancelled Voter Affidavit Cards," Code DA 424-425, Cabinet X, Drawer 5, Row 4, St. Louis City Hall Archives).

Tax Rolls

Tax rolls are another valuable resource. They may be used for a variety of purposes, such as a substitute for census records. To interpret the information you find, examine laws that govern tax rates. For example, in the antebellum period the rate for a poll tax on free people of color was sometimes twice that of whites. If you have not been able to determine the race or status of the person you're researching, a higher tax rate may suggest the person's racial status.

Tax lists may be arranged alphabetically and may show an individual's name and property location, amount of tax, or value of real estate. The rolls may also provide the number and value of slaves or tax on other personal property. For instance, Virginia records that began in 1782 provide names of white and free nonwhite heads of households over twenty-one years of age, the numbers of slaves over and under sixteen years, and other data. Some early Virginia personal property tax lists (1782–1786) include a slave's first name, age by category, and the person who was to pay the tax.

Oral History

Oral history provides invaluable information. Stories are often handed down from generation to generation, and the family historian tries to confirm these traditions through genealogical sources.

A few of the published oral histories or bibliographies of autobiographies that are available in public or university libraries demonstrate the value of this method of research. Among those that may be consulted are George P. Rawick's *The American Slave;* Belinda Hurmence's *Before Freedom;* Robert S. Starobin's *Blacks in Bondage;* Charles L. Perdue, Thomas E. Barden, and Robert K. Phillops' *Weevils in the Wheat;* Russell C. Brignano's *Black Americans in Autobiography;* and John W. Blassingame's *Slave Testimony.*

SECONDARY SOURCES

Printed secondary sources usually refer to newspapers, periodicals, books, microfilm, and newsletters. They are important for several different reasons.

First, they direct you to actual records that can then be examined for accuracy and details. Also, by checking published accounts of records someone else has already discovered, you may save endless hours duplicating the research. In some cases, original records may no longer exist. Finally, you may not have access to original records or be able to travel to the repositories where the records are housed. One of the fundamental weaknesses of secondary sources is that they sometimes contain errors.

The library is one of the better sources of information, with its broad collections of books, magazines, newspapers, and pamphlets. Larger libraries often have film and record collections. Trained librarians can help you use specific items for research.

A bibliography from the library can provide a general guide to sources for your research. Some guides will, for example, tell you what kinds of military records are available, what types of data they include, and where in the archives they are located. If you're researching a surname, bibliography surname histories can help.

Newspapers

Although we have already discussed newspapers, you should note that a number of historically black newspapers—along with guides to help you locate them—are available. Especially valuable are the following publications: Georgetta Merritt Campbell's *Extant Collections of Early Black Newspapers: A Research Guide to the Black Press;* Neil E. Strache's *Black Periodicals and Newspapers: A Union List of Holdings in Libraries of the University of Wisconsin and the Library of the State Historical Society of Wisconsin;* Frankie Hutton's *The Early Black Press in America, 1827 to 1860;* Donald M. Jacobs's *Antebellum Black Newspapers;* Warren Brown's *Check List of Negro Newspapers in the United States (1827–1946);* and North Carolina Central University's *Newspapers and Periodicals by and about Black People: Southeastern Library Holdings.* One of these guides might mention *The Colored Tennessean* (later *The Tennessean*) which was published from 1865 to 1867 and contains information on slavery and advertisements to help locate displaced persons.

Periodicals

Numerous periodicals can assist you, including historical or genealogical journals, quarterlies, and magazines; the scope can be national, state, or local in orientation. The coverage of each varies, depending on their professional or scholarly status. Some may publish Bible, church, cemetery, county, military, funeral home, school, and organization records; census indexes; newspaper abstracts or indexes; deeds or bills of sale of slaves; cohabitation or impressment records; lists of free nonwhites; or manumission records. Periodicals accept articles dealing with sources, methodology, or family histories. Some periodicals contain a query section where members looking for information on their ancestors solicit help from other researchers. (Sometimes researchers may obtain information from individuals that might not be found in courthouses or archives. In addition, this approach might introduce the researcher to someone working on the same family, who might be willing to share the results of their research.) Recently published books are also reviewed in journals. Indexes to many of these periodicals are available at public, genealogical, or university libraries. Notable among these is Michael B. Clegg and Curt B. Witcher's *PERiodical Source Index* (PERSI).

The *National Genealogical Society Quarterly* has published excellent articles dealing with African American genealogy. Genealogists are encouraged to read them and to apply the same methods used by others in their work. The *Journal of the Afro-American Historical and Genealogical Society* and the *Journal of Negro History* publish materials specifically oriented toward non-whites. Magazines like *The Genealogical Helper* and *Heritage Quest* cover a wide variety of topics of general interest to family historians. Many more periodicals are aimed at the national, state, or local level.

Newsletters

Newsletters offer current information concerning the affairs of a specific organization and the events of other genealogical or historical groups. Genealogical and historical societies publish newsletters on a regular basis, often monthly or quarterly. They may provide noteworthy information on a member's activities or contributions to the field of genealogy, forthcoming conferences, queries, book reviews, computer programs, repositories, calendars of events, and family reunions. Newsletters may also contain brief articles and lists of library acquisitions.

Books

Historical or genealogical books are valuable sources. The former place ancestors in proper historical perspective and may show how national, state, or local events affected their lives. Some books may serve as guides for those who want to publish a family history or locate abstracts of records. Bibliographies in books help readers locate sources that might otherwise be overlooked.

Books published on a variety of subjects—including indexes to records; censuses; compiled genealogies; archival and library guides, including guides to African American research; church, county, or family histories; directories; biographies; and many more topics—are available in public, genealogical, or university libraries. For instance, you may consult *Bibliography of Sources for Black Family History in the Allen County Public Library Genealogy Department* (available at the Allen County Public Library, Ft. Wayne, Indiana), or the guide to African American genealogical research published by the South Carolina Department of Archives and History in Columbia, South Carolina.

It is clear that secondary accounts play an important role in genealogical research. Identifying relevant books and articles should be one of every researcher's goals. These works may help you locate information about different types of sources or methods of research, or they may contain the one piece of data necessary to complete a family group sheet.

LAY DOWN BODY

REPOSITORIES

Family historians should become familiar with all types of repositories, including those at the local, state, and national level. Among these are university, public, and genealogical libraries; archives; historical or genealogical societies; and museums. The sources they house can be very useful to researchers looking for information on their ancestors. State archives or historical societies may contain records not available in other places; they also have materials common to other libraries. Some city archives house governmental or other records. The city of St. Louis, for example, maintains a microfilm library containing tax rolls, voting and probate records, and other documents that may not be available at other locations. Each facility may contain primary and/or secondary sources, and guides to some of these facilities are available. For instance, Debra L. Newman's *Black History* deals with civilian records in the National Archives, while the catalog *Black Studies* deals with National Archives microfilm records. Card catalogs, many of which are computerized, can be used to access the holdings of various repositories. One can search for specific authors, titles, or subjects. Reference librarians and archivists are available to provide assistance.

When you start your research, find and visit repositories in the geographical region where your ancestors resided, as well as those in the community where the family currently resides. Facilities in both areas may contain local and national sources. Librarians in the genealogy or local history section may be able to direct you to other libraries, archives, or organizations that can provide further help.

Guides showing the location of each department or section in the library are one of the aides that such facilities have to offer. It is important to see what materials are available and how they are arranged in a particular repository. Books and periodicals may be arranged by one or more classification systems. In addition, manuscript collections may be arranged by county agency or organization; and some have inventories. Certain collections have sources that are specific to African Americans. For instance, in the Civil War files of the Dexter P. Tiffany Collection at the Missouri Historical Society in St. Louis are free Negro bonds that often include physical descriptions and occupations.

Ask the right questions when visiting a library or other repository. In a university library, for example, it may be best to ask where the local history section or the microforms department is located. If you were to ask where the genealogy section is located, the response might be that there is none. However, if the question is rephrased as stated above, you may be directed to several sections with useful information. On the other hand, while a good public library may have a separate section devoted to local history and genealogy, they may have another area for such microfilms as censuses, newspapers, or county records. You also should ask whether the library has a special collection dealing with African American history or genealogy. Vertical files in some libraries or historical societies may contain newspaper clippings. These articles might otherwise be overlooked or not located if newspaper indexes are not available. The files may provide information concerning church or family histories, or other topics related to African American history, such as slavery.

Certain repositories have important African American sources. The Mississippi State Archives has an index to the labor contracts entered into by former Mississippi slaves after the Civil War. The original documents are part of the records of the Freedmen's Bureau at the National Archives. The Amistad Research Center on the Tulane University campus in New Orleans, which specializes in the history of African Americans, houses original manuscripts, letters, family papers, organizational records, photographs, and other materials. The holdings of the Southern Historical Collection at the University of North Carolina at Chapel Hill, and the libraries at Duke University and Louisiana State University, contain many valuable antebellum resources, some of which have been microfilmed; and printed guides provide access to the records that deal with the purchase and sale of slaves, marriage and family life among slaves, and slave genealogies. The Schomburg Center for Research in Black Culture, a branch of the New York Public Library, holds records from African American churches.

Various repositories throughout the country maintain records created by anti-slavery organizations and their activities. Abolition society papers may show places of origin, ages, births, deaths, and marriages. Such documents are located in the Maryland Historical Society, the Chicago Public Library, and the Southern Historical Collection at the University of North Carolina at Chapel Hill.

When beginning genealogical research, you should not expect to find one book that has all the answers concerning your family history, nor should you expect librarians to do the research. Librarians may suggest certain materials but will recommend that the researcher do his or her homework *before* going to the facility and have a general idea of names, places, time periods, and the particular genealogical information he or she desires.

OTHER SOURCES

If you wish to hire a professional genealogist, there are several ways to locate one. You may obtain names from the roster of certified persons issued by the Board for Certification of Genealogists; the list of accredited genealogists offered by the Genealogical Department of the Church of Jesus Christ of Latter-day Saints in Salt Lake City; the directory of the Association of Professional Genealogists; advertisements in genealogical publications; or lists maintained by historical or genealogical societies and libraries with genealogical collections. When contacting a professional in writing, it is best to include a self-addressed, business-size, stamped envelope and a brief overview of what work is needed.

LAY DOWN BODY

Information on family associations is also available. Consult Elizabeth Bentley's *Directory of Family Associations* or *Everton's Genealogical Helper* magazine's annual March/April listing of family associations and family periodical publications.

In short, a wide variety of sources are available to researchers of African American families. Family historians are encouraged to examine all types of documents—primary and secondary—including, but not limited to, census, church, court, vital, military, and cemetery records. Researchers are urged to identify potential records, whether they are located in local, state, or national repositories, and then carefully examine them. Without question, African Americans have a traceable ancestry and the wealth of information that may be uncovered and recorded can be used as the basis of your family tree.

Creating a Family Tree

Much of the research gathered from books and archives, talks with close and distant relatives, and the examination of other records can be used as the seeds of a family tree. The family tree, when completed, will provide an at-a-glance look at where relatives, living or dead, are in relationship to you and to each other. The tree shows how you are linked by blood or marriage to each of your relatives. Until this very important step is completed, the question "Who am I?" is not fully answered.

Most of us want to know who our relatives are, and genealogy is interesting, even fascinating. But discovering information about past family members is important and useful for other reasons. In particular, concerning legal matters, a carefully coded family tree can be of the utmost help in regards to the law of inheritance.

In cases where the deceased dies without having made a will or where it is important to determine the line of descent, the search is facilitated if a well-documented family tree is available. There are instances on record, in fact, where persons have attempted to inherit property by masking the truth about their family connections, assertions that a family tree would negate. Also, when persons attempt to falsify their background in order to gain status by claiming to be part of an important family, a family tree can help present the truth.

Don't be discouraged if many of the relationships are not full, but are "half" or "step" relations. For example, when one parent in a family dies or when parents get divorced, a second family may be started. The children of the second family—the half brothers and sisters—can be so designated. Also, in cases where a stepfather or stepmother brings stepbrothers and stepsisters to the family table, make such entries and design your chart so it will be all inclusive.

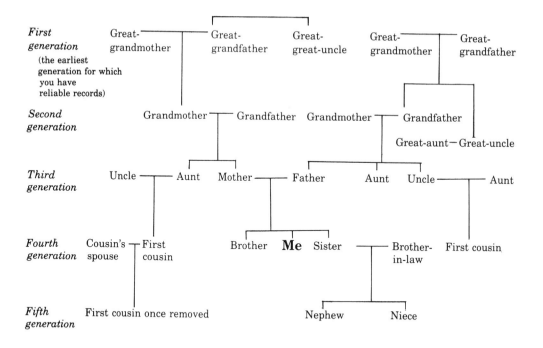

First generation
(the earliest generation for which you have reliable records)

Great-grandmother — Great-grandfather — Great-great-uncle | Great-grandmother — Great-grandfather

Second generation

Grandmother — Grandfather | Grandmother — Grandfather

Great-aunt — Great-uncle

Third generation

Uncle — Aunt | Mother — Father | Aunt | Uncle — Aunt

Fourth generation

Cousin's spouse — First cousin | Brother | **Me** | Sister — Brother-in-law | First cousin

Fifth generation

First cousin once removed | Nephew — Niece

FAMILY RECORDS AND CHARTS

The "Family Record" form included here will help you gather the information you will need to construct and display your family tree in a graphic, well-organized manner.

The larger family tree illustration, called a *pedigree chart* or *lineal* family tree, records only your direct ascendents. Rosemary A. Chorzempa, who first published these charts in her book *My Family Workbook*, explains that in the chart, you are number 1, your father is number 2, and your mother is number 3. A father is two times his child's number; a wife is one more than her husband. Thus all men are even numbers, and all women are odd numbers.

The smaller illustration, called a *collateral* family tree, shows all your relatives—not just your direct ascendents. Write each name in full, along with complete birth and death dates, and add ancestors as you discover them and new family members as they are born or married into your family.

A family tree is a living thing; it will continue to grow, and you can continue to add information as you discover it.

PEDIGREE CHART

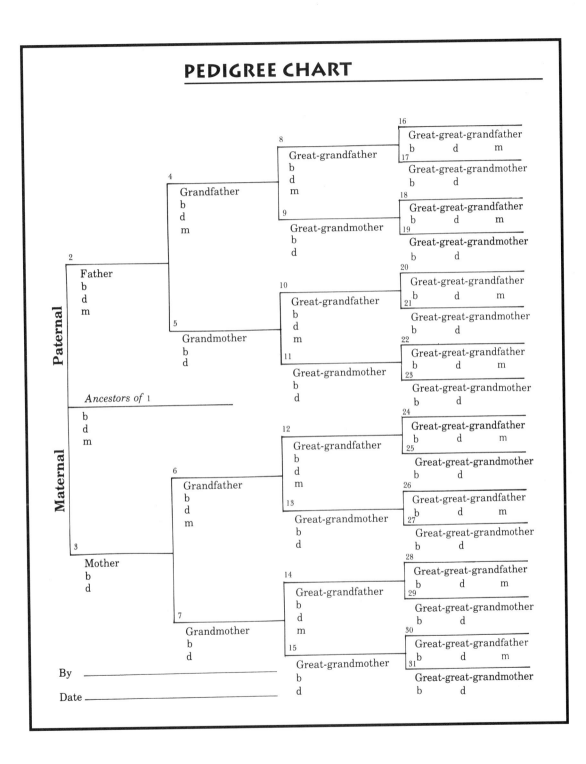

Paternal

Maternal

2 Father
b
d
m

Ancestors of 1
b
d
m

3 Mother
b
d

4 Grandfather
b
d
m

5 Grandmother
b
d

6 Grandfather
b
d
m

7 Grandmother
b
d

8 Great-grandfather
b
d
m

9 Great-grandmother
b
d

10 Great-grandfather
b
d
m

11 Great-grandmother
b
d

12 Great-grandfather
b
d
m

13 Great-grandmother
b
d

14 Great-grandfather
b
d
m

15 Great-grandmother
b
d

16 Great-great-grandfather
b   d   m

17 Great-great-grandmother
b   d

18 Great-great-grandfather
b   d   m

19 Great-great-grandmother
b   d

20 Great-great-grandfather
b   d   m

21 Great-great-grandmother
b   d

22 Great-great-grandfather
b   d   m

23 Great-great-grandmother
b   d

24 Great-great-grandfather
b   d   m

25 Great-great-grandmother
b   d

26 Great-great-grandfather
b   d   m

27 Great-great-grandmother
b   d

28 Great-great-grandfather
b   d   m

29 Great-great-grandmother
b   d

30 Great-great-grandfather
b   d   m

31 Great-great-grandmother
b   d

By _____

Date _____

FAMILY RECORD

Place photo above

- ❏ Myself
- ❏ Mother
- ❏ Father
- ❏ Sister
- ❏ Brother
- ❏ Maternal Grandmother
- ❏ Maternal Grandfather
- ❏ Paternal Grandmother
- ❏ Paternal Grandfather
- ❏ Extended relation (aunt, uncle, cousin, niece, nephew, etc.):

FULL NAME _____

NICKNAME _____

NAMED AFTER _____

ADDRESS _____

SOCIAL SECURITY # _____

FATHER'S NAME _____

MOTHER'S NAME _____

DATE AND PLACE OF BIRTH _____

DATE AND PLACE OF DEATH _____

PHYSICAL DESCRIPTION _____

MARRIED TO _____

ON (DATE)   AT (PLACE) _____

NAMES OF CHILDREN _____

OCCUPATION AND PLACE OF EMPLOYMENT _____

HOBBIES AND SPORTS _____

OTHER INTERESTING FACTS _____

PRESERVING HISTORIC CEMETERIES

DEATH COMES AND TOUCHES ALL—

NOT IN AN ANGRY MOOD THAT BRINGS OBLIVION

BUT IN A REVERENT HUSH THAT QUIETS PAIN.

FOR, AS THE NIGHT DRAWS ON,

SHOULD WE NOT REST A WHILE

UNTIL THE TRIUMPH OF A BRIGHTER DAWN?

—EDNA CULLINS, "PRESERVATION"

The customs, tales, stories, and songs of today and times past paint an engaging portrait of the men and women who created them. Besides their value as entertainment, these acts of the imagination hold messages—serious messages—of both despair and hope. For many people who are concerned about the preservation of African American history as a means of understanding themselves and their future as a people, burial grounds mirror many important customs. The genealogist who visits cemeteries and reviews valuable burial records will gain precious insight. Such visits can reveal critical findings, often opening the way to further fruitful investigations. The destruction of burial grounds is a threat to a heritage about which few written records remain, a heritage in danger of being lost. By preserving African American cemeteries, we are

Crispus Attucks and the Boston Massacre

Crispus Attucks, a black man, was the first to give his life at the commencement of the American Revolution. Eighteen years previous to the breaking out of the war, Attucks was held as a slave by Mr. William Brown of Framingham, Massachusetts and from whom he escaped about that time, taking up his residence in Boston. The Boston Massacre, March 5, 1770, may be regarded as the first act in the great drama of the American Revolution. The presence of the British soldiers excited the patriotic indignation of the people. Led by Crispus Attucks, shouting, "The way to get rid of these soldiers is to attack the main guard; strike at the root; this is the nest!" they rushed to King Street and were fired upon by Captain Preston's company. Crispus Attucks was the first to fall; he and Samuel Gray and Jones Caldwell were killed on the spot. Samuel Maverick and Patrick Garr were mortally wounded.

continued on next page

sustaining the memories of the folk ways they represent; the sermons, prayers, and testimonials are expressions of life's hardships, its stresses and strains, and, in the end, its beauty.

People with the greatest stake in the historic preservation of cemeteries are those who use cemetery data for reasons other than remembrance. Cemeteries as fields of history, cultural landscape, religion, folklore, anthropology, and even folk art, show patterns of change over time. Students of these areas seek to understand social status, family and community values, customs, and precedents. Rather than visiting cemeteries to obtain a single fact, such as a date of death, we find historians and others viewing the cemeteries as "communities of the dead."

As we have seen, particularly in the history of the Sea Islands cemeteries, considerable effort is being expended in fighting the elements of both nature and politics to maintain the integrity of black burial grounds. Often a single family member, small families, groups of advocates, or sometimes even entire communities will move forward to prevent a cemetery's destruction, whether by regularly raising funds, evoking community awareness, or designating clean-up days. Hope remains alive; the will to remember the past is ever constant. "Do not forget" has become the traditional chant of the historic cemetery advocate.

Richard E. Meyers, a writer for the *Journal of the Association for Gravestone Studies,* considers "communities of the dead" to be a challenge to the researcher: "Far more than merely elements of space sectioned off and set aside for the burial of the dead, cemeteries are, in effect, open cultural texts, there to be read and appreciated by anyone who takes the time to learn a bit of their special language."

Much can be ascertained from cemetery artifacts regarding the ethnicity and mores of the people who once populated the surrounding region. Church cemeteries, as well as community cemeteries, reflect all types of significant information about those interred there. In most cases, people buried in church cemeteries during the same generation knew each other as family or friends, shared the same religion, and interacted with each other during the course of their daily lives. To a lesser extent, the same is true of the smaller community cemeteries.

LAY DOWN BODY

Preservation methods and require-ments vary in accordance with the ceme-tery involved. For example, in large cities, which house larger cemeteries, there tends to be an immeasurable amount of broad-based information available, but less communal informa-tion. And persons interred in military cemeteries have a wide diversity of back-grounds—different ethnicities, religions, and residences—but share common mil-itary experiences.

Some cities and states give ceme-tery restoration a high priority. The Boston Parks and Recreation Depart-ment, for example, hosts an annual "Tour de Graves," a twenty-five-mile bicycle tour of Boston's historic burying grounds. The city has sixteen historic burying grounds; seven date back to the 1600s, three to the 1700s, and six to the 1800s. Several remained active well into the twentieth century. The burying grounds are located in neighborhoods city-wide, and three are sites along the city's historic Freedom Trail.

Proceeds of the Tour de Graves (and the Petit Tour de Graves) go directly toward the restoration and conservation of these sixteen burying grounds. The Boston Parks and Recreation Depart-ment's Historic Burying Grounds Initiative is the largest municipal cemetery restoration project in the United States.

Historic cemetery preservation is still an emerging field, stimulated by the urgent need to safeguard irreplaceable cultural resources threatened by imminent loss. The city of Boston's historic burying grounds may very well comprise the largest collection of historic cemeteries owned by any U.S. municipality. The Boston Experience, as it is called, is set forth in the *Manual for Historic Burying Grounds Preservation,* which provides a comprehensive guide for those interested in the subject. As pointed out by the *Manual's* writ-ers and editors, in addition to containing some basic "how to" information, it is primarily a presentation of the "why tos" of burial-ground preservation. Chapter headings range from "Getting Started" and "Grave Marker Inventory and Analysis" to "Master Plan" and "Implementation."

continued from previous page

Three days after, on the 8th, a public funeral of the martyrs took place. The shops in Boston were closed; and all the bells of Boston and the neighboring towns were rung. It is said that a greater number of persons assembled on this occasion than were ever before gathered on this con-tinent for a similar purpose. The body of Crispus Attucks had been placed in Faneuil Hall, with that of Caldwell, both being strangers in the city. Maverick was buried at his mother's house on Union Street; and Gray at his brother's on Royal Exchange Lane. The four hearses formed a junction in King Street; and from there the procession marched in columns six deep, with a long file of coaches belonging to the most dis-tinguished citizens, to the Middle Burying Ground, where the four vic-tims were deposited in one grave, over which a stone was placed with this inscription:

Long is in Freedom's cause the wise contend,

Dear to your country shall your fame extend;

While to the world the lettered stone shall tell

Where Caldwell, Attucks, Gray, and Maverick fell.

—WILLIAM WELLS BROWN, *The Negro in the American Rebellion*

What directly follows is information from the section "Getting Started."
For those who wish to follow through on obtaining an historic designation,
we encourage you to contact Boston's Historic Burying Grounds Initiative.

Getting Started

Successful historic burying ground preservation involves becoming aware of
the complexity of the issues. The first step in the preservation process
requires identifying all foreseeable problems. After several informal meetings
to assess the situation, concerned parties should involve the owner of the burying ground or those responsible for its continuing maintenance. Local and
state preservation agencies can be called upon for technical assistance. Three
important issues to focus on are markers, site features, and management issues.

MARKERS

How old are the markers, tombs, and memorials? Are several kinds of stone
or other materials present? What do their conditions appear to be? What significance do they possess in terms of both artistry and social history? Has an
inventory or a history of the burying ground been prepared?

SITE FEATURES

What is the character of the setting? Is it simple and rural, with tall unmown
grass and informally placed trees; or more formal, with a designed path system, planting plan, and features such as ornamental gates or signs? Is the
topography relatively flat or hilly? Are views into, within, or out from the
cemetery important features?

Does the cemetery exhibit a unified style characteristic of development
over a short period of time, or show features that indicate long-term evolution, perhaps over more than a century? Do accretions over time add to or
detract from the character of the site? What are the general conditions of
trees, fences, walls, paths, signs, and other site features?

MANAGEMENT ISSUES

Who owns and who maintains the cemetery? What regulatory agencies have
jurisdiction over the site, such as a local historical commission or state
archaeologist? Are access and security adequate? How many visitors does it
receive? Is over-use or under-use a concern? Is increased public awareness or
site interpretation needed? Who will pay for preservation activities? Who can
supervise or perform them? What about other kinds of support, such as the
formation of a friends of the burying ground group?

Preservation Terminology

For purposes of burial ground preservation, the following definitions regarding processes apply:

Preservation refers to activities that help perpetuate and care for historic burial sites, including planning, maintenance, documentation, and education.

Conservation refers to mechanical and chemical processes used to treat damaged markers and other cemetery structures.

Restoration may occasionally apply to burial grounds, although it implies significant intervention, which should be avoided whenever possible. When a mausoleum, for example, has deteriorated to the point where a partial rebuilding is required, restoration is appropriate. True restoration includes documentation and research to determine the original appearance of the artifact, its structure, and the treatment required.

Stabilization refers to treatments executed to retain the greatest cultural and structural integrity of the artifact and the site overall, with a minimum of intervention into the historic fabric. In some cases it may approach restoration, although it generally does not include replacement of non-structural detailing. Most marker repair may be classified as either conservation or stabilization.

A "Shopping List" Approach to Planning

In addition to its sections on "Getting Started" in cemetery preservation and "Preservation Terminology," the Boston Experience *Manual* sets forth a comprehensive list of interrelated areas of concern that comprise; a "shopping list" approach to preservation planning. Such areas include "Marker and Tomb Conservation," "Protective Measures," "Vandalism and Security," "Landscaping and Site Improvements," "Engineering Interpretation," "Maintenance," "Fundraising and Manpower Support," and "Resources of State Historic Preservation Organizations."

As staff members of the Boston Parks Department and Boston Landmarks Commission worked with local preservation agencies and advocacy groups to determine the preservation needs of the city's sixteen historic burying grounds, a comprehensive list of tasks and interrelated areas of concerns began to emerge within the central task of mapping out a philosophy of conservation:

MARKER AND TOMB CONSERVATION

Determine the extent and types of damage; do a grave-marker inventory, including an inventory of specific materials: slate, brownstone, granite, brick, marble, etc. Determine options for recutting and replacing markers; develop a policy to determine which stones will be selected for repair, and the method of restoration and storage for damaged stones and fragments. Make proposals as to how, who, and where methods of maintaining the grounds can be used to reduce further damage.

PROTECTIVE MEASURES

Make up a grave marker inventory. Apply for National Register listing, if appropriate. Determine gravestone rubbing policy and/or prohibition. Find out about access to funding; decide upon a public education and involvement policy. Find out about state and local laws protecting graveyards and grave markers; is it appropriate to adopt a local ordinance to enforce any prohibition of reproduction and/or removal of significant gravestones?

VANDALISM AND SECURITY

Determine any misuse of grounds—vandalism, loitering, occupation by homeless individuals. Look at fencing, lighting, tree canopy, police surveillance, neighbors, abutters. Are there local regulatory signs supervision and enforcement repair policies concerning graffiti, tombs, or overturned or broken stones?

LANDSCAPING AND SITE IMPROVEMENTS

List the site's aesthetic and physical condition, including access and circulation. What about the pruning, feeding, and other care of mature trees; the possible introduction of new trees or seasonal plantings (flowers); the desired length of grass/sod/ground cover; the effects of shade trees on gravestones (i.e., roots, visibility, soiling); or soil erosion and compacting problems? Check for historical accuracy—are landscape elements such as fencing and decorative iron retained and/or restored? Should they be repaired or replaced with the same or other material? Should stone walls be heightened or should they be repaired, repointed, replaced, or made solid? What types of gates, stone steps, gateways, handicapped access, and pathways are used?

What are the current materials? What is best for maintenance, upkeep, longevity, safety, and historical accuracy? What about location: what will cause the least damage to grounds, stones, etc., for a logical circulation pattern? What is the lighting like? Are there special-effects or floodlighting? What is the effect of lighting on adjacent structures? Is it vandalproof? What is the location of fixtures and attachments and what is the cost of electricity? Are benches inside and/or outside and, if so, what is the type and location? Are there trash receptacles? What about signage: what is the appearance, location, and safety factor of any signs or interpretive markers? What about rodent extermination? Is the facility locked or open? And what is the ease of visitation and access to keys?

LAY DOWN BODY

Determine engineering requirements: what is the deterioration of retaining walls, tomb structures, and drainage or irrigation systems? What about on-site maintenance and safety factors: are there walls along public ways, open tombs, or ground subsidence?

INTERPRETATION

Determine objectives for an informational signage system and its value as a public education or fundraising tool. Is protection of historic markers and plaques provided on-site? Are original gravestones displayed off-site and replaced by on-site reproductions? Should there be brochures? Who provides litter pick-up?

MAINTENANCE

Coordinate trash removal and mowing techniques with landscaping restoration/gravestone conservation. Weigh the efficiency vs. precision of clipping, weeding, or other maintenance methods. Should there be specialized training of maintenance personnel in simple conservation techniques, such as fragment collection or resetting sunken/tilted stones?

FUNDRAISING AND MANPOWER SUPPORT AND RESOURCES

The Massachusetts Historical Commission determined its potential funding sources to be foundations, charitable trusts, descendants, corporate donors, the Boston city budget, and the federal government. Who pays for what? How are funds matched with needs? Is it feasible to phase in projects as funding becomes available, or to use volunteer sources—"friends" groups, youth groups, local civic organizations, et al? Which local businesses/contractors might be willing to donate services or supplies? Is professional project management needed for documentation, fundraising, implementation, or record-keeping?

Preservation Philosophy and Strategy

In addition to using a "shopping list" approach, it is important to develop a preservation philosophy. In order to establish an overall mind-set in regard to restoration, a series of questions needs to be formulated and then answered. Answering such questions will result in a foundation on which to build a preservation philosophy. Some suggested questions are as follows.

- What kinds of information should be collected to formulate a plan for restoration?

- How should this data be standardized?

- Should restoration include recreating now-illegible markers?

- What are the criteria for choosing stones for repair and how many should be chosen?

- Should exceptionally significant stones be reproduced and removed from their original location?

- Can original stones removed from the burying ground be stored or put on exhibit near the site of origin?

- What about reproduction of grave markers for commercial purposes?

- What kinds of information are needed for public education?

- Should the burying ground be restored to one period in time or should it show a historic continuum?

- What additions should be made for visitors to the site, such as benches or interpretive markers?

- Should regulations regarding picnicking, gravestone rubbing, or the presence of dogs be considered?

- Is handicapped access adequate?

- Are current plantings in keeping with the original design?

- Are some maintenance practices harmful to the markers, such as scraping by lawn mowers; removal of graffiti using harsh chemicals, abrasives, or high-pressure wash; or the use of pesticides, herbicides, or fertilizers around gravestones?

These pertinent questions deserve very serious thought; each and every answer is important in the formulation of a comprehensive restoration philosophy and program.

After you've clearly established a preservation philosophy, your next step is to develop a preservation action strategy. In other words, how much work is the individual or group willing to do? Sometimes priorities are obvious due to safety reasons: Open tombs or retaining walls in danger of collapsing require immediate attention. Other priorities must be organized in view of the preservation philosophy.

L A Y   D O W N   B O D Y

Creating a Master Plan

Comprehensive planning is essential, though each city and town—and even each burying ground—have needs that vary. The responsible stewardship of Boston's sixteen burying grounds, for instance, required a formal master plan, one that accommodated phased implementation over a number of years and provided the basis for developing annual budgets for capital improvement well into the future.

For preservation of a single burying ground the planning product need not be as formal. However, the process should be equally comprehensive. Every burying ground has a unique and complex set of interrelated issues. Action addressing one problem in an isolated manner has the potential to create a different problem down the road. For example, the use of acid to remove graffiti on marble monuments has resulted in the stone's deterioration to the point that carvings have become damaged; likewise, planting trees in the vicinity of underground brick tombs has caused damage decades later when their expanding root systems have broken through the tomb's masonry walls.

A master plan is long-term. Designed to be future-oriented, it must necessarily allow for flexibility. Priorities change, as can preservation philosophy, technology, and available support. Consequently, the budget limitations that usually necessitate proceeding with historic preservation projects in phases can actually prove beneficial, enabling new techniques—such as those developed through monitored pilot or outdoor laboratory projects on carefully chosen gravestones or masonry tombs—to add to our ability to care and plan for the future.

Grave Marker Inventory and Analysis

A grave marker inventory is a key element in developing any burying ground preservation program. This inventory, in the form of a final report, provides a working document containing accurate data about the number of grave markers, the types of materials used on the site, the historical and artistic significance of such markers, and the conditions of both the grave markers and the burying ground site at project inception.

The challenge of any inventory is to amass a large amount of data within a format that can be adapted for a variety of uses. In Boston, the need for consistency in dealing with sixteen geographically separate sites containing over twelve hundred grave markers was especially important. This resulted in the development of a standardized inventory form containing categories for recording inscriptions and other physical data. To facilitate the use of inventory data in planning for grave-marker conservation, a detailed *conditions assessment* is particularly useful. During the Boston project, for example, the initial inventory form was revised to incorporate specialized conditions terminology developed by the consulting masonry conservator.

An information booklet on preservation written by Lynette Strangstad, a specialist in the preservation of historic burial grounds, also provides in-depth information on all aspects of the subject. The following are excerpts:

> In the last decade, increased public interest and concern for our threatened burial sites has resulted in the development of this new area of historic preservation. Due to the recent nature of this develop-ment, relatively little written information is available and locating professionals knowledgeable about the preservation of historic burial sites can be difficult.
>
> The publication of the National Trust for Historic Preservation is designed to meet the need for information that both the general citizenry and professionals may have when considering the preservation of historic burial grounds. Basic knowledge of the field is offered to help organizations and individuals understand the significance of historic burial grounds, identify concerns relevant to their preservation, and recognize methods appropriate to their conservation.
>
> Cemeteries and graveyards, often visited as parks and historic sites, are places to commemorate the dead—whether family member, friend, or historic figure—and to reflect on the past. Visitors often find these sites peaceful and serene settings in which to spend a pleasant afternoon. Historical burial sites offer this, of course, and much more. Such sites yield vast amounts of information regarding our bicultural, historic, artistic, and architectural heritage.

Understanding and Respecting the Site

The first recommended action in any preservaton project is to understand the site. In the preservation of historic burial grounds one must understand the nature of the grounds in relation to the surrounding physical environment and its cultural context. Next—and particularly if the historic significance is not at first apparent—one must search diligently to obtain a broader understanding of the history of the surrounding area. Discoveries of unexpected artifacts, including cultural artifacts, may be of great help in determining the particulars relating to the history of the site. In short, all preservation work should take place with the greatest caution, to assure that no information is lost to future generations of researchers.

The National Trust suggests that only professional archaeologists, sensitive to the requirements of historic burial sites and familiar with the burial customs and practices of ethnic groups, should undertake below-ground archaeological investigation of historic burial sites. Since any soil disturbance will also disturb the landscape surface, including relic plants, all landscape inventories must be completed prior to beginning any archaeological work. Shallow soil samples taken as part of a preservation project—perimeter

LAY DOWN BODY

samplings taken in conjunction with the repair of a wall or fence, for example—may provide valuable information regarding earlier buildings or activity alongside the burial site. Likewise, shallow samplings taken within the burial ground can be used to locate lost burials or identify earlier walkways, walls, monuments, or buildings.

The excavation of burial sites for scientific investigation raises many moral and ethical questions. The conservative viewpoint holds that excavation of burials is acceptable only in cases of inadvertent discovery—human remains found in an otherwise unmarked spot during road construction, for example. Such discovery should result in a respectful move of the remains to a suitable burial location. Most archaeologists, however, feel that such discovery legitimately may be used for scientific inquiry.

Although now less acceptable, it has been common in the past for burials—particularly of paupers or ethnic groups including African Americans and Native Americans—to be unearthed and examined in such an inquiry. But disturbing the burial places of their ancestors is abhorrent to most groups; the African-American tradition that firmly resists disturbing burial grounds in any way survives to this day. Such traditions should always be respected when planning burial ground preservation efforts.

Cultural Context and Physical Setting

Whether in a busy metropolitan area, near a small factory town, next to a tiny white church surrounded by cornfields, or in a neglected and forgotten wood, the burial ground's cultural context and physical setting are important considerations in determining the direction take by preservation efforts. Is the burial ground on a flat, featureless plain? Is it bordered by tall pines or cedars? Or is there a profusion of mature vegetation enclosing the site? Is it a rolling, rambling, romantic setting straight out of a Victorian novel? Or is the setting severe, almost sterile, in its simplicity?

Examining the burial ground within its larger physical context results in a fuller understanding of the site's historical evolution. It enables accurate interpretation of the site, and a more realistic plan of its future use. If the graveyard is bordered by a pine or oak forest, for example, the acid generated by these species of trees has a potentially detrimental effect on marble and limestone markers. On the other hand, such trees could also provide some protection from a road or factory that produces pollutants even more damaging to these stone types. It is as inappropriate to remove the trees as it would be impractical to move the road or the factory, but both must be addressed in any preservation project.

In most cases little can be done to alter properties adjacent to a burial site, although occasionally circumstances may require action. For example, the owner of a contiguous property may dispute a property line. Research and physical investigation can sometimes clarify original boundaries that may have become unclear over the years. This is particularly important when the disputed area contains burials that are now considered to be outside the graveyard.

Changes to adjacent property may affect the burial ground even if no burials are directly threatened. Rerouting a nearby drainage ditch could result in erosion of the soil due to run-off; and constructing a large building nearby could significantly alter the site visually. It is reasonable, appropriate, and, in some cases, essential to address any proposed changes to adjacent real estate by attending planning commission meetings, discussing problems with local government officials, and working with them toward a solution.

Features of the Site

Once the broad context of the site is understood, but before specific preservation planning can begin, it is essential to undertake an evaluation of the burial ground's features, including entrance gates and perimeter walls, ironwork, enclosure gates and fences, masonry plot enclosures, vegetation, roadways and walkways, retaining walls, open spaces, buildings, and the markers themselves. Each feature requires careful study in order to understand its importance within the context of the entire site and to aid in developing a useful, comprehensive, and appropriate preservation plan.

ENTRANCES

The entrance is the visitor's introduction to the graveyard. Be it through elaborately wrought black iron gates or between two large rocks of moss-covered granite, an important statement is made to visitors at the entrance of the site. Except for security or legal reasons, a simple site that has stood for many years without a perimeter fence, walls, or gates should remain so. Wrought iron, cast iron, or early twentieth-century wire fences and gates may surround more elaborate cemeteries. Other sites may have walls of brick, stone, coquina, tabby, or wood. Each of these styles and materials provides significant information regarding the site's historical period, the availability of materials, the representative culture, and local craftsmanship. In addition, the perimeter can determine a guided point of entry, security, boundary definition, and aesthetics.

PLOT ENCLOSURES

Within the burial ground, the variety of fence-types and other plot definitions and enclosures may reflect the sophistication of the site, the era in which it

LAY DOWN BODY

was most active, the availability of materials and craftspeople during different historical periods, individual expression, the relative wealth of those buried at the site, and other historical, artistic, and demographic information.

VEGETATION

Understanding the importance of vegetation to a site is essential to site preservation. A mature tree canopy is often a site's most significant organic feature and the one most important in creating its character. It is also an important historic feature, since in many cases trees were planted as memorials, as part of the original site plan, or even as part of an earlier restoration effort. In all cases, these are sufficient reasons to retain existing trees and mature shrubs. Smaller vegetation, too, such as low-growing shrubs, perennial flowers, and ground covers, can be of historical significance, having often been planted as a memorial. Traditional graveyard plantings include such evergreens as cedars, pines, hollies, and spruce; deciduous trees such as crape myrtles, oaks, and maples; lilacs and old-fashioned shrub roses; and perennial flowers such as irises, lily-of-the-valley, and peonies. Common succulents include hen-and-chicks, live-for-ever, and creeping sedums. In many cases, particularly in graveyards that have been untouched or neglected for considerable periods of time, early varieties of plantlife that still flourish at the site have become rare elsewhere in the local or regional landscape. Sometimes such relic plants serve as the only marker, standing over a grave site as a living tribute to the deceased.

GRAVE MARKERS

As the most obvious feature of any burial ground, grave markers are the objects most commonly earmarked for preservation. Most people recognize the significance of large stone monuments honoring prominent individuals, markers representing well-known historical figures, markers intricately carved by talented artisans, and curiosity pieces to which bits of local folklore or other mystique are attached. However, these are only a few of the markers included in the overall picture. In order to understand the history of any particular site and region, an understanding of the total assemblage of markers is essential. Each marker is another piece of the puzzle. When sufficient pieces are lost, no matter how insignificant each alone might be, the puzzle cannot be completed and the full history of the site and the region is unattainable.

Less understood, but often of even greater importance than stone markers and monuments, are the pioneer markers of early settlers. These, along with other vernacular expressions, were commonly made of wood, shell, stone, or cast concrete as a unique expression to be lovingly placed on a grave site by a family member or other mourner. In preserving a site, no marker is insignificant. Many small pioneer markers, important by virtue of their scarcity and cultural importance, are overlooked, misunderstood, or discarded by well-meaning individuals untrained in recognizing marker types and their significance. The grave goods found in African-American and other ethnic burial grounds are such examples.

TREE AND VEGETATION SURVEY

Together with its accompanying vegetation conditions assessment, the tree and vegetation survey is used in identifying and recording all forms of vegetation within a cemetery. Part of the historical record, it is used for maintenance and management. The survey is conducted by a horticulturist, consulting arborist, landscape historian, or preservation landscape architect familiar with both historic plantings and the preservation of landscaping in historic burial grounds. Sometimes urban foresters or country or university extension services are able to offer needed guidance. It is essential that the professionals chosen for such a survey be familiar with historical vegetation found in burial grounds. Many landscape architects, for example, are more familiar with planning than plantings and with modern hybrids rather than with the earlier varieties sometimes found in old burial grounds, but infrequently grown today. Native wildflowers, grasses, and other vegetation may remain from the pre–settlement terrain, particularly in sparsely populated areas.

The survey is designed to document the location, variety, size, age, and condition of plant species. It outlines general maintenance and recommends treatment for the various plantlife grown on the site. It also recommends removal of invasive, weedy, or scrub vegetation and may contain notes as to the historic character of various plantings. Surveyors should conduct the survey during at least three seasons: spring, summer, and fall. Some plants may be easily overlooked if the survey takes place during only one growing season.

Maintaining and Preserving Burial Sites

According to the National Trust for Historic Preservation, there are a variety of ways to maintain a cemetery. The following is reprinted from their newsletter, *Information:*

GRAVE DEPRESSIONS

Shallow depressions in old burial grounds are often actually grave depressions. While it is advisable to in-fill sink holes or holes left by the removal of diseased trees, grave depressions should be retained. Often they are the only evidence of otherwise unmarked graves. Since no burial may be considered unimportant, information regarding each must be preserved and care taken before altering any aspect of the terrain.

IRONWORK MAINTENANCE

To maintain existing ironwork, sound areas of the metal need to be cleaned and primed. Once iron surfaces are free of oils and grease, salts, dirt, and loose rust deposits, and the surface is allowed to dry, a rust inhibitor may be applied directly to rusted surfaces without sandblasting or extensive sanding. Elimination or reduction of the sanding step is cost-effective, since time is saved. It is also sound as a preservation policy, since as much as possible of the deteriorating iron is retained and re-adhered to the sound surface. The question of whether or not to paint the ironwork, and if painted, what color to use, can be answered through a *paint analysis,* a procedure performed by an expert in the field to determine what colors were applied to structures at the time of their construction. The state historic preservation officer may be of help in finding a professional to assist with paint analysis.

When existing ironwork structures, such as fences, are not complete, a preferred preservation solution is to repair and maintain the remaining work rather than add historically incorrect substitutes.

ROAD AND PATH MAINTENANCE

Roads and paths, particularly in nineteenth-century cemeteries, are often a key feature in the cemetery's landscape design; as such, their preservation and maintenance are essential. Such preservation includes maintaining existing widths and contours, the small triangles or circles often found at path intersections, and the original paving surfaces. Brick gutters should be maintained rather than ignored or eliminated. Introduction of asphalt for the convenience of modern vehicles seriously alters the site and erodes its integrity. To preserve certain existing roadways, traffic can sometimes be limited to pedestrians only. Replacement of original crushed stone or early brick with new brick pavers or other paving materials likewise compromises the site. If brick was the original material, roads or paths should be resurfaced with as much of the original brick as possible and reproduction brick that matches the original in color, size, texture, and strength, intermixed as necessary. When a custom-made brick is required, restoration brick firms have little difficulty in producing good replica brick. Brick and gravel paths and roadways need regular maintenance. Especially important are monitoring and repair or correction of erosion problems.

ADAPTING FOR CURRENT USES

Because tourists and other interested persons are among the most common visitors to burial grounds, minor adaptations to accommodate them, such as benches and trash receptacles, can enhance the burial site as well. In Victorian cemeteries, cast-iron benches and cast-iron or wire trash receptacles might be appropriate at strategic points. In an earlier, simpler burial ground,

Cleaning Burial Markers

When to clean: Determine the nature of soiling agents: lichens, fungi, vines, and other biological growth that can obscure inscriptions. They may promote acidic surface conditions or actually feed on stone material. Carbonaceous deposits may cause gypsum to form.

Who should clean: Cleaning is generally undertaken by conservators prior to stone treatment. Cleaning may be undertaken by maintenance personnel, plot owners, and volunteers following a brief workshop illustrating correct methods and materials.

How to clean: Unstable stones: Leave for a conservator or leave alone. Stable stones in good overall condition: Begin by flooding stone with clean water. Sometimes water alone or water and a soft-bristled brush is enough. If a cleaning agent is desired, use plain household ammonia diluted with water 1:4. Always complete the process by rinsing thoroughly with clean water. Gypsum may be removed with continuous extra-low-pressure water application.

continued on next page

such accommodations are best left outside near the burial ground's entry. Placement and choice of these element requires careful consideration; obviously, an orange plastic industrial drum with "Trash" gaily painted on it in white letters is not a fitting enhancement to any historic burial ground.

URBAN GREEN SPACES

Uses beyond tourist visitation are important and, indeed, probably essential to the survival of many sites. Burial grounds are typically visited by genealogists, history buffs, and people interested in gravestone carvings. In urban areas, cemeteries and early burial grounds provide open areas that offer urbanites the tranquility and respite found in tree-lined, grassy areas. Delightful places for strolling or bird watching, burial sites also serve as minor habitats for wildlife, particularly small creatures such as birds and squirrels. Some nineteenth-century cemeteries also serve as botanical gardens. Such uses are very much in keeping with the original intent of the site and serve today's public admirably as well.

SIGNAGE

Signage is an important aspect of the visitor's overall experience during his time spent at the cemetery grounds. Signs should be uniform throughout and should reflect the style of the era most appropriate to the burial ground. In most cases, simple, clear, unobtrusive signs are best suited to burial sites and, wherever possible, should be limited to the entryway. The use of numerous signs throughout the site, in addition to being disruptive, compromises the site's historical integrity unless signs were similarly placed at a very early date in the site's history. In many cases, a style similar to that used by the National Park Service at its historic sites is most appropriate: effective, simple, and clear.

The content of signs is primarily informative. Sometimes a map at the entryway can effectively direct visitors to points of interest. Historical information is also useful. In addition to providing visitor information, signs can

LAY DOWN BODY

also set forth state regulatory policy. In some cases, a direct statement of what is or is not allowed is appropriate. Often, however, a positive approach which involves visitors and asks them to take a personal interest in the site is more effective. Remind visitors that the site is both historic and sacred ground that deserves care and respect. A note about the fragility of the site may be appropriate as well.

REGULATIONS

Regulations apply primarily to visitors and delineate appropriate behavior, hours of operation, and acceptable maintenance procedures. They are generally site-specific and may vary greatly from one location to the next. Site regulations might open the yard at 8 or 9 a.m., and close at dusk. A notice that trespassers apprehended after such hours will be prosecuted may aid the monitoring efforts of local police and reduce vandalism.

continued from previous page

What to remove by hand: Encroaching vegetation that keeps markers damp (trim historic vegetation; remove scrub vegetation), and vegetation in mortar joints or seams.

What to avoid: Cleaning sugary, cracked, split or otherwise unsound stones with muriatic acid, household bleach, household detergents, pressure cleaning, unidentified chemicals, sandblasting, stone refinishing. letter recutting, paint, sealants, metal implements, and biocides.

What to use: Rubber gloves and goggles, nylon or tampico scrub brush, cleaning solution of plain water or common household ammonia and water diluted 1:4, tongue depressors, cotton swabs, spray bottles, and garden hoses.

NATIONAL TRUST FOR HISTORIC PRESERVATION, *Information*

Gravestone rubbing should be strongly curtailed or eliminated due to the potential long-range damage to markers. Irreparable and significant damage has been done by people who thought themselves both careful and knowledgeable. In addition to the damage caused by pigment residue, most visitors are not able to accurately distinguish between sound stones and unstable ones. Because of the potential damage, rubbing is best avoided altogether.

It is essential to the well-being of the burial site—for legal clarity, for proper site maintenance, and for permanent archival records—that any governmental body with jurisdiction over an active burial ground enforce any existing ordinance or, if necessary, implement a new one, mandating the recording of all new burials within each cemetery under its jurisdiction. The burial record should include, at minimum, the name, location (mapped), and date of the burial. Obviously, no burials should be allowed in otherwise claimed spaces. A permit to bury, issued following proof of ownership of the proposed grave space, should be required at the site before a burial can take place. Such records, appropriately maintained by the city or county and upheld with the mutual cooperation of the governmental body and the burial site administration, bear the force of law. Other regulations appropriate to effective management and care of the site should also be developed.

ADDITIONAL ACTIVITIES

Other current uses, particularly of the larger Victorian sites, include organized activities: tours, holiday and memorial observances, community pic-
nics, fund raisers such as walks or runs, and more. Such activities, when managed by informed, sensitive groups working as custodians of the site, can add
much to the overall value of such historic cemeteries as a community
resource without adding damage to the site.

Such expanded use of burial grounds is desirable both to the site—well-
visited sites are less subject to the destruction caused by vandals and derelicts
than are less-visited sites—and to local residents. Activities draw individuals
to the site who may not otherwise come to know and appreciate burial
grounds. They create a vested interest by individuals in protecting and promoting the site. In addition, they broaden the base of community support
needed to speak up, either when inappropriate changes are proposed or when
much needed funding is required. In the long term, preservation of historic
burial grounds is impossible without the broad-based interest of the community. Carefully managed, hosting activities on the site of early burial grounds
can benefit both the historic site and its modern-day visitors.

BURIAL SOCIETIES AND LODGES

I SING—

FOR FAR TOO MANY WRONGS ARE LEFT UNRIGHTED

AS BLACK FOLKS BEND BEFORE THE SCOURGE OF HATE

AND SEND ENTREATING PRAYERS UP TO ANOTHER,

BEGGING AND PLEADING FOR A KINDER FATE;

WE NEED TO KNOW, AS SAMSON DID OF OLD,

THAT OUR OWN STRENGTH CAN BREAK THE GIANT HOLD

THAT KEEPS US DOWN BENEATH THE FEET OF MEN,

FEARING TO RISK, LEST WE BE HURT AGAIN—

SO I MUST SING.

—RUBY BERKLEY GOODWIN

Burial societies and lodges served as the precursors to modern-day insurance companies for America's black communities, filling the important gaps in security and peace of mind created by racial discrimination. In exchange for a monthly, or in some cases weekly, premium or dues, these organizations guaranteed their members health care in the event of sickness or accident. Members provided support for the disabled and worked together to plant or harvest crops for a fellow member unable to do so. Many of these societies, which also supported schools for black children, became, in fact, the social and religious

267

center of some black communities. But perhaps most importantly, they contracted to guarantee a proper funeral and burial for their dues-paying members. "Without a doubt their major concern was the death benefit; making sure their members received not only a decent but a special burial," says Robert L. Harris, professor of Afro-American History at the African Studies and Research Center at Cornell University.

Burial societies developed in both urban and rural settings, mainly to counter the discriminatory practices that prohibited African Americans from sharing white health facilities. Their importance to the community stems from the belief that the soul of an African American would eventually return to the mother continent—but only if the body was given a proper and respectful send-off. Hence a great deal of attention was given to burials. Elaborate funeral ceremonies, such as the famed funeral parades in New Orleans, complete with trumpeters and singers, were the order of the day.

These institutions almost always had a religious or spiritual flavor. "Many of these societies developed prior to the formal development of black churches and filled a gap in social and religious areas for the black communities," explains Harris. But as the black churches began to grow, they slowly took over many of the functions of the societies and lodges, including burials. Some societies and lodges themselves evolved into local churches.

Melville H. Herskovits was a distinguished professor of anthropology who taught on the faculties of Columbia University, Howard University, and Northwestern University prior to his death in 1963. The author of many articles and books, including *The Myth of the Negro Past,* he was the founder of the first university program of African studies in the United States. In describing the importance of burial insurance and burial societies, Herskovits maintained that the principle that life must have a proper ending as well as a well-protected beginning is the fundamental reason for the importance of the funeral in Negro societies. This results from several causes, the most important being the widespread African belief in the power of one's ancestors to affect the living.

H. W. Odum, writing in his *Social and Mental Traits of the Negro,* published in 1910, recognized the important place accorded to death within the mores of the Negro community:

> It is a great consolation to the Negro to know that he will be buried with proper ceremonies and his grave properly marked. . . . There are few greater events than the burial, and none which brings the community together in a more characteristic attitude. The funeral is a social event, for which the lodge appropriates the necessary expenses.

About the Mississippi community of the 1930s, Hortense Powdermaker notes in *After Freedom:*

> Burial insurance is usually the first to be taken out and the last to be relinquished when times grow hard. It is considered more important by

the very poor than sickness or accident insurance, although the latter is becoming more important.

The benevolent secret societies of the Negroes, with their special stress upon burial ceremonies, may have had a faintly African origin. Ulrich B. Phillips states in *American Negro Slavery* that they were also strongly influenced by white orders like that of the Masonic Temple. There may well have been similar lodges among the enslaved that left behind no tangible record whatsoever. Those in which the colored freedman figured, however, were slightly more affluent, formal, and conspicuous. Such organizations were as much a recourse for the enhancement of social prestige within the black community as they were a network for mutual aid.

The founding chapter of the Brown Fellowship Society at Charleston in 1790 (which is described more fully later in this chapter), with a membership confined exclusively to mulattos and quadroons, appears to have prompted free blacks to found an organization of their own in emulation. Phillips writes that, by 1835, there were over thirty-five such lodges in Baltimore, with memberships ranging between thirty-five and 150 men and women. The tone and purpose of these lodges can be gathered in part from the constitution and by-laws of the Brown Fellowship Society or from the Union Band Society of New Orleans, founded in 1860 with the motto "Love, Union, Peace." The Union Band Society's officers included a president, vice-president, secretary, treasurer, marshal, mother, and six male and twelve female stewards; its dues were fifty cents per month.

Members joining a lodge were pledged to obey its laws, to be humble to its officers, to keep its secrets, to wear the society's regalia on occasion, and to live in love and union with fellow members: "to go about once in awhile and see one another in love."

A Pauper's Burial in Trinidad

A story was often told about an incident that occurred in the Trinidad village of Toco during the summer of 1939. An extremely poor man, whose wife and children no longer lived with him, was found lying, dead, on the floor of his shack. Since he had no relatives and belonged to no insurance society, his burial was left to the officials charged with the care of paupers. In the tropics, a corpse is ordinarily buried in early morning or late afternoon. During the day following the man's death, public works carpenters could be heard hammering on "de box" they had been hired to make. After they had finished their work, the young men who had made the crude coffin lay the man's body inside, placed the box on their shoulders, and, with no concern to form a procession, walked down the road with it to the cemetery and laid it on the ground until the grave was dug. Then they lowered it, refilled the hole, and went on their way. Indignation and pity for the deceased was voiced on every hand. Expressions of opinion were heard from all members of the village. One minor official said: "It wasn't right to put him in the hole just like he wasn't human, it wasn't right of the ministers to stay away, and it wasn't right nobody laid him out."

No one was surprised when, one day shortly afterward, some children, who had stopped after school to gather fruit from beneath a tree growing in front of the pauper's hut, ran with fear as, glancing into the branches, they "saw" him glowering at them. And the door of his poor hut, blown open by the wind, remained unshut as folk sedulously avoided what must be a residence haunted by an angry, dissatisfied, vengeful spirit.

Any member three months' in arrears of dues would be expelled unless, upon his plea of illness or poverty, a subscription could be raised to meet his deficit. It was the duty of all to report illness to the membership; the function of the officer's mother was to delegate members for the nursing. The secretary saw to the washing of the sick member's clothes and paid for such work, as well as the doctor's fee, from the lodge's funds.

The marshal had charge of funerals, and was given the power to commandeer the services of such members as might be required. He could fee the officiating minister not more than $2.50, and draw pay for himself along a similar schedule. Negotiations for the custody of the corpse and the sharing of expenses with any other lodge were provided for in case of the death of a member who had fellowship in more than one organization. A provision was included that when a lodge was given the body of an outsider for burial, it would furnish coffin, hearse, tomb, minister, and marshal at a price of fifty dollars, all told. The stress on matters of death in the by-laws, however, didn't necessarily signify that the lodge was more funereal than festive. A Negro burial was as sociable as an Irish wake.

In an article by St. Clair Drake and Horace R. Clayton called "Urban Burying Leagues," the authors contend that the burial association represented the impact of a southern cultural pattern upon the northern community. In the South, the church "burying leagues" and lodges had, by 1920, been replaced in many areas by associations organized by local undertakers. Each member paid weekly or monthly dues, and the undertaker guaranteed an impressive burial. The founder of a Chicago burial association defended the innovation thusly:

> There was a need for one here in Chicago. You know they are a common thing in the South. Since the Depression, you will find more people in funeral systems than previously carried life insurance. I suppose it's because they had to cash in the policies for what they could and didn't have any protection left.

The largest burial association in Chicago was founded in 1922 by an undertaker with an eye for increased business. At that time, masses of African American migrants to the city were unprotected, except for lodge benefits. Many who had insurance policies had been forced to let them lapse or had cashed them in. While white companies charged exorbitant premiums, northern Negro companies had not yet attained sufficient prestige to inspire confidence in their potential customers. Into the breach stepped the burial association, offering a policy which, while without a "turn-in" or borrowing value, assured the holder of a funeral, required no medical examination, and imposed no age limit. The Depression made burial societies even more popular, since when an insurance policy was turned over to the association in lieu of paying dues, it did not need to be listed as an asset when its owner applied for relief.

LAY DOWN BODY

Burial societies existed primarily to assure its members that there would be money for their funeral. Granted, there was added social status conferred upon members of burial societies, but the dues that were paid assured these members that they would not be neglected at death. But often, even if the interment was immediate, the funeral ritual was sometimes delayed. Herskovits describes some slaves' manner of honoring the dead:

> One of the big days among our people was when a funeral was held. A person from New Jersey who was not acquainted with our customs, heard it announced that: "Next Sunday two weeks, the funeral of Janet Anderson will be preached." "Well," said the stranger, "how do they know that she will be dead?" The fact was, she was already dead, and had been for some time. But, according to custom—a custom growing out of necessity—the funeral was not held when the person was buried. The relatives, and friends, could not leave their work to attend funerals. Often persons would be buried at night after working hours. If the deceased was a free person, and the immediate family could attend a weekday funeral, there might be others, both friends and relatives who could not attend, hence, the custom became general.

The Brown Fellowship Society

In 1990 the members of the Brown Fellowship Society commemorated their 200th anniversary with a grand celebration. Brown member Herbert A. DeCosta Jr., born in Charleston, South Carolina, and a descendent of Richmond and Benjamin Kinloch, is an architect specializing in reconstructing old mansions. On October 13, 1990, DeCosta, one of Charleston's most prominent residents, delivered an address commemorating the organization's anniversary:

> We are pleased to pay tribute to the resourcefulness of the founders of this group, who organized as a sick and death benefit society, and, we can imagine, enjoyed a measure of camaraderie at the same time. Although, today, we may not understand or agree with all of the rules and regulations of the original society, we must remember that they reflected the pattern of society when the organization was founded.

> We also honor our ancestors who kept the organization alive for two centuries, making changes in its structure as needed to accomplish this feat.

> Nonetheless, it is still admirable, but hard to believe that 200 years ago on November 7th, our forebears gathered together to form a society to help themselves in times of sickness, misfortune, and death. Although they were considered free persons of color, we know that they lived in a world of shadow, constantly fighting to retain the degree of freedom they enjoyed.

Further, it is hard to believe that 200 years ago there were free persons of color who could read, write, and express themselves in such an articulate manner as so clearly shown in the beautifully handwritten minutes of the Brown Fellowship Society.

It is hard to believe that 200 years ago, while some of our ancestors were trying to free themselves from the shackles of slavery, others owned property and operated successful businesses in the city of Charleston.

Finally, it is also hard to believe that 200 years ago the members of this society were successful and independent enough to meet at 12 o'clock noon and sit down to a meal at 3:00 in the afternoon.

So, today, 200 years later, we the descendants and relatives of these early members, commemorate the founding of this society by meeting at 12 o'clock noon and will sit down to a meal, the Lord willing at 3 o'clock this afternoon. . . . May the accomplishments of our forefathers, in spite of tremendous adversity, be an inspiration for us and for future generations.

Burial societies and lodges were important historically because they provided a major service to the community. Although for all intents and purposes many of these groups no longer exist, some, as in Charleston and on St. Helena Island, are still functioning. In the 1700s persons of color in several states, both southern and northern, were met with great opposition when they sought to bury their loved ones. The reaction to this denial provided the impetus for founding many of these groups. The first and most prominent of such burial societies was Charleston's Brown Fellowship Society.

The society's original cemetery on Charleston's Pitt Street no longer exists, having been lost to commercial development. Several tombstones have been moved, however, to a quiet plot in the city's Magnolia section. Although the society briefly changed its name to the Century Club in 1890 to mark its 100th anniversary, it returned to its original name in the 1940s, the same time that it began accepting women as members.

Robert L. Harris Jr., of Cornell University's African Studies and Research Center, has written about the society. In his essay, "Charleston's Free Afro-American Elite: The Brown Fellowship Society and the Humane Brotherhood," included in the society's 200th anniversary commemorative booklet, the story of the Brown Fellowship Society is fully told.

The Brown Fellowship Society was founded in 1790 by five charter members: James Mitchell, George Bampfield, William Cattel, George Bedon, and Samuel Saltus. These free African Americans belonged to the white St. Philip's Episcopal Church where they worshiped, were baptized, and married, but, unlike the white members of the church, could not be interred in the burial ground.

L A Y   D O W N   B O D Y

The society was organized as a voluntary association with the motto "Charity and Benevolence." Between 1790 and 1844 it admitted 131 men to its ranks. During that fifty-four year span, forty-eight of its members died, twenty-five were excluded, and six resigned, leaving an active membership of fifty-two men.

The most prominent case of exclusion from the society occurred in 1817. George Logan, who had joined the Brown Fellowship on October 2, 1800, was expelled when the association discovered and confirmed his collusion in the sale into slavery of a free black man named Robinson. The society labeled Logan's conduct "base and notorious," but granted him a hearing at which he failed to defend his conduct satisfactorily. He was subsequently banished and any claims or benefits for himself or his heirs were nullified. This particular action in reprimanding one of its own demonstrates the organization's concern for the rights of all free African Americans in Charleston in addition to those of its in-group.

Rules and regulations for the Brown Fellowship Society were established on November 1, 1790. The following preamble well describes the frustration and discontent of the society's five originators:

> Whereas we, free brown men, natives of the city of Charleston, in the State of South Carolina, having taken into consideration, the unhappy situation of our fellow creatures, and the distresses of our widows and orphans, for the want of a fund to relieve them in the hour of their distresses, sickness and death; and holding it an essential duty of mankind to contribute all they can towards relieving the wants and miseries, and promoting the welfare and happiness of one another, and observing the method of many other well disposed persons of this State, by entering into particular societies for this purpose, to be effectual, we therefore, whose names are underwritten, do comply with this great duty, have freely and cheerfully entered into a society in Charleston, and State aforesaid, commencing the first of November, 1790, and have voted, agreed and subscribed to the following rules for ordering and conducting the same.

Rules I through XI discuss, in detail, the organizational structure, duties of the officers, payment of dues, voting, and other privileges and procedures. Rule XII, which follows, speaks more specifically of illness and death:

> In case sickness afflicts any member, it shall be the duty of the Stewards, in conformity to the 7th rule, to call on the sick, examine their circumstances, and finding he is in need of assistance from the Society, he shall be entitled to, and allowed a weekly sum of not less than $1.50, by an order from the President, Vice President, or any one presiding in their absence, to the Treasurer, in order to be given to the sick member by the hands of the Stewards, and if he dies, the Stewards shall attend in like manner, as before mentioned, after which he shall report the case to the

President, or presiding officer, who shall order a meeting immediately, and consult on the management of the funeral; and in case the circumstances of such deceased member be low and indigent, that a decent funeral cannot be afforded out of their own estate or effects, the President or presiding officer shall have power and authority to appoint a committee, to regulate things in as frugal a manner as possible, for the funeral, which charges shall be paid off of the Society's funds, in such manner as before stipulated. Every member in Charleston shall attend the funeral, with a Black crepe around the left arm, by invitation from the Secretary; and on neglect (if able) to attend, he shall be fined in a sum not exceeding twenty-five cents, payable at the next meeting, unless a good and sufficient excuse be then made.

It is clear, therefore, that the Brown Fellowship Society was a pioneering effort. Its members paved the way for an important and powerful method of joining together, pooling resources, developing friendships, and easing the burdens that each knew must be faced at death. By studying their rules and regulations and reading their preamble, one can see and even feel the strictness and the seriousness of the procedures. Everything—from their attendance to their dress code to their demeanor—was carefully outlined. Monetary penalties were imposed for violations.

Because of the society's careful attention to record-keeping, persons researching their backgrounds would do well to make use of their records and books. Brown Fellowship's minutes are all written in precise, beautiful, and legible penmanship.

Today the Brown Fellowship Society has evolved into a commemorative organization comprised mostly of descendants of families who belonged during its heyday more than a century ago. With a membership of about twenty people by the mid-1990s, it now meets on an irregular basis, no more than two or three times a year. Dues are no longer charged and the society is no longer involved in the burial business. "The society has evolved from a group that helped people in time of sickness and assisted with burials to a social organization," says current president Herbert DeCosta. "We are certainly not a burial society anymore." He adds, "There is a great tradition that may soon pass and our culture will be worse off for it. This is some of our history that is worth preserving."

Humane Brotherhood

A rival organization to the Brown Fellowship Society, called the Humane Brotherhood, organized in Charleston, South Carolina, in 1843. The Humane Brotherhood had forty-two members consisting exclusively of blacks and mulattos and listed, as was the system at the Brown Fellowship Society, by certain specific data. Members of these two organizations were traced in the 1850 and 1860 federal manuscript census for Charleston, the 1848 city census, city directories, and the 1859 and 1860 city taxpayer rolls. The sources yielded date and age, occupation, value of real estate, slave holdings, place of birth, and complexion. Such information makes possible comparisons between the two associations within Charleston's broader free African American population.

The Humane Brotherhood's preamble explained its purpose as "alleviating the couch of pain, and helping a brother when distressed." It further resolved "That we, free dark men of the City of Charleston, do form ourselves into a compact body for the purpose of alleviating each other in sickness and death." The death benefit to a deceased member's family was twelve dollars for a decent burial—Brown Fellowship provided sixty dollars for widows. Surviving members had to wear a mourning cloth for thirty days. Widows could collect a twelve-dollar annuity, while orphans were to be supported and educated until they were ready to take up a trade under apprenticeship to a Humane Brotherhood craftsman.

The Brown Fellowship Society and the Humane Brotherhood each maintained burial plots on Charleston's Pitt Street, adjoining each other but separated by a fence. Brown's burial plot operation was more extensive; they provided services for subscribers who did not belong to the organization.

According to the commemorative booklet honoring their 200th anniversary celebration, major differences between the two associations, in addition to complexion, wealth, and slaveholding, were age and occupation. Humane Brotherhood members were 12.9 years younger than their Brown counterparts. Their mean age in 1850 was 33.6 years, as opposed to 46.5 years for the Brown Fellowship. On the whole, Humane Brotherhood men were artisans in the employ of others; the fact that most Brown Fellowship men were shopkeepers and small businessmen helps to explain their greater wealth.

Though no one is able to say so with complete certainty, surviving members of other South Carolina societies and lodges believe that the Humane Brotherhood no longer exists.

The Bury League

In *The Book of Negro Folklore*, edited by Langston Hughes and Arna Bontemps, Julie Peterkin describes the Bury League as a cooperative society that grew out of the Negro's sincere desire for an elaborate and respectful funeral. Every neighborhood had a local chapter headed by a "Noble Shepherd," and the members paid a small sum each week to a common fund that provided enough funds for the next funeral. The Noble Shepherd kept the "treasury," a black tin box with a lock and key; once a month, when the treasury was heavy with dues, he took it over the river and emptied it into the hands of the Leader of the Flock, who owned and drove the automobile hearse and provided fine, store-bought coffins and white stones to stand at the head of the graves.

Bury League members, Peterkin explained, are required to attend every burial unless hindered by providence. They all wear white gloves, the women carry white paper flowers, and the Leagues' officers, who carry the banners of the organization, wear large badges.

The Leagues' moderate dues must be paid promptly, and every member must visit the sick and take presents of money or food. To fail in the least of these obligations means expulsion from the league, but nobody fails. The reward for complying is a fine coffin, a journey to the grave in the automobile hearse, and a tombstone.

Before the Bury League was organized, coffins were simple pine boxes made by the plantation carpenter and hearses were farm wagons drawn by mules. Nobody was buried before the sun had "set in the grave" to make it sweet for the last long sleep. The services were long, with much mourning and praying and singing, and fat lightwood torches provided visibility for the burial and the march round and round the grave.

All this has changed with time: The Bury League's membership is now large and the hearse has to travel all over the country. Some roads are rough, the hearse sometimes refuses to run, and it has taken as many as three people to their graves in one day. There no longer the time to wait on the setting sun; people now have to trust in Jesus to make their graves sweet and restful. Times have indeed now changed, but change has been for the better, for poor people used to have a much harder burden to bear when death took those dear to them.

The members of the Bury League are not alone in their attitude toward death. Most people crave a proper burial, and pride often plays a part in making funerals so expensive that families are left with uncomfortable debts. Unscrupulous undertakers of all races have made fortunes out of the feelings surrounding death that attend every human creature.

Peterkin continues her delightful story, combining the frivolity of a spirited imagination with reality. She explains that the Negroes delight in making a good appearance before their fellows, but when death takes one of them, their pride is accompanied with fear that their failure to give the departed a proper burial will result in disaster for the lonely spirit on its way to a final home. This fear is probably a lineal descendant of the old African belief that without proper rites for its protection a soul may be hindered by other spirits from finding its destination and become a pitiful wanderer on the face of the earth. A proper funeral ceremony is believed to be of great help in enabling a soul to find the right road, either to heaven and God, or to hell and Satan. Otherwise, the spirit of the deceased will haunt houses, burial grounds, and lonely roads, thereby frightening the very people it loved best on earth.

As a rule, spirits resemble the bodies they occupied in life. The most unfortunate ones become plat-eyes and change quickly from one shape to

LAY DOWN BODY

another: Now a dog, then a horse, a man without a head, a warm cloud, or a hot smoke that suffocates all living creatures. "Plat-eyes" fear nothing and stop at nothing. Wise people and beasts flee from them, for "a coward never totes broke bones."

People with vivid imaginations are often terrified by apparitions that walk at night when the moon is young. The vicinity of cemeteries is carefully avoided after dark and so are places where people have met with fatal misfortune. Animals have "second sight" and can see spirits, but only people born with cauls over their faces have this keen vision.

One particular story has been handed down from among the members of the Bury League. While it has varied in content through the retelling, the tale's sense of fun heavily salted with superstition remains the same in Peterkin's rendition:

One Saturday evening a plantation mother who had second sight sent her two small sons on a trustworthy mule to the crossroads store to fetch home the week's supply of groceries. She warned the boys to hurry home before sundown, since a young moon was due to shine and set spirits to walking all over the country. The boys put the paper bags of rice, sugar, white flour and coffee all together in a large crocus sack so that none would be dropped on the way home.

The lonely road ran through thick woods that looked scary, but the mule walked along quietly until the sun dropped and a young moon [shone] in the sky. Then he began to back his ears and switch his tail. Just as they came in sight of the spot where a man had been mysteriously killed years ago, the mule stopped short in his tracks and would not budge. At first the boys thought he was being contrary, so the older one got a stick and frailed his sides, then beat him on the head, but the beast only rolled his eyes and snorted like he smelt something dangerous. They did not know what to make of such carrying on until a warm gust of air passed over their faces and a small white cloud floated across the road right in front of their eyes.

The hair on their heads stood up and pushed off their hats, for the cloud smelled like smoke from burning sulfur. The mule shivered and leaped backward with hoarse hee-haws, and tried his best to talk. The boys fell off his back and the groceries tumbled into the road. They did not tarry to pick up the groceries or hats but scrambled onto the mule's back just as he struck out for home. He had always been too lame and broken-winded to go faster than a walk, but he galloped like a colt until he reached home, then he fell down flat in the yard where he laid all night gasping for breath.

The mother did what she could to comfort him, then she thanked God on her knees that the poor beast had sense like people and brought her sons home safe instead of letting them be smothered by death by the evil-smelling cloud. It was undoubtedly the spirit of the man who had been secretly killed years ago. His strange end was due to turn him into the most dangerous of all ghostly things, a plat-eye.

The groceries and hats stayed where they fell until the sun shone the next morning, for spirits of all kinds, even plat-eyes and hags, dread sunlight and hide in [the shadows] until first dark comes. The incident furnished the preacher with a subject for his sermon the next Sunday. He explained that if the dead man had been given a proper burial, instead of being hurried into the ground with not even a church deacon to pray over his body, he might have been a harmless "ha'nt" instead of a plat-eye which changes from one ugly thing to another as it strives to harm innocent people.

The moral: The dead are helped by thoughtfulness just as the living are, and the very poorest people must struggle to pay insurance dues to the Bury League, not only for themselves but for every member of their families. This, then, is the message: the payment of dues is important. The power and fright-value of the story is forceful, and it remains an interesting tale. Another story that has been told:

[A] black father came to get the plantation carpenter to make a box for his dead baby. He was pitifully grief-stricken because the child had not been "insured" in the Bury League, and since he lacked money to buy a nice coffin the baby was condemned to be laid away in a simple box of pine boards. As he helped to saw the short lengths and plane them smooth, he sobbed over his "bad mistake" that kept the child from being put away right.

The carpenter tried to console him, for the child was too young to have sinned and was bound to reach heaven; death levels everything and makes a home-made pine box as soft a bed as a Bury League coffin. The father shook his head and sobbed as he explained that he and his wife and every other child in his house were Bury League members. Times were so hard and money so scarce, it pinched him to pay all their dues, but he did it. This baby was so healthy he never thought it would sicken and die. It was his only boy child, too, the flower of his flock, the child he ever loved best. Nobody ever saw a finer little boy child or one so smart for its age.

The mother took more pains with him than any child she ever birthed. Three or four times every day she left her work in the field and went home to suckle him. And now, this failure to provide a proper burial would work the child heavy harm. No common sickness killed him, for he was ailing only one day and night.

Some people thought the mother was to blame because she would not wean him when she started breeding again. Others thought maybe her breast milk was too hot or poisoned with weariness from hoeing grass so long in the sun. That could not be so. The mother was an able woman and never minded sun-hot or hard work when she was carrying a new child. Evil spirits must have killed the little boy child, for they saw how his parents loved him more than the little gal-children. They loved him more than life itself, and now their hearts were pure broken because he was dead and would be buried in a home-made box.

The mother believed some jealous-hearted woman with no child to equal him had put a "black hand" on him. A strong healthy child would not die so quick unless somebody cast a spell on him or a spirit tricked him into leaving this world. It was hard to think anybody could be mean enough to do such a damage to an innocent little baby, but evil spirits are all over the land. They know everything about everybody, and they pleasure themselves with causing sorrow.

Tears leaped out of the father's eyes as he lifted the little pine box and put it on his head to take home. Its small weight was slight for his strength, but his broad shoulders dropped and his feet stumbled along the smooth path as if they bore a heavy burden. The carpenter groaned with pity as the short, narrow box balanced on the father's head made a stark pattern against the sunset sky. Then he set about boiling water to scald the tools that had cut and nailed together the little coffin boards.

This Peterkin story is sad and mournful, but like her next story, it mixes reality with a logical imagination:

The earth from which people spring clings to their feet no matter where they go, and will try to fetch them back home. The Negroes delight in taking journeys, but a dread of being sent home "cold in a

The Cemetery As a Spiritual Symbol

As seen across the rural areas that have traditionally supported an African American population, the cemetery is very special. Not only is it the realm of the deceased, but it is also where we find the strongest material demonstration of African-inspired memories. In earlier times, the attitudes and practices manifested by African Americans derived from their belief that the deceased could, in some way, affect the lives of families and friends still living. Because of this, it has always been important to take care in the planning of the funeral and the burial.

Strong feelings about the last rites led to the formation of many of the burial societies. Burial insurance was usually the first to be taken out and the last to be relinquished when times grew hard. It was considered more important by the very poor than sickness and accident insurance.

The book *Afro-American Tradition in Decorative Arts*, a publication of the Cleveland Museum of Art, points out that "a proper funeral must be conducted with decorum and respect. The deceased must be honored and his remains treated with dignity and reverence. To encounter Afro-American graveyard decoration is to witness a physical manifestation of strong religious belief. The cemetery gives us a glimpse of the spiritual force that has ever been the source of hope and inspiration for black America."

box" often keeps them from tarrying long when they go away. When a message came from a town some miles away saying "Diana dead. No insurance. Promised to send her home," everybody cheerfully contributed something to bring Diana's body home "right." The next day a fine hearse and automobiles filled with Diana's friends made a long funeral procession that moved toward the river bridge which marks the town's limit. The elegant vehicles halted at the bridge, where they were met by a pitiful line of wagons and carts drawn by mules and oxen. Diana's body in a fine coffin was taken out of the hearse and put in one rickety wagon. The mourners got out of the automobiles and climbed into broken-down wagons and carts. The humble procession went slowly across the bridge and followed the highway until it reached the narrow winding road which led to the country graveyard where Diana wanted to lie.

These simple people could not afford the hearse and automobiles for the whole journey, but they had done the best they could to give Diana's soul a good start on the way to its eternal home.

When the original graveyard became full another one had to be started, which upset the members of the Bury League terribly. There is a powerful superstition that the first person buried in a graveyard never rests easy. Peterkin again lets the reader enjoy the make-believe aspects of her stories while still providing thought-provoking innuendo. Superstitions here are not trivial beliefs to be disregarded or laughed away; this one involves everybody's peace of mind.

Nobody knows what would have happened if an old woman who was respected by everybody in the community had not come forward and said that she was willing to lie first in the new graveyard. She had thought the matter over. She knew her time on this earth was almost out, for lately, one rainy day she was walking home and her dead husband came and held an umbrella over her. It meant he wanted her to come with him. She would trust the master to take care of her. He knew she had tried to live a good life and would see to it that her last long sleep would not be restless.

[The old woman] had never joined the Bury League or accepted changes that crept into the plantation. Her old baptizing robe, made when she was baptized many years ago, had been put away carefully in her trunk to serve as her shroud. Time had yellowed and weakened the cloth, so it was hardly fit to serve as a pattern, but she bought new white cloth, and asked a "seamster" to make a robe exactly like it. When the shroud was made and pressed with a "laying-out head rag" to match it, she bought a pair of white gloves and new shoes to wear with them. She examined them all carefully, then put them in the trunk to wait. "I'm all ready for de journey now," she said with a gentle smile.

LAY DOWN BODY

She talked of this journey as if she were going home to live forever, not only with God and Jesus and the angels, but with her father and mother and husband and the children who had gone on before. All her treasures were kept in the trunk where the shroud was laid. She took them out and gave all away except a pretty blue china mug wrapped in a clean white cloth. This was to be kept until a white lad whom she had nursed and tried to teach and train should marry and have a son. The mug had been saved for the little boy child she had hoped to nurse like his father and grandfather before him.

As she unwrapped it her mind went away back into the gentle past, and she told how, forty years ago, when she was a middle-aged woman, a group of Polish people came to the neighborhood to farm. Only one was a woman and she had children, one of whom was a beautiful, red-cheeked blue-eyed girl child. Soon after they came, the girl child sickened and died. The mother mourned in a strange language, but her grief was something any mother could understand. She refused to have the child buried in the white people's graveyard, but laid her away in a shady spot on the edge of the woods near a little waterfall that made music day and night. [Only a] lonesome grave told where the child had so loved to wade in the clear water, and gather pebbles and pick white violets that bloomed along the banks. The poor woman would not believe [it when she discovered that] the stream had stolen the child's spirit although it was plain enough to everybody else.

The child's death made the Polish people unhappy there and they decided to go away. When the mother said good-bye she left the china mug for a keepsake. It had been a parting gift to the little dead girl from an old grandmother in Poland. The old trunk had held it for over forty years, and now it must be kept for the white lad's first boy child or for his first grandboy in case he got only girl children. No girl child must ever own it, for it brought bad luck to one and it might do the same thing again.

Trees and bushes hid the little Polish girl's grave long ago, but sometimes when a thin young moon shows in the west her singing can be heard above the music of the water, and the words of her song are strange, same like those of her mother.

When [her memory of the] story of the cup ended, the old woman slowly wrapped it up again, as she added, "When I first thought on leavin' dis world, one mind told me to stay until Christmas when my white baby will come home from school; but my other mind said I better go spend Christmas in heaven wid my own li'l chillen. Maybe li'l chillen don' grown up in heaven, but my white baby is done tall, like a man. I would like to look in his blue eyes one more time. I ever dream 'bout em same like I dream 'bout de chillen I birthed my own self. I won' forget em when I get up yonder. I'll pray for em same like I pray for em here, Gawd bless em." It was useless to argue with her about staying until her white baby came home. Her mind was made up.

Her last request was, "After I'm laid out do watch my eyes so dey won' crack open an' scare de li'l chillen what comes to look a last look on my face." She refused to eat and drank only enough water to wet her dry lips, but she reached heaven in time for Christmas. Her burial was one of the greatest celebrations the plantation has ever known. She was not a Bury League member, but the Bury League hearse brought her coffin, and the Bury League members marched behind it carrying banners and white paper flowers. The sun set in her grave to make it sweet, and pine torches made light to fill the dirt in. When the low mound of earth was smoothed and the Bury League white paper flowers laid on it, things she prized on earth were put with them: a clock that had not ticked for many years, the cup and saucer she used, a glass lamp filled with kerosene, and a china vase holding fresh blossoms from those growing around her doorstep.

When the funeral sermon was preached, some months later, the church could not hold the congregation. Windows and doors were crowded with people who strained their ears to hear the preacher describe the welcome she received from God and Jesus, her parents and friends, her husband and children, when the angels flew through heaven's gate with her soul. People rocked their bodies from side to side and hummed the tune of "I'm gwine home to die no more" while the preacher told how she walked on golden streets, and flew down the sky on her strong white wings to watch over those she loved on earth.

Funeral sermons are never preached at a burial, but, rather, afterward at church on a following Sunday. The sermon tells with utter frankness whether the deceased is happy in heaven or wretched in hell, or driven by pains far worse than torment to roam through the air, without rest or peace day or night. Peterkin ends her description of the Bury League with a gentle finale, a striking description:

> The old graveyard, unused and deserted, waits for Judgment Day on the edge of a hill that drops to the river with a steep fall called "Lover's Leap." Below it lie untamed miles of swamp where the river bends into Devil's Elbow, or swollen by rains, makes a vast yellow lake that uproots and drowns the swamp's undergrowth. Yellow stains high on the trunks of tall trees mark the height of its flood long after it has passed. But no flood can reach the old graveyard.
>
> Spring shows early in the tender, misty green of willows that mark the river channel where strong roots clutch swamp mud and strive to hold the unruly stream to its rightful road. Maples flame scarlet, poplars make bright yellow splashes, wood duck quack gaily, turkey hens call gobblers who deserted them and their children in the fall to gang

LAY DOWN BODY

together all winter like carefree bachelors. Then the old graves sunken with waiting so long for Gabriel to blow his trumpet and clothe old bones with living flesh are sprinkled with blue violets; tangles of yellow jessamine drop golden bells and crab apple thickets send down showers of fragrant pink petals to lie among carved wooden heads of wheat placed on some of the graves long ago. Nobody knows who carved them or why the wood lasts so long, but everybody knows they are symbols of eternal life carved by somebody who believed that some day "The trumpet shall sound and the dead shall be raised incorruptible . . . and this mortal must put on immortality."

Sea Island resident Billie Burn writes about the three secret lodges or orders on Daufuskie Island, South Carolina. They included the Oyster Union Society, the Knights of Pythias "Pity," and the Odd Fellows. The Oyster Union Society was begun in October of 1919 to financially benefit the oyster gatherers and shuckers when they became sick or disabled and couldn't work. The Knights of Pythias was begun in 1916 and ended circa 1934. The Odd Fellows started in 1927 and ended about three years later.

Once these organizations were established, reports Burn, meetings were held once a month in the Maryfield Praise House on the grounds of the First Union African Baptist Church. Dues were one dollar per month. Soon the members bought a vacant two-story building known as the "Hall" and the meetings were held there. The Oyster Society always met downstairs—they had women members who dared not go upstairs where the other orders, who had no female members, tended towards the boisterous.

The members of all the orders would have parties and sell shrimp, crabs, and have oyster roasts—anything to make money to help with the expenses of illness, including medicine, doctor bills, and, should the worst happen, to aid the family should there be a funeral.

The Oyster Society outlasted the other two. With its members gradually dying through the years, there were so few members by 1980 that the society was finally abolished. The treasury money was divided equally among those who were still living; the hall and the land were sold in 1981.

The Knights of the Wise Men Lodge

"The Knights of the Wise Men Lodge," a paper prepared by Laura Hansen for the Sea Island Preservation Project at Penn Center, provides a comprehensive look at this fraternal order, organized in 1870. Provided with financial and farming assistance, lodge members also enjoyed social functions and fellowship in addition to fulfilling their mission to establish a common treasury. Between 1870 and 1930 more than thirty other such benevolent societies were formed on St. Helena

Island. Today, only the Knights of the Wise Men Lodge, Ladies Union, and Rome of Victory Society continue to function as burial aid societies. The following is taken from Hansen's treatise:

> During the reconstruction era (1863–1877), burial-aid societies flourished in African American communities and were an essential aspect of [black] life well into the twentieth century. By the 1930s there were some thirty-seven burial societies found in the sea islands alone.
>
> In 1889, the Knights of Wise Men purchased a quarter-acre plot on the old Corner Plantation in St. Helena, for eight dollars. Sometime thereafter they built the first of two structures. The first was a two-story frame building.
>
> At its height in the early 1920s, the Knights of Wise Men Lodge had more than 350 members, representing almost every plantation community on St. Helena Island. Many of the communities had burial aid societies of their own, but the Knights of Wise Men's prominent location at the Corner gave it a special prestige. Located at the intersection of Highway 21 and Lands End Road Drive (historically Church Road, and now known as Martin Luther King Drive) and in close proximity to Penn Center, the Corner Community has been the commercial center of St. Helena since at least the 1860s. Most shopping was done here, and a number of other transactions such as public record keeping and loans and credit activity, took place here as well.
>
> The lodge building is situated at the rear of the Green (now known as the King Park), the traditional gathering place for island-wide celebrations. Around 1940, the wood building burned and was replaced shortly thereafter by a concrete block structure. Members were "taxed" to provide the building fund, and local bricklayers were hired to construct the new hall in similar fashion to the first one. The major design change was to place the stair to the second story on the outside and at the rear of the building to allow members to come and go without intruding on the first floor tenants.
>
> Following the 1940 hurricane, in which many Island buildings were heavily damaged, other societies and lodges used the Knights of Wise Men hall for their meetings while waiting on repairs. Like most burial aid societies, the Knights of Wide Men exemplified the cooperative ideal. Members paid monthly dues for which they were assured a substantial use of their money for their funeral and family. In the early years, this money was usually more than enough to cover burial expenses. Dues were twenty-five cents per month for most of the first part of the century. In recent years, they have increased to $1.25. The death assessment in the early years was one dollar; today it is four dollars. It was optional for members to purchase stock in the lodge. The lodge's stock certificate is printed on an elaborate and beautifully rendered full-color image of the Biblical wise men. At the time of this certificate, circa the 1930s, a share of stock sold for $5. Upon a member's

This historic building,
belonging to the Knights
of the Wise Men Lodge,
is no longer in use.

death, his family was paid the full value of his stock. During the past twenty years or so, the Knights of Wise Men have organized excursions to raise funds, primarily for building maintenance, expenses, and taxes. These events included oyster roasts on the Green and bus trips to Myrtle Beach. . . .

Lodge brothers would deliver and administer medicine, and they would take a member to the Savannah hospital by boat if necessary. All the while, they would see that the farm and household chores, like chopping wood and caring for animals, were maintained. All of this was carefully organized. The lodge's plantation committees would make assignments when "one of theirs" was sick. Two at a time, the members would sit with the patient. Each night two more would come to serve. The rotation would move from plantation to plantation and would start over again if the illness continued for that long.

The Knights of Wise Men were leaders in the islanders' eyes. Perhaps the most prominent resident of St. Helena, Dr. Y. W. Bailey, was the lodge's treasurer for many years, until his blindness in the 1950s. A native of St. Helena, Dr. Bailey was the area's first black doctor, and the island's only doctor for much of the twentieth century. He is fondly remembered as a doctor and as an officer of the Knights of Wise Men. Officers often served for many years, as long as they were serving the lodge well in the eyes of the other members. Appointment to membership in this lodge, like most, came through member recommendation. They were the "wise men." While the origin of the lodge's formal name is unknown, one long-time member likens it to the wise men seeking for Jesus Christ, and the stock certificate image would support this.

Ceremony was a fundamental component of the burial aid societies' organization. Their meetings were formal and standardized, as was their role at members' funerals and the annual "turning out." Monthly meetings were held every second Friday at the lodge hall, presided over by the Arckon, or president, who used a gavel to call the meetings to order and to keep order throughout the proceedings (unruly behavior was subject to fine). The room was arranged like a church with the president facing rows of wooden benches; the secretary and treasurer sat to his side, much like deacons in a church. During the 1920s and 1930s there were usually thirty to forty members in attendance. The opening prayer was offered by the chaplain, and was followed by the lodge song, "Blessed Be the Name of the Lord," kept in its own separate book. Business was conducted regarding recruitment, building mainte-nance, etc.; dues were collected (monies were kept in a bank in Beaufort); and reports on sick or distressed members were made by the plantation committees. If new members were being inducted, a secret initiation ritual involving stations was performed. Throughout the meeting a doorkeeper admitted latecomers only if they knew the secret rap. If a death was reported, there was a death assessment, and plans were made for the attendance at the funeral.

The Knights of Wise Men would often meet at their lodge hall prior to a funeral service. In their required dress—black trousers, jacket, tie and shoes, ceremonial hat, and special Lodge badge worn with the black side forward—they would march as a group to the church. There they performed their funeral rites, including songs and a speech on the member's character as a brother in the lodge. At the burial site, the Knights of Wise Men would file by the grave, each dropping a palm leaf or flower onto the coffin. They occasionally acted as pall bearers or helped make the coffin. There was a moment when the Knights of Wise Men would announce to the family the amount of money they would receive from the lodge, and a promise was made that within sixty days, the Knights would deliver that sum. The president and pos-sibly other officers would later call on the family to deliver the money. Attendance at funerals was mandatory, and absence was subject to a fine of up to $5.

L A Y   D O W N   B O D Y

The ceremony and ritual was in part imitative of organizations of European origin, such as the Masons and other guilds. The Masons and the Odd Fellows were the oldest black fraternal orders. Organized by free blacks in Boston and New York, respectively, these organizations were chartered directly from Europe after rejection by the American white orders. They thrived in northern cities, and even established lodges in a few Southern ones. Free southern blacks during the antebellum period also organized a number of mutual benefit societies, which were less ritualistic than the orders, and were instead specifically concerned with fulfilling "their obligations to the deceased...and to assure their own avoidance of a pauper's burial or, worse, disposal of their body to a medical school."

The legacy of the sea islands burial aid societies is an intangible system of values—values of individual and community responsibility, cooperative welfare, and dignity in life and death. For the Knights of Wise Men, this legacy is also a collective memory of the hundreds of community leaders who were members through the years, which is embodied in the tangible artifact of its lodge hall. Since 1889 the hall, first the frame building and then the block one, has been a central component of St. Helena life. It stands as quiet testimony to the actions of the Knights of Wise Men and the values they represent. The Knights of Wise Men Lodge has plans to dissolve, as its membership continues to dwindle. The count now is about fifteen to twenty men. They meet only occasionally, at Scott Community Hall. They also own property in the area. Theirs is a wonderful history, a great tradition, that is no longer viable in today's fast paced, unstructured society. The Knights of Wise Men will not be forgotten as they take their place in the annals of history. The hall, however, could continue to function as an active and vital component of community life at the Corner. Its reuse would be a most appropriate example of cultural continuity in the face of inevitable change.

In the northern United States, burial societies and lodges began to lose their role to churches in the decades following the 1830s. Because of slavery and the suppression of many mainstream black churches in the South, however, this same evolution took place at a much slower pace; southern burial societies were still active up until the Civil War. As the year 2000 approaches, the few remaining burial societies and lodges are approaching extinction.

Harry Mack, a current member of both the Knights of the Wise Men Lodge and the Young Men's Social Club—two societies on South Carolina's St. Helena Island that now barely function—believes that these organizations now function more like social clubs, places where an aging membership can go to reminisce and keep the traditions of oral history alive. For amateur genealogists seeking to trace a family tree or burial sight, Mack admits that the burial societies of today would probably be of little use.

In the South at least, few written detailed records of such societies and lodges have survived. There is at least one exception. The Brown Fellowship,

The History of Dissolved Lodges

During the early days of burial lodges, several traditions were common to such organizations. During a funeral procession, for example, the society's members walked behind the body of the deceased, which was carried by an oxen cart or mule- or horse-drawn wagon, singing and waving green branches on their way to the graveyard.

The lodges were established for many purposes, such as caring for sick and disabled members; relieving other family members by sitting up all night with a sick member; distributing monetary benefits to cover the costs of burying the deceased; cooking, washing, and cleaning the house; and harvesting any crops in the field during planting season.

Among those lodges since dissolved were **The Women Labor Union**, an all-female labor union established in 1907; **The Blue Mountain Lodge**, whose members were both male and female, which was established in the early 1900s; **Little Supreme**, with both male and female members, established in the early 1900s; **Household of Ruth**, an all-female organization established in the late 1800s; **Oak Tree Lodge**, with both male and female members, established in the 1800s; and **Little Bethlehem**, with both male and female members, established in the late 1800s.

perhaps the best known of all black burial societies, kept detailed minutes of its meetings through the decades. Those minutes are now housed in the archives of the College of Charleston.

Lodge and society members of St. Helena still pay dues, usually less than three dollars per month, and the clubs still pay out a token burial benefit—usually less than $300—but their role as the black community's life-line, insurance company, and social center has long since passed to others. "There are a few of us holding on to these traditions," says Mack. "But with all the facilities—things like hospitals, schools and everything—we can't get new people to join. They don't need us for much."

"We really don't do burials or funerals any more," Mack continues. "Before, many years ago, people needed our help. Now they don't need so much help. Back in the old days, there were no hospitals, not many doctors. There really was no place to go if you got in distress. Things are way different today."

By 1995 the Knights of the Wise Men lodge had fewer than forty members, none younger than age sixty. The lodge usually meets once a month. Club dues are one dollar a month. There is a special $2.50 "debt assessment fee" in the event of a member's passing to cover the club's payment of its standard $150 death benefit.

Ladies Union

The Ladies Union of St. Helena Island remains active as a burial society; dues are still collected monthly. Their creed and their responsibilities remain similar to those of the Knights of Wise Men, with whom they have maintained a good relationship. It is no longer just a women's union, having partially combined with the Young Men's Social Club many years ago. The purpose of these united groups is to pay dues to cover burial expenses, but these days the dues only partially cover the rising costs of a funeral. Still, the Ladies Union and the Young Men's Social Club are probably the most prosperous of South Carolina's surviving burial societies.

Mothers and fathers often enroll their small children in the group and begin to pay their dues. The bookkeeping is done carefully and meticulously. It's estimated that close to two hundred members meet on the first Sunday of every month at their well-kept hall, near the Orange Grove Baptist Church and the Capers Community. When the women have a "turning out"—their term for the club's annual celebration—the men join them, and vice versa. Although men and women meet in the same hall, their activities, except for the turning out, are separate.

"We still visit the sick and we still give people something when they are buried, but it isn't really much," says club member Harry Mack. The standard burial benefit is $250. He says the club's main efforts and much of its resources are aimed at maintaining the hall, which is used for recreation and rented out for special events. "The young just don't want to join us. They just don't care about tradition."

The Ladies Union and the Young Men's Social Club meet at Scott Community Center on St. Helena Island.

Rome of Victory Society

The Rome of Victory Society at 21 Seaside Road, St. Helena Island, was founded in 1896 by Elizabeth Richardson, a local resident and landowner. The society, originally set up to assist families with burial arrangements and to attend to the sick and needy, boasted more than three hundred members at its peak, but by 1995 membership had dwindled to less than thirty people, all over the age of sixty.

Surviving members are not sure how the organization came about its name. "Elizabeth Richardson named it and I'm not sure anyone today remembers why," said George Austin, a member of the society who was signed up by his mother right after his birth in 1910. "I guess it had to have a name and that name was as good as any other."

Austin said the Rome of Victory Society has had no new members in years and now faces bankruptcy. Dues are $1.50 per month. Members still meet every other month but do little charity work. "We still take care of the sick, but we can't do as much as we used to. There isn't the money or the people," said Austin. The society continues to contribute money toward the burial expenses of members. The standard payout is $150, down from $200 just a few years ago.

Like other burial societies on St. Helena, the Rome of Victory Society owns a lovely building in the Cuffy community that is used for meetings and is rented out occasionally for church services and fund-raising dinners. "This society is dying out and I don't see how it can survive for much longer," said Austin. "Young people are not interested. They are out in the world now. Some don't even care about going to church."

L A Y   D O W N   B O D Y

FUNERAL AND BURIAL CUSTOMS: TRENDS FOR A NEW TOMORROW

WE ARE SO FOOLISH ABOUT DEATH. WE WILL NOT LEARN

HOW IT IS WAGES PAID TO THOSE WHO EARN,

HOW IT IS GIFT FOR WHICH ON EARTH WE YEARN

TO BE SET FREE FROM BONDAGE TO THE FLESH;

HOW IT IS WINNING HEAVEN'S ETERNAL GAIN.

HOW IT MEANS FREEDOM EVERMORE FROM PAIN,

HOW IT UNTANGLES EVERY MORTAL MESH

WE FORGET THAT IT MEANS ONLY LIFE—

LIFE WITH ALL JOY, PEACE, REST AND GLORY RIFE,

THE VICTORY WON AND ENDED ALL THE STRIFE.

—AUTHOR UNKNOWN

Social customs and cultural attitudes toward death continue to evolve, even in our more enlightened, less superstitious age. Three significant issues—cultural, environmental, and business concerns—affect the day-to-day and long-term operations of burial grounds in particular. This chapter will examine how each of these concerns influences private, municipal, and national cemeteries.

Cultural concerns have had a significant effect upon burial practices and procedures since the pre–Civil War days. The range of customs and traditions is wide, varying from region to region and culture to culture. Traditions that have become established have sprung from the local residents' strong ethnic heritage, the result of nature's impact on the surrounding landscape, or reactions to changing attitudes over time. In addition, several traditions were born of practicality; the lack of technical expertise in earlier times left little chance for experimentation and progress in the operation of cemeteries.

Environmental concerns, likewise, have had a significant impact on the entire field of burial ground management, especially in the areas of cemetery properties and procedures. There was little genuine awareness in earlier times of the destructive forces now known to cause decay and deterioration. In time, however, cemeteries have become much more alert to the impact of the environment and have put in operation various methods of defense.

Business concerns have ranged from becoming more financially savvy to, in essence, going into the "death care business." In fact, in some instances small "corner" establishments have grown to become major industries within this modern-day milieu. Many small and independent cemeteries remain intact, however, and have no interest in becoming a part of a mega-company operation.

Municipal cemeteries remain viable alternatives to privately owned cemeteries. There is no sign, however, of a surge in activity to promote these many city-owned cemeteries. Although they are viewed as potentially viable business ventures, such burial grounds encounter many of the same problems as the privately owned cemeteries.

The national cemetery system has plans to expand, however, and several new properties are on the drawing board. In spite of the increased number of cemeteries in the system—from 103 in the 1970s to more than 114 in the 1990s—many of them are now closed for interments because of the lack of space. For some who already have family burial sites, second interments in single graves or cremation of remains may be all that can be accommodated.

As with any other business, today's cemeteries must also offer security. To that end, some have installed high-tech security systems designed to shield the property from unwanted intruders and would-be vandals. While some perpetrators target specific cemeteries or grave sites, most do only random destruction; African American cemeteries, as a whole, have not been targeted as a specific group.

Both municipal and national cemeteries are currently being presented with interesting challenges. Although municipal cemeteries show a slow, steady growth, the national cemetery system has found itself faced with an almost constant need for expansion. Many more families of veterans now select national cemeteries over local burial grounds because of the increased knowledge and understanding of the system and its benefits and provisions.

L A Y   D O W N   B O D Y

In the twenty-first century, writes William H. Whyte in *Cemetery Management* magazine, one characteristic of the American marketplace will be diversity. One way the industry can meet this changing marketplace across the United States will be to offer a broader product line, contends Whyte, who also predicts that the area where change will be most dramatic will be cremation. As recently as 1970, most cemeteries did not need to offer specialized inventory for those selecting cremation. However, cemetery managers are urged to continually reexamine such policies and practices and to keep in mind the cemetery's heritage.

Cultural Concerns

Dubbed by journalist Maria Dickerson as the "Culture of Death," people-oriented concerns are important both to those in the cemetery business and those involved in auxiliary services to the industry. Dickerson, writing in the *Detroit News,* finds sharp contrasts between the death rituals of the past and modern-day practices. Death rituals continually evolve and serve as a mirror of societal changes, as a look into the past will illustrate.

Mourning periods of a year, sometimes two, were routine up into the nineteenth century. Death was so frequent among early colonists that it was planned for far in advance. Upon the birth of a child, many families put away a cask of wine to be used for the offspring's wedding or funeral—whichever came first. And the early European custom of giving small mementos of the deceased to mourners was transplanted to the New World, where it quickly took root and grew out of control. Some eighteenth-century families nearly spent themselves into the poorhouse, passing out jewelry, scarves, gloves, books, and other gifts to mourners, while widows were literally eaten out of house and home by ravenous relatives.

PREPARING THE DEAD

The bodies of the deceased were almost always prepared at home, where young children could be exposed to the sobering influence of death. Adolescents served as pallbearers for their peers well into the early part of the twentieth century. Children who died of infectious disease were sometimes held up to the nursery window so playmates could say good-bye.

The old custom of watching over the body of a loved one from death until burial was not only a spiritual vigil but a practical one as well, since the "deceased" weren't always dead. Colonial annals are peppered with anecdotes of comatose "corpses" who revived before they were buried. This vigil was known in many cultures as a "wake," a term that is thought to have derived from a Celtic word meaning "the watching."

Offerings to the Dead

The mode of decoration used in African American graveyards is so different from what is commonly expected in a cemetery that the graveyard may not be recognized for what it is. A report of the Institute of Archeology and Anthropology at the University of South Carolina included the following evaluation: "A man was dispatched to check out the area (Charlestowne Landing) and he returned reporting that there didn't appear to be anything there other than some late nineteenth-century and twentieth-century junk scattered throughout the area."

Writing off the area turned out to be an unwise decision. What the man viewed as "junk" turned out to be an important black graveyard site with a wide variety of offerings. Far from being heaps of garbage, funeral offerings are sanctified testimonies; material messages of the living intended to placate the potential fury of the deceased.

Preserving the bodies of the deceased, whether for sanitation, viewing, or religious purposes, has preoccupied humankind since ancient times. The first American settlers generally buried their dead quickly, thus avoiding the need for preservation. But because relatives sometimes had to travel long distances to attend funerals, early colonists also experimented with several crude methods of embalming, according to the *History of American Funeral Directing,* a seminal work on U.S. death history. Those techniques included disemboweling the corpse and filling the body cavity with charcoal, immersing the body in alcohol, or wrapping the deceased in a cloth soaked with alum. The tidier, simpler principal of refrigeration supplanted these methods once ice could be manufactured with ease. "Cooling boards" and coffins with special ice cavities became the standard until well into the mid-nineteenth century, even as medical pathologists were making great advances in chemical embalming. Then came the Civil War, which changed everything as both North and South had to face death on a massive scale. The process of transporting the bodies of soldiers fallen in battle long distances back to their homes and loved ones spurred the demand for chemical embalming. The battlegrounds of Manassas, Shiloh, Antietam, and Gettysburg were, in effect, the birthplace of modern mortuary science.

The Civil War gave Thomas Holmes, the "Father of American Embalming," the opening he was looking for to introduce safe, sanitary chemical embalming. Unfortunately, Holmes's breakthrough spawned a flurry of fast-buck artists and charlatans. Civil War chronicler Francis Lord once commented that Washington, D.C., was plastered with "ghastly advertisements of embalmers" who flocked to the battlefields distributing handbills like expectant vultures. One shameless entrepreneur erected billboards along the route used by soldiers marching to the front. "When a staff member pointed out their demoralizing influence, General Butler ordered the embalmer to desist from this method of advertising," Lord wrote.

Some seemingly modern twists in death rituals are really just updated versions of age-old customs. The lavish 1988 send-off for reputed cocaine dealer Richard "Maserati Rick" Carter—who was laid out in a casket outfitted with rubber car tires and a chrome Mercedes-Benz front grill—is not unlike

the ship burials once reserved for ancient Viking warriors. Death historians note the fact that families today still bury their loved ones with religious objects, jewelry, pictures, tools, and sporting equipment—as humankind has done for millennia. In fact, sending a loved one to his final rest without a personal token is considered unusual.

Mourning periods of a year, or even more, were considered routine into the nineteenth century. Widows were expected to don black clothing, wear somber expressions, and shun all social events. It was both a show of respect for their deceased spouse and an acknowledgment to the community that these unattached women stood somewhere outside the normal social milieu in a patriarchal society.

Americans no longer bury the living along with the dead through such prescribed mourning periods. Still, something has been lost in our rush to dispense with the deceased and "get on with our lives," as the 1990s mantra goes. People who mourn excessively today are sent to grief counseling for their "problem." Employer-paid bereavement leave is a few days at most. The radical shift from one year of mourning to one day in the space of only a century makes a statement on the priorities of America's evolving culture.

While our culture's seeming coldness is partly the result of weathering the loss of family and friends to two world wars within our recent past, the changing nature of the funeral industry has also had its effect. Corporations are busy buying up independent funeral homes, cemeteries, and mausoleums, pursuing the standardized, chain-store approach that has worked in everything from muffler repair to fast food. Can undertaking franchises outlets be far behind?

Some death historians worry that the American funeral could become less solemn if corporate culture and death culture ever become synonymous. "Caring for the dead is *the* most sensitive job," Mr. Huntoon, a mortician from Pontiac, Michigan, believes. "Flipping hamburgers and changing oil filters isn't the same as showing empathy for the family, going the extra mile with personal service. . . . If we ever start treating our dead like toxic waste, Lord help us as a society."

Environmental Concerns

Modern-day concerns have shifted in focus from those of centuries, or even decades, past. Today Americans are becoming more aware of the impact of many years of misuse and abuse of natural resources upon our planet. This misuse has taken its toll on the life and survival of many burial grounds. While a concern over industrial pollution wasn't of great significance in small towns and rural areas, natural weathering, neglect, and the encroachment of hungry land developers have been particularly harmful to the traditional cemeteries of the 1800s and early 1900s. These churchyard and neighborhood burial grounds were especially affected by such "elements" when funds to legally protect or routinely clean and maintain the grounds were not forthcoming. This shortage of funds forced a kind of neglect that could not be remedied. Fortunately, these burial grounds were less likely to suffer the vandalization of more urban areas because the entire community had a distinct relationship with the cemetery.

As cities have started assuming more responsibility for their own cemetery properties, and laws and regulations have been enacted to govern them, the large urban cemeteries have been able to provide various degrees of care, many becoming gardens of beauty. However, it is difficult to control troublesome vandalism by gangs and groups that enjoy this kind of destruction of property. In addition, increased industrial pollution causes "fallout" materials that are harmful to markers and stones.

CHEMICAL POLLUTION OF CEMETERIES

Concerns about the environment now reach even beyond the grave and are troubling the cremation and cemetery business, writes Warren E. Leary in the *New York Times:*

> More than 2 million people die each year in the United States. Those responsible for disposing of the remains say their work is increasingly constrained by federal, state and local laws aimed at protecting air, land and water quality.

> Some environmentalists have questioned the industry's effects upon the living, wondering, for example, if buried bodies might contaminate underground water or if cremation could be a source of toxic air pollutants.

> The American Cemetery Association expressed concern: "As an industry, we are concerned because environmental issues generally are the issues of the 1990s. We don't anticipate any serious environmental problems now, but we follow issues such as reauthorization of the Clean Water Act to see if there are any changes that could affect us."

> Because of concern about underground water pollution, questions have been raised about formaldehyde and other chemicals in embalmed bodies seeping into local water tables.

> In addition, blood and other body fluids removed during embalming, which may contain infectious agents or toxic chemicals used to treat cancer and other diseases, are usually flushed into the regular sewer system.

L A Y   D O W N   B O D Y

No one is sure how many cemeteries there are in the nation, but industry estimates put the number between 75,000 and 100,000. These vary in size from small churchyard plots to large military and municipal establishments.

Federal officials have discussed plans to drill in some cemeteries to check water quality, but industry spokesmen said they did not expect any adverse findings.

Most graves are lined with concrete, brick, metal or other materials that should separate caskets from any groundwater in places where it could be a problem. In addition, unpublished findings from test borings done in cemeteries in Canada indicate no groundwater problems.

CEMETERIES AND WATER POLLUTION

The "Washington Report," a recent Canadian report by Stephen Morgan and Robert M. Fells, finds cemeteries don't significantly contribute to water pollution. The Ontario Ministry of the Environment (MOE) published the results of its study, "Cemeteries and Groundwater: An Examination of Potential Contamination of Groundwater by Preservatives Containing Formaldehyde." The MOE's Water Resources Branch conducted a "groundwater renaissance sampling survey" by using six well-sites located downgrade from cemeteries.

Based on a survey of standard burial practices in populated areas of Ontario, it was determined that 90 percent of the human remains in the cemeteries involved in the survey were embalmed and then placed into a casket. "Caskets range from soft to hard woods to steel. Steel caskets are hermetically sealed. The casket may be placed into a concrete vault and sealed with impermeable caulking."

The report is also based upon various calculations, including the following: A quantity of approximately one quart of a two-percent solution of formaldehyde is used in the embalming process; there is a maximum burial density of five hundred bodies per cemetery acre; the six wells tested are located in sandy shallow areas down grade of cemeteries; the wells ranged in depth from 3 to 24 meters (approximately 10 ft. to 79 feet) the burial time ranged from a century to eight years ago; and the distance ranged between 500 and 2,000 meters.

Water samples from the survey sites were analyzed for evidence of formaldehyde, nitrates, and phosphates. The report concluded "that cemeteries are not a significant source of groundwater contamination by formaldehyde. In addition, the calculated loading estimate for formaldehyde and nitrates being released from cemeteries supports a low potential for groundwater contamination."

Harvey Lapin, legal counsel for CANA, writes that the federal Environmental Protection Agency (EPA) is proposing to regulate crematories under the Environmental Protection Laws in an adverse manner. Seven Draft Reports were issued. Crematories are featured in the seven reports. Based on the limited information available, the EPA is proposing that crematories be required to update existing facilities in three stages to house state-of-the-art equipment over the next few years, while also stressing strong combustion and emission controls.

CITIES RUNNING OUT OF BURIAL SPACE

Cemeteries in urban and suburban areas are also experiencing a critical lack of grave space. Burial grounds located in New York and Boston have, for years, warned that the year 2000 will see a complete lack of burial space in these and other cities. Because of increasing land costs and stringent zoning laws, cities cannot continue to set aside large tracts of land for use as cemeteries.

Expected and unexpected solutions to the problem have been voiced. As far back as 1975, D. W. Peabody noted in a *New York Times* article that he thought "the ideal thing would be to bury bodies immediately after death, without embalming them, in places where they could disintegrate naturally, and the elements return to their respective cycles." An architect in New Jersey drew up plans for a cemetery in which coffins and vaults would be eliminated; bodies would be wrapped in shrouds or burial cloths and buried in the earth. The cemetery he envisioned would resemble a park with trees planted as grave markers. "Such a cemetery would never have to expand to make room for more and more concrete burial vaults," he points out. "There would be almost no limit to the number of burials. Human compost, like all other kinds, returns very quickly to life again."

Society's traditional respect for the dead, as well as modern burial practices, would, of course, prevent such pragmatic scenarios from being considered by most tradition-minded people. However, mausoleums are now universally acceptable, as are cremations. But while there is an increasing acceptance of these alternatives, the conventional cemetery remains the prime choice of most Americans. Even though a plot of cemetery land is expensive, as indicated, people are willing to pay the price to be buried in the earth.

ENVIRONMENTAL CHALLENGES AND CREMATION

The problems regarding cremation are slightly different than those of in-ground burials but still of concern to environmentalists. The cremation industry faces its biggest environmental challenge from the passage of state-dictated air quality laws that are tougher than current federal standards. One

man heavily involved in interactions between the state congress and the industry is Bob Wise of West Virginia. California and Florida, states with large death and burial industries because of their large, elderly populations, have the strictest laws affecting crematoriums, explained Wise. "I don't see anything in federal environmental law that will be a big problem for the industry," he predicted, "but state laws will be the most stringent."

A statement by Clean Water Action, a Washington-based environmental, non-profit group, reflects Wise's belief:

Clean Water Action, Greenpeace and other environmental groups raising cautions about emissions from crematorium smokestacks are encouraging tougher monitoring and regulation.

Greenpeace, for instance, has accused medical officials and federal regulators of not keeping close track of people with plutonium-powered heart pacemakers.

If people are cremated with those devices, the groups say, dangerous radioactive particles could be released into the air. . . . [A]lso people are worried that crematorium emissions might contain mercury from dental fillings, toxic heavy metals from cancer chemotherapy and other dangerous substances.

We would encourage states to pass rigorous laws, controlling emissions from crematoriums.

CREMATION AS AN ALTERNATIVE TO BURIAL

Jack Springer, executive director of the Cremation Association of North America (CANA) is familiar with the questions people frequently ask about cremation. Why do people really choose cremation? Answer: "People in this country are dying older. Just a decade ago, 10 percent died over eighty years old; now more than 20 percent of the population dies over eighty. They look at cremation as less expensive," he continues. "They have outlived many of their friends and family. Older people often live far away from where they grew up." Springer believes that cemeteries will become obsolete: Because a casket funeral doesn't hold the same social weight it used to, cremation begins to look simpler and make more sense economically, socially, and ecologically.

This trend is not as evident in African American cemeteries. For example, although several funeral directors in the Metropolitan Detroit area note an increase in families requesting cremation, they maintain that the percentage is minimal. These morticians indicate that a significant number of families with African roots who request cremation after death are also making more frequent visits to their homeland. Included in their wills is often a request to return their ashes to Africa. However, the casket funeral and the ground burial remains far more popular than cremation or the more expensive mausoleum burials.

In her presentation at the seventy-sixth annual CANA convention, Joanne B. Hawkins stated that African Americans have a full-service funeral most of the time. Imbedded in the African American community and reflected in the tradition of Negro spirituals, the focus has always been on the fact that what comes after leaving this earth is superior. Death is an important rite of passage; the funeral rite must contain suitable emotional impact.

Still, some blacks are choosing cremation. African Americans have traditionally sent their loved ones "home" (to where they originally came from) after death. Home could be Louisiana, North Carolina, Georgia, or Montana. There would, of course, be a service wherever the deceased was living at the time of death; then the body would be sent "home" where there would be another service.

Cremation provides a much more efficient and cost-effective manner of sending the person home. Also, in certain cases (as when the cause of death was a disfiguring accident), cremation can be performed with no viewing of the body. A memorial service as elegant and reflective as with a traditional cemetery burial generally follows.

The February 1994 edition of *American Cemetery* magazine included an article by M. R. Sandy, called "Cemetery Geology." In it, Sandy states that cemeteries are a veritable treasure-trove to the geologist—that the history of the earth can be told from a cemetery's monuments and features. Studying Woodland Cemetery in Dayton, Ohio, Sandy discovered that headstones, obelisks, and mausoleums crafted from rock quarried in North America, or in far-off places such as Africa, Asia, and Europe could be found at the site.

Paul Laurence Dunbar (1872–1906), acknowledged as the first black writer to receive international acclaim, is buried in Woodland Cemetery. The cemetery was founded in 1841, and has approximately one hundred thousand monuments covering 247 acres. Sandy describes the markers of Wilbur and Orville Wright, world famous for developing and performing the first powered flight in 1903. Dunbar, he says, was a classmate of Orville Wright in Dayton's Central High School's class of 1890. Dunbar's grave marker is glacial erratic, or "field stone," deposited by melting glacial ice at the end of the Ice Age, approximately 17,000–20,000 years ago. The erratic is granitic in composition, with cross-cutting veins. The author explains that this rock was probably eroded from the Canadian Shield and transported by glacial ice.

THE EMBALMING DISPUTE

The effect of embalming fluids on cemetery soil was, and still is, a topic of major dispute. The following article by Melissa Johnson Williams and John

300

LAY DOWN BODY

L. Konefes, first printed in *American Cemetery* magazine, discusses the environmental aspects of embalming.

Many past practices have come back as problems, including indiscriminate waste disposal, asbestos use, and persistent pesticide use on land and water. In many cases, the "bad" practice was originally done with good intent: waste disposal as an improvement in visible sanitary conditions and removal of hazards, asbestos as a very good fireproof material, and pesticide use to curb damaging insects and weeds.

Even further back in our history, arsenic embalming began as a sanitary practice, and a practical means to preserve the body until burial or for transport. Considering that the alternative was use of ice, arsenic embalming was a significant improvement. What the embalming practitioners, or undertakers, did not consider were the long-term effects of placing significant amounts of arsenic in concentrated burial areas—cemeteries.

Gravestone Group Develops Headstone Database

There are many benefits to computerizing cemetery records. Burial records can be located in seconds on "fields," such as "First name," "Last name," and "Maiden name." A list of Civil War veterans at a given cemetery can be generated in minutes. The location of a gravestone can be found with a simple clacking of a key.

One less obvious benefit is protecting records. It is truly sad when cemetery records have been destroyed in a fire, tornado, or other disaster. This can be avoided by entering records into a computer database and duplicating them on a floppy disk or tape and storing them off site. Genealogists and gravestone researchers have been using computers as a research tool for about a decade. But the exchange of data between researchers has been hampered by a lack of standards for gravestone data bases. The Association for Gravestone Studies (AGS) has been working for about a year to establish a standard database software program for recording gravestone information. . . .

continued on next page

The advent of embalming brought with it a new era in funeral service. Families who once had to bury their loved ones quickly to prevent the spread of disease or before the body started to decompose would now plan funeral services that allowed family members from out of town to attend or to allow the body to be returned home.

Advertisements of this new "process" made a variety of claims—"Bodies embalmed by us never turn black," and "will remove all offensive odors, whiten the body, restore it to a natural sleeplike appearance." The latter was made by Dr. Thomas Holmes, the man considered to be the father of American embalming. He manufactured his own fluid called The Innominata, which proclaimed to be "guaranteed to contain no poison." Nearly 130 years later it would be discovered that his fluid contained a high amount of arsenic.

The search for a formula to preserve the dead human body did not begin in the United States. It is well documented back to early Egypt

continued from previous page

The AGS database standard springs from a research project that began five years ago. The goal of the project is to log data from every gravestone in Rhode Island. Thirty volunteers have been working on this. During its first 200 years, most of Rhode Island's cemeteries were small farm graveyards. Thus, of 3,200 cemeteries in the state, 3,000 are family cemeteries, with four to twenty burials. More than 2,500 are abandoned and overgrown, in the woods and fields, on private and public land. As of May 1995, 260,000 gravestone inscriptions in 2,663 cemeteries had been recorded and entered into the computer database (used by many genealogists at the Rhode Island Historical Society). The AGS database standard allows for entry of all obvious gravestone data: date of death, age, relationships, and location or cause of death. It also contains information like dimensions (height and width); composition (slate, marble, granite); condition (good, fair, poor); shape of top (round, square, fancy); status (upright, down, broken); carving (skull, angel, urn); and legibility (good, fair, poor). (The AGS database contains code letters for these characteristics and will reject invalid codes.)

continued on next page

and proof of its success still exists today. Throughout medical history the need for such a preservative is also well documented. Modern medicine would not be where it is today without dead human bodies to use for anatomical dissection and exploration.

During the course of the American Civil War, Dr. Thomas Holmes was engaged by the medical department of the Union Army to set up battlefield embalming tents to return home the bodies of Union dead. Because of the large and extensive territory of the Civil War, many were trained to carry on the embalming. Holmes provided the fluid which initially "some protégés of Holmes" contended contained arsenic and zinc chloride. Holmes throughout his lifetime vehemently denied this and wrote extensively against the use of these and other poisonous agents. Holmes never patented his fluid which he contended would then give others his formula. Test results from a 1990 sample of a body embalmed by Holmes indicated arsenic in the remaining tissue at 2.8%, and it was probably the major embalming agent!

Burials during this time period were made primarily on wood coffins that were put directly into the ground of local or church cemeteries. There were few metallic burial vaults or casket cases used and the Fisk Cast Iron Coffin was in limited use around the country. Towards the end of the 19th century, metallic cases were more widely used, particularly in urban areas.

As these wood coffins and metal cases disintegrate or corrode because of exposure to moisture and shifting cemetery ground, what are the possible consequences of twelve pounds of arsenic being absorbed into the soil and surrounding groundwater?

This question had not been raised until nearly 100 years after the widespread and continuing use of arsenic in embalming preparations. With more emphasis being put on environmental hazards and safety this question is now up for consideration.

LAY DOWN BODY

Arsenic was widely used as an embalming ingredient from about 1880 to 1910. Burials occurred in wooden coffins or metal containers that could degrade in the underground environment. These containers are subject to corrosion, and will eventually deteriorate. Arsenic, a basic element, will not change or degrade, but must remain with the buried body, or move into the environment. As the containers degrade, water moving downward through soils of cemeteries can dissolve arsenic. A logical conclusion is significant potential for groundwater contamination at many locations throughout the U.S. from arsenic-embalmed bodies.

Without an extensive review of public agency or private funeral establishment records, accurate determinations of the number of arsenic-embalmed bodies present in the nation's graveyards is impossible. Even if records were made available, they may not contain sufficient information to verify use of arsenic in certain cases. And the effort to obtain such information would be enormous. To understand the potential impact, let's focus on a hypothetical cemetery in a modest-size town. It is reasonable, for the period 1880 to 1910, to assume that 2,000 people died in that time period. If 50% of those were embalmed with arsenic, using six ounces of fluid per person, then the cemetery contains 380 pounds of arsenic. If the embalmers in the area used more arsenic, such as three pounds per person, then the cemetery would contain over one ton of arsenic. In either case, this is a significant amount of a potent, toxic material to find in the ground at one location.

Arsenic-embalmed bodies can release the toxic metal as rainfall percolates through the soil, into degraded burial containers, and on down to

continued from previous page

A database normally has a "date" field allowing an entry in a format like, 09/15/1852. This can be a problem when the entire date cannot be read, because the database will not accept incomplete or invalid dates. This problem is solved on the AGS database by entering dates in this format: 15 SEP 1852 [if any of the three parts cannot be read, the part or parts can be left out]. (The computer checks to see that the month entered is one of the 12 valid months, and that the sequence of numbers-to-letters-back-to-numbers is in place; it will not permit deviations from this sequence.)

North Burial Ground in Providence has been in continuous use since 1700. It includes 110 acres of slate, marble, sandstone, and granite monuments marking graves of some of the city's earliest and most influential citizens.

In summer, genealogists flock to the cemetery office looking for records, which were not kept until 1848. A computer in the office is now loaded with the above-mentioned software; data on most of the earliest gravestones has been transcribed by volunteers. Before records were computerized, thousands of early gravestone inscriptions were accessible only to those willing to trek through the cemetery. The program being used to store and search at North Burial Ground is an early version of the program to be offered by AGS.

continued on next page

continued from previous page

Another cemetery with computerized records is Rhode Island Veterans Memorial Cemetery, which contracted with my business in 1993 to develop a computer program to store data on veterans buried there. The program stores enlistment place and date, discharge place and date, and war served. It also stores data on future burials and next of kin, with mail-merge options. One feature visitors here especially like is the veteran's memorial card—a map printed by the computer which includes the location of the grave, military record, and birth and death information.

In closing, it is clear genealogists look forward to the day when all cemeteries have records on computer. For some of the dead, the gravestone carries the only written record of their life.

—JOHN E. STERLING, *American Cemetery*

the shallow groundwater table. Such periodic releases of arsenic can occur over many years, and may be accelerated as burial containers degrade.

Based on the knowledge of embalming and burial practices, it is reasonable, from the standpoint of an environmental engineer, to assume that arsenic contaminated remains can have a significant impact on soil and groundwater. Certainly, if hundreds of pounds of arsenic pesticides were thought to be buried at a site, action would be taken to verify and determine the extent of contamination. But with the justifiable sensitivity toward cemeteries and burial sites, little has been done to assess potential impacts on soil and groundwater resources.

Business Concerns

The public concept of a cemetery is as a plot of ground set aside for the burial of the dead. But what is a cemetery, in business terms? A cemetery is considered a special-purpose property: a burial park for earth interments, a mausoleum of crypts or vaults, and/or a crematory. The proper valuation of cemeteries, mausoleums, crematoriums, and the like on a balance sheet can serve a variety of purposes, including the determination of leverageable equity. Few cemeterians would say that their property, with whatever services it offers, couldn't use some restoration and revitalization. Roads need repaving. Dead trees need to come down. Headstones need to be realigned. The mausoleums' masonry needs to be repointed. The problem, of course, is money. The expenses to maintain a burial ground through several generations are not insignificant.

Some cemeteries were mismanaged during the last century, run by people with little or no business acumen and no interest in acquiring any. Some established no perpetual care or endowment funds until states passed laws requiring them to. The legacy of this lack of foresight is the struggling cemetery of the late twentieth century.

In the past, a funeral at a smaller church or neighborhood cemeteries incurred no particular burial costs. Consequently, the founders had no thought of profit making. Only recently have "white" cemeteries in cities like Detroit been receptive to the burial of African Americans. As cemetery grounds in those urban areas were purchased by African Americans in the early twentieth century, these new owners were motivated more by necessity than by the bottom line on a balance sheet.

In those same cities, now occupied anywhere from 60 to 90 percent by African Americans, cemetery owners direct their public relations campaign toward the black market; the bottom line is now, realistically, profit making. In general, most burial grounds are purchased for the purpose of earning income on the sale of grave plots and articles of implementation. Encouraged by the tax-free status of cemetery property and the sometimes low costs of large acreage in agricultural and rural settings, big businesses have been developed.

National Public Radio's *Morning Edition* aired a program entitled "Death Care Business Is Big and Getting Bigger" on December 1, 1993. Much of the discussion was between the reporter and an analyst for the Chicago Corporation Brokerage House, who specializes in "death care," the current preferred term for the funeral and cemetery business.

The analyst reminded listeners that the first baby boomer turns sixty-five in the year 2010, and that demographics, for this industry in particular, become very compelling beyond that. Overlooking the sobering fact that one has to die to be a customer, a look at the trends in the death care industry reveals many similarities to other growth industries. Such potential for profitmaking is something that institutional investors feel particularly comfortable with.

We now spend $8 billion a year burying our dead, cremating them, and memorializing the more than two million Americans who die each year. By the year 2030, one-fifth of our population will be over age sixty-five. While medical advantages have delayed mortality, health care experts don't expect much more good news there. Instead, the good news, certainly profit-wise, can be found in death care. Three large companies heard the good news early on and started buying up funeral homes and cemeteries around the country. The brokerage analyst reported that these companies' stocks increased in value by 40 percent in 1993 alone. While big investors might be hesitant at first, the demographics of the situation remain enticing.

DEATH CARE CORPORATIONS

One of the big three death care corporations described on NPR's *Morning Edition* is Stewart Enterprises, based in New Orleans. A regional representative for Stewart Enterprises travels through Pennsylvania, Virginia, West Virginia, and the Carolinas, looking for possible cemetery properties to buy. One of the company's current holdings is Fôrt Lincoln, the largest cemetery in the state of Maryland. It is situated on the outskirts of Washington, D.C.

Fort Lincoln has several burial operations. These include a large, hilltop mausoleum and a three-story stone building with a tower, arched openings, stained glass windows, and handsome burial chambers. Many customers, of course, prefer less lavish burials, but even these are not cheap. The average cost of death care at Fort Lincoln in 1995 ran to about $5,700.

The place of business at Fort Lincoln includes a new funeral home—the cemetery was without one until it was purchased by Stewart. Now it boasts what the NPR analyst called a "combo operation," a logical retailing development. Such combinations are based on a superstore concept and adapted to the death care industry. A couple can prearrange their respective funerals, select merchandise for service options, and then literally walk right next door to the cemetery to select a ground plot or mausoleum space.

The NPR reporter stated that such operations are why large companies like Stewart are doing so well. They have the money to advertise extensively, they can afford to buy funeral homes and cemeteries from families who want to get out of the business, and they realize economies by sharing some costs among several facilities. The funeral home at Fort Lincoln Cemetery opened in 1992 and was turning a profit by 1994. It has benefitted from a built-in market; of the hundreds of families using the cemetery every year, a certain percentage will use the funeral home.

Trends in the cemetery industry in the United States have paralleled other industries in the areas of growth and acquisition. In addition to Stewart Enterprises, two other multi-million dollar corporations are rapidly growing: SCI (Service Corporation, Inc.) and The Loewen Group. These corporations have also been purchasing cemeteries and funeral homes throughout the country. Some are also active in related industries, such as casket manufacturing, cremation, and memorialization.

The days of church burial grounds and local funeral director–owned cemeteries are rapidly fading. It has become easier for owners to sell than to maintain expensive properties, fund perpetual care trusts, adhere to increasingly rigorous EPA and OSHA regulations, and operate in an increasingly litigious society. In some cases, families will be the losers in this battle for growth and acquisition. There will be less personalized service; the local undertaker who has served families more than two generations will cease to be available for comfort when the bereaved come calling. This is not to say that large corporations will not be courteous and offer counseling and follow-up care. Large organizations that focus on death, burial, and related services have large, well-trained sales counselors who excel in marketing their products and services. How many of us can say that we don't need what they are offering? Everyone who has passed childhood is a potential target of a good mailing and/or telemarketing campaign. Obviously, such pre-arrangement is smarter, cheaper, and less stressful than contacting death care providers at the time of need.

LAY DOWN BODY

Pre-arrangement has become the preferred choice for families, funeral homes, and cemeteries. Choosing caskets, graves and services immediately after a loved one has died is the worst possible time to make important decisions. If the family had approached the funeral director or cemeterian during the previous year, or sooner, arrangements would be complete, some costs would be lower and balances could then be paid with less strain and anxiety.

BURIAL ALTERNATIVES IN FLORIDA: A MODEL FOR THE FUTURE?

Charles Strouse, a staff writer for the *Miami Herald,* wrote in his article "Alternatives to Burials on Increase":

> More and more Dade residents are rejecting traditional burials and taking an alternative approach after death. The number of people in Dade County who opt for cremation, a sea grave, or who donate their bodies to science has been rising consistently during the past few years, according to the Dade County medical examiner's office.

Saying the increase in burial alternatives is reflective of nationwide trends, Strouse cited such reasons for the increase as rising costs for burials, a decrease in available land, greater acceptance of cremation, and a more mobile society whose families don't necessarily have special, meaningful places in which to bury their members. Commenting on the local and nationwide trend, Strouse continued:

> In Dade, the cremation rate is 20 percent, or one in every five deaths. Both state and county records confirm the number is rising. The nationwide rate is 17 percent, and that has nearly doubled since 1980.

> But Dade's rate is lower than in the rest of Florida, where about one in three bodies are cremated. Experts say blacks and Hispanics, who make up the bulk of Dade's population, have traditionally shunned cremation.

> "There was a time when it was unheard of for anyone with a Hispanic name or for an American black to ask for cremation," said Joseph Davis, Dade's medical examiner for thirty-five years. "But now I'm seeing more and more of them."

Municipal Cemeteries

The Norfolk, Virginia, cemetery exemplifies the municipal cemetery system and tradition in the United States. Like Oak Ridge Cemetery in Springfield, Illinois, the final resting place of President Abraham Lincoln, the Norfolk cemetery is an old and historic site. Although one of the country's oldest municipal cemeteries, it still shares the same plight as others of its type. Some of these are large, some small, some operate efficiently, others are struggling, yet each of these city-run burial grounds faces similar difficulties as they move towards the next century.

Norfolk established its first city cemetery on fourteen acres just north of the city boundary. Today, it owns and operates eight cemeteries totaling 350 acres. The initial venture, started in 1825, was born of necessity, as no private cemeteries provided this service. These early burials were provided at a minimum cost with no thought of maintenance of the grounds. As Norfolk's population expanded, area were set aside for wealthier families; likewise "Strangers and Paupers" sections were designated for the underprivileged.

Today, municipal cemeteries and private cemeteries find themselves competitors. City cemeteries, offering services at prices below break-even levels—the city absorbs the losses—are not only unfair competition for private cemeteries, but are a bargain for a few paid for by every resident taxpayer. In the past few years, however, municipal budgets have become strained, and cemeteries such as Norfolk have begun facing the same concerns over funding cemetery operations and the future provision of services and maintenance as their private cemetery counterparts.

The shift from providing a community service to running a viable business necessitates an almost paradigmatic change of philosophy. The cost of operating cemeteries like Norfolk has far outpaced income, and the cemetery operators realize that changes must be made. To remain competitive after raising prices, the cemetery operators must become sensitive to the needs and wishes of the public in developing new programs and services. To this end, they have begun offering such things as marker sales, flowers, and marker cleaning; the long range plan is to develop a care fund. Cemetery administration is being empowered to fine-tune prices and the product/service mix as necessary to compete with the private sector. Norfolk has a difficult task ahead in its move from a municipal service to a business.

FUNDING OF MUNICIPAL CEMETERIES

LuAnn Johnson writes in *American Cemetery* magazine that common perceptions about municipal cemeteries are two-fold. First is the attitude of the community itself, which views such cemeteries as a public service, giving little thought to their operation. Secondly, people closer to the problem, such as cemeterians and those involved in community affairs, recognize these cemeteries as a drain on tax dollars that are seldom managed as a business. Private cemeteries see public-owned cemeteries as unfair competition.

Most municipal cemeteries are funded through tax dollars, putting them in competition with other city departments for their revenue. Small city-owned cemeteries may not have full staff, while larger municipal cemeteries often lack resources and knowledge to perform efficiently. In some

L A Y   D O W N   B O D Y

instances, the cemetery manager is a municipal employee who lacks the specialized expertise to operate a cemetery.

Most all the problems common to municipal cemeteries stem from inadequate or nonexistent care funds. If such care funds can be established with the cooperation of city officials, the cemeteries will eventually become self-supporting. It is in the best interest of all in the community, especially taxpayers, to cease viewing municipal cemeteries as public services and view them as viable business ventures.

Municipal cemeteries should be able to charge a rate for goods and services comparable to those in the private sector; likewise, they should provide the same well-cared for and attractive grounds as private cemeteries. Also, their personnel must keep abreast of legislation and regulations affecting cemeteries, and need to become aware of what the American Cemetery Association (ACA) and their state associations can offer. The American Municipal Cemetery Council, a suborganization of the ACA, is also an excellent resource for its members and those who request assistance. Funds should be provided for membership in these organizations.

National Cemeteries

The U.S. Department of Veterans Affairs manages 114 cemeteries, and either the Department of the Interior or the U.S. Army runs fourteen other national cemeteries. The National Cemetery System began in an effort to cope with the many casualties caused by the Battle of Bull Run in 1861. When the battle ended, it was obvious that space would be needed to lay out graveyards. The first national cemeteries were set up for Union soldiers in Alexandria, Virginia; Philadelphia, Pennsylvania; New Albany, Indiana; Fort Leavenworth, Kansas; and Sharpeburg, Maryland, the site of the Battle of Antietam, where 4,476 Union soldiers were killed in one day's slaughter.

By 1863 there were eight more cemeteries, including one on the site of the Battle of Gettysburg; in 1864 Arlington National Cemetery was established for those dying in hospitals surrounding Washington, D.C. Of the nearly 360,000 Union soldiers killed in the Civil War, only 101,736 graves were registered in national cemeteries. However, by June 1866, 87,664 additional remains had been discovered on various battlefields, buried where they had fallen; they were reinterred at forty-one national cemeteries. By 1870 there were almost three hundred thousand Union soldiers buried in seventy-three national cemeteries.

By an act of Congress in 1872, burial rights in national cemeteries were granted to "all soldiers and sailors of the United States who may die in destitute circumstances." In March 1873, the act extended burial rights to all honorably discharged veterans of the Civil War and provided one million dollars for headstones—in white marble or granite—to mark each grave at each national cemetery. San Francisco National Cemetery was laid out in 1884, and was the first national cemetery on the west coast. By the end of the 19th century, soldiers killed in the Spanish-American War and the Philippine insurrection were frequently brought to Arlington or San Francisco National Cemetery.

By 1920, "All soldiers, sailors, or Marines dying in the service of the United States . . . or who served or hereafter shall have served during any war in which the United States has been . . . engaged, and, with the consent of the Secretary of War, any citizen of the United States who served in the army or navy of any government at war with Germany or Austria during the World War and who died in such service or after honorable discharge therefrom, may be buried in any national cemetery free of charge."

In 1929 more cemeteries were planned and in October 1943 a bill was introduced in Congress requiring at least one national cemetery in each state. After much debate in Congress and protests from the private cemetery sector, the bill died. In 1948 Congress again extended national cemetery burial privilege eligibility, this time to wives, husbands, widows, widowers, and dependent children of eligible veterans and some reserve officers. In 1960, because of lack of space for expansion, Congress replaced its policy of separate grave sites for family members to one grave site per family.

During the Vietnam War era, President Johnson asked the Department of Veterans Affairs (VA) to improve all veterans' programs, including the National Cemetery System; in 1973 the National Cemeteries Act was the beginning of a new era for America's national cemeteries. The law required that all but two of the cemeteries—Arlington and Soldiers Home—be transferred from Army control to that of the VA, which also assumed responsibility for providing headstones and markers.

A plan was submitted to Congress in January 1974, calling for the establishment of one regional cemetery in each of ten standard federal regions. The first four regional cemeteries were established in Texas, Missouri, Colorado, and Oregon. In the years following, the requirements of the regional cemetery concept were fulfilled.

THE MARKER BUSINESS

The Veterans Administration was put in charge of the Government Headstone and Marker Program. From the first congressional directive in 1873, which stated that a permanent marker should be provided for every grave in a national cemetery, more than five million headstones have been provided.

In fiscal 1992 alone, the Office of Memorial Programs within the Veterans Administration delivered nearly 303,000 headstones and markers.

L A Y   D O W N   B O D Y

Of these, 24 percent were placed on graves in national cemeteries, 71 percent were delivered to private cemeteries, 3 percent to state veterans' cemeteries, and 2 percent to other federally operated cemeteries.

Currently twenty-five memorial companies supply headstones and markers to the government. Eleven manufacture granite markers, two make bronze memorials, five make flat marble markers, six manufacture upright marble markers, and one makes bronze niche covers. Contracts are awarded on a state-by-state basis for terms of one year with two one-year renewal options.

Many people have voiced continued concern and confusion over the issue of the veteran's marker benefit. In answering a letter to the editor of *American Cemetery,* the magazine notes that:

> There are no charges for national cemetery services provided to veterans and certain other eligible family members. These services include burial space, whether in-ground, full-length, or cremation or columbarium niches, together with perpetual care and the provision and installation of a variety of headstones, markers, and niche covers or plaques.

> Of course, these services depend on availability of burial space and the type of headstones or markers used in the particular national cemetery.

> The law, Title 38 U.S. Code, directs the Veterans Administration to provide government headstones or markers at the expense of the United States for the unmarked graves of any individual buried in national, [military] post, and state owned veterans cemeteries.

> The same law authorizes furnishing government headstones or markers in private cemeteries for veterans, but excludes the surviving spouse. The VA is not authorized to pay the cost of installing a veteran's headstone or marker in a private cemetery.

> When a non-veteran spouse predeceases the veteran and burial in a national cemetery is chosen, a government head stone or marker is provided and installed. When the veteran dies and is buried in the same grave site, the headstone or flat stone marker is destroyed and replaced with a new one.

> We have found over the years that because of our high volume and lower costs for markers, this is generally the most economical way to provide the second inscription. Bronze markers and columbarium niche plaques are returned to the manufacturer for credit to the government after the new marker with both inscriptions is installed. When a non-veteran spouse predeceases the veteran and burial in a private cemetery is chosen, the VA is not authorized to provide a headstone or marker. When the veteran dies and is buried in the same grave

site, the VA is authorized to provide a headstone or marker. Placement and installation is at the discretion and cost of the cemetery and next-of-kin. The change suggested by Mr. Goldblatt—that is, provision of a VA marker or headstone for the non-veteran spouse buried in a private cemetery—would require Congress to change the law governing the headstone and marker program.

It becomes apparent that the funeral and burial business is by no means static. Significant changes in each of its facets—cultural, environmental, and business concerns, municipal cemeteries, national cemeteries, and the marker business—have had a direct effect on the whole. Historic and rural cemeteries retain an important place in the development of the industry, but it is the large, urban cemetery that reflects, to a greater extent, the many changes wrought throughout the years. While all cemeteries find themselves knowledgeable about such cultural and political changes occurring within our evolving society, it is the growning concern over environmental issues that weighs most heavily on the continued existence of the traditional burial ground.

L A Y   D O W N   B O D Y

Abrahams, Roger D., ed. *Afro-American Folklore: Stories from Black Traditions in the New World.* New York: Parthenon Books, 1985.

The African American Presence in New York State: Four Regional History Surveys. Albany: New York African American Institute, State Univ. of New York, 1989.

American Cemetery Management (January 1994).

American Genealogical Research Institute. *How to Trace Your Family Tree.* New York: Doubleday, 1973.

Angelou, Maya. *Maya Angelou: Poems.* New York: Bantam, 1986.

Association of African Museums. Lecture, Dallas, Texas, September 1991.

Atlanta Historical Bulletin 20, no. 2. (summer 1976).

Bancroft, Frederic. *Slave Trading in the Old South.* Maryland: J. A. Furst Co., 1931.

Bates, Angela. "New Promise for Nicodemus." *National Parks* (July/August 1992).

Beaman, Alden G. "Rhode Island Black Genealogy: Inscriptions from the Negro Section of the Common Burial Ground, Newport." *Rhode Island Genealogical Register* 8, no. 2 (October 1985).

Beaufort Gazette: 1991.

Bennett, Lerone, Jr. *Before the Mayflower.* Chicago: Johnson Publications, 1966.

Blockson, Charles L. *African American State Historical Markers (Philadelphia Guide).* Philadelphia: The Charles L. Blockson Afro-American Collection/William Penn Foundation, 1992.

——— "Nowhere to Lay Down My Weary Head." *National Geographic* (December 1987).

The Boston Experience: A Manual for Historic Burying Grounds Preservation, 2nd Edition. Boston: Boston Parks & Recreation Department, 1989.

Botsch, Robert E., and others. *African Americans and the Palmetto State.* Columbia: South Carolina Department of Education, 1994.

Brown, Cynthia Stokes. *Ready from Within: Septima Clark & the Civil Rights Movement.* California: Wild Trees Press, 1986.

Brown, William Wells. *The Negro in the American Rebellion: His Heroism and His Fidelity.* New York: Citadel Press, n.d.

Burn, Billie. *An Island Named Daufuskie.* Spartanburg, South Carolina: Reprint Company Publishers, 1991.

Byers, Paula K., ed. *African American Genealogical Sourcebook.* Detroit: Gale Research, 1995.

Bynes, Frank. Interview, Savannah, Georgia, August 1991.

Cantor, George. *Historic Black Landmarks: A Travelers Guide.* Detroit: Visible Ink Press, 1991.

Carawan, Guy, and Candie Carawan. *Ain't You Got a Right to the Tree of Life?* New York: Simon & Schuster, 1966, 1989.

"Cemetery Management," *American Cemetery Association* 54, no. 2 (February 1994).

"Changing Philosophies: Is the Municipal Cemetery to Be a Community Service or Business?: City of Norfolk Cemeteries." *American Cemetery* (December 1991).

Chorzempa, Rosemary. *My Family Tree Workbook: Genealogy for Beginners.* New York: Dover, 1982.

Cohen, Hennig. "Burial of the Drowned among the Gullah Negros." *Southern Folklore Quarterly* 22 (1958).

Consumer Reports. Funerals: Consumers' Last Rights. New York: Norton/*Consumer Reports,* 1977.

Cooley, Rossa B. *School Acres.* Westport, Connecticut: Negro Universities Press, 1930.

Cremation Chronicles 1, no. 1 (1991).

Cunningham, Montrose. *Public Information Office.* Dallas: State Department of Highway and Public Transportation, 1994.

Curry, Major General Jerry P. *The Crisis* 92, no. 1 (January 1985): 28.

Daise, Ronald. *Reminiscences of Sea Island Heritage.* Orangeburg, South Carolina: Sandlapper Publishing, 1986.

"Dallas Project Restores Forgotten Freedmens Cemetery." *American Cemetery* (January 1991).

Deas-Moore, Vennie. "Treading on Sacred Grounds." *National Historic Trust and Preservation Society Information Series* 76 (1993).

"Death Care Business Is Big and Getting Bigger." *Morning Edition* (radio broadcast). National Public Radio, December 1, 1993.

DeCosta Herbert, and others. *History of the Brown Fellowship Society and the Human Brotherhood.* Charleston: Brown Fellowship Society, 1990.

Detroit Free Press: October 12, 1993.

Detroit News: July 29, 1990; July 1993; May 14, 1995.

Dickerman, G. S. "A Glimpse of Charleston History." *The Southern Workman* 36, no. 1 (January 1907).

Dunbar, Paul Laurence. *The Complete Poems of Paul Laurence Dunbar.* New York: Dodd Mead, 1952.

Ellsberry, Daniel. "The City of Savannah's Four Cemeteries: Cemetery Management." *American Cemetery Association* 51, no. 12 (December 1991).

Emanuel, James, and Theodore L. Gross. *Dark Symphony: Negro Literature in America*. New York: Macmillan, 1968.

Estell, Kenneth. *African America: Portrait of a People*. Detroit: Visible Ink Press, 1994.

Family Tree Maker: User's Tutorial and Reference Manual. Freemont, California: Banner Blue Software, Inc., 1993.

"Final Resting Places of Famous Blacks." *Ebony* (February 1979).

Fordham, Monroe, ed. *The African American Presence in New State History*. Albany: New York African American Institute, State Univ. of New York, 1989.

Frazier, Evelyn McD. *A Guide for Amateur Genealogists*. Jacksonville, Florida: Florentine Press, 1974.

"Geographica." *National Geographic* (February 1993).

George, Carol V. R. *American Visions* 12 (1986).

Godolphin, Vincent. "The Henrietta Marie." *About ... Time* (August 1993).

Greene, Robert Ewell. *Swamp Angels: A Biographical Study of the 54th Massachusetts Regiment*. N.p.: 1990.

Guthrie, Patricia. *Catching Sense: The Meaning of Plantation Membership among Blacks on St. Helena, S.C.* New York: Univ. of Rochester, 1977.

Guines, Kevin, and Beth Parkhurst. *African Americans in Newport, 1660-1960: A Report to the Rhode Island Black Heritage Society*. Providence, Rhode Island: Black Heritage Society, 1992.

Hamilton, Virginia Van de Veer. *Alabama*. New York: Norton, 1977.

Hampton, Henry, and Steve Fayer. *Voices of Freedom*. New York: Bantam, 1990.

Hanson, Laura, *A History of the Knights of the Wise Men Lodge*. St. Helena, South Carolina: Sea Island Preservation Project of Penn Center, 1995.

Harrison, Henry. *Negro Voices*. New York: Poetry Publisher, 1938.

Hawkins, Joanne B. "You Always Go Home Again." *American Cemetery* (November 1994).

Herskovits, Melvin. *The Myth of the Negro Past*. Boston: Beacon Press, 1958.

Historic Oakland Committee, Inc. *Join Historic Oakland—Your Gateway to Oakland*. Atlanta, Georgia: Historic Oakland Committee, 1991.

Holloway, Josiph E., ed. *Africanisms in American Culture*. Bloomington and Indianapolis: Indiana Univ. Press, 1990.

Holt, Rackham. *George Washington Carver: An American Biography*. New York: Dudley Doran, 1943.

Hughes, Langston, and Arna Bontemps, eds. *The Book of Negro Folklore*. New York: Dodd Mead, 1959.

Illinois Generations: A Guide to African American Heritage. Chicago: *Chicago Sun Times*/Performance Media, 1993.

Island Pocket: December 1994.

Johnson, LuAnn. "Municipal Cemeteries: A Change in Perception." *American Cemetery* (December 1991).

Jones, James H. *Bad Blood.* New York: The Free Press, 1981.

Kelsoe, Joe. *Black Civil War Casualties.* Nashville, Tennessee: N.p., 1991.

Korotin, Gayle. "The People's Advocate." *Christic Institute, South* 12, no. 2, (March/April 1991).

Lapin, Harvey I. *The Cremationist of North America* 27, no. 4 (1991).

Law, W. W. Interviews, Savannah, Georgia, 1991.

Leland, Elizabeth. *The Vanishing Coast.* Winston-Salem: John F. Blair, 1992.

Litwack, Leon F. *North of Slavery: The Negro in the Free States, 1790-1860.* Chicago: Phoenix Books, 1961.

Maynard, Joan, and Gwen Cottman. *Weeksville Then & Now.* Weeksville: Society for the Preservation of Weeksville & Bedford Stuyvesant History, 1983.

Meriweather, Louise. *The Freedom Ship of Robert Smalls.* Englewood Cliffs, New Jersey: Prentice Hall, 1971.

Meyer, Richard E., ed. *Markers XII.* Worcester, Massachusetts: *Journal of the Association for Gravestone Studios,* 1995.

Morgan, Stephen L., and Robert M. Fells. "Washington Report." *American Cemetery Association* (August 1992).

Moseley, Robert L., ed. *Greenwood Cemetery—100th Anniversary Celebration* (pamphlet). N.p: Greenwood Cemetery, 1988.

Murphy, Beatrice M., ed. *Negro Voices: An Anthology of Contemporary Verse.* Brooklyn, New York: Polygon Press, 1938.

Nash, Gary, and others. *The American People: Creating a Nation and a Society.* New York: Harper & Row, 1996.

"National Cemeteries Date to Battle of Bull Run." *American Cemetery* (August 1994).

Newport Daily News: August 19, 1994.

New York Times: October 29, 1984; August 13, 1990; July 28, 1991; September 3, 1991; October 10, 1991; December 1991; May 23, 1993; November 11, 1993; February 10, 1994; April 2, 1995.

Nichols, Elaine, ed. *The Last Miles of the Way, 1890 to Present: African American Homegoing Tradition.* Charleston: South Carolina State Museum, 1989.

Nordmann, Chris. "Basic Genealogical Research Methods and Their Application to African Americans." *African American Genealogical Sourcebook.* Detroit: Gale Research, 1995.

North Buxton's 64th Annual Homecoming & Labour Day Celebration. Brochure printed by North Buxton Centennial Community Club, September 3, 1988.

Oppenheimer-Dean, Andrea. Article in *Historic Preservation* (January/February 1995): 29.

Pearson, Elizabeth Ware, ed. *Letters from Port Royal, 1862-1868,* New York: Arno Press, 1969.

Perry, Charlotte Bronte. *The Long Road.* Windsor, Ontario: Summer Printing, 1967.

Phillips, Ulrich Bonnell. *American Negro Slavery.* Baton Rouge: Louisiana State Univ. Press, 1918.

Plain Dealer: October 9, 1993.

Powdermaker, Hortense. *After Freedom.* New York: N.p., 1939.

Pransky, Judith. "Looking at History along the Main Line." *Main Line Times* (November 26, 1992).

Preserving Black Heritage for Future Generations. New Orleans: Mount Olive Cemetery, n.d.

Putnam, John J. Article in *National Geographic* 164, no. 6 (December 1983).

Quarles, Benjamin. *The Negro in the Making of America.* New York, Macmillan, 1964.

Redd, Rev. A. C. List of Africanisms in African-American funerary practices.

Reid, David, ed. *Sex, Death and God in L.A.* New York: Parthenon, 1992.

Riverside Cemetery Inscriptions, 1830-1975. Jackson: Mid-west Tennessee Genealogical Society, 1975.

Robbins, Arlie C. *Legacy to Buxton.* Ontario: Ideal Printing, 1983.

Roediger, David R. "And Die in Dixie: Funerals, Death and Heaven in the Slave Community, 1700-1865." *Massachusetts Review* 22 (1981): 163-83.

Rose, Willie Lee. *Rehearsal for Reconstruction: The Port Royal Experiment.* Oxford: Oxford Univ. Press, 1964.

Rosengarten, Theodore. *Tombee: Portrait of a Cotton Planter.* New York: Quill/Morrow, 1986.

Rowson, Denise, and others. *Reclaiming Yesterday: The Geer Cemetery Project.* Durham, North Carolina: Durham Service Corps., 1992.

Sance, Melvin M., Jr., and others. *The Texians and the Texans.* San Antonio: Univ. of Texas Institute, Institute of Texan Cultures at San Antonio, 1975.

Savannah Morning News: December 31, 1992.

Scarups, Harriet Jackson. "Learning from Ancestor Bones." *American Visions* (February/March 1994).

Sheumaker, Helen. "The Gravemakers of Nicodemus Kansas as a Test of Black Town Isolation." Master's thesis, Univ. of Kansas, 1988.

Smith, Janet. "Rocking the Boat." *Hilton Head Island Monthly* (February 1991).

The State (Columbia, South Carolina): May 22, 1992.

Strangstad, Lynette. "Preservation of Historic Burial Grounds." *National Historic Trust and Preservation Society Information Series* 76 (1993).

Summerville, James. *Educating Black Doctors: A History of Meharry Medical College.* Univ. of Alabama Press, 1983.

Sun Sentinel (Fort Lauderdale): December 20, 1992; December 30, 1992.

Tavining, Mary A., and Keith E. Baird, eds. *Sea Island Roots: African Presence in the Carolinas and Georgia.* N.p.: African World Press, 1991.

Tennessean (Nashville): December 16, 1990: February 9, 1992.

Thompson, Sharyn. *Florida's Historic Cemeteries.* Tallahassee: Historic Tallahassee Preservation Board, 1989.

To Walk the Whole Journey: African American Cultural Resource in South Carolina. South Carolina Department of Parks, Recreation and Tourism/South Carolina State Museum, 1991.

Ulack, John Michael. *The Afro-American Tradition in Decorative Arts.* Cleveland: Cleveland Museum of Art, 1978.

Venator, Rolayne, and Paul B. Williams. *South Atlanta—A Short Developmental History.* N.p.: N.d.

Walker, Alice. *In Search of Your Mother's Gardens.* New York: Harcourt, 1984.

Wallis, Charles L., ed. *Words of Life.* New York: Harper & Row, 1966.

Washington Post: July 27, 1991; April 29, 1993; May 17, 1993; March 1994; April 30, 1995; May 1995.

Wells, Ida B. *Crusade for Justice,* edited by Alfreda M. Duster. Chicago: Univ. of Chicago Press, 1970.

White, John. "Veiled Testimony: Negro Spirituals and the Slave Experience." *Journal of American Studies* 17 (1983).

———"Whatever Happened to the Slave Family in the Old South?" *Journal of American Studies* 17 (1983).

Whyte, William H. "The 21st-Century Cemetery." *Cemetery Management* (May 1994).

Williams, Melissa Johnson, and John L. Konefis. "Environmental Concerns of Older Burial Sites." *American Cemetery* (February 1992).

Wilson, G. A. "The Religion of the American Negro Slave: The Attitude toward Life and Death." *Journal of Negro History* 8 (1923): 41-71.

Wilson, Samuel G., and Leonard V. Huber. *The St. Louis Cemeteries of New Orleans.* New Orleans: St. Louis Cathedral, 1993.

Wright, Roberta H. *Detroit Memorial Park Cemetery: The Evolution of an African American Corporation.* Southfield, Michigan: Charro Book Co., 1993.

Wright, John A. *St. Louis—Black Heritage Trail.* N.p.: Ferguson-Florisant School District, 1990.

Wynn, Linda T. "The Boyhood Home of Alex Haley." *Courier* 24, no. 2 (February 1986).

INDEX

Anderson, Ralph 143
Anderson, Webster 109
Angeles Abbey Memorial Park
    123, 182
Angeles Rosedale Cemetery 183
Angelou, Maya 225
Antebellum Black Newspapers 241
Archdiocese of New Orleans
    Sacramental Records 208
Archer, Dennis 166
Arlington National Cemetery
    34–6, 309
Arlington, Virginia 34–6
Asbury, J. C. 175
Ashe, Arthur 179
Ashe, Mattie C. 179
Association for Gravestone Studies
    (AGS) 301–2
Association for the Study
    of African American Life
    and History 112
Association of Professional
    Genealogists 244
Atkins, John W. H. 180
Atlanta Baptist Female
    Seminary 126
Atlanta, Georgia 123–7
Attucks, Crispus 250–1
Augusta, Georgia 127–9
Austin, George 290
Azusa Street Revival 183

B

Bacon, Jerome 174–5
Bad Blood 152
Badger, Roderick D. 126
Bailey, DeFord 139
Bailey, York W. 92, 286
Bala Cynwyd, Pennsylvania 175
Ballard, Florence 171
Balton, K. R. 150
Bampfield, George 272
Bancroft, John 77
Banneker, Benjamin 176
Banner Blue Software Inc. 196
Baptist Tabernacle Church 77
Barbour, Lucille 122
Barden, Thomas E. 240
Barnett, Alice 153
Bartlett, Annie M. 80

Bates, Angela 162
Bayley, John 58
Baylor, Julia 148
Beard, Matthew 183
Beaufort Memorial Burial
    Association 80
Beaufort National Cemetery 73, 74
Beaufort, South Carolina 73–83
Beckett, J. Campbell 175
Bedon, George 272
Before Freedom 240
Belcher, Edwin 115
Bell, Barbara L. 237
Bellefontaine Cemetery 159–60
Belleville, Michigan 171
Bentley, Charley 57
Bentley, Eddie 57
Bentley, Elizabeth 245
Bentley, Janie 57
Bentley, Mingo 57
Bentley, Robert 57
Bethel, Elizabeth 221
Bethlehem Cemetery 140, 142
Bethlehem Methodist
    Church 142
"Beyond the Orphanage" 238
Biddle, John 172
Big Antioch Cemetery 228
Big Bethel African Methodist
    Episcopal Church 127
"Big Sixteen" 28–30
Biggs, William 77
Biography and Genealogy
    Master Index 237
Birmingham, Alabama 149–51
"Birth Registrations of Children
    of Slaves" 216
Bishop England 105
Black Americans in
    Autobiography 240
Black Biographical Dictionaries,
    1790–1950 237
Black Biographical Sources: An
    Annotated Bibliography 237
Black Biography, 1790–1950 237
Black Center 134
Black History 243
"Black Holocaust, The" 34
Black Infantry in the West, The 223
Black Masters: A Free Family of Color
    in the Old South 228
Black Miners Cemetery 38–9

Fripp Cemetery 46, 55, 87
Fripp, Richard Fuller, Sr. 55
Frunkin, Sid 171
Fugitive Slave Cemetery 123, 189
Fugitive Slave Laws 184

G

Gadson, Marie 100
Gaines, Wesley J. 126
Galloway, Alfred C. 139
Gannett, W. C. 99
Garr, Patrick 250
Garvin, Richard 135
Gaston, A. G. 149, 150
Gaston, Deacon 101
Gates, Henry Louis 237
Geer Cemetery 122, 130–3
Geer, Jesse B. 130
Geer, Polly 130
*Genealogical Abstracts from Tennessee
     Newspapers* 229
Genealogical Helper, The 242
*General Index to Compiled Military
     Service Records of Revolutionary
     War Soldiers* 219
George Washington Carver
     Foundation 151
Georgia 14–15, 46, 110–20, 123–9
"Georgia Registrations of Free
     People of Color" 230
Ghana National House of Chiefs 8
Gilmore, Martin 77
Ginsberg, Harry N. 15, 116
Givens, James 51
Gladden, Freeman 110
Glass, H. H. 143
Glory 77
"Go Down Death" 2, 19
"God's Little Acre" Common Burial
     Ground 178
Golconda, Illinois 166
Goodwin, Ruby Berkley 267
Gordon, Edythe Mae 121
Government Headstone and Marker
     Program 310–2
Grace Truth Bible Chapel 87
Graceville, Florida 34
Grant, Doris 60, 61, 62, 63, 66
Grant, Joseph 45
Grant, Moses 60
Grant, Sarah 45

Graves, Antoine 126
Gravestone database 301-4
Gray, Fred 152
Gray, Pierce 82
Gray, Samuel 250, 251
"Great Negro Plot" 5
Green, Alex 77
Green, Bobbie 61, 62
Green, Charles 77
Green, Jacob Benjamin 105
Green, Karen Mauer 232
Green, Kit 94
Green, Mazie 96
Green, Pheobe G. 97
Green, Sarah "Margu" Kinson 17
Green, Shields 17
Green, Walter 73
Green's Shell Enclosure 62, 63
Greenberg, Alan 8
Greene, Ervin 92
Greenpeace 299
Greenwich Cemetery 120
Greenwood (Co-Haven) Cemetery
     see Co-Haven Cemetery
Greenwood Cemetery 134, 135–9
Greenwood, Peggy 238
 Greenwood, Val D. 202
Greenwood-West Cemetery 134,
     135–7, 139
Gregoire, Emmanuel V. 157
Gregory, Winifred 229
Guide for Amateur Genealogists, A
     192
Gullins, Edna 159
Guthrie, Patricia 87, 88, 90
Gwinett, Buttin 114

H

Haig's Point Cemetery 46, 55–6
Haig's Point Plantation 55
Haley, Alex 140–2
Haley, Bertha 141
Haley, Simon Alexander 141
Hall, Charles 109
Hall, Lyman 114
Hall, Walter P. 177
Halstead, Elizabeth 10
Halstead, Underhill 10
Hamer, Fannie Lou 31–2
Hamilton, Jane 54
Hamilton, May 56

LAY DOWN BODY

Price, John 16
Price, Samuel E. 78
Prince, Robert 13, 14
Prince of Tides, The 74
Providence Church 153
Providence, Rhode Island 303
Public Cemetery 148–9
Puce, Ontario 123, 189

Q

Quarles, Frank 126

R

Railroad Retirement Board 237–8
Randolph, Benjamin F. 106–7
Randolph Cemetery 42, 106–8
Randolph, Curtis 172
Rawick, George P. 240
Readville, Massachusetts 76
Reason, Charles R. 78
Reave, John Bunyan 175
*Reclaiming Yesterday—The Geer
    Cemetery Project* 131–3
"Record of Details of Free Negroes,
    Camp of Instruction at
    Richmond, 1864" 222
"Records of Slave Claims
    Commissions,
    1864–1867" 221
Redd, A. C. 127
Redd, S. C. 19
Redford, Michigan 167–70
Reed, D. W. B. 138
Reed, William B. 138
Reeves, E. S. 148
Reeves, Garth 148
"Register of Claims of United
    States Colored Troops,
    1864–1867" 221
"Register of Free Negroes Enrolled
    and Assigned, Virginia,
    1864-1865" 222
"Register of Slaves Impressed,
    1864–1865" 222
"Registers of Officers of United
    States Colored Troops,
    1863–1865" 221
Reid, David 182
Reimonenq, Louis 158
Relyea, Captain 75–6

*Researcher's Guide to American
    Genealogy, The* 202
*Revolutionary War Pension and
    Bounty Land Warrant
    Application Files* 219
Reynolds, Hobson 176
Rhode Island 177–8, 302, 303, 304
Rhode Island Historical
    Society 302
Rhode Island Veterans Memorial
    Cemetery 304
Richards, Fannie 172
Richards, John D. 172
Richardson, Elizabeth 289, 290
Richmond Hill Cemetery 51
Rideout, Charles 78
Riley, Benjamin 54
Riley, Elizabeth 53
"Ring shouts" 32
Ripley, Tennessee 142
*River Roads to Freedom: Fugitive Slave
    Notices and Sheriff Notices
    Found in Illinois Sources* 229
Rivers, Bennie 81
Rivers, Hector 81
Rivers, Josie 81
Rivers, Norman 118
Riverside Cemetery 139–40
Riverview Cemetery 153
*Road That Led to Somewhere,
    The* 190
Roark, James L. 228
Robbins, Dennis 186
Robinson, Ida 175
Robinson, James 173
Rome of Victory Society 284,
    289–90
Roots 142
Rosa B. Cooley Health Clinic 90
Rose Hill Cemetery 73
Rosedale Cemetery
    Association 183
Rosedown Baptist Church 155, 156
Rosedown Baptist Church
    Cemetery 155–6
Rosengarden, Theodore 83
Rosenwald Fund 153
Roslyn, Washington 38–9
Ross, Joseph B. 220
Rossi, John 7
Roth, Herman J. 157
Rouzan, Mamie Austin 155

LAY DOWN BODY